ENCOUNTER WITH ISRAEL:
A Challenge to Conscience

ASSOCIATION PRESS
New York

ENCOUNTER WITH ISRAEL:

A Challenge to Conscience

ALICE
and
ROY
ECKARDT

With maps drawn by Alice Eckardt

ENCOUNTER WITH ISRAEL: A CHALLENGE TO CONSCIENCE

Association Press, 291 Broadway, New York, N.Y. 10007

Standard Book Number: 8096-1783-8
Library of Congress Catalog Card Number: 79–132395

 2

PRINTED IN THE UNITED STATES OF AMERICA

For
REINHOLD NIEBUHR
in thanksgiving

Preface

THE AIM OF THIS BOOK is to foster understanding of today's Israel and her people, and to contribute to responsible moral and political decisions respecting that country and her place in the Middle East.

Our intended audience extends to those who know little about Israel and those who know much. Although this has made our work difficult, we hope that the consequent need for both breadth and depth will have aided rather than hindered the exposition.

We are indebted to the editors of Association Press for the invitation to prepare this study and for their advice and criticism. Our gratitude is also expressed to innumerable persons in several lands—Jews and Arabs, Muslims and Christians—for their willingness to talk with us, their counsel, their hospitality, and their tangible aid. A complete roster of names would fill several pages; space permits only a partial list: Karl Baehr, Fuad Bahnan, Philip Berman, Harry Brunger, Mrs. Margaret Cantieni, Rhoda and Jack Cohen, Aref El-Aref, Basil Ennab, James Feron, Darinka and William Gardiner-Scott, Gershon Givoni, Rita and Alan Graham, Hugh R. Harcourt, Yehoshafat Harkabi, M. N. Hawary, Mrs. Nancy Nolan Abu Haydar, Father Jean Roger Hene, William Holladay, Salim Jubran, Elias Koussa, Mussa Kteily, Mrs. Sylvia Landress, Ammon Linn, Thérèse and Yona Malachy, Mrs. Inam Mufti, Anwar Nuseibeh, Bishop Karekin Sarkissian, Jean and Peter Schneider, Abraham Shachar, Michael Shashar, John M. Snoek, Ernest Stock, Bertha and Romain Swedenburg, Ibrahim Taktak, Miriam and Uriel Tal, Marc H. Tanenbaum, Moshe Unna, Ephraim E. Urbach, Alisa and Zwi Werblowsky, Georgina and Douglas Young, and Narda and Ze'ev Zimerman. We thank Susan Dunn, Patricia Girke, and Doris Wilkinson for their assistance in readying the manuscript for publication.

It is scarcely needful to add that as the authors we bear exclusive responsibility for the data and judgments offered in this book.

We trust that the results of our efforts will not disappoint the many colleagues, friends, and critics who have helped us, and that they and others will find in these pages much to ponder.

ALICE and ROY ECKARDT

Contents

Maps

1. Preparation for a Portrait

HOW DID ISRAEL come to be? What is the relation of today's State of Israel to ancient Israel and to later Palestine? What is it like to live in Israel? What major issues face the nation in the 1970's? What moral, political, and religious judgments may be brought to bear on our subject? What challenges does Israel bring to the world at large? These questions are central to any balanced understanding of Israel and, secondarily, of the situation in the Middle East. They are therefore the key questions to be considered, successively, in the present study.

The Point of View

A man's true home is the place where he wills to live and at the last readies himself to die. (Some men never find such a home.) Here is an immigrant who, setting foot upon the soil of Israel for the first time in his whole life, is certain that he has come home. How is this conviction possible?

Perhaps only Jews can supply compelling answers to the question. We who have composed this book are not Jews but gentiles, and not Israelis but Americans. However, we endeavor to represent Israel through the eyes of Israelis, to mediate between the reader and the Israelis, and in some instances between the reader who is an Israeli and other Israelis. This has made inevitable the inclusion of many controversial issues. Stress is placed on questions and replies that come from different, and often contrary, sides.

Our reporting of opposition to Israel from various quarters, particularly from the Arab world, is necessary to the description of Israeli life. Our incorporating of criticisms of Israel does not mean any lack of sympathy. Frequently, human beings reserve their criticisms for those they love or for whom they are concerned. It is often observed that the greatest critics of Israel are the Israelis, for many of whom complete self-expression is a wonderful new experience. At the same time, we are aware that the people of Israel have grown weary, and properly so, of having their country continually subjected to inspection, evaluation, and

13

advice by strangers. Books on Israel by outsiders are, unavoidably, part of the intrusion. The only justification for this particular volume is our persuasion that Israel remains in great need of sympathetic representation.

Perhaps the word "portrait" best identifies the present effort. A portrait weds objectivity to interpretation. It is not free of the artist's own self, yet it does everything possible to perceive its subject truthfully. Needless to say, we are speaking ideally. Others must decide whether our portrait is good or bad. John Sargent reputedly defined a painted portrait as the "representation of a person with something the matter with the mouth." No portrait can entirely escape distorting its subject, any more than it can encompass the whole of the reality it seeks to depict.

Portrayers ought to confront their subject face-to-face, as we have done on several successive research visits to Israel and the Middle East where much of the initial preparation for this book was undertaken. Beyond our meetings with a number of Israelis, we have talked to many persons "on the other side" from Israel's, including severely critical Arabs, both within Israel and within the "West Bank" of the Jordan. On both sides, in Israel, Jordan, and Lebanon, we have consulted with educators and religious leaders, Arab refugees and administrators of refugee camps, army personnel and *kibbutz* members, labor leaders and social workers, diplomats and government employees and spokesmen, housewives and students, and lawyers and journalists.

Beyond the portrayed and the portrayer stand those who view and react to the portrait. Third parties bring along their own ideas and sentiments, and they face the same risks of partisanship that confront the portrayer.

Few contemporary topics generate as much emotion, irrationality, and rancor as does the subject before us.[1] Some will automatically condemn any presentation of Israel once it dares to suggest that the life of that State is justifiable. For such opponents, the very existence of Israel is at best a mistake and at worst a crime. They will not be moved or satisfied at all by such criticisms of Israel as are included in the course of this study—save for the "criticisms" we report that consist of categorical denunciation. They will, if consistent, do whatever they can to ensure Israel's demise. It is hardly necessary to record that the present volume will carry no weight with those of the above persuasion.

The judgment that, without open-mindedness, there is no way to understand Israel applies not alone to her foes, but also to those enthusiasts for Israel who, in their worst moments, are outright chauvinists. We believe that enmity toward Israel and uncritical adulation of her are both, in varying degrees, to be fought. Israel has the same right to life that any country has. But Israel is not God, nor even a Messiah. To be pro-Israel, in the sense of acknowledging and praising Israel's integrity and freedom, one does not have to be anti-somebody else or blind to Israel's problems and faults. To celebrate the reality of Israel, even to have love for her, is not to abandon concern for other human beings, least of all Israel's enemies.

Much of the writing on our subject today concentrates upon the justification (or rejection) of Israel, her combat and her trials, rather at the expense of her givenness. Perhaps this is to be expected, since so much of her story is a lesson in travail, an agonizing struggle to win through to recognition and independence. The description of Israel must differ markedly from accounts of nations whose life is more or less placid and secure. Just because she faces serious internal challenges and grave external threats, any discussion of Israel must make a large place for these very problems. To ignore her continuing peril would be to paint a frivolous and unreal portrait. It would mean ignoring the cardinal need to take into full account, and to be responsibly informed about, the ongoing and grievous international conflicts of the Middle East.

Nevertheless, to focus exclusively upon the international situation and particularly the hazards to the nation would mean a failure to consider the integrity of Israel in and for herself. Much of what ought to be known and remembered about Israel transcends her efforts to fend off the attacks of enemies, however chronic the attacks and however ruthless the enemies. Adequately to portray the life of a people is to do much more than attend to its anxieties and constantly plead its case. In sum, what is demanded is objective recognition, critical celebration of the national fact, yet with heedfulness of Israel's threatened place as a nation. Our hope is to balance her reality and her cause.

No discussion of the State of Israel can escape religious considerations or controversy. At the same time, Israel simply cannot be understood from an exclusively religious perspective (unless religion were to be inflated to stand for the total life-and-death concerns of a nation). We are engaged in this volume with the overall life of a *laos,* a people. Accordingly, our work is much more of a venture into secularity than a narrowly "religious" effort. Once this is made clear, it becomes safe (or at least possible) to say that one major purpose of our exposition is to contribute to the contemporary dialogue between Christians and Jews, a dialogue that, happily, has begun to extend to Muslims. That our study should have been commissioned by a publishing house that includes Christian literature among its diverse offerings is itself indicative of widespread current interest in Jewish-Christian relations within the world of religion, and, more specifically, of a concern in some Christian quarters for an understanding of Israel and her problems.

At this juncture a decisive reservation must be inserted. While it is true that religious faith has had an incomparable place in the very inspiration of a reborn State of Israel, we do not believe that Israel's unquestionable right to life as a sovereign nation can be validated or proved through theological absolutism, the contention that once upon a time "God gave the land" to the people of ancient Israel, unqualifiedly and for all future history. Those who, either as Christians or as Jews, identify "religious Zionism" in terms of theological absolutism, and then seek to promote that point of view, will find that we disagree with them. We are not "Christian Zionists." That is to say, we oppose any view that seeks to prove by religious arguments the claim of any people to a piece of land. (In Chapter 22 that viewpoint is identified as "territorial fundamentalism.") The rights of Israel as a sovereign nation must be authenticated in a quite different way. In this connection, many who resort to the term "Zionist" convey the impression that they are somehow ignorant of the reality of the State of Israel. Today the words "anti-Zionist" and "Zionist" largely refer to positions either hostile or friendly to Israel, a country that has had renewed independence for over two decades.

It must be emphasized that the vast majority of Israelis, however much they are devoted to their country, are not apostles of theological absolutism. Hence, in dissociating ourselves from that point of view, we do not violate the promise to try to represent Israel through Israeli eyes.

We further intend to show that a purely "nonreligious Zionism" is not possible. That viewpoint neither permits us to apprehend the meaning and significance of Israel as a human phenomenon nor does justice to the reality and role of faith in the celebration of Israel.

Our opposition to "religious Zionism" and to "nonreligious Zionism" alike is intimated at various points in the book, and a constructive alternative taking us beyond both those views is developed in Chapters 21–23.

The Heritage

To be a man in society is to ask and receive some kind of answer to a question that addresses itself to all men: How have we been brought to our present place as a community or a nation?

If the question is the same for everyone, the answers are, of course, radically divergent. The story of every people is unique in that, whatever the parallels with other stories, the single and developing structure of events that the one people shares is duplicated nowhere else. Histories do not repeat each other exactly. Side by side with common experiences and common fates, there are always peculiarities.

It would be foolish to argue that the attitudes of the people of Israel toward their past are exempt from all comparison with the attitudes of other peoples, or that Israelis are necessarily more dedicated to or concerned with their past than are other nations of men. But this does not exempt us from grappling with the uniqueness of Israel.

In order to meet responsibly the issue of how Israel has come to her present place as a nation, we have to raise a further question: Must a person be a Jew in order to qualify as an authentic Israeli? This issue will pursue us, sometimes explicitly and sometimes implicitly, all through our work. It is, indeed, among the most poignant problems that confront Israel today.

Were the issue merely one of citizenship, the answer would be easy, and it would be "no." About one-seventh of the population of Israel is composed of non-Jews. These people are just as much citizens of the country as are Jews. However, the further we descend from surface levels of identification to deeper levels of historical meaning and destiny, the less certain is the above negative reply. Thus, it would simply be incorrect to say that non-Jewish consciousness or ideals played a crucial, positive role in the resurrection of the State of Israel in 1948. (This is not to lose sight of the ironic truth that the present political-geographical shape of Israel is primarily a consequence of Arab behavior.[2])

Significantly, the events of 1948 are identified as the initiation of the Third Jewish Commonwealth. It is Jews who have provided the decisive motivations, energies, and characteristics of independent statehood. It would be erroneous and artificial to proceed as though Israel as a nation were not decisively Jewish. The collective life of non-Jewish Israelis is largely shaped by a basically Jewish ethos.

Now we are in a better position to approach the question of the historical origins and meaning of Israel. Any effort to gain understanding of the roots and the life of the people of Israel has to reckon with the fundamental Jewishness of the country—as, analogously, one would have to concentrate upon the Arabness of the Jordanians or the Latin American character of the Bolivians.

Our answer, then, is that the long history of the Jewish people comprises the essential bond between the Israel of the 1970's and the Israel of antiquity.

We are entirely aware that the reasoning here is sometimes called into question. Critics ask: What can modern Israelis have to do with the ancient Israelites? We are aware as well that at the opposite extreme from these critics are those who insist that the Israel of any time is, in effect, a single, living body (as in the sentiments of some religious Israelis).

If it is misleading to claim in this latter fashion an absolute identity between biblical Israel and the modern State of Israel, it is infinitely more misleading to try to separate the two realities. Among Israeli Jews there is a shared body of experience and conviction sufficient to sustain, at least in a probationary way, the answer we have given.

The most telling consideration is not the feelings or ideas of outsiders, including even those who are historians, but instead the reply that the overwhelming majority of Israeli Jews, together with their brothers beyond Israel, give to the question: What are our roots as a people?

Among Israelis today the conviction is pervasive that they are recapturing the ancient past of their people—not through some impersonal repetition of that past, and not without awareness of the tolls that history exacts from men, but in a creative way that looks ahead at the same time that it looks back. This conviction has captured the souls and minds of Israelis. It suffuses the very air that one breathes in the land today. Yesterday is the foundation of today; today is the free child of yesterday; tomorrow is the promise of yesterday and today. In holding to such a confession, Jew and Israeli are the one man.

The Jewish people take the historical process with utmost seriousness. As James Muilenberg points out, all the men of Israel live a narrative life.[3] He is referring to the early biblical period, but he could just as readily be speaking of today.

The great numbers of Jews approach the long history of Israel, of the Jewish people, as a living reality. That is to say, the Israeli's existential understanding, his life-and-death comprehension of himself, is grounded in a story that began in very ancient times. His encounter with the past enables him to make sense of his own life experiences. And through his experiences today he is brought to recognize identities with the past. Thus is he a participant in the living story. He is its continuing interpreter. The roots of Israel are his roots as a man. Indeed, among the nations of the Middle East, his is the only one that "bears the same name, speaks the same tongue, upholds the same faith, inhabits the same land as it did 3,000 years ago." Israel is organic to the texture and the memory of the Middle East.[4]

The final choice in 1948 of "Israel" as the nation's name was historically and morally auspicious. The ancient and the contemporary have been drawn together in the fact of rebirth. The Israel of our time is possessed of powerful symbolic and substantive cultural, psychological, and spiritual bonds with the past. And yet, today there is much that is new, while tomorrow will see even more new things.

Many persons outside Israel possess a highly limited awareness and knowledge of the land and its history. Not so most Israelis. Everyone absorbs the heritage, even those few who consciously reject the past or appear indifferent to it. (These people discovered within themselves the past's compelling power when the Old City of Jerusalem and other parts of the ancient land became accessible to Israelis after June, 1967.)

Here is why a study of appropriate events from the past, together with their interpretation by Israelis, can go far to convey what it means to be a Jew in Israel today, and especially why there is so deep an attachment to the land. (We consider the historic roots of Israel in Chapters 2–5, and the more contemporary story in Chapters 6–17.)

It is important to emphasize that the existential attitudes of Israelis to their history, their drive to make the past live again in their own being, is by no means a psychological fabrication. The truth is that past events and experiences find moving parallels within the present generation.

At this preliminary stage of our dialogue, brief exemplification will suffice.

The seemingly impossible task assumed by Moses of unifying and motivating the Hebrew slaves of Egypt more than three millennia ago finds a striking counterpart in the challenge placed upon the Zionist pioneers and the State of Israel to restore hope and incentive to the survivors of modern oppression (in Europe and in countries of the Middle East), to give them the promise of a new life, and to integrate them, as well as many others, into one society.

Events of the past, particularly of the biblical past, come alive in the festivals and observances of the present.

Sukkot (Feast of Tabernacles) is one of three pilgrim festivals in which Jews of ancient times would go up to the Temple in Jerusalem. Today pilgrims come from all over Israel and beyond, and assemble at the Western Wall. Sukkot commemorates the safe passage of the Israelites through the Wilderness of Sinai from their bondage in Egypt.

Just as King David once "danced before the Lord" while bringing the Ark of the Covenant to Jerusalem (II Sam. 6:14), so today in the streets of Jerusalem men and boys go before the Torah scrolls with singing and dancing. The occasion is the celebration of Simhat Torah, marking the end and the recommencing of the cycle of reading the Torah in the synagogue.[5]

Many of the festivals are at once national and religious. They are both universally Jewish and concretely Israeli. The period between Rosh Hashanah (New Year) and Yom Kippur, the solemn Day of Atonement, witnesses nation-wide attendance at religious services and observance of the ten days of penitence.

Thus are we confronted by objective bonds between the Israel of the distant past and Eretz Yisrael (the Land of Israel[6]) today. Any who deny these bonds are being unhistorical and incorrect. Further, they are refusing to take seriously the standpoint of Jews within and beyond Israel, and thus they manifest a lack of sympathy.

In the novel *Mila 18* by Leon Uris the testimony of an old rabbi is cited: "The words 'I believe' mean 'I remember.' "

Yet there remains a contrast between the Israeli Jew and other Jews. It is an obstinate difference of geography. After all, the Mount of Tabor is *here*, the Cave of Elijah is *here*, the Western Wall of the Temple enclosure is *here*. These sites are not in Paris or Capetown or New York. Jews from *there* must journey *here* if they are to incarnate the history within the physical story of their own lives. Time is brought alive under the aegis of space. It is not the Israeli who makes pilgrimages—except at home.

The Defiance of Fate

It is often said that, by all reasonable historical and sociological expectations, the Jewish people should have long ago departed from the stage of history. To assert that Jews have endured because the world's persecutions have forced them to band together and to take all necessary measures to survive is to be unfair to Jewish self-understanding and integrity. Other peoples have been persecuted and have simply disappeared.

Despite centuries of suffering—persecutions, mass slaughter, captivities, exiles —this people lives. The very resurrection of Israel in our time is a revolt against historical probabilities (as well as being a vindication of age-old historical hopes). How is such collective defiance of death possible? Why has this people refused to cooperate with fate and die? There are mysteries here. Mysteries invariably laugh at attempts to comprehend them completely through historical understanding or any other form of explanation. Yet history may offer us vital clues.

The main thing is that a great series of coincidences had to be created, coincidences between historical event and human response. Obviously, had the given events never occurred within and near the geography that is now Israel— had the ancestors-to-be gone off somewhere else—any historical or moral case for the State of Israel would be meaningless. Although no people has endured into the modern age without a land to which it is in some way related,[7] the primordial events in themselves together with their sequels could not have been sufficient. The order of happenings had to be joined by a believing appropriation of these happenings. The persuasion of the bond between Eretz Yisrael and the Jewish people not only helped the Jews to survive but also made today's Israel a historical possibility.

Men had to keep coming along—a hundred years, a thousand years, several thousand years after the initial events—to claim, or at least to confess, "In these events our people had a beginning. Through these events and their tomorrows we have been granted our existence and we seek to fulfill our destiny."

PART I
The Roots of Israel

2. From Abraham to the Romans

AN ISRAELI was recently heard to remark, "In those days we had twelve tribes." Here is epitomized Israel's link with the past. The man was speaking of an epoch more than three thousand years in the past. What tale is more poignant than the Jewish people's struggle to secure a homeland for at least that much time?

The Beginnings

From the time of the first migrations of Hebrew tribes into the area, and long before the Bible was composed, there have been Jews in the land of Palestine. (The change in name from "Hebrews" to "Jews" involved a later historical development, when one part of the nation—Judah—became the essential core of the Jewish state.) For many, the history of Israel begins as long as four thousand years ago. The reference is to the first patriarch of the Jewish people: Abraham.

Scholars have debated for years whether "Abraham" and the names of the other patriarchs point to actual historical individuals or are collective names for the ancient tribes. But there is no argument over this statement: *"Jewish tradition* has it that the history of Israel begins with the call of God to Abraham."

According to the tradition, Abraham migrated from his home in Haran on the upper Euphrates River. Any and every event (or presumed event) can be interpreted either religiously or extra-religiously. Expressed in extra-religious terms, it would appear that Abraham and his family came to surrender a settled and comfortable city life, returning to a more nomadic existence.[1] His trek southwestward to Canaan probably coincided with similar journeys of related Aramean tribes. "A wandering Aramean was my father" (Deut. 26:5). Expressed in religious terms, the "going out" from Haran constituted an obedient response to a summons from Yahweh, and the entry into Canaan became the beginning of the possession of the "promised land" by "the people of God."

23

Go forth from your native land
and from your father's home
to a land that I will show you.

I will make of you a great nation,
bless you and make great your name,
that it may be a blessing.

I will bless those who bless you,
and curse those who curse you;
and through you shall bless themselves
all the communities of the earth.[2]

Beyond the weight attached to the reputed promise by God to "give this land" to Abraham's descendants (Gen. 12:7), Israelis have other important reasons of a symbolic kind for their attachment to the Abraham-Isaac-Jacob tradition. Thus, we have the story of the near-sacrifice of Isaac (Gen. 22:1–19), which is associated, whether accurately or not, with the City of Jerusalem (Mount Moriah being considered the site of the Temple). Again, there is the significance of the country's very name. Was it not the grandson of Abraham whose name was changed from Jacob to Israel (Gen. 32:22–28)? The man Israel is, after all, the etymological father of the modern State, and his twelve sons are the foundation stones of the Jewish people.

The "patriarchal period" (perhaps extending from 2000 to 1400 B.C.E.[3]) was a time of continuous movement for the Hebrew tribes, including one or more journeys down into Egypt, during an era of drought and famine.

Whatever one's conclusions respecting the actual happenings during the period before the sojourn in Egypt, the Exodus from Egypt, culminating as it did in the experience at Mount Sinai, stands out as the really crucial event in the creation of Israel as a nation, from the perspective of Jewish self-understanding. Prior to the Exodus, the Hebrews had not developed the kind of group identification that issues in creative common action. With the Exodus, all this began to change.

Once again, we can read the story in either nonreligious or religious ways. It was probably in the thirteenth century B.C.E. that an Egyptian pharaoh (whose identity is still uncertain) came to the throne. Looking with fear and distrust upon the Hebrews living in Goshen, he subjected them to miserable servitude. Moses, a Hebrew or Israelite by birth but a member of the royal Egyptian household by adoption and upbringing, was angered at the treatment meted out to his people, and determined to lead them to freedom.

Religiously expressed, when God "heard the groaning" of the people under the pharaoh's heavy hand, he "remembered his covenant with Abraham, Isaac, and Jacob," and resolved to bring his people "up out of that land to a good and broad land . . . flowing with milk and honey, to the place of the Canaanites, the Hittites, the Amorites, the Perizzites, the Hivites, and the Jebusites" (Exod. 2:24; 3:8). For this purpose, he raised up a deliverer in the person of Moses, under whom the people made good their escape from the land of Egypt.

Testimony to the preeminent place of the Exodus in Jewish historical consciousness is found in the words of the Seder, the ceremonial celebration observed by Jews everywhere at the beginning of Pesach (Passover): "We were Pharaoh's slaves in Egypt, and the Lord our God brought us forth from there with a mighty hand and an outstretched arm."

According to the Exodus tradition, at the "mountain of the Lord" somewhere in the desolate Sinai Peninsula, Moses confronted his people—who evidently had been quite uncomprehending and had become severely demoralized due to their wanderings and suffering in the wilderness—with the awesome challenge to become "a kingdom of priests and a holy nation" (Exod. 19:6). In the tradition, most sublime of all is the link between Sinai and the receiving of the Torah, the very instruction of God himself. The Covenant between God and his people was sealed. By dint of threats, pleas, denunciations, and promises over the ensuing forty years, Moses recalled the people again and again to their promise to serve God as well as reminding them of God's own faithfulness and providence.

Invasion, Exile, Return

Moses never made it to the promised land; he could only behold the land from afar. It was left to Joshua, in the latter part of the thirteenth century B.C.E., to ensure the Israelites' reentry into Canaan, on the heels of evident military successes. However, the Hebrews did not, and could not, supplant the local populations. Living side by side with these other peoples and their tempting gods, Israel's faith in Yahweh was continuously put to the test. It often failed. Moreover, the initial unity that had been painfully forged during the journey through the wilderness was threatened by the scattering of the twelve tribes into various parts of a land where travel and continued contact were made difficult (and sometimes dangerous) by desert, mountainous areas, and hostile peoples.

After much controversy over the wisdom and probity of having a king, the monarchy was instituted toward the close of the eleventh century B.C.E. under Saul. David, the most celebrated of the rulers, succeeded in developing a united nation with a centralized administration. Under his leadership the army was finally able to defeat the Philistines. It was primarily the hammer blows of these Phoenician people against the Hebrew tribes that forged the twelve links into a solid chain[4]—just as the Arab attacks of the twentieth century have intensified Israeli unity.

David's charismatic qualities and astuteness enabled him to hold together and bring prosperity to a dominion extending in the North from beyond Mount Hermon and Damascus (probably to the Euphrates River), through Transjordania to the Gulf of Aqaba in the South. (See Map One.) Perhaps most significant for the future of Israel and the Jewish people was David's capture of Jerusalem from the Jebusites. He made this stronghold his capital, a city that had had no prior connection with any of the Hebrew tribes and was therefore devoid of favoritism for any one tribe. David installed the "Ark of the Covenant" upon a rocky eminence in Jerusalem, thus making the capital a holy city. Containing the Tablets of the Law, this chest was Israel's most sacred religious object, representative as it was of the very presence of the God of the Covenant. It is reputedly upon this particular site that Solomon, David's heir, placed the "holy of holies," an inner sanctuary for the Ark and the heart of the Temple. Two other traditions

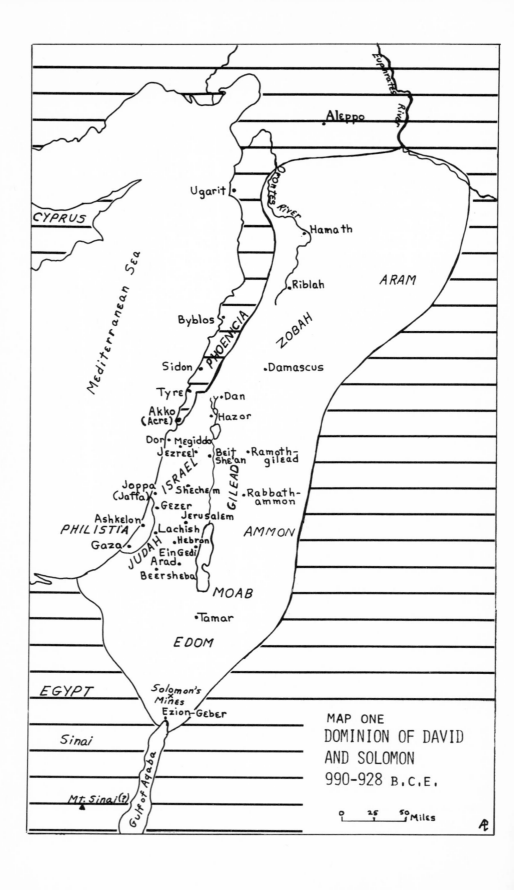

MAP ONE
DOMINION OF DAVID
AND SOLOMON
990-928 B.C.E.

0   25   50 Miles

are associated with this rock: Abraham's aborted sacrifice of his son Isaac, and Muhammad's ascent and return through the "seven heavens" many centuries later.

The political and religious bond of the Jews with Jerusalem has been preserved across the centuries: "If I forget thee, O Jerusalem, let my right hand wither" (Ps. 137:5). Today the Western Wall of the Temple precinct is the magnetic center of Jerusalem, just as Jerusalem is the magnetic center of Israel.

Solomon concentrated on peaceful development of the nation, broadening its cultural outlook and character and widening its international contacts through commerce. His fleet sailed from Ezion-Geber (today's Eilat) on the Gulf of Aqaba to Africa, Yemen, and India. He developed copper and iron mines in the Negev; today's Timna Mines operate in the same region. Solomon hired Phoenician architects from Lebanon to construct his palaces and even the Temple for which he is most remembered.

In addition to successful revolts in some outlying areas, there were disruptive power struggles during Solomon's reign. Taxation and work levies proved more than the people were willing to bear. Upon Solomon's death in 922 B.C.E. the country split in two. The southern part, Judah, retained Jerusalem. The northern part preserved the name of the former united kingdom of Israel, with its capital finally established at Samaria near the ancient shrine of Shechem. The divided people vacillated between enmity and cooperation.

Now and again, from Elijah in the ninth century to Ezekiel in the sixth, the celebrated biblical prophets gave voice to their pleas for justice in the land, threats of divine judgment, and in some instances assurances of hope and divine deliverance in the future. No other nation has ever made heroes of a group of men who rebuked and denounced it mercilessly, including its rulers, for the immorality that betrayed its own religious imperatives. The prophets' insistence that righteousness alone exalts a nation makes them venerated today by religious and nonreligious Israelis alike.

Even if Israel and Judah had somehow been resolute enough to meet the stringent moral demands of the prophets, or to unite in some other way, it is doubtful whether the two small kingdoms could have survived. Already in the early years of the prophetic period the star of Assyria rose in the East. The Assyrians conquered Israel in 721 B.C.E., deported nearly 30,000 inhabitants, and resettled the region with captives from other parts of the spreading empire.

Judah continued for a time. Although it was a vassal state, it succeeded in preserving the traditions of the Hebrew nation and the cult of Yahweh. However, some four generations after the demise of Israel, Judah also met defeat, at the hands of the now-ascendant Babylonians. Jerusalem fell in 587 B.C.E. and Solomon's Temple was destroyed. The First Jewish Commonwealth had terminated. But Jewish life in the land did not end. Gilead, the Galilee, and the northern Negev remained largely Jewish in their populations. The conquerors carried off to Babylon community leaders, the cultured elite, and skilled craftsmen. The wealth of the nation was confiscated. Poor peasants were left behind to eke out a living as best they could in a ravaged land, and at the mercy of enemies from Moab, Edom, and Samaria.

Probably most Jews of the Exile settled more or less comfortably into Babylonian society, which was apparently quite open and tolerant, while others retained their ethnic and religious identity. Some Jews prayed only to return to their homeland, resisting every temptation to assimilate. Surrounded as the Jewish people were by an alien culture with strange gods, many of them were made newly conscious of the uniqueness of their own faith and of the God whose merciful concern followed them wherever they went. They resolved to preserve that faith and their own identity as a covenanted people.[5]

There began to emerge in this time two significant innovations: the synagogue and the rabbinate. These twin institutions were born from necessities occasioned by separation from the Temple and its priestly-led rituals. The synagogue and the rabbinate continued to fill a need even after the Exile and the restablishment of the Temple and the priestly cult. As a local meeting place providing communal worship and the study of the Scriptures, the synagogue spread the understanding of the Jewish faith among ordinary people. The rabbinate furnished local teachers and biblical expositors. When Jews had to live in alien surroundings, the necessary adaptation of the Torah to new conditions was provided by the rabbis as learned men. Together, synagogue and rabbinate were to serve to ensure the survival of the Jewish people and their faith beyond as well as within the homeland.

Beginning in 538 B.C.E. the Persian ruler Cyrus, conqueror of Babylon, encouraged national groups to preserve their uniqueness. He not only permitted but urged the Jews to retain their faith and even to return to their homeland. He presented them with the confiscated Temple vessels in order that these might be returned to Jerusalem. Here was the initial step in what was eventually to become the Second Jewish Commonwealth, a new Judah.

A Second Commonwealth

Zerubbabel, a descendant of King David, led one of the first bands of returning exiles (by tradition, about 50,000 in number). He rededicated the altar at Jerusalem, and began reconstruction of the Temple. Armed opposition from non-Jews stopped the work for a number of years, until the extraordinary efforts of the priest-prophets Haggai and Zechariah finally prevailed upon the people to complete the Temple (516 B.C.E.). It was a "humble, plain, undecorated" affair, and yet it proved of great significance in the reviving of Jewish hopes and faith.

Of equal import was the task of purifying both religion and people from corrupting influences. The methods used were a rigorous observance of the Torah and an abandonment of marriages with non-Jews. The salient figure in this effort was Ezra. By tradition, he returned from Babylon some fifty years after the initial band of Jews, leading some eighteen hundred exiles and armed with priestly and civic authority conferred by the Persian king. Ezra saw to it that specially trained men read and explained the Torah in public places on each market day. He revived the celebration of Sukkot. He laid the foundation for the Great Synod (Knesset Hag'dolah), which transferred religious authority from the hereditary priesthood to the scholars and gradually created normative Judaism. As for the abrogation of mixed marriages, this action was undertaken for religious and moral reasons alike. In those times such marriages implied a sanctioning of the partner's pagan religious rites, which included idol worship, religious prostitution, and even infanticide. These practices, together with the mass orgies frequently involved, had often enticed Jews away from obedience to the commandments of Yahweh and the moral imperatives central to the Covenant. On the other hand, the incipient tendency here toward a closed society met a certain opposition in this time, as the books of Ruth and Jonah testify.

Under the aegis of Persia, the Jews of Babylon, Egypt, and a revived Judah found themselves under a single political authority, with freedom to travel and exchange ideas.[6] With peace regained and the Temple rebuilt, Jerusalem once again became the center of Jewish life within the small region of Judah, which itself gained a considerable degree of autonomy lasting over three centuries, even during the suzerainty of the Ptolemies of Egypt.[7] Under the newly favorable conditions the land was redeveloped and irrigation systems and terraces rebuilt. Towns and cities grew, as did the population. The developing forms and institutions of the Jewish religion spread through much of the nation. Proof that Judaism was able to gain secure allegiance would be shown later on in the resolute struggles against its suppression.

For Jews outside the land, especially those in close contact with Greek civilization, Judah retained a special significance not unlike that of today's Israel in the eyes of world Jewry. Judah provided an extra dimension and meaning for Judaism, to which Diaspora Jews remained faithful even while they acceded to many Greek ways. Judah sustained their nationhood. It kept alive the memories of their shared past. Furthermore, the Temple at Jerusalem was still the center of worship and celebration for Jews everywhere.[8]

As an independent Jewish culture grew in strength within the homeland, it was suddenly faced in the fourth century B.C.E. with the same challenge of Hellenism that had been confronting Jews elsewhere. In 332 Alexander the Great swept through Judah on his way to Egypt and forced it out of its isolation. After his early death the Ptolemies of Egypt gained suzerainty over Judea (as it now became generally known) and continued to import Hellenizing influences. Many upper-class Jews, including priests, were captivated by Greek interests and modes of living, but not so the masses of the people. As Sachar writes, every people of the ancient world succumbed sooner or later to the allurements of Hellenism except "the stubborn little folk of Palestine."[9]

However, the victories over Ptolemy by the Seleucids of Syria boded ill for the Jews. In 175 B.C.E., with the nation already divided over Hellenization, Antiochus IV sought to compel all his subjects to adopt Greek ways. The Temple of Yahweh was dedicated to Zeus. Swine were sacrificed on the altar, and Jews throughout the land were ordered to do the same, a most loathsome practice in their sight. Imperial troops plundered the Temple treasury, carrying off Jewish sacred objects and destroying Torah scrolls. A false rumor of the Emperor's death inspired an uprising. The traitorous priests were slain and the Temple cleansed. Antiochus thereupon determined to wipe out Judaism. His legions slaughtered many Jews and enslaved others. The Jews responded by rebelling. In 166 B.C.E. at Modin, northwest of Jerusalem, the priest Mattathias acted to abolish the pagan sacrifices. He and his sons, who became known as "the Maccabees," led a revolution. In 165 they succeeded in liberating the Temple mount and rededicated it to Yahweh. Here was one of history's first wars for religious freedom. It remains, accordingly, of abiding significance for Israelis and Jews everywhere. The event is commemorated each year at Hanukkah, the Feast of Lights.

Peace proved to be as elusive then as it is today. Fierce warfare alternated with periods of truce until 141, when the Seleucids capitulated. Simon Maccabeus was confirmed by a Jewish assembly as both ruler of a sovereign state and high priest. The Hasmonean Dynasty had begun. As Seleucid power declined, the Hasmonean rulers gradually expanded the boundaries of their land, and finally controlled much of the area once ruled by King Solomon. (See Map Two.)

The exuberance of the Jews over their rewon independence was reflected in active proselytizing for Judaism. Some of the more joyful songs of the Book of Psalms seem to come from this time. For seventy years the Second Jewish Commonwealth remained in a state of well-being. However, her own rulers were sowing the seeds of strife and final destruction. Simon's son, John Hyrcanus, violated Maccabean ideals by engaging in such policies as enforced conversions of conquered tribes, destruction of the Samaritans' temple, and the oppression of neighboring peoples. The successors of Hyrcanus were even worse. They aroused the antagonism of their own people, with the Pharisees in the forefront of the opposition. When exercised by Jewish rulers, tyranny and pagan practices were even more abhorrent to Jews than when engaged in by foreigners.

A series of civil uprisings erupted, only to be met by merciless retaliations. Thousands of Jews were either killed or exiled by Alexander Jannaeus, their own king. Finally, in 63 B.C.E. the Roman general Pompey was called upon by Pharisee leaders to assume control of the country in the interests of peace and security. The King's followers together with others dedicated to the Commonwealth strongly resisted. When the Roman legions at last broke through the Temple walls, it was the Sabbath. Most of the defenders would not desecrate the day even in self-defense. In consequence, the blood of thousands of pious Jews was spilled. The Second Jewish Commonwealth was ending as it began, with the people's refusal to abandon allegiance to Yahweh and the Torah.

The leaders who had besought Rome's aid were to be sadly disillusioned. The Roman domain itself became engulfed in civil strife. Because Jews supported the Parthians in a temporary defeat of Rome in Syria and Palestine, the Romans, upon returning in victory, slaughtered thousands of Jews. They then installed Herod as King of Judea. His reign of thirty-five years produced many social and economic benefits. Nevertheless, even the magnificent Temple he rebuilt could not overcome the people's hatred of him. It was more than a matter of offense because of his Idumean ancestry. The Jews were shocked by Herod's terrible acts of cruelty, even to his own family.

The Common Era

According to the New Testament, Herod ordered the slaying of all male children "in Bethlehem and in all that region who were two years old or under" (Matt. 2:16). When the Kingdom was divided upon Herod's death in 4 B.C.E., Archelaus was assigned Judea, Samaria, and Idumea. After Archelaus was ban-

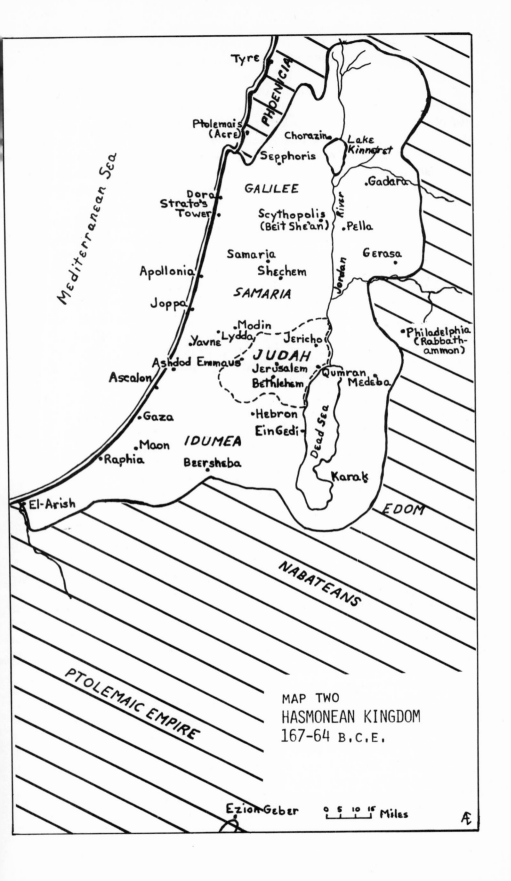

Tyre

PHOENICIA

Ptolemais
(Acre)

Chorazin

Lake
Kinneret

Sepphoris

Mediterranean Sea

GALILEE

Gadara

Dora
Strato's
Tower

Scythopolis
(Beit She'an)

Pella

River

Samaria

Shechem

Gerasa

Apollonia

SAMARIA

Joppa

Jordan

Modin

Lydda

Jericho

Philadelphia
(Rabbath-
ammon)

Yavne

JUDAH

Ashdod Emmaus

Jerusalem

Qumran

Medeba

Ascalon

Bethlehem

Gaza

Hebron
EinGedi

Dead Sea

Maon

IDUMEA

Raphia

Beersheba

Karak

El-Arish

EDOM

NABATEANS

MAP TWO

HASMONEAN KINGDOM
167-64 B.C.E.

PTOLEMAIC EMPIRE

Ezion-Geber   0 5 10 15 Miles

Æ

ished, the region was placed under Roman procurators, whom the Jews resented greatly.

In Galilee, where the tetrarch Antipas ruled, a ferment of nationalist and messianic expectations contributed to Jewish unrest and to actual uprisings. Not strangely, Jesus of Nazareth found responsive crowds in that region. Yet it is understandable that his career and death went largely unnoticed in the land as a whole. For there were many Jewish prophets and reformers, a number of whom were killed by the Roman authorities as threats to their rule. (We do not here imply any disparagement or negation of the Christian testimony that Jesus was "more than a prophet.")

The capable and sympathetic rule of Herod Agrippa lasted only three years (41–44 C.E.). The procurators who followed had no sympathy for Judaism and oppressed the Jews financially, politically, and religiously. During the intolerable administration of Gessius Florus, rebels seized the Temple, the Roman citadel, and the Herodian palace, while another band captured the stronghold of Masada above the Dead Sea. The land was once again under Jewish control. A four-year struggle ensued before Vespasian and his son Titus could subdue the populace and reconquer Jerusalem, by then reduced to ruins including the Temple. The last Jewish stronghold in Jerusalem fell in 70 C.E. Today's visitor to Rome will see depicted upon the Arch of Titus the victory procession with the confiscated Temple menorah.

The Roman celebration was somewhat premature. Several Jewish strongholds still resisted. The last to fall was Masada, where fewer than a thousand Jews, including women and children, held out for almost three years more. At last, faced with certain defeat, and either enslavement or death by torture, the survivors committed mass suicide. A hopeless cause gained a certain vindication through the weapon of self-destruction, which robbed the Romans of the *coup de grâce*. The epic of Masada is foremost in the consciousness of Israelis today. Their watchword is: "Masada shall not fall again."

For all their harshness, the Roman overlords did not seek to exterminate the Jews or even to eradicate Judaism. Thus, at the very time Jerusalem was being sacked, the religious leader Johanan ben Zakkai was permitted to establish at Yavne (Jabneh) an academy devoted to the preservation of the Jewish heritage. But sixty years later the Emperor Hadrian made renewed opposition inevitable by forbidding circumcision and starting to build a Roman city to replace Jerusalem. Simon Bar Kochba, with the blessing of the esteemed Rabbi Akiba, led the Judeans in a second revolt against Rome. The evidence suggests that Bar Kochba was hailed as the Messiah. The people, fired by religious zeal, looked for the end of suffering and the coming of God's Kingdom upon earth.

Initially, the revolt was phenomenally successful. The Jews regained control of Jerusalem and rededicated the altar. But then Rome's greatest military figure, Severus, was called from Britain. His legions finally smashed the rebellion. Bar Kochba and Akiba were put to death. Probably a half-million Jewish lives were sacrificed, not just in battle but in indiscriminate massacres and the gladiatorial arenas of the Empire. So many remaining Jews were sold into slavery that the price of slaves dropped sharply.[10]

The land itself was devastated, especially in Judea. Trees, vineyards, and fields were ruthlessly destroyed. Hundreds of villages and towns were levelled. Famine and disease killed untold numbers of survivors of the war.

In 135 C.E. the autonomy of the Jews in their homeland ended, a condition that endured—with one brief interruption in the seventh century—until the twentieth century. The very name "Judea" was expunged in favor of "Palestine" ("country of the Philistines"), after the ancient enemies of the Hebrews. The Roman city of Aelia Capitolina was erected upon the ruins of Jerusalem. A temple to Jupiter covered the Temple area, the most holy site of the Jewish people. So much as a visit to the city meant death for Jews—save on the ninth day of Ab, anniversary of the Temple's destruction, when for a fee Jews were permitted to visit the site and mourn the event. (This is the origin of the phrase "Wailing Wall."[11]) All connections between the Jewish people and their land were thus intended to be severed forever.[12]

Furthermore, Hadrian was determined to stamp out Judaism, having found in it the very key to Jewish resistance. For three years his troops hunted down religious leaders and scholars, and all who gave evidence of observing their faith. However, in 138 C.E. Antoninus Pius, Hadrian's successor, rescinded the prohibitions and once again acknowledged the Jewish community's right to observe and teach its faith. The attitudes of the rulers changed so much that in 211 C.E. Palestinian Jews were granted Roman citizenship along with other residents of the area.

The rabbis had been struggling to keep alive the remembrance of the Temple. After 135 the difficulty of the task increased immeasurably. The very survival of Judaism and the Jewish people in their homeland was in question. Whenever a more sympathetic or relaxed administration permitted, pilgrimages to the Temple site were encouraged. The festivals of Pesach, Shavuot (observing the giving of the Torah), and Sukkot—traditional pilgrimage occasions—received especial attention. The Seder service was revised to include prayers for Jerusalem and the Temple. The ram's horn (shofar), formerly used at the Temple, was introduced into synagogue services. The language of Aramaic was barred from synagogues and higher schools, and was replaced by Hebrew. In fact, the speaking of Hebrew became equal to living in the land as evidence of Jewish piety—a striking parallel, as we shall see, to the twentieth century. Emphasis was put upon the Sabbatical Year when tithes were abolished, debts cancelled, and the land allowed to lie fallow, with everything that grew of its own accord becoming public property.

For centuries the southern part of the country had been the spiritual and commercial center of Jewish life, and the most populous area. But now it was so barren that most survivors had fled to Galilee, while others relocated in the Negev. It was in the North that the new Jewish centers of learning were to develop over the next few centuries, until Babylon became the seat of Jewish scholarship due to Christian persecutions of Palestinian Jewry.

The two Jewish wars with Rome also affected relations between Judaism and the new Christian, or Nazarene, sect. The developing break between the two sides was made that much more final by the destruction and scattering of the Jewish-Christian congregations of Jerusalem and other towns, as well as by the refusal of the Nazarenes to follow Bar Kochba in the second uprising.

Christian theologians were to look back upon the Roman destruction of the

Jewish nation and fancy that they saw in it God's judgment upon his people for failing to accept Jesus as the Messiah. The French historian, Jules Isaac, has effectively argued against such a simplistic rendering of events on the part of innumerable Christian spokesmen. Isaac emphasizes the obvious point that the dispersion of Jews beyond Palestine extended over many centuries, starting seven hundred years before the beginning of Christianity. And he stresses a fact even more significant for our present study: that whether we speak of the first century or of the second century C.E. or even of later, the Jews have never been entirely dispersed from their ancestral homeland. In sum, the contentions of the Christian apologists involve "a theological myth without the slightest foundation."[13] Despite the falsehoods and prejudice in such a reading of history, or perhaps because of these elements, the theologians' claims were, unhappily, to help ensure future persecutions of Jews at the hands of a religiously, socially, and politically dominant Christendom.

3. Neglected Years, Renascent Years

THE IMPRESSION is sometimes conveyed that very little of consequence took place in Palestine over the long period from Roman times to the early modern era. More critically, it is often presumed that Jews had no real influence or presence in the region during that period. Both notions are quite false. They help prevent a proper understanding of Israel and the Middle East today.

A Persisting Community

One evidence of the resilience of Jewish life in Palestine in the centuries following the Second Roman War is the great amount of building. Remains of some of the new villages and synagogues built during the second to sixth centuries have been excavated and bear testimony to the on-going life of the community.[1] (See Map Three.) Another evidence of Jewry's vitality in the land is the authority it retained in religion and even to some extent in politics. During some periods local self-rule was permitted, and Jews held high office. More important, the Romans acknowledged a descendant of Hillel as president of the rabbinical assembly, which after the Temple's destruction succeeded the Sanhedrin. In the next generation the Romans accepted the Jews' affirmation that the holder of this office—at that time, Rabbi Judah—was the head of the entire Jewish community. Here was a new focus for Jewish life. The office became a kind of symbolic substitute for the Temple and Jerusalem. More significantly, "the theocratic conception of the Jewish people, and the intimate association between their political survival and their religious loyalty were preserved."[2]

The most crucial and creative work of these years is still to be mentioned. The whole foundation of post-biblical Judaism was laid by the rabbis of Palestine, culminating in the work of Rabbi Judah. By 200 C.E. he finished the massive task of collecting and codifying the teachings of the most respected sages and scholars of preceding generations.[3]

While the Jewish community was revitalizing itself in Palestine and adapting

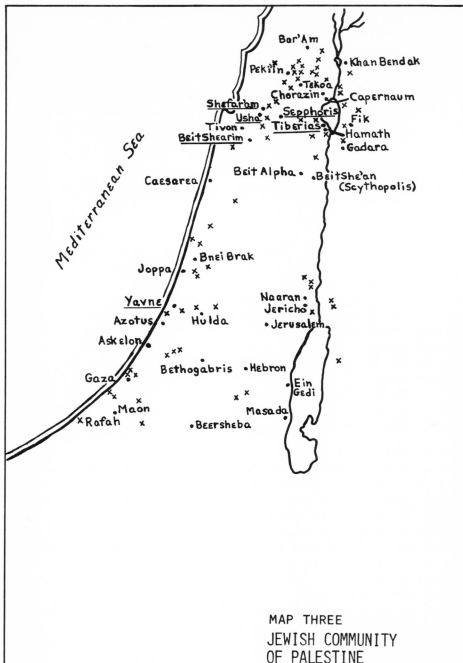

Bar'Am

Pekiin × × × •Khan Bendak
× × ×
× ×
× •Tekoa
Chorazin • × •Capernaum
Shefaram • × × × Sepphoris• × •Fik
Usha •× •Tiberias• ×
Tivon• × × × •Hamath
BeitShearim • × •Gadara
×

Beit Alpha • ×BeitShe'an
Caesarea • (Scythopolis)
×

×

×
× ×
•Bnei Brak
Joppa • × ×
×

Naaran• × ×
Yavne • × × × Jericho• × × ×
Azotus• × •Jerusalem
Askelon• Hulda
× × ×

Gaza• Bethogabris •Hebron
× × •Ein
× × Gedi
•Maon × × Masada ×
×Rafah × •Beersheba

MAP THREE

JEWISH COMMUNITY
OF PALESTINE
2ND – 6TH CENTURIES

×   Additional
         Communities
Usha   Locations of
        Rabbinical Assembly

0 5 10 15 Miles

its religious forms to new conditions, the new child of Judaism, the Christian church, was spreading elsewhere in the Roman world. Emperor Constantine ended the persecution of the church in 312 by recognizing Christianity as one legitimate religion of the Empire.[4] In 380 Theodosius I made Christianity the only acceptable religion. Formerly persecuted, Christians now became the persecutors—of pagans, Jews, and Samaritans. By 438, public offices and professions were closed to Jews. Slaves and freedmen were forbidden to convert to Judaism, and Jews were barred from marrying Christians. The erection of new synagogues was disallowed, only the most essential repairs of existing structures were permitted, and any synagogue that had been seized and consecrated as a Christian church (even by an unruly mob) could not be restored to its original owners. Subsequent legislation removed citizenship rights from all non-Christians of the Empire, thus denying them equality before the law.

Until the early part of the fourth century the church's presence was little felt within Palestine. Then numbers of Eastern Christians began to appear. Some came as pilgrims; others were monks intent on remaining.[5] This influx disrupted the relative placidity the land had enjoyed since 138. Rancorous divisions over theological matters, an affliction of the early church, became manifest here. The Eastern monks were especially intolerant and even violent over issues of theology, often climaxing their verbal disputations with pitched battles. During the fifth century, Palestine was wracked by this kind of violence. And the monks needed very little encouragement to turn upon the Jews, whom they had come to identify as killers of the Savior. Synagogues and entire villages were set ablaze, and not infrequently the inhabitants were massacred.

Ever since the third century the Jewish community, along with other provincials of the Empire, had been economically hard-pressed by heavy taxes, an avaricious bureaucracy, and a generally declining economy. The Palestinian population had borne an even heavier financial burden than other provinces because large concentrations of Roman troops were garrisoned there to fight the Persian enemy. Now, harried by discriminatory legislation and subjected to mob violence, numbers of Jews of Palestine—many of whom could trace their tenure of the land to Joshua's time—began reluctantly to emigrate to Persia to escape the combination of religious, political, and economic tyranny. Such emigration increased in the sixth century as a result of Emperor Justinian's measures to force conversion to Christianity.

Within the country a vast population shift occurred. The South, which normally held the largest Jewish population, made a very slow recovery from the depredations of the second war with Rome. Even as late as the fourth century, Jews may have been in a minority there, whereas in Galilee they doubtless constituted the majority. Almost all of the land was farmed by Jews, even when the ownership was held by the State or Roman landlords. Christian writers in the early fifth century complained of the small number of Christians living in the land and deplored the dominance of Jews and Samaritans. The Jewish community was vigorous enough to rebel occasionally against repressive laws or foreign officials in the fourth and sixth centuries. By the seventh century, however, the Jewish population had dwindled considerably. Yet when the Persian army attacked the Eastern Roman Empire (now called Byzantium) in 614, large numbers of Palestinian Jews were on hand to take up arms to bring about the defeat of their Christian oppressors.

Evidence of the size of the Jewish community in the land is thus attested, both by its military role and by the promises the Persian victors made to it: the Temple could be rebuilt, and Jerusalem could once again become the capital of an autonomous Jewish province. Unfortunately, Persia was unable to hold her new territories. The Byzantines reconquered them within fifteen years. The fighting and religious strife during these years brought devastation once again to the cities (including much of Jerusalem), villages, and agricultural land. Christian and Jewish religious buildings alike suffered great damage. The country was half-emptied of its population.[6]

The Coming of the Arabs

The Byzantine and the Persian empires were alike so debilitated that neither could withstand the onslaughts beginning in 636 of Arabs who were followers of the new religion of Islam. Here were primitive desert men who, like the Hebrew tribes in their initial conquest of Canaan, were able to subdue more culturally advanced peoples. But there was an essential difference: The first Arab conquerors actually opposed Arab settlement of Palestine (Filastin in Arabic), and only wanted to dominate the country politically and economically. Even after this policy changed and settlement was encouraged, no rapid transformation occurred. Arab historians such as Ya'quibi and Ibn-Hawqual, writing at the close of the ninth and the start of the tenth centuries, indicated that Arabs were not yet the dominant people. Probably for at least a century and a half, Eastern Christians remained the majority population, with Jews and Samaritans as substantial minorities. (An earthquake of the eighth century destroyed thirty synagogues in Tiberias alone.) Foreign mercenaries and the intrusion of desert tribes added to the complex situation.[7] Despite all the adverse conditions of the first three and one-half centuries of Islamic rule, Palestinian Jews remained a sizable community until as late as the twelfth century, as the Crusaders were then to attest.[8] Nevertheless, the Arab conquest was decisive because inevitably it brought about the expropriation of land held and worked by Jewish and Christian owners or tenants (including religious sites), and introduced a new national (and religious) majority. The residual Jewish character of the country was ended and replaced by an Arabized population by the eleventh century.[9]

Muhammad had exterminated entire Jewish communities of ancient origin in the Arabian peninsula because they refused to accept his religious claims. But his generals and successors were much more lenient, unless confronted by opposition. As a matter of fact, Jews, Samaritans, and reputedly heretical Christians in Palestine and Syria at first welcomed the Muslims for delivering them from their erstwhile oppressor, Byzantium.

The Arabs adopted from the Persians the millet system of allowing internal autonomy to religious communities under their control, though with a status subordinate to Muslims. Christians and Jews alike were forced to remain unobtrusive in their observances so that the "true believers," the followers of Muhammad, would not be disturbed. The first caliph allowed Jews to supervise the Temple site in Jerusalem, and, apparently, to build a synagogue nearby.[10] But within a few years the Arabs rescinded this decision and claimed the site for themselves. Between 685 and 705 they erected the magnificent Dome of the

Rock commemorating Muhammad's ascent through the "seven heavens," and in the eighth century the Mosque of el-Aqsa on another part of the mount.

The fact remains that the Arab rulers made it possible for the Jews to return to Jerusalem. Though kept from the Temple area, Jews were able to purchase the slope of the Mount of Olives for use during religious festivals and as a burial place.

At Tiberias during the seventh and eighth centuries, revitalized Jewish scholarship produced the final Masoretic text of the Hebrew Bible, which became the definitive version for Christians as well as Jews.

Unhappily, the tolerance of the Muslim conquerors was succeeded fairly soon by intolerance and fanaticism among lower levels of Islamic society, as well as by increasing hostility from within the caliphate once the capital was moved from Damascus to Baghdad in 762. Christians and Jews alike suffered the consequences: repression, humiliation, extortion, confiscation, and violence. Nor did political peace last. Within a hundred years the Islamic Empire,[11] which had stretched from the Atlantic to the Indian Oceans, broke up into a number of kingdoms.

With the Arab conquest of Palestine, the land lost its individuality, and except for the Crusader Kingdom of Jerusalem in the twelfth century, never regained it until the early 1920's. As a remote corner of successive empires, the region suffered continuing neglect. It also became a battleground for various parties: warring Arab clans, rival claimants to the caliphate, Bedouin raiders, and invading Turkish tribes. This general state of affairs continued, unbelievably enough, for more than a thousand years, with devastating effects upon people, land, and culture. The grandeur of consecutive imperial capitals at Damascus, Baghdad, and Cairo never extended to the region of Palestine, nor was any influence exerted by the so-called golden age of Arab-Jewish collaboration in Spain.

Arabs generally looked upon agriculture as demeaning work. Consequently, despite the great fertility of Palestine at that time, the government showed almost no interest in its proper cultivation. Arab peasants who gradually settled there possessed only primitive knowledge of farming. Soil erosion and the deterioration of terraces and irrigating systems went on apace, a process that became more and more catastrophic as the centuries passed.

Within a few years after the Fatimids of Egypt gained control over Palestine in 973, conditions worsened.[12] Early in the eleventh century Caliph Al-Hakim sought forcibly to convert or expel both Jews and Christians. He desired his domain to be exclusively Muslim, an extreme to which no other Muslim ruler ever went. He ordered the destruction of all synagogues and churches.

Crusaders, Mamelukes, Ottomans

The demolishing of churches, including the Church of the Holy Sepulcher in Jerusalem, helped prepare the way for the infamous Crusades, which over a period of two hundred years impelled hundreds of thousands of European Christians to "save the Holy Land from the infidel."

The army of the First Crusade arrived in 1098 and set about slaughtering the populace without regard for religion, sex, or age. Even native Christians were given no quarter. When Jerusalem fell in 1099, Muslims and Jews alike were massacred. The Jewish community was burned alive in its synagogue. In proportion to their numbers, Jews suffered the greatest losses because, mistakenly as it turned out, they had fled to the cities as the normal foci of protection where they fought alongside the other local defenders. Yet it was on the cities that the Crusaders concentrated their attacks, and thence reprisals. Catastrophe struck Jews not alone in Jerusalem but in Haifa, Acre, Jaffa, Lydda, Hebron, and other fortified towns. At Ramla and Jaffa they were scattered as refugees. Only those in Caesarea, which city opened its gates, and those in the Galilean villages escaped.

The laws of the Crusaders' Latin Kingdom of Jerusalem prohibited Jews from owning land, and only a tiny minority of Jews were allowed to live in Jerusalem. On the other hand, following the original Crusader destructiveness, there was some betterment in the fortunes of all the surviving local people. As a minority in the country, the Crusaders found that the cooperation and services of the populace were essential. For about one hundred years, and in the face of almost constant warfare on the frontiers, the Latin rulers were able to provide internal security and justice in the courts. Commerce and agriculture prospered due to improved markets.

The thirteenth century witnessed considerable Jewish immigration. After the Kurdish leader Saladin conquered Jerusalem from the Crusaders, he invited Jews to return to the city. Many responded, including 300 French and English rabbis. Following yet another ruination of the city in mid-century—this time by Tartars—the famous Spanish rabbi Nachmanides reestablished the Jerusalem Jewish community, which was never again to be totally eliminated. At the same time a French rabbi settled in Acre with his *yeshiva* of some 300 students. Spanish and German Jews followed.

When the Christian overlords were finally evicted, government by administrative decentralization and local autonomy protected by a system of law was replaced once again by the arbitrary and often irresponsible rule of a central royal court. Even when the ruler was himself a responsible man, he failed to achieve necessary control over the lower bureaucracy, particularly in the outlying regions. This political deficiency obtained for hundreds of years—under the Mamelukes[13] of Egypt (1260–1517) and again under the Ottoman Turks (1517–1917). An important consequence for our concerns is that while both these dynasties were often sympathetic to the indigenous Jewish populace, and sometimes encouraged settlement by Jews in Palestine, they never marshalled the necessary administrative machinery to protect or promote such interests. The local officials lacked any genuine concern to improve the region. The people as a whole—Muslims, Jews, and Christians—remained at the mercy of these men, who sought by every means to reap a continuing harvest in taxes, fees, and bribes. The successive dynastic rulers were themselves not completely innocent, since they received sizable shares of these funds.

Generation after generation, conditions deteriorated in most Muslim provinces away from the capital cities. In Palestine, the cities and fertile plain along the coast were deliberately laid waste by Mameluke rulers. Bedouin raids became increasingly frequent and destructive, and more and more land went out of cultivation. Olive and date palm trees were wantonly, or at least stupidly, put to the axe. Herds of goats devoured crops and natural vegetation. Internecine village warfare grew and tribal blood feuds flourished. Marauders and brigands became more blatant as officials became more lax. The Ottomans instituted a policy of punishing nonpayment of taxes by sacking whole villages and destroying trees and crops. This practice forced the abandonment of ever more land by people who could no longer support themselves on it. Even greater Bedouin infiltration was thus invited, and this completed the circle of destruction. The losses were greatest within the Christian and Jewish communities, although Muslims were by no means spared.

To all this man-made destructiveness must be added certain so-called natural calamities. From the thirteenth to the sixteenth centuries many droughts and plagues of locusts brought famine. The Black Death raged in the fourteenth century. During the Mameluke period some two-thirds of the population perished in these and other ways.

It may well be the case that not until Mameluke rule did Palestine become a predominantly Muslim country. And it was probably not until the Ottoman era—nine or ten centuries after the original Arab conquest—that the country "acquired a substantial Arab population," in the ethnic sense.[14]

During the fourteenth and fifteenth centuries, increasing numbers of Jews took up residence in Palestine, in spite of the difficulties of sustaining life there. The Ottoman Turks deliberately opened their lands to Jewish immigration. This meant salvation for many thousands of European Jews, especially in the sixteenth century, by which time Christian persecution, forced conversion, and expulsion of Jews had reached a zenith. (By the sixteenth century many Christian countries had simply banished their entire Jewish populations.) Yet equal numbers of Jews met death while seeking to reach the East.

Most of the newcomers settled in the major cities of the Ottoman Empire where they could carry on with accustomed means of livelihood. Other Jews went on to Palestine despite its dreadful condition. Jewish populations were augmented in Lydda, Ramla, Tiberias, Hebron, Gaza, Acre, Beit She'an, and Jerusalem. But the greatest center of settlement proved to be the city of Safed in the Galilean hill country. During part of the sixteenth century Safed became the spiritual center of Jewry. However, it was sacked by Bedouin and Druses[15] in the next century. In addition, an imperially-supported settlement of Jews upon the land around Tiberias was wiped out by bands of brigands.

In the eighteenth century newly immigrating Jews from Smyrna and Poland resettled Safed and Tiberias, as well as adding to the populations of Jerusalem and other cities. Yet by the early nineteenth century the abuse and neglect of hundreds of years had brought the land of Palestine to almost total ruin. This intolerable situation meant enforced emigration for Jew, Muslim, and Christian alike. A land that had supported 3,000,000 people in Maccabean times could now sustain no more than 500,000.

Fresh Beginnings

In the early nineteenth century a fresh wind stirred. A brief period of Egyptian control of Palestine opened the door to travelers from the West, to biblical scholars and archaeologists, and to founders of Christian schools and hospitals.

The motivation behind much of the newcomers' activity was missionary: to convert Muslims and Jews to Christianity. There was also concern for the religious education of the native Christian population. To this end, Bibles in Arabic were distributed. Much less opposition to these efforts came from the Muslim Sultan than from the Eastern churches.

British sympathy for the return of Jews to their homeland was expressed as early as 1838 when the seventh Earl of Shaftesbury urged the great European powers to facilitate that return. Others went so far as to advocate a sovereign Jewish state. Much public and official support was forthcoming for the general idea, even from the other powers and from such a personage as former President John Adams. It was viewed as "a generous and noble act," a solution to conflicts in the area, and a means of alleviating human misery in that part of the Ottoman Empire.[16]

Unfortunately, no Jewish organization was capable of undertaking such a vast enterprise. However, there was significant new Jewish interest in the land during this period. Hasidim from Poland came to settle.[17] The British Jew, Sir Moses Montefiore, paid several visits to Jerusalem, and through his personal bearing and eminence did much to restore a sense of dignity to the downtrodden Jews of the city. He also extended moral and financial support to new enterprises, such as the first modern Jewish settlement outside Jerusalem's walls.[18] Sir Moses and Adolphe Crémieux of France were successful in intervening with the Sultan in behalf of Damascus Jews who were threatened by mob violence. Further, the British Government assumed responsibility for the safety of Jewish people in the domains of the corrupt and ineffectual Ottoman rulers. The result was that for the first time in approximately seventeen hundred years Jews were given the same protection that external authority had long provided other nationals and religious communities in the area. In addition to Great Britain, several states, including the United States, intervened to protect the Sultan's non-Muslim subjects.[19]

European powers were now paying renewed attention to the Middle East because of its strategic position astride the bridge to Africa, India, and the Far East, and the financial and imperial interests there at stake. Although the Sultan was too weak to resist the demands of the European nations, mutual jealousies preserved his Empire.

New projects for revitalizing the wastelands of Palestine came from two groups: Christian pietists (particularly millenarians) and native-born and immigrant Jews.[20] Unfortunately, the Jerusalem Jews who purchased land for cultivation north of Jaffa at Petach Tikvah lacked proper agricultural knowledge. Some Russian and Rumanian Jews who had settled in Galilee were not only inexperienced in farming but suffered from the climate and from malaria. Thanks to Baron Edmond de Rothschild of France, agricultural experts were sent from Europe, and some measure of success was finally achieved.

In the mainstream of thought in the Jewish Diaspora[21] was the age-old persuasion that God would one day gather his scattered people to their homeland and restore Eretz Yisrael immediately prior to the advent of the Messiah and the messianic age. In the interim, the exiles were to pray for the coming of this time and the welfare of the land. They continued to mourn their expatriation and to long for the return. Such rabbinic teaching was not interpreted to mean that

Jews could not return to the homeland if they wished to do so.[22] Nevertheless, the emphasis upon a divine form of deliverance had precluded any mass movement to the ancestral home. There were, of course, brief times when the belief in the imminent appearance of the Messiah excited whole Jewish communities and led them to prepare for the expected return.

In Europe, a coincidence of developments was revolutionizing Jewish attitudes toward the land of Zion. At the end of the eighteenth century the French Revolution quickly turned the thinking of Jews in Western Europe to a new kind of messianic hope: the advent of an age of emancipation, full equality for all, and the fulfilling of Jewry's mission through its contribution to humanitarian betterment everywhere.[23] During the nineteenth century in Eastern Europe, socialism captured the imagination of some Jews in the same way. The collective society was held to enshrine the Hebrew prophets' vision and demand of equal justice.

The first of these two dreams was abruptly ended for many by the widespread, virulent antisemitism in "enlightened" France revealed by the Dreyfus Affair (1894–1906).[24] The second dream was shattered, or at least its fulfillment was delayed, for many Russian and other Jews by the czarist regime's abetting of pogroms visited upon the Jewish people in 1881 together with the passing of extremely harsh anti-Jewish laws the following year. Tens of thousands of Jews fled to the United States, Canada, South Africa, and Western Europe. (Ironically, Germany appeared as a land of hope.) But for other Jews the time had come to "go home" to Eretz Yisrael no matter what the conditions there.

Even before these events, a few nineteenth-century Jewish leaders had called for a revision of thinking about the homeland and for appropriate action. A colonization society to implement immediate settlement and a tract on behalf of Jewish nationalism instead of assimilation were two of the early attempts. Leo Pinsker preceded Theodor Herzl in proclaiming the need for a Jewish state in order that Jews might have the respect of the world and, with other peoples, a sovereign defender of their rights. For Pinsker, such a state was vitally necessary to the "auto-emancipation" of the Jewish people from an imposed "ghetto mentality." Among the consequences of these efforts was the founding of the Lovers of Zion (Hoveve Zion), which sent Russian and Rumanian pioneers to Palestine in the nineteenth century. However, the overall impact and results were negligible.

Herzl and the New Zionists

Something new was needed if the Jewish love for Zion was to attain concrete realization. The inspiration came in the person of Theodor Herzl (1860–1904). In the beginning Herzl hardly seemed to be the man for the task. As an emancipated and assimilated Viennese Jew, he knew very little of the plight of Jews in Eastern Europe. He had been assuming that enlightenment and education would soon put an end to any lingering remnants of antisemitism.[25] However, as a journalist he was assigned to the trial of Captain Dreyfus. In the years that followed, he witnessed with dismay the terrible wave of antisemitism that was set in motion by this affair and that threatened to engulf France. In a complete reversal of his life-outlook, Herzl concluded that Jews would never be safe anywhere until they had a national home. Such a home would not only give them recognition as a nation; it would also provide a haven in times of trouble. Once large numbers of Jews were removed from other lands, Herzl reasoned, those remaining as citizens by choice would not face the same enmity.

With the fervent enthusiasm of a convert, Herzl immediately gave voice to his new convictions. His famous pamphlet, *The Jewish State,* has been reprinted many times. For Herzl, not only would the Jewish people benefit from the vitality released by such a creation; all mankind would reap advantages from it. To bespeak political sovereignty for the Jewish people was not an entirely new idea. But for a Western Jew to do so and to reject immigration to the West, and for there to be people prepared to listen—these things were certainly new.[26]

Almost overnight, a new—and yet not new—national movement was born. The logical name for it was "Zionism"—not an essentially new term any more than was the phenomenon itself.

The Zionist movement was not at all alien to the spirit of the times. It accorded well with other nineteenth-century (and twentieth-century) struggles for the recognition of national identity and the self-determination of peoples. This explains why most of the early opposition to Zionism came not from outside the Jewish community but from within.[27] Many Orthodox Jews insisted that the return to Zion had to wait upon divine intervention, while believers in assimilation feared that a Jewish nationalist movement would prejudice their position and aggravate antisemitism.

Having been reared in a nonreligious environment, Theodor Herzl was totally unaware of the emotional and spiritual ties that bound untold numbers of Jews to Eretz Yisrael. Indeed, for him Palestine was not the indispensable anchorage of the Jewish state. But at the First Zionist Congress in Basel, Switzerland in 1897 the opposite view prevailed. Despite the fact that the Jewish communities of Eastern Europe had suffered terrible adversity and loss of life in the previous two decades, and still lived under the threat of the sword, the representatives of these communities refused to allow consideration to be given, even as a temporary measure, to any place but the ancestral land.

Herzl appealed to the Sultan of the Ottoman Empire to permit Jews to settle in Palestine as a corporate entity. The Sultan bluntly refused. Upon receiving this rebuff Herzl turned for help to various foreign offices. Only the British responded positively. They first offered land at El Arish in the Sinai Peninsula, but this offer was withdrawn when it was learned that water resources would be insufficient. Great Britain then offered the highlands of Uganda. This alternative was, for obvious reasons, unacceptable to Zionists. Although both places were out of the question, this episode represented the first time that a modern government had officially recognized the Jews' need of, and right to, a land of their own.

The Zionists disagreed over more than the question of whether to accept a temporary abode outside Palestine. There was the fundamental issue of whether to hold back until the entire scheme had gained outside, official sanction or to follow the pioneering course of instituting immediate though small-scale land purchases and settlements. The latter position won out, through the convergence of three claims: that only Eretz Yisrael could arouse the enthusiasm among Jews that was the precondition of success; that any authentic nation must be able to boast a specific, identifiable political entity and demonstrable, practical results;

and, on religious and historical grounds, that only the land of Zion was justified.

A permanent executive committee was elected to carry on the day-to-day work of the Zionist Organization. Following upon Herzl's untimely death, and in face of his lack of success with the Sultan,[28] the Zionist executive concentrated its efforts on buying land, preparing immigrants for the kinds of labor they would have to do, helping settlers, establishing schools and hospitals, and seeing to the teaching of Hebrew.

Whenever the Jewish National Fund bought land, it retained ownership in behalf of the Jewish people, and simply made it available or rented it to settlers. Socialists in the movement could try out on such land their principles of social and economic organization and reform. This was how the first two *kibbutzim*, Degania and Kinneret, came to be established in 1909. Such collective settlements, which have become a most noted feature of the new Israel, were peculiarly suited to the conditions of the time. The land was begging for just such sacrificial toil in order to regain its historic productivity.

Other beginnings were made. The founding of the Anglo-Palestine Banking Company immediately met a great need for available development funds and the reinvesting of profits. The new town of Tel Aviv, destined to become Israel's largest city, was begun in 1909 upon a barren expanse of sand. From 1880 to 1914, in quiet and unspectacular ways, the Jewish communities of Palestine increased markedly in number and size. The population rose from 25,000 to almost 100,000. Enterprises varied more and more, from agriculture through crafts to business ventures. The people became much more self-supporting. A social revolution was occurring. It brought new hope to Jews, new vitality to the land, and improvements in health, in opportunities for livelihood, and in the standard of living. All inhabitants, Arabs as well as Jews, benefited from these endeavors. In general, relations with the Arabs were quite helpful to both sides.

Exactly what political form the new undertakings would take was an open question. Though the Zionists of this time and later had many dreams, they were also realists. There seemed much promise that a genuinely bi-national society, such as many of the early Zionists optimistically foresaw, could be created. Hopefully, the Middle East as a whole would experience a renaissance sparked by the rebirth of the Jewish people in their land. Jews would be able to look out upon the world with a self-confidence and dignity impossible under conditions of sufferance and persecution. Jew and Arab, Christian and Muslim would be the benefactors of a new spirit and program of cooperative action.

But suddenly there was tragedy.

4. The Great War and Its Sequels

THE CATASTROPHE that descended upon Europe with World War I spread quickly to the region of our interest.[1] Germany's desire to expand eastward and Turkey's fear of the Russians made the two countries allies. Consternation struck the British. Their colonial interests in India and the Far East, the Suez Canal route, and oil supplies from the Persian Gulf were all put in jeopardy. These threats together with the isolation of Russia from her allies in the West made inevitable a military campaign in the Middle East. The Turks acted promptly and ruthlessly there to forestall insurrections and prevent support for Great Britain and Russia. Leading Arab nationalists were rounded up and executed.

In Palestine many Jews were jailed, tortured, or put to death for suspected sympathy toward the Allies. As citizens of countries with whom Turkey was at war, most Russian and Rumanian Jews in Palestine were forced to flee to Egypt for British protection. The Jewish population of 90–100,000 in 1914 was thereby reduced to about 55,000 in 1918. However, many agricultural settlers and older communities remained. Trees were ruthlessly cut down for the wood-burning locomotives, and crops and livestock were seized. At once, the fruits of a half century of the most arduous labor were lost. Zionist endeavor suffered a terrible setback.

Power Maneuverings

For all their hatred of the Turkish overlords, the Arabs were almost equally fearful of European imperialism. In consequence, they were fundamentally unsure which side to support in the War. At this juncture began the long series of negotiations, agreements, and misunderstandings that were to contribute to the deadlocks of the period after World War I and that even today help condition attitudes. Secret British-French, British-Arab, and British-Zionist agreements were made. These contradicted each other. Negotiators remained in ignorance of terms that were being worked out elsewhere, while each party evidently retained its own interpretations and reservations respecting the meaning of the agreements.

Great Britain's outlook and behavior during and immediately after the War involved much more than naked self-interest. Her leaders assumed that she could somehow aid the Arabs and the Jews together. To many Britishers, the interests of the two parties did not appear irreconcilable. In point of fact, these interests could have been reconciled had the Arab world as a whole been prepared to acknowledge the unique relationship between Jews and the land lying between the Jordan-Dead Sea Valley and the Mediterranean Sea. Since the particular Arab leaders with whom the British early negotiated were willing to recognize that relationship, the Government in Whitehall had some reason for optimism.

Of great influence upon Britain was a liberalism characterized by a new appreciation of the yearnings of oppressed peoples for freedom. A number of Britishers, including those who proved able to influence political policy, had come to know and admire Arabs, and to share the Arab dream of a revitalized people. Many of these same persons also understood and were in sympathy with Jewish aspirations for a sovereign nation. Whether Great Britain, once given a free hand in the Middle East as a whole, could have finally satisfied both peoples is a fruitless question. The opportunity was never given her because her French ally was to demand an equal role in the ultimate settlement and development of the region.

The French interest in the Middle East went back hundreds of years.[2] As a result of French involvement and expenditures in the Syrian part of the Ottoman Empire, her leaders anticipated that this area would eventually become part of greater France, with its own representatives in the National Assembly.

Under stress from the War, the British felt bound to go along with France in a division of the region into two parts. Not only did this decision conflict with the Arab dream of a large nation-state, it made the Arabs increasingly skeptical of Western promises. It was also a first and decisive means of preventing the satisfaction of the hopes of Arabs and Jews alike.

As the British-French agreement was being worked out in 1915–1916, the British independently reached some understandings with certain Arab leaders, chiefly Hussein ibn Ali, who as Sherif of Mecca was a significant Muslim leader. Hussein sought British support for an independent Arab state covering—in terms of present-day political divisions—part of Turkey, all of Iraq, Syria, Lebanon, Jordan, Israel, Saudi Arabia, and the small states on the Persian and Aqaba gulfs. Britain consented to help foster Arab independence but with an important triple proviso: The agreement would apply only to areas where she could act without detriment to her ally France;[3] it would not apply to parts of the Arabian coast; and it would not apply to an area along the Mediterranean coast (interpreted by the Arabs to mean, roughly, the Lebanon of today).

Sir Henry McMahon, the mild British representative, failed to state specifically that Palestine was to be an additional exception, though he asserted later on that he had "every reason to believe, at the time, that the fact that Palestine was not included in my pledge was well understood by King Hussein."[4] Arab leaders proceeding on the basis of the McMahon-Hussein correspondence could hardly be expected to read McMahon's mind—or, for that matter, Hussein's. This explains why—to get ahead of our story—the Arabs had justification for complaining in 1921 that Britain had failed to keep her word. Yet the British Government felt eminently justified in keeping Palestine separated from that part of the Mandate where she acknowledged Arab hegemony, and in withholding immediate self-government for Palestine. Sherif Hussein and, through him, his sons Feisal and Abdullah, were prevented from charging Great Britain with a breach of faith, because in a further diplomatic exchange with Hussein, the British explicitly stated that Palestine was *not* to be included in the future Arab nation-state. The British spokesman, D. G. Hogarth, made this specific assertion in January, 1918 upon being sent from General Allenby's headquarters to talk directly with Hussein, who had meanwhile become King of the Hejaz.

Hogarth made it clear that his Government looked with favor upon the fulfilling of Jewish aspirations to return to Palestine, and that "in so far as is compatible with the freedom of the existing population, both economic and political," Great Britain was determined that "no obstacle shall be put in the way" of the realizing of this ideal. Hogarth further pointed out that "the Moslem-Christian-Jewish character of Palestine necessitated the establishment of 'a special regime . . . approved by the world.' "5 Unfortunately, this important understanding was not made public and therefore did nothing to make the situation clear for the Arabs.

The crucial question of whether Britain intended an autonomous Jewish state in Palestine and not simply a "national home" was not cleared up at the 1918 meeting, and perhaps could not have been at so early a stage.

The Balfour Declaration

It had been only two months—to return to our original chronology—since the British Cabinet had agreed upon the Balfour Declaration. This famous policy statement of November 2, 1917 was set down in a letter from Lord Balfour to Lord Rothschild, the latter a leader in the Jewish community in England. It affirmed:

> His Majesty's Government view with favour the establishment in Palestine of a national home for the Jewish people, and will use their best endeavours to facilitate the achievement of this object, it being clearly understood that nothing shall be done which may prejudice the civil and religious rights of the existing non-Jewish communities in Palestine, or the rights and political status enjoyed by Jews in any other country.

According to Ronald Bryden,6 the Declaration constituted a watered-down version of the original draft prepared by Balfour, Mark Sykes, and others, a draft that had categorically declared for "the reconstitution of Palestine as *the* National Home of the Jewish people" (emphasis added). The qualifying phrases regarding the rights of non-Jewish communities, and the status of Jews elsewhere, were included largely at the insistence of Lord Curzon, who was, in part, concerned over the possible reactions among India's 80,000,000 Muslims. Yet, objectively speaking, the two reservations are identifiable as ways of reassuring two groups: respectively, the Arabs and Christians of Palestine, and Jews outside Palestine. In all probability, the actual wording had this reassurance as at least part of its purpose.

The fact remains that the changes finally agreed upon made the Declaration ambiguous and subject to manipulation in ways that the Government had hardly intended originally. In his memoirs David Lloyd George makes all this clear. The words "National Home" meant a Jewish state in Palestine, provided that the Jews should have in the meantime taken advantage of the opportunity offered them and become a majority of the inhabitants. Any arbitrary restrictions upon Jewish immigration or purchase of land were unthinkable to those framing the policy,[7] or, a few years later, to those at the Allies' San Remo conference when the Balfour Declaration was made an integral part of the British Mandate.

Unfortunately for all concerned, none of this was spelled out. Here was another fundamental blunder. As Bryden comments, even though the ultimate intention of the Balfour Declaration was the establishing of a Jewish state in Palestine, the British Government had not publicly committed itself to that goal. As events were to turn out, Britain's real problem—and the consequent tragedy for Arabs and Jews—arose from the illusion that she could be spared having to take sides firmly and irrevocably. However, it is certainly the case that the British position at this time advocated equality for the two peoples regardless of political boundaries.

A further complication was that no deadline was stipulated for adjudging when and whether the Jews would have taken sufficient advantage of the opportunities given them.

Yet none of this can change the momentous character of the policy decision behind the Balfour Declaration. The British Government had officially recognized "the existence of a historic Jewish right in the country and promised to assist the Jewish people in its development. . . ."[8] More than that, the Government was fostering the right of the Jewish people to reestablish themselves as a sovereign nation in Palestine.

Whatever criticisms may be made of the Balfour Declaration's wording or of the ways it was to be applied in the future, its significance remains. That significance can only be seen against the backdrop of nineteen centuries of the displacement, misery, and ostracism of Jews. At the same time, acceptance of the Jewish claim to the land must also be recognized as a successful culmination of years of dedicated effort by Chaim Weizmann, leader of the Zionist Organization. A Russian-born Jew who had made England his home, Weizmann held fast to the belief that Great Britain was Zionism's ultimate hope. Just as Herzl was the father of modern Zionism, so Weizmann was the father of the State of Israel (and ultimately her first president).

In October of 1917 President Wilson had sanctioned the general principles of the forthcoming British proposal for a Jewish homeland. Both the other major allies, France and Italy, accepted the principle and policy of the Balfour Declaration shortly after its publication. Such Asian countries as China and Siam approved Zionist aspirations. Even Pope Benedict XV offered approbation, although in a somewhat qualified way.[9]

On the other side of the war lines the Turkish Government sought to gain Jewish support by issuing a statement affirming its allegedly traditional friendship with Jews (in point of fact, it had been responsible for anti-Jewish decrees since the latter part of the nineteenth century). Germany went even further, assuring the Jewish people that Turkey planned to foster the settlement of Jews and even local self-government in Palestine, under the laws of the Ottoman Empire.[10]

As news of the Balfour Declaration gradually penetrated the Arab world, a great shock wave built up. According to Christopher Sykes, even the Jews of Palestine who had been living under the Turks could not believe that the Declaration was devoid of ulterior motives. Could anything but manipulation be expected from a government? As Sykes comments, "it is unlikely that at any time from 1917 to the present day, a single Arab has believed that altruism, idealism, or a regard for justice played any part at all in a British policy favouring a Jewish National Home. The people of the Middle East preferred to seek an explanation in a myth and a truth"—the myth of British imperialist aims encircling the globe, and the truth of Britain's concern over the Suez Canal.[11]

Only the Husseins were undisturbed. They trusted the British to carry out the promise to further Arab independence, and they were not greatly concerned with how Palestine would finally fit into the overall scheme. The Emir Feisal, who was to be the Arab emissary to the Paris Peace Conference, had a cordial meeting with Chaim Weizmann in June, 1918. They agreed that both their peoples' national yearnings could be satisfied equitably and that nothing but mutual benefit would accrue from cooperation. This accord was noted by Feisal in a statement published in *The Times* (London) on December 12, 1918 and in a memorandum to the Peace Conference meeting the following month. Feisal affirmed that in their principles Jews and Arabs are "absolutely at one." Feisal did not insist upon immediate self-government for Palestine, either separately or as part of a larger state. He acknowledged the temporary need for a protectorate during the ensuing transitional period.[12]

Feisal's remarkable readiness to cooperate with Zionists was spelled out in greater detail in a written agreement with Weizmann in early January, 1919. This actually stipulated a Palestine separated from "the Arab State" by boundaries to be worked out by a jointly-approved commission, and "duly accredited" Jewish and Arab agents of the respective territories who would maintain relations and undertakings on a "basis of cordial good will." Furthermore, the "fullest guarantees for carrying into effect the British Government's Declaration of the 2d of November, 1917 would be written into the Constitution and Administration of Palestine." Included, of course, would be the encouraging of Jewish immigration to Palestine "on a large scale, and as quickly as possible to settle [Jews] upon the land through closer settlement and intensive cultivation of the soil." At the same time, the rights of Arab peasants and tenant farmers would be protected, and they would receive assistance in bettering their economic situation. The Zionist Organization also promised a two-fold assistance program to "the Arab State": an economic survey commission that would recommend development schemes for both areas, and help in "providing the means to put such plans into operation." Then Feisal added an important codicil: He would not be answerable for failing to carry out the agreement if Arab independence was not granted.[13]

The original Syrian delegation to the Peace Conference had allowed that a federal relationship might be granted to Palestine if a Jewish majority developed there. But the "General Syrian Congress," which met in July, 1919 and claimed to represent Muslims, Christians, and Jews, took a hard line against any such arrangements: "We oppose the pretensions of Zionists to create a Jewish Commonwealth in the southern part of Syria, known as Palestine, and oppose Zionist migration to any part of our country; for we do not acknowledge their title but consider them a grave peril to our people from the national, economical, and political points of view." The Congress opposed any separation of either the Lebanon or Palestine from Syria, and—significantly, in light of later French action—denied any French assistance to, or jurisdiction over, their country.[14]

In March of the following year the impatient Arab nationalists sought to present the Peace Conference with a *fait accompli* by having another "General Syrian Congress" choose Feisal as King of United Syria, that Kingdom to include Palestine, Transjordan, and the Lebanon. The weakness both of Feisal's position as an Arab leader and of his own political integrity was revealed when the Arabs succeeded in forcing him to go against his former commitments and to back a policy that was at once anti-Zionist, anti-French, and anti-British.

The Irreconcilables

A month later the Allies met to arrange temporary administrations in the Middle East even though they were still battling Turkish forces. The actions of the Syrian Congress were rejected. The British stood firm on the Balfour Declaration and insisted on its being included in full in the description of her Mandate. (The Declaration was thus implicitly given acceptance by all nations attending the Conference.) Transjordan and Palestine were made into a single British Mandate. (See Map Four.)

France had no intention of being excluded from the Middle East. She insisted that the Lebanon and a reduced Syria be assigned to her mandatory control. In July of 1920, French troops marched into Syria, evicted Feisal, and quite ruthlessly ended Syrian independence. This action was a formidable blow to Arab hopes for a great nation-state.

Although Great Britain has been excoriated for her later behavior in Palestine, France must bear the blame for making virtually impossible any real settlement of the Middle Eastern problem. From her demands of 1915–16 down through her actions in the 1920's, she antagonized and frustrated the Arabs.

Arab bitterness was exacerbated toward any and every outsider, and particularly toward those who would be considered guilty of throwing additional obstacles in the path of Arab unity. Zionist Jews were in this respect a natural enemy. They were seen as part of a subtle stratagem to keep the Arab world in suppression by new overlords from the West.[15] Of further consequence, energies that might ordinarily have gone into the development of a greater Syria (with or without Palestine and the Lebanon) were concentrated upon wresting Palestine from the British and the Jews.

British actions also were such as to focus Arab hostility on western Palestine. As compensation for Feisal's loss of Syria the British made him King of Iraq. But that throne had already been promised to his brother Abdullah. Then, to placate the brother and his followers, the British acceded to Abdullah's takeover of the emerging Arab state of Transjordan, which Britain created by slicing off the eastern part of the mandated territory of greater Palestine. With a territorial boundary now running down the Jordan Valley, and with two different govern-

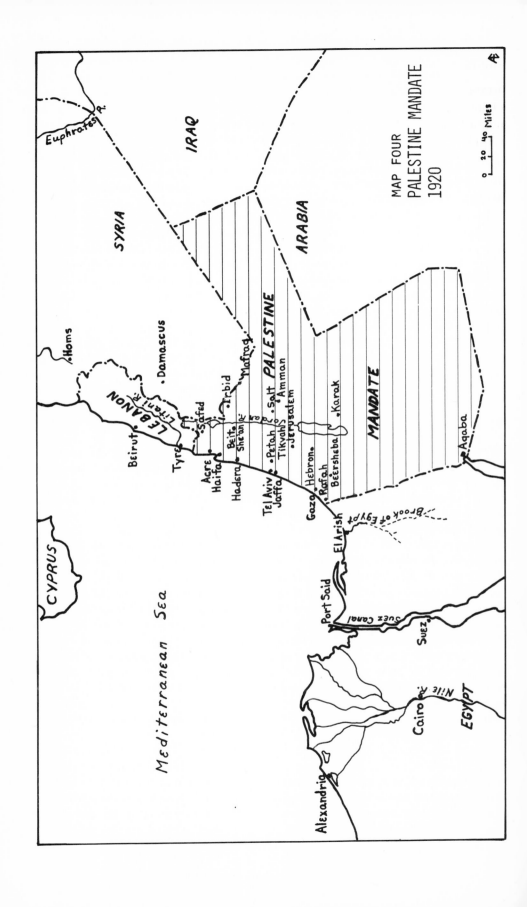

MAP FOUR
PALESTINE MANDATE
1920

0   20   40 Miles

CYPRUS

Mediterranean Sea

SYRIA

IRAQ

Euphrates R.

Homs

Damascus

LEBANON

Litani R.

Beirut

Tyre

Safed

Irbid

Mafraq

Acre
Haifa

Beit
Shean

Hadera

PALESTINE

Tel Aviv
Jaffa

Petah
Tikvah

Salt

Amman

Jerusalem

MANDATE

Gaza

Hebron

Karak

Rafah

Beersheba

El Arish

Brook of Egypt

ARABIA

Aqaba

Port Said

Suez Canal

Suez

Nile R.

Cairo

Alexandria

EGYPT

ments involved (the British Mandatory Administrations of Palestine to the west and the Emirate of Transjordan to the east), there was lessened likelihood that Britain could persuade Arab landholders of western Palestine to accept equally productive land in Transjordan in exchange for any land sold to Jewish settlers.[16]

The new situation also greatly increased the difficulty of reconciling Arab and Jewish interests. Previously, a sizable territory had offered a reasonable hope of national realization for both peoples. But as the Middle East was being subdivided, the pressures increased within the greatly restricted region west of the Jordan River. No self-government was being permitted in this smaller area, yet Jews were being allowed to develop their own institutions. Several generations of pioneering Jews had already done much to redevelop the land and its economic life. In consequence, Arabs were naturally attracted to move there. They came in unrestricted numbers from across the Jordan as well as from Syria. Improved work opportunities and greater security were the result of both Jewish and British efforts.

Evidently, the British Government was either unaware of the full impact of the division or chose to ignore it. Of course, in issuing the Balfour Declaration the British had committed themselves to a unique and delicate experiment. It was an attempt, as Balfour himself declared, to right an ancient wrong done to the Jewish people. The Jews would at last have full opportunity to recreate their own national home in the original homeland, as at the same time the rights of present inhabitants were honored.

To help insure the success of the experiment, the British would have to establish relationships with leaders and individuals who gave promise of furthering a moderate position. The Hussein family had originally been chosen because of their religious eminence, political ambitions, and apparent willingness to accept Jewish immigration and even some form of national home for Jews. Even though the Husseins obviously could not speak for the Arab people as a whole, neither could any others. (Tragically, leadership and representative bodies had been suppressed by the Turks.) However, there were to be fateful consequences in the fact that the Husseins were not Palestinian Arabs but outsiders.

The gravest error of British leadership was its underestimating the force of Arab nationalism, especially in Palestine. The British were under the illusion that the Arab world could and would adjust to Jewish settlers as long as the newcomers entered the country with sufficient gradualness. Britain paid far too little attention to two hostile meetings: a gathering of Arab notables in Jerusalem in 1919 at which a national home for Jews and the separation of Palestine from the rest of Syria were rejected with equal vigor; and the third Palestine Arab Congress of Muslims and Christians in 1920, which rejected any and every Jewish claim to a place in the land.[17] The delegates to the latter meeting insisted that Palestine belonged exclusively to the Christian and Muslim worlds.

Fortunes of the Twenties

The British also greatly underestimated the determination of the Zionists. Enthusiasm was the most potent Zionist weapon for ensuring sufficient immigration to supply visible proof of Jewish dedication to redeveloping the ancient home. But the Zionists were quite fearful that Jewish response from overseas would be insufficient and hence that their new opportunity would be irretrievably lost. From 1919 to 1923, the most Jews to reach Palestine in any one year numbered only 8,500.

Weizmann's point that it would take several generations to build a viable Jewish nation in Palestine was of course a truism. Sizable increases in numbers of Jews were, nonetheless, an immediate necessity to ensure favorable starts in community-building, to develop the country's resources, and to offset the marked growth in Arab population.

Unfortunately for the Zionist cause, the new Soviet Government acted to forbid the emigration of Russian Jews (and also outlawed Zionism). The great masses of Jews in Russia, among the most ardent Zionists anywhere, could not join the other settlers of Zion. In Germany the Weimar Republic seemed secure and Jews felt no need to leave. They were actively working for the success of German democracy. The rights of minorities were proclaimed within treaties signed with the newly created nations of the post-war years and with the former enemies of the Allies. This led many people to the gratuitous conclusion that antisemitism and the oppression of minorities belonged essentially to the past. The general optimism of the early 1920's not only served to check emigration to Palestine—hardly the most comfortable place to live anyway—but influenced a number of persons to shrug off the difficulties and frictions in the Middle East as reflecting a merely temporary stage of readjustment and development.

As a matter of fact, conditions in Palestine did greatly improve in the years from 1919 to 1929, even after the financial crisis of 1926. In the early 1920's, while Europe was suffering from recessions and inflation, the Middle East was prospering. Cooperative Zionist settlements carried forward their work of draining malarial swamps and bringing additional land under cultivation. Irrigation projects were initiated. There was crop, seed, and livestock experimentation. Great effort was expended in rebuilding the soil and reforesting the barren countryside. The Mandatory Government built roads, developed the harbor at Haifa, and improved sanitation and water supplies. There were only scattered incidents of violence between Arabs and Jews, mainly in 1920 and 1921. Zionist leaders were extremely conscious of the need to develop ties with the Arab community, and did all they could in this direction. Often relations between the two peoples were cordial on the local level, although cooperation along institutional or official lines was absent.

On the other side, the Arabs boycotted all attempts by the British authorities to get them to participate in a joint legislative council. This refusal was in a sense self-defeating, for two reasons: As the majority group, the Arabs could have easily dominated whatever advisory political decisions would be made; and the boycott kept the Arabs from creating institutions of self-government and political responsibility in competition with Jews. That no responsible bodies were enabled to develop over the years was to become one factor in the failure to realize a Palestinian Arab state in keeping with the 1947 Partition Plan of the United Nations and agreed to by the Jews.

Jewish institutions covered a wide range: local town councils, an educational commission, an elected assembly and executive (the Va'ad Leumi) to cope with domestic concerns, an elected Chief Rabbi and rabbinical council for religious matters, and, at the top, the Jewish Agency as stipulated in the Mandate.[18]

Despite the improvements of the twenties, about 13 percent of Jewish immigrants turned around and became emigrants. From 1925 to 1928 almost 33 percent of erstwhile immigrants left the country. After that, departures dropped rapidly. Immigration and emigration were as much affected by external factors as by local conditions. For example, when in 1925 Russia temporarily relaxed its law against emigration, over 34,000 Jews entered Palestine, as compared with some 13,000 the previous year. Again, in 1926 a financial collapse occurred in Poland. This had wide repercussions within Palestine's economy. The capital funds of immigrants were cut off and there was a frightening rise in unemployment. In consequence, of the 14,000 persons who had entered Palestine in that year, 7,000 were forced to leave again.

During the ensuing period of depression and joblessness (first in Palestine and then, starting in 1929, in the entire Western world),[19] immigration stayed below 5,000 each year, and in one year the net gain was practically nil. Even so, 165,000 Jews were living in Palestine by 1929, compared to the 55,000 of 1918.

Afflictions of the Thirties

Beginning in 1932, rising totalitarianism across much of Europe together with disillusionment over expectations of better treatment of Jews brought steady increases in immigrants to Eretz Yisrael: 10,000 in 1932; 30,000 in 1933; 42,000 in 1934, and almost 62,000 in 1935.

Meanwhile, Arab hostility and resentment were intensifying. This was particularly the case among the middle classes, which had been denied top governmental and civil service positions by the presence of the British and also had to compete with Jews in the professions. After the financial crisis of 1926 and the resultant high unemployment, urban and agricultural workers blamed any dislocation and economic trouble on the Jewish immigrants. Peasant fears of losing land, while not completely groundless, were aggravated and manipulated by Arab leadership.

The most potent force to be utilized in stirring up active opposition to Jewish settlers and British officials alike was religion. This weapon was used with great effectiveness, particularly after 1928, by the Muslim Grand Mufti, Haj Amin Al-Husseini. One of the most terrible blunders of the British was the appointing of Haj Amin to this leadership position, ignoring the fact that a British court had already convicted and sentenced him for helping the Arab anti-Zionist riots of 1920. For years, Haj Amin succeeded in deceiving British administrators into believing that he was a sincere, moderate religious leader. In reality, he was an unscrupulous seeker of power, willing to stop at nothing to gain his own ends. He stirred up religious fanaticism, confiscated Muslim charitable funds, and used these to hire mercenaries and assassins. These men were employed to attack Jews and British personnel and to murder Arabs whom the Mufti suspected of being moderates or personal opponents.

The success of the Mufti's strategies was first evident in the bloody events of 1929. A minor incident at the Western Wall in Jerusalem was cunningly used to convince Muslims that the Haram esh-Sharif (the Temple mount with the Dome of the Rock and the Mosque of el-Aqsa) was in imminent danger of being taken over or destroyed by the Jews. The riots that spread rapidly over the entire country gave every evidence of a carefully planned conspiracy. Several Jewish settlements were ravaged. Safed suffered extensively. But the worst attack was on the religious and thoroughly non-Zionist community of Hebron. While the Arab police looked on, a band of Arab assassins massacred and mutilated sixty men, women, and children, and wounded at least that many more.[20]

The year 1929 is generally regarded as pivotal. Maurice Samuel identifies the riots as the "first concerted attempt to destroy the Jewish homeland." The point is that the Arab leadership had hoped for a general uprising of the 800,000 Arabs against the 160,000 Jews. While this did not happen, Samuel points out that Jewish-Arab relations were never to be the same. "The Arab leadership had, in the literal sense, tasted blood; and it had become too keenly conscious that its aspirations were not wholly repugnant to the administration. It had also become convinced that it had found the right method: violence."[21]

A breakdown in British-Jewish relations also followed from the events of 1929, due to a British failure to distinguish between the attacked and the attackers. To make matters worse, the new Colonial Secretary now advocated restrictions upon the Jews, despite the truth that they were the victims.

When Parliament rejected proposals limiting Jewish immigration and land purchases, and insisted that the Balfour Declaration be honored in its original intent, British-Arab relations deteriorated. In 1933 Haj Amin Al-Husseini, now convinced that Zionism could not succeed without British support, resolved to concentrate his forces against the mandatory power instead of Jewish settlers. He instigated riots and attacks upon the Mandatory Administration in four cities. Curiously enough, the generally benevolent British attitude toward the Arabs was unaltered.

Apparently hoping that the violence had intimidated the authorities, a group of Arab mayors subsequently demanded the immediate creation of a legislative council (which they had refused or boycotted on three previous occasions). This demand fitted the High Commissioner's own plans, but he needed Parliament's approval as well as the cooperation of Jews and Arabs.

The Arab leaders quite openly declared that once they had sufficient power, they would annihilate the Jewish national home. This avowal led both the Jews and the British Government to oppose the Arab demand for a legislative council.

Arab violence, which had only temporarily subsided, broke out again in April, 1936. Jews were the first targets but soon the British suffered further attacks. The Mufti and the Arab Higher Committee called a general strike that lasted six months. Terrorist bands were joined by the unemployed. By 1937, the rebels controlled much of the country. The British District Commissioner for Galilee was assassinated in broad daylight. At last, the Mandatory Administration accepted the solid evidence proving the Mufti's responsibility, evidence the Zionists had been offering for years. But irreparable damage was already done: the functionaries of religion, Muslim and Christian, had effectively wedded antisemitism and anti-Zionism. The furies of fanaticism were unleashed. Religion-inspired hatred and denigration of Jews had been given concrete application. Any Arab moderates who might have agreed upon some kind of settlement had been either assassinated or silenced in other ways.[22]

From 1936 to 1939 the activities of Arab terrorists against Jews, British, and moderates among their own people became more and more fierce. Christopher

Sykes reports that the largest group of casualties in the final troubled years before World War II were Arabs, and at least a quarter of those who lost their lives were murdered by their own fellow-Arabs.[23]

The terrorists attacked Jewish settlements, mined roads, burned crops, uprooted orchards, and ambushed, beat, and murdered innocent people, including children. Buses were forced to travel in convoys escorted by armed vehicles.

Reference may be made here to the Haganah (literally, "self-protection"), the Jewish defense force, which protected outlying and isolated settlements. Though technically illegal, it was actually called into service by the British to help put down the Arab rebellion of 1937.

The Jewish answer to Arab attacks and to an increasing British movement away from the principle of the Jewish national home was two-fold: a strictly-observed and self-imposed policy of restraint (havlagah), which meant fighting only in self-defense; and a rapid expansion of the number of communities established. (Havlagah is further discussed early in the next chapter.)

New communities were needed to meet the continued influx of refugees. In addition, these communities constituted a de facto claim on the land, a claim that seemed ever more in peril of repudiation by the British Government as well as through Arab behavior.

The serious threat to life and security demanded a new technique for building the Jewish settlements. Within a single day's time prefabricated communal buildings and a combined water and watch tower were erected, and defense perimeters were marked out. By nightfall the new community was in a position to defend itself. One is reminded of the days of Nehemiah, when those who rebuilt the city walls worked with one hand and in the other hand held a weapon (Neh. 4:17). During 1937-39 more settlements were started than in any previous period. Thus did the Jews of Palestine demonstrate their courage and their determination never to be uprooted again from their ancestral homeland.

5. Resurrection

WHEN NEW OUTBREAKS occurred in Palestine in 1936, the Government promised to send a royal commission under Lord Peel to investigate the underlying causes and to suggest remedies. The Commission arrived at the end of the general strike and during a short truce in the Arab rebellion. Until the very end, the Arabs boycotted the hearings. At the last the Grand Mufti (who was still in good standing with the Administration) was persuaded to present the Palestinian Arab case.

Futility and Terror

The Peel Commission became convinced that the Mandate was not workable, and that no unity was possible between the two peoples without betraying national aspirations on both sides. And so in their 1937 Report the members made an alternative proposal: to partition the country. Here lies the historical and practical significance of the Peel Report. For this was the first time that the partition of Palestine was publicly espoused.

Specifically, a Jewish state would be formed along the coast from north of Jaffa to the border of Lebanon, but excluding Haifa and Acre. A somewhat truncated Galilee would be included together with a small chunk of coastal land south of Jaffa. A British mandate would continue over a small area from east of Jaffa to Jerusalem and Bethlehem, and over the northern towns of Tiberias, Nazareth, Safed, Haifa, and Acre. All the rest of Palestine, including Jaffa, Gaza, Hebron, Beersheba, and the entire Negev, would be annexed to Transjordan. (See Map Five.) Since numbers of Arabs were living in the territory proposed for the Jewish state, the Commission recommended their relocation to Arab areas, if necessary by force. Because the Jews held the most fertile land, the new Jewish state would be required to pay a yearly subsidy to Transjordan.

The deficiencies in such an arrangement were as obvious as they were serious. The proposed Jewish state would be very tiny; it would be cut off from most

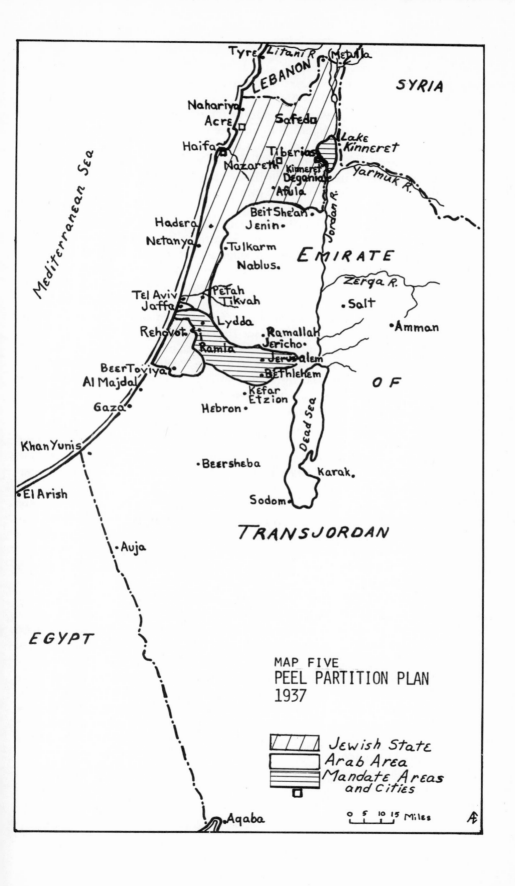

MAP FIVE
PEEL PARTITION PLAN
1937

Jewish State
Arab Area
Mandate Areas
and Cities

0 5 10 15 Miles

natural resources (including water) and have hardly any room for growth; it would be in two pieces; its only sizable town would be Tel Aviv; and its borders would be unnatural and indefensible.

The Zionist Congress, meeting a month after the Peel Report appeared, was prepared to reject it out of hand. But such were Chaim Weizmann's powers of persuasion that he was able to get the Congress to empower its Executive to negotiate with the British Government for other terms that might be acceptable to a new Congress. Despite the niggardliness of the Peel proposal, by the close of the Zionist session there was, significantly enough, more acceptance than rejection of the general purport of the scheme.

Where the Government had anticipated the most support—in Arab quarters—it met total rejection. The Arab Higher Committee refused categorically to consider any partition scheme. Thus was the stage set for a conference in September of 1937 involving 400 delegates representing every Arab state save Yemen. At the meeting the unanimous and uncompromising assertion was made that Palestine was an integral part of the Arabian homeland and could not be partitioned without Arab consent. The representatives further demanded the end of the Mandate and the annulment of the Balfour Declaration.

From the start, the debate in the British Parliament had been very unfavorable to the idea of partition put forward by the Peel proposal. Partition was seen as creating a dangerous and unfeasible situation. The advocates of a Jewish state could not accept such a restrictive plan. Since there was almost no support, the Government decided to withdraw the proposal.

Meanwhile, the Arabs had resumed terrorist attacks (it was after this that the District Commissioner for Galilee was murdered). The Government finally decided to take stern measures against Arab rebel bands. It also dissolved the Arab Higher Committee.[1] The Mufti fled to Syria whence he continued to direct terrorism and rebellion (with no hindrance from the French).

In the meantime, the Jewish Agency had resolved not to be goaded into the kinds of acts of terrorism that the Arabs were committing against innocent people. Such acts would only make a rapprochement that much harder. The Zionist leaders had, accordingly, adopted a policy of *havlagah*: self-restraint, patience, and endurance. Self-defense was essential and just, but indiscriminate reprisals were not to be condoned.

For some years the Zionist leadership was able to sustain this humane policy. But as Arab terrorism intensified—it was encouraged and supported by Nazi Germany and Fascist Italy—a small, militant minority among the Jews refused any longer to abide by *havlagah*. They struck back in kind. They argued that the terrorism was working in the Arabs' favor because of the nature of the British administration's response. The Government had instituted restrictive measures against the Jews, such as sharp limitations upon immigration, despite the plain fact that Jews were not the instigators of the trouble but the victims. Therefore, so the argument ran, the Arab terrorists would have to be stopped. The militants further insisted that in Arab eyes, Jewish restraint was a contemptible sign of weakness.

The horrendous acts of the Nazis were making most essential a refuge for European Jewry. Almost every nation had all but closed its doors to Jews.[2] And at this most fateful moment the very "national home" that had been promised to the Jews in 1917—a pledge reasserted by the League of Nations in 1923 and upheld by its Mandates Commission during the 1930's—was being increasingly barred to those in dire need. Jews who were prepared to sacrifice everything to save fellow-Jews were being prevented from doing so by the British Government. In contrast to the almost 62,000 Jews enabled to enter Palestine in 1935, only 50,000 were granted legal entry during the entire three-year period that followed. Each succeeding governmental decision carried additional reductions both in permitted immigration and in the areas of Palestine open to settlement. On a number of occasions the Mandates Commission rebuked Great Britain for contravening the conditions of the Mandate. The rebukes had no effect.

Betrayal and War

In May of 1939 the Government headed by Neville Chamberlain issued a White Paper. In the very face of infinite and terrible need, the sponsors of this document callously restricted the immigration of Jews into Palestine to 10,000 persons annually for the succeeding five years, plus an additional 25,000 from Nazi Germany and Austria to be admitted when the High Commissioner so determined. After the five years, no immigration at all would be permitted unless Arab consent were forthcoming. At the end of ten years, if conditions warranted, Palestine would become independent.

The White Paper at once crushed any hopes the Jewish people might still have had that Palestine could be the freely-entered haven for Europe's distraught and persecuted Jews, and it sounded a note of doom for Jewish aspirations of free nationhood in Palestine. Yet its authors had the effrontery to include the claim that Great Britain was in these ways meeting the obligations of the Balfour Declaration.

Very many members of Parliament dissented. The White Paper was accepted only because Parliament did not want to cause the Government to fall at a time of peril and world crisis. The League Mandates Commission found the White Paper contradictory to the intent of the original Mandate—but to no avail.

In 1940 an addition to the White Paper severely restricted the areas in which Jews—wholly legal immigrants—could buy land.

Jewish response to the White Paper was that it was a total betrayal, not only of Great Britain's earlier commitments but of simple justice. Because of the severe restrictions upon immigration into any "independent Palestine," a minority of Jews would be subject to an Arab majority at least double its size. The majority had already been inflamed against the Jews, and the Arab leadership had clearly enunciated its plans to rid the land of the Jewish minority. The Arabs had rebelled against the mandatory authorities and caused great bloodshed and destruction, and yet they were being appeased at the expense of peaceful residents who had suffered so grievously and yet had not rebelled.

Even though the Arab governments and the Grand Mufti's party did not publicly accept the White Paper,[3] it is highly significant that rebellion died down in Palestine. Further, for all the Arab interest in victory for the Fascist nations, the Arabs refrained from operating behind British lines in the Middle East. The war years were, indeed, the most peaceful ones the country was to know between 1929 and 1949.

When World War II erupted a few months after the publication of the White Paper, Jews were caught in a grievous dilemma. On the one hand, they had to support Great Britain in the struggle against Germany and Italy. On the other hand, the Jews were only too sorrowfully aware that the British, by their inhuman policy were contributing to the destruction of thousands of innocent Jewish lives. David Ben Gurion formulated the only course open to Jews: They would fight the War as if the White Paper did not exist, and fight the White Paper as if the War did not exist.

With respect to the first dimension of this policy, when forced to choose between the narrower goal of independence and the broader issue of Jewish survival, the Jews did not hesitate to support the Western allies.[4] And yet, far fewer Jews were enabled to join the battle against Hitler than yearned to do so. There was concerted external opposition to a separate force under a Jewish flag. Yet large numbers of Jews enlisted as individuals. By 1942, some 12,000 Palestinian Jews were in the service of the Allies, as compared to fewer than 5,000 Arabs from a population thirty times greater than the Jewish population. Almost 30,000 such Jews served during the War.[5]

With respect to the second part of Ben Gurion's formula, the Jews made every effort to help their brethren escape occupied Europe and get to Palestine. Yet only a small number succeeded.[6]

The Break With Britain

Their pre-war experiences had taught the Jews of Palestine to be highly suspicious of British intentions respecting the Mandate. During the War the Jews were given no reason to change this attitude. Nevertheless, they did hope that the full revelation of the Nazi extermination camps and the program of genocide would mean such world-wide revulsion that even the British Government would be forced to raise the bars against immigration into Palestine. The Jews knew better, however, than to pin all their hopes on humanitarian protestations. If their long history had not once and for all proved to them humanity's wicked complicity in, and disregard of, Jewish suffering, then certainly the unqualified diabolism of the Nazis, abetted by the world's conspiracy of inaction and silence, should have provided the final demonstration.

In his role as President of the Jewish Agency, Chaim Weizmann sent a memorandum to Winston Churchill in May of 1945, the month that saw the end of the War in Europe. The communication called for the implementing of the so-called Biltmore Program approved just three years before by a large conference of Zionist and non-Zionist Jews. The Biltmore Program called for renunciation of the 1939 White Paper, creation of a Jewish state in Palestine, unrestricted immigration, and reparations to be paid by Germany. This last measure was to begin with the turning over to the Jewish Agency of all German property in Palestine.

Churchill replied that any such decision would have to wait upon a peace settlement. By mid-June of 1945 when the Agency sent its next petition—for the immediate granting of 100,000 immigration visas for European Jewish survivors—an election campaign was in progress in England, and no action was taken. Churchill had always been a friend of the Zionists, although as a sterling advocate of the British imperial tradition his aims and methods were hardly identical with theirs. Whether events would have taken a different turn under his leadership is a question made academic by his defeat in the election.

The men of the Labour Party were unknown to the Zionists. However, the Party's pre-election convention offered the most unequivocal endorsement of a Jewish state in Palestine, of immigration, and of land sales ever given by any party. Zionist hopes were therefore raised high when Labour carried the election so decisively. But these hopes were suddenly dashed when the new Foreign Secretary, Ernest Bevin, openly opposed the entire endorsement. Not a single visa over the 2,000 still available under the White Paper would be issued. Nor would the restrictions on land purchases be changed.

President Truman's plea that the British immediately open the doors of Palestine to 100,000 survivors of Hitler's death camps fell on deaf ears.[7]

The Zionists were now given no choice but to identify the British Mandatory Administration as the enemy. War-trained commandos created an underground for rescuing the survivors of the death camps and other Jews who had managed to stay hidden during the worst years. The refugees would be smuggled past the British blockade. Jewish organizations were called upon to give all possible support for the transporting of refugees to embarkation points, the purchasing or leasing of ships (those that were procured often turned out to be no more than rotting shells), the supplying of food, clothing, and medicines, and the restitution and support of the new arrivals in Palestine.[8]

Such clandestine activities were obviously necessary and morally justified if the pitiful remnant (less than twenty-five percent) of Europe's once-flourishing Jewish communities were to be saved. This was made poignantly clear when the nations of the world refused to make room for the refugees. Even if these people had wanted to return to their former homes, at best only bitter memories awaited them. At worst, they frequently met with new instances of antisemitism even to the extent of murderous pogroms. Eretz Yisrael was their one chance of salvation.

The British authorities remained determined to carry out the White Paper provisions. This would put the Jews of Palestine at the complete mercy of the Arabs. The Mufti had returned to the Middle East and was once again acting as leader of the Palestinian Arabs. Thus, only a horrible repetition of Nazism awaited the Jews, and within their ancient homeland itself.

Throughout the War, the Haganah and other groups obtained and hid arms and ammunition. Young and old were trained secretly for defense against attack. Now, training for sabotage against British installations was also instituted. Although forced into offensive operations, the Haganah, functioning under the Jewish Agency, remained from beginning to end an army of self-defense. Even when fighting the severest forms of Arab terrorism, the Haganah tried its best to avoid the taking of life.[9]

By contrast and most regrettably, two extremist factions—the Irgun Zvai Leumi and the Stern gang—refused to accede to the policy of *havlagah*. The official Zionist bodies denounced the increasing terrorist measures of these Jewish groups but could do little to stop them.[10] The terrorists brought incalculable harm to the Zionist cause.[11]

In September, 1945 the Haganah actually agreed to work with the Irgun and the Sternists in sabotage operations. Although part of the purpose here was to try to keep these extremists under control, it also reflected the growing desperation of increasing numbers of Palestinian Jews. Terrorist tactics seemed the only recourse before the British rigidity that was flouting human need and compounding human suffering. However, it must be noted that the Haganah-terrorist alliance lasted only one year, at the end of which the Haganah and the Jewish Agency vigorously denounced the extremist groups. In the very midst of continuing suffering and humiliation, *havlagah* won the day.

The Defection of Britain

With a solution to the Palestine question fatefully eluding all parties, an Anglo-American Committee of Inquiry was formed toward the end of 1945. The Committee was called upon to make yet another investigation of Palestine, but also to assess the actual condition of European Jewry and to submit definite recommendations regarding immigration.

In December of 1945, before the Committee had begun its real work, the Congress of the United States adopted a resolution enjoining the American Government to secure "free entry of Jews" into Palestine, with "full opportunity for colonization and development, so that they may freely proceed with the upbuilding of Palestine as the Jewish National Home." Thus, the resolution went much beyond merely asserting "a" national home "in" Palestine.[12] At the same time, President Truman issued a special directive to expedite the admission of European refugees into the United States. However, the standing laws covering immigration—laws that operated directly against persons most in need of admission—were not changed for another two and one-half years. Consequently, very few Jewish refugees were admitted to the United States.

Americans are hardly in a position to cast stones at the behavior of other nations, including Great Britain, toward Jews before and during World War II.[13]

The Report of the Anglo-American Committee in April, 1946 advocated the immediate admission into Palestine of 100,000 Jewish refugees, the continuance of immigration, and the abolishment of land regulations. It also rejected a Jewish state, an Arab state, and the partition of Palestine. Curiously enough, the Committee sought to ground these latter, negative political judgments upon religious considerations: "Palestine is a Holy Land, sacred to Christian, to Jew and to Moslem alike; . . . Palestine is not, and can never become, a land which any race or religion can justly claim as its very own."[14]

Against all the evidence of the wretched mandatory years, not to mention the centuries before, the Committee clung to the utopian notion that Jews and Arabs could be constrained to live side by side in peace on the land without the political sovereignty that any such peace in fact required. Accordingly, the Committee recommended the retention of the trusteeship until the proposed arrangement could be worked out.

Since the United States had made clear that it would assume no obligation for Palestine, the plain implication was that Great Britain would have to continue to bear the responsibility. But, in truth, Britain was now in no condition to carry the cost of an effective administration.

Perhaps the connecting link in all the actions of the British authorities during the Mandate period—certainly before the final years of strife—was their illusion that they could in some way resolve the Jewish-Arab conflict in Palestine, or at least that the conflict could somehow be solved through the power of fundamentally decent behavior. This illusion was compounded by the gratuitous assumption that they could give simultaneous acceptance to the Arab cause and the Jewish cause. The British became the victims of their tacit idealism and their hopeless vacillation. Of course, we must not ignore the extent to which the Middle East had been used as an instrument for the furtherance of Britain's own interests.

In a word, the British had proved themselves unacceptable to Arab and Jew alike. Accordingly, while the Labour Government's refusal to abide by the Anglo-American Committee's recommendations is to be chronicled as a fact, the final irrelevance of that fact must also be recorded.

Following upon one last proposal,[15] the British Government gave up on Palestine. In February of 1947 Ernest Bevin announced a decision to turn over the Mandate and all its problems to the United Nations as successor to the League of Nations.

On to Independence: The Third Commonwealth

In May, 1947 the United Nations Special Committee on Palestine (UNSCOP) was appointed to make recommendations to the General Assembly. Eleven nations were chosen for membership.[16]

The investigators found that they "could not divorce the question of a Jewish commonwealth from the fate of the dispossessed Jews of Europe. Nor could they bypass the historic claims of the Jewish people, especially when they were placed against the over-generous territorial grants that the Arabs had received after World War I."[17]

In contrast to the lack of realism in many earlier recommendations, the Committee came to the view that neither a federated state nor a bi-national one was any longer possible—if either had ever been possible. The only solution the majority of the members could agree on was partition.[18]

There were to be two independent states linked by a ten-year treaty of economic union. With the stated purpose of avoiding the unhappy business of uprooting entire populations, and yet of providing the Jewish state with sufficient size for growth and self-support, the UNSCOP plan called for a complicated geography. The proposal has been variously described as "crazy quilt," "checkerboard," and "a twined serpent." In the central portion the coastland was to be Jewish, while north of Haifa and south of Jaffa the coast would be Arab. The pattern was to be reversed inland, where the eastern half of Galilee and a large section of the Negev would be Jewish, while the entire central inland area extending to the Jordan River and the Dead Sea would be Arab. However, Jerusalem was to be excluded from Arab control; it would be "internationalized." (See Map Six.)

The Arab leadership denounced with equal vehemence the majority and minority reports. But the Zionist Congress voted to accept the UNSCOP scheme, despite the fact that the territory to be assigned to the Jews was considerably less than that proposed by the Jewish Agency in 1946. The Agency now went along with the Zionist Congress and sanctioned the recommendation of the U.N. Committee.

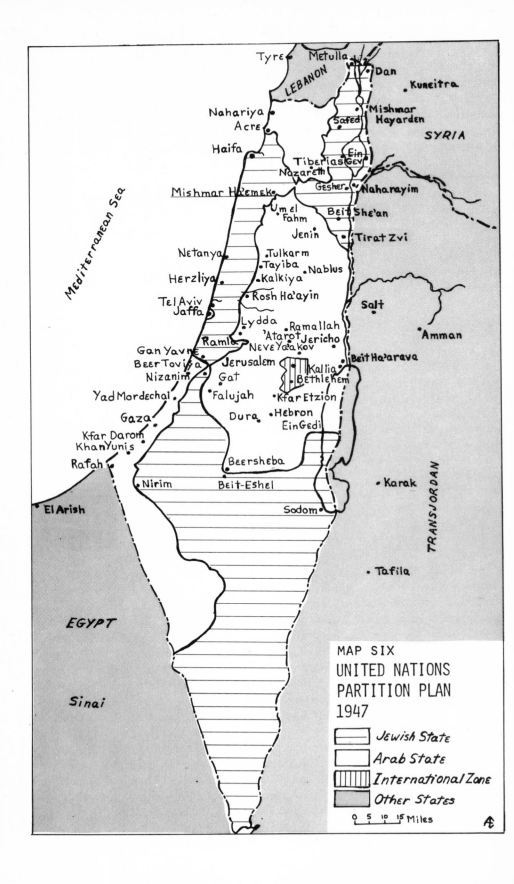

Tyre • Metulla
LEBANON
• Dan
• Kuneitra
Nahariya
Acre
Safed • Mishmar Hayarden
SYRIA
Haifa
Ein Gev
Tiberias
Nazareth
Mishmar Ha'emek
Gesher • Naharayim
Um el Fahm
Beit She'an
Jenin
Tirat Zvi
Netanya
Tulkarm
Tayiba
Nablus
Herzliya
Kalkiya
Tel Aviv
Rosh Ha'ayin
Salt
Jaffa
Lydda
Ramallah
'Atarot Jericho
Amman
Ramle
Neve Ya'akov
Gan Yavne
Jerusalem
Beit Ha'arava
Beer Toviya
Kallia
Nizanim
Gat
Bethlehem
Yad Mordechai
Falujah
Kfar Etzion
Dura
Gaza
Hebron
Kfar Darom
Ein Gedi
Khan Yunis
Rafah
Beersheba
Nirim
Beit-Eshel
Karak
El Arish
Sodom
TRANSJORDAN
EGYPT
Tafila
Sinai

Mediterranean Sea

MAP SIX
UNITED NATIONS
PARTITION PLAN
1947

Jewish State
Arab State
International Zone
Other States

0 5 10 15 Miles

In the course of attempts to appease the Arabs and obtain agreement, the suggested borders were reshuffled before the plan was actually presented to the General Assembly of the United Nations. The consequence was that 500 square miles originally allotted to the Jewish state were reassigned to the Arab state. The Jewish Agency even accepted this concession. But when the General Assembly met to debate the issue, representatives of the seven Arab member-states threatened reprisals if partition were voted, and they attempted to use their oil resources and available military bases as bargaining devices.

On November 29, 1947, the day set for the vote at the United Nations, the outcome was in great doubt. An affirmative vote by two-thirds of those voting was required to pass the resolution. Several delegations changed their votes more than once. One delegation, upon receiving news of its home government's fall, cast a vote contrary to instructions originally given it. The United States and the Soviet Union became strange bedfellows: they joined in voting for partition. Ten nations abstained, among them Great Britain.

At the end of a day of high drama the partition plan stood approved by a vote of 33 to 13.

The rejoicing of Jews throughout the world knew no bounds, despite the knowledge that bitter struggle and much suffering lay ahead before the Jewish state could ever win through. The sublimity of the moment is reflected in the following description of two scenes:

> In the midst of the ruins of Italy's Fascism, at the base of the Arch of Titus, which was erected two thousand years before to commemorate the extinction of a stiff-necked people, five thousand Jews gathered, the survivors of other crematoria, to express their gratitude at the miracle of resurrection. In Egypt, undaunted by Arab threats, Jews rejoiced in the shadow of the Cairo museum where reposed the famous parchment stile of Mnepthah, one of the earliest of the Pharaohs. He had written thirty centuries before: "Israel is no more," using the term "Israel" for the first time in recorded history, introducing Israel with the salutation of an epitaph. But in 1947 the Jews of Egypt were still there to hail a United Nations decision that seemed to offer new opportunities to attest their indestructibility.[19]

On November 30 the Arabs, as expected, initiated hostilities. Mobs and guerrillas attacked Jews in Haifa, Tel Aviv, Jaffa, Lydda, Jerusalem, and in the open countryside; by the end of the week, 105 had been killed. Simultaneously, mobs in other parts of the Arab world—in Aden, Aleppo, Baghdad, Beirut, and Damascus—fell upon Jewish communities and property (especially homes and synagogues). A *jihad* (holy war) against the Jews was proclaimed at the Muslim University in Cairo, and from Damascus the Grand Mufti called for a general strike in Palestine, thus encouraging further mob action. The prophecy of Sir John Glubb (Pasha Glubb) of some eighteen months before—that the entire Muslim world would be set aflame by the Palestine issue—was gaining the first of many authentications.[20]

Any hope that the United Nations decision would bring concord was soon lost. Oddly enough, within the ranks of the three traditional contenders of Palestine—Arab, Jewish, and British—a definite impression prevailed that there would not be a general Arab-Jewish war.[21] (Ben Gurion took notable exception to this view.) Among supports for the expectation was the disunity among leaders of the Arab States. In addition, both the British and the Jews were in secret contact with King Abdullah of Transjordan, who, with the backing of Iraq, hoped to annex the Arab territory of Palestine for the benefit of Palestinian and Jordanian Arabs alike. Abdullah acknowledged that Zionism had in fact succeeded in creating a Jewish state and that accommodations would therefore have to be made to the new reality. (It is ironical that Abdullah's own country was later to become one of the chief belligerents against Israel.)

None of the optimists allowed for the fanatical opposition to Zionism and a Jewish state that a twenty-year campaign of propaganda and hatred had nurtured throughout the Arab world. As still today, the Arab leaders were as much the prisoners of their past words and deeds as the masses were of the lies and distortions that had assailed them for years. Insofar as the rulers of the Arab states may not have wanted war—their overestimation of Jewish military strength had them seriously doubting whether they could win—they found themselves forced into war by a combination of influences: mob and guerrilla action already in progress, the pressures of fanaticism, and their own past performances.

While refusing to permit the United Nations to intervene and assume obligations, the British authorities just about abdicated their own responsibilities. Although they were maintaining capable armed power in the country, the British made no real effort to stop the battles raging everywhere.[22] Jewish-held weapons were seized under the law. Yet shipments of arms were maintained to Egypt, Iraq, and Transjordan. Only a secret purchase of Czech arms by the Jewish Agency in the Spring gave Jewish defense forces an adequate supply.

Since the Arabs had made it very clear that they would not accept a Jewish state in a partitioned Palestine, and since they had failed to establish a government of their own, in March of 1948 the American delegation to the United Nations announced withdrawal of its support for partition and recommended temporary continuance of the trusteeship.[23] However, no U.N. action was taken along these lines, and the proposal was dropped.

As the British withdrew from Palestine, they turned over the majority of their posts to Arab forces. Great Britain announced that May 15, 1948 would constitute the date of her final withdrawal. However, the High Commissioner and his staff sailed one day earlier. Accordingly, in Tel Aviv on Friday, May 14, just before the start of the Sabbath, the Chairman of the Jewish Agency Executive, David Ben Gurion, stood before a special assembly of the Va'ad Leumi and read the Proclamation of Independence of the State of Israel. (See Appendix to this volume.)

Israel was immediately invaded on all sides by Arab armies. Egyptian and Iraqi forces attacked the borders, adding their troops to those of Lebanon, Syria, and Transjordan already inside the country. Although the Jewish forces had held off since December numerous Arab attacks in many areas, they had also lost some territory and settlements. Jerusalem was in mortal danger of capture; at the end of the fighting, only West Jerusalem was to be in Israeli hands.

Save for three truce periods, bitter warfare continued until the end of 1948. (See Map Seven.) It was not until early 1949 that peace of a sort came to the new State,[24] following upon terrible sacrifices and suffering—all this despite firm assurances of the world community through the United Nations that Israel's independent existence was both just and wise. Six thousand Jewish lives were sacri-

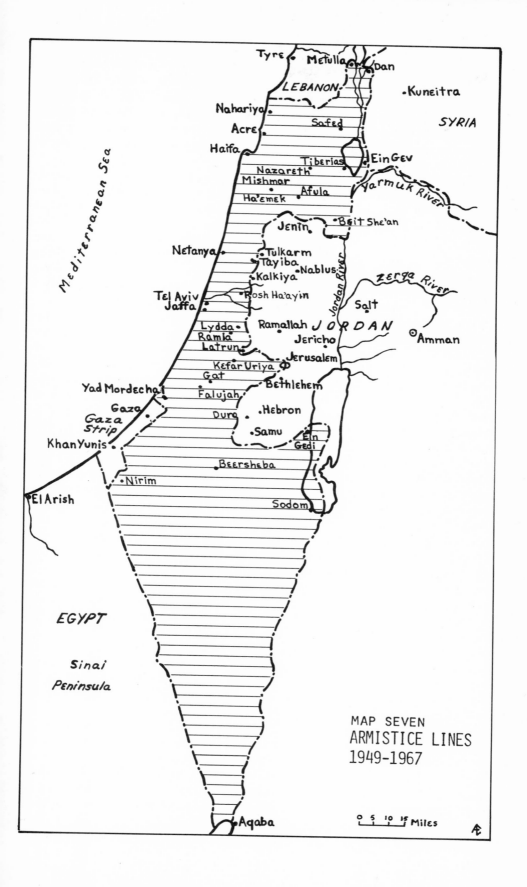

MAP SEVEN
ARMISTICE LINES
1949-1967

ficed in the War for Independence—the equivalent, in terms of comparative populations, of 2,000,000 American lives today.

Just before the Armistice Agreement with Egypt, Israel had become a parliamentary state. On February 15, 1949 David Ben Gurion was confirmed as the first Prime Minister, and Chaim Weizmann as the first President. At last, resurrection had come to Medinat Yisrael, the State of Israel.

PART II
The Life of Israel

6. The Polarities of Israel

IN OUR STUDY of the roots of Israel, it seemed wise not to go on to chronicle separately the period since 1948 but rather to treat the appropriate historical data after that year as integral parts of the many topics to be covered in the remaining chapters. Our basic concerns are contemporary. (It was not possible to include within the foregoing chapters all salient historical materials from before 1948. These materials are also given a place within the chapters that follow.)

As a transition from our survey of the story behind Israel to a study of Israeli life and times, we refer to some basic contrasts. While any country can be described through the use of polarities, that device is particularly applicable in our subject. For the Israeli lives in a world whose contrasts are striking.

The vividness and the significance of these contrasts are intensified by the smallness of the country. We are dealing with a land only slightly larger than the State of New Jersey. Israel does not exceed 265 miles from north to south, and 70 miles from west to east. The small size of the country is naturally of great influence upon her life and outlook; it tends, for one thing, to make for a centralized society. Israel is in many respects like a large family.

The Environment

The visible environment of Israel may not be the most decisive consideration, but its inevitability justifies reference to it at the outset.

There is the vastness of the Mediterranean seascape and of the mountains,[1] and there is the closeness of the alleys and shops of one or another city. The stark and even harsh quality of much of the land is elsewhere relieved by the gentleness of rolling hills and the sweep of great plains. The cities and towns teem with humanity (and animals); some 82 percent of Israel's population is classified as urban. One-seventh of her people live in one city: Tel Aviv. Yet quickly one enters upon the isolation of the rural and wilderness regions. To the north lie lush forests and farmlands; to the south is the "veritable moonscape" of the desert. A yearly average of 40 inches of rain falls in Galilee; in the Negev the amount is less than 10 inches. Moving from the clear, cool air of the Jerusalem heights, one encounters the leaden, furnace-like air of the Dead Sea Valley, which is further below sea level than any spot on earth. All in all, the terrain and climate are such that the land ever faces the threat of deterioration. Human vigilance and hard work are a constant necessity for countering this threat.

Young State, Old Land

Israel offers a unique contrast between youth and age.

The oft-heard sentiment that every Israeli tends to identify himself as a kind of archaeologist is more truth than humor. Indeed, archaeology has become a national pastime in Israel. But it is more than an interesting hobby. Consciously or unconsciously, it reinforces the identity of the contemporary Israeli with the ancient land he now inhabits. No one's home is very far from historical sites or ruins extending back several millennia. The Jews of Israel—along with the Arabs of the region—-look upon themselves as a people deeply rooted in the ages. Much in their way of life still reflects the habits and standards of olden times.

On the other side, everywhere Israel exudes youthfulness and modernity. With several other Middle Eastern nations, she attained her present independence as a state only after World War II. Not until 1969 did she "come of age" and celebrate her twenty-first birthday. One major peculiarity of Israel is the gap of almost two thousand years between the end of the Second Jewish Commonwealth and the formation of the Third. But the youthfulness of Israel, in marked contrast to several of her neighbors, centers primarily in the overriding zeal with which she has been fashioning a country out of virtually nothing. To be an Israeli is to share the excitement of participating in this creation, yet upon foundations that lie within the far past. The visitor to the land is quickly caught up in the excitement. For all the antiquity, Israeli reality is a young, developing thing. Even archaeology, not normally known as a practical subject, is often put to the service of such contemporary purposes as land development and military endeavor. (Such current application of archaeology is quite unique to Israel. Nor may we forget that the archaeological encounter with one's ancestors is, in a sense, a rediscovery of oneself.)

Perhaps the deepest impression one brings away from Israel is that of indefatigable energy. This is a nation on the move. However unwarranted or oversimplified is the charge that Israel constitutes an unjust intrusion into the Middle East, there is at least one element of truth in the assertion: the dynamism of the life of Israel is most conspicuous in contrast to much more placid, socially undeveloped, and even fatalistic domains outside. Israel is not easy on able people who are unprepared or unwilling to work hard. Special esteem is reserved for the doers, the resourceful ones. It is not strange that Israel, in consequence, has come to have so much appeal among young people from other lands (non-Jews as well as Jews).

The paradox of youth and age is nowhere felt more vividly than in the marked cessation of effort on the Sabbath. Once each week much in the youthful nation turns toward its ancient tradition. In Israel the openness of present and future meets the commanding power of antiquity. The mood that abides is not so much one of building as it is one of rebuilding. Life in Israel is a restless pendulum swinging from yesterday to today to tomorrow, and back again.

East and West

There is also a noteworthy contrast between East and West.

Israel is set in the center of the Middle East. It is often asserted that Israeli life is more Western than Eastern: the political institutions, the technology and science, the economic system, and education. However, many things cannot be easily comprehended under Western categories: a number of the social traditions, the institution of courts for the different religious communities, the Hebrew language, the foods, a great deal of the music, art, and religion, and, perhaps most important of all, vast segments of the populace.

Well over half of the total population in Israel consists of Jews from Middle Eastern countries and North Africa. The phrase "Oriental Jews" is often used for these people, but this is misleading. "Middle Eastern Jews" is much more accurate. For simplicity's sake, we shall speak of "Eastern Jews" in contrast to "Western Jews."[2]

The expectation of a greater and greater salience of Easterners over Westerners in Israel in the 1970's rests upon two decisive considerations: the much younger comparative age of Easterners; and higher birth rates among Eastern Jews as against Western Jews, as well as among Israeli Arabs as contrasted with Israeli Jews.

There is the moot question of whether the increasingly dominant numbers of persons born in Israel are "Eastern" or "Western." Probably most native-born citizens think of themselves neither as Easterners nor as Westerners but simply as Israelis. It seems safe to conjecture, however, that if and when peace comes to the region, Israel will become much more an intrinsic part of the Middle Eastern world. In fact, this has been her expressed desire throughout her short history. Today, at any rate, Israel as a whole is a complex mixture of Eastern and Western influences and behavior.

One and Many

Akin to the above is the contrast between the unity of the people and their diversity.

Israelis are bound together by vital if unpretentious loyalties. The reasons for this are many. They involve, in combination, the long and compelling historical and religious heritage that we have reviewed, the challenge of fashioning an entire country anew, and a solidarity induced by the threat of neighbors who are enemies. The country is too small to permit the development of ardent regionalism, with its tendency to cause conflicts. A further consideration of relevance is the marked group cohesiveness that is at once characteristic of Middle Eastern peoples in general and consistent with the historic ethos of the Jewish people.

On the other hand, the populace of Israel manifests almost incredible diversity, a fact that enhances the fascination of our subject. Small nations tend to be more or less homogeneous. But that is the last characteristic we could assign in the present case (unless we are thinking in completely non-ethnic terms). The inhabitants of Israel come from over one hundred countries of origin. Involved are "all manners of Jews, a virtual Babel of colours, customs and tongues."[3] Never in history has a small nation taken in so many immigrants in so short a span of years. The result has been formidable and even painful disparities in language backgrounds, accustomed standards of living, national and ethnic outlooks, and degree of cultural sophistication. At a recent festival in Jerusalem a friend of ours from Haifa, looking around at the mélange of people present, exclaimed, "Every once in a while I must forcibly remind myself that we are all Jews." But the unity is there, beyond all the differences.

Individual and Group

A closely related contrast is that of extraordinary individualism as against marked group consciousness.

Doubtless the paradox is made possible, in large measure, by a religio-historical tradition that insists upon both the dignity of the individual and the moral imperative of social concern, the individual as fashioned in the divine image and Israel as a covenanted, spiritual reality. Indeed, the group possesses no substance apart from its members, and the individual finds no meaning for himself apart from the group.

Individuality is so regnant in contemporary Israel that sometimes it almost seems to flirt with self-flagellation at the personal level and anarchy at the social level. Israelis are fairly obsessed by freedom of self-expression. Self-criticism is a notorious habit among the people, as is the vociferous criticism of all things political and social. One basic reason why generalizations about Israeli life are hazardous—including all the ones ventured in this book—is the potent individualism of the people.[4]

On the other hand, while all peoples allow a certain place for individual dignity and initiative, few have succeeded in creating, right alongside the individualism, genuinely collectivist institutions. Israel has achieved this, primarily through its renowned *kibbutzim* (singular, *kibbutz*, literally "gathering"). There is no disposition here to idealize these voluntary collectivist communities, much less Israeli society as a whole, and few Israelis would wish to do so. Yet the fact that many people are enabled to choose between more individualist forms of socio-economic endeavor and life on a *kibbutz* serves as one viable means of reckoning with the perennial human problem of individual interests versus corporate demands and social values.

The Inward and the Outward

An elusive but influential contrast is Israel's intense self-concentration versus the breadth of her outreach.

On the one side, we are met with certain parallels to any form of historical adolescence. The adolescent nation, like the adolescent individual, has to marshal enormous resources of self-centeredness to the end of emerging as a capable and self-assured adult. The Israeli problem is aggravated by the menace of surrounding foes. Here is a people nurtured by a long tradition of anti-militarism and yet forced to become a nation of soldiers. (The Israeli armed forces are for the most part a militia of civilian reservists. Young men must now devote thirty-six months to active military service; unmarried women, twenty-four months.[5]) Within the first two decades of her modern existence, Israel had to fight three wars for her survival (1948, 1956, and 1967). Mounting burdens of defense continue to beset her economically and politically. It is entirely understandable that the young-old nation of Israel should be engaged in a rigorous pursuit of self-understanding, including new ways of behaving and thinking.

The other side of the contrast is made possible by the fact that the Israelis are legatees, willing or unwilling, of the highest moral standards, which transcend and often contend against their own self-interests, and which potentially encompass all mankind. Fortunate is the adolescent whose parents stand for universal ideals. This condition makes possible an impact upon humanity out of proportion to Israel's modest size. The moral dilemmas such a heritage poses for a tiny nation—its power politics, its encounters with foe and friend, its modes of survival—are as baffling as they are challenging.

Respecting Israel's reach beyond herself, it is relevant to point out that in the very midst of a desperate struggle for her survival, she continues to engage in significant programs of cooperation and counsel with developing countries in Asia, Africa, and Latin America, sharing her skills and educational and training facilities.

Certainty and Uncertainty

Israel is divided and united by the competing psychological forces of certainty and uncertainty.

There are the assurances that derive from freedom and the anxieties that stem from vulnerability, with the whole affair complicated by this new-old people's search for national identity. In Chapter 1 we alluded to the immigrant who at last finds himself at home in Israel. No comfort is firmer for Israeli Jews than the ability to say, "I can be myself here. I am accepted." For several thousand years the Jews of the world have lived under the threat of persecution and destruction at the hands of dominating and hostile majorities. In Israel all this is changed. The fear is gone. Free men walk the land. In this respect, though it is not the only one, Israel is already a success story. For the first time in centuries a generation of Jews has been reared for whom antisemitism has no immediate personal significance or consequence.

Once the certainties are taken into consideration, the fact remains that Israel is no more than an oasis in a desert of the world's hatreds. The joys of freedom are countered by forebodings of travail, amidst increasing numbers of casualties from enemy aggression, even without full-blown warfare. The Israeli's unqualified acceptance within his own national household is matched by abiding insecurities and dangers from without.

Again, whether they are within Israel or elsewhere, Jews continue to feel themselves on wrongful trial before the world with its double standards. Israelis have learned of these double standards from bitter experience. The world accepts without substantive reservation the reality and sovereignty of most countries. Yet, after initial support for the renewed State of Israel by the international community, many nations now stand arrayed in opposition to her. The threat of Israel's obliteration by enemy neighbors is an ever-present Sword of Damocles. As a nation, Israelis find themselves much alone in the world. The irony of these people is their deep and historic attachment to a land within wider surroundings where they are made to feel so alien. The land that embraced the stranger is itself a stranger in its own region; the walls of hostility that bar passage from Israel to Lebanon, Syria, Jordan, and Egypt "are no less barriers to national normalcy than the ghetto walls of Europe in their day."[6]

In the present phase of our deliberations we are not entering upon the question of the justification or lack of justification in the positions of those who are hostile to Israel. Here we are concerned only with the life-and-death outlook of Israelis today.

We must add one further qualification: It would be misleading to conclude that the constant threat against Israel's life has destroyed or even weakened the people's morale. A friend in Jerusalem wrote to us recently (after a number of Arab terrorist attacks against Israeli civilians): "The central factor in the present situation is precisely the wonderful, steadfast spirit of our people—its optimism, vigor, and strength of character. Despite continuous acts of terrorism and war, the people remain assured of the justice of their cause and do not show the slightest sign of demoralization."

The Secular and the Religious

There is, finally, the prominent contrast between thoroughgoing secularity and abiding religiousness.

Jewish religious institutions within Israel are continually subject to opposition and criticism. Many Israeli Jews insist that they are a national reality no different in kind from any other people. There is no guarantee that secularity will not become the dominant way of the future in Israel, as is happening throughout much of today's world. Attention is often directed, for example, to the alleged turn among Israeli youth away from traditional spiritual interests. On the other hand, Jewish religious observance is a massive fact in Israel, and this applies to many young people as well as to older persons. Judaism has always been marked by its devotion to human concerns and values. Because of this, any final division between secular existence and the life of faith is untenable, just as is any attempted divorce between Jewish peoplehood and Jewish religiousness. Nevertheless, a contrast and even a certain conflict between secularity and religiousness is a truth of experience in Israeli society today. The serious issues posed by this situation call for scrutiny in later pages.

The contrasts just sketched do not cover the whole ground. These and other polarities are fundamental to Israeli life—at least for our particular time. The elements referred to serve to remind us of the complexity of our subject.

7. From Many Lands . . .

THE LEADERS OF ISRAEL have been concentrating upon the following objectives:

1. Israel as a national home open to Jews from anywhere. Encouragement of Jewish immigration into the ancestral land.

2. Social justice and equality for minorities within a Jewish state, in contrast to the age-long persecution of Jews at the hands of hostile majorities.

3. A viable compromise between religious and nonreligious forces and interests.

4. An effective, democratic political system.

5. A firm economy that will eventually be free of outside intervention and subsidies.

6. Security for Israel and peace with her neighbors. Partnership with the Arab states in fostering well-being and prosperity throughout the Middle East.

7. Continuing cooperation between the Jews of Israel and those of the Diaspora.

8. A recognized place for Israel within the world community, including contributions by Israel to the welfare of other nations.

We discuss and appraise the above objectives in the following chapters.

The Conglomeration

Israel is a congeries of human beings committed to the task of becoming one people. We are about to consider the vital issue of social integration in Israel. "Integration" is here construed in broad terms to mean the entire task of fashioning a new and unified society.

In approaching this question, we have to bear in mind a number of factors: the modern historical and social origins of the State, particularly the immigrant background of contemporary Israel; the trials of settling the immigrants; the directions in which Israeli society is developing, with particular respect to the origins of the population and to diverse social goals; and the various social and psychological problems of, and inevitable conflicts among, different ethnic and social groups.

The idealizer may tell us that Israel has already achieved unity and solidarity as a nation. The political, social, and religious structures and achievements we are reviewing in these pages can be offered in support of that argument. Reference was made in the last chapter to the marked group cohesiveness in Israel. But such factors do not, unfortunately, make the problem of social integration in the country any less serious or difficult. With their own history of absorbing innumerable ethnic groups, Americans can readily sympathize with this problem. They will also understand the desires of particular groups to preserve their own heritage and identity.

No country in today's world approximates the vast ethnic and cultural heterogeneity of Israel (a diversity that itself contrasts with the much more homogeneous Jewish community of Palestine in the pre-1948 period). The country is for the most part immigrant-created. Still today, almost two-thirds of Israel's Jewish citizens are immigrants.

The origins and foundation of the modern Jewish state were very largely Russian. Indeed, until World War I, Zionism remained primarily a movement of Russian Jews. The German Jews contributed primarily to organization and ideology. Under the pressures of antisemitism, many Jews left Russia. While most of them went to Western countries, a significant number went to Palestine, then under Turkish control. From this latter group came a nucleus of strong leadership. These "founding fathers" of the new Israel were committed to certain political, social, and moral ideals that continue to exert great influence upon Israeli life:

1. *Zionism,* the building of an independent Jewish nation boasting a viable economy and cultural autonomy. The creation of such a state was looked to as the only solution to antisemitism and to the marginality and rootlessness of the Jewish people.

2. *Socialism.* Political independence was not an end in itself. The immigrant founders aimed for the reconstruction of human society. There was to be cooperative enterprise and social and economic equality. Labor, and particularly physical labor, was extolled, and the "simple life" became a distinctive element of the new society. As one immigrant has put it, "Our mind was on the rehabilitation of *adam* and *adamah* [man and soil]." The workers were organized into the Histadrut, the General Federation of Labor. The goal was what we now call a "welfare state," with publicly owned and directed industry at the forefront. Romanticism and economics were wedded in an odd but appealing union.

3. *Pioneering.* Alex Weingrod describes this ideal as expressive of the merging of Zionism and socialism. The pioneers possessed "an almost evangelical enthusiasm; they were passionate in their dedication to national and social ideals. The physical hardships of their lives, and the opposition they faced, also solidified the bonds between them: outbreaks of Arab terror, or opposition to Turkish or British rule, drew them closer together. . . . [Strong communal feelings] epitomized the formative period. But it was mainly the dedication that the immigrants shared in building a new nation that lent the com-

munity its keen sense of common purpose."[1] The ideals of personal moral responsibility and service were at the fore.

In this formative period there were, of course, social and cultural differences. But these were not significant at the time. The pioneering element was dominant; the religious and Eastern groups remained at the periphery.

In the years between the two world wars the entire ethnic situation changed decisively. From 1925 to 1940 the Jewish population of Palestine rose from 122,000 to 470,000. Most of the new people were not self-selected; they represented a broad spectrum. The majority of them were refugees from oppression in Europe. Thousands of Polish Jews entered Palestine in the 1920's and 1930's. German Jews, fleeing the Nazi terror, began to come in. Many of these people represented middle-class values and were anything but socialists. The Germans in particular regarded themselves as possessed of a high culture, and tended to develop and settle in segregated communities (for example, sections of Haifa).

It must be emphasized, however, that during the 1930's the version of Zionism for which the original pioneers stood remained the dominant one in Palestinian Jewry. While some foreign Zionists were prepared to settle for a homeland and haven without political independence, the Jews of Palestine demanded an autonomous commonwealth.[2]

An unforeseen development accompanied the refounding of the State in 1948. An overwhelming Jewish majority was handed to Israel. Had the Arabs accepted the United Nations partition decision, Jews would have had only a small majority.[3] And had ordinary population trends been allowed to take their course, today Israel would possess an Arab majority. But with the Arab-initiated hostilities, thousands of Arabs fled from the areas allotted to the Jewish state by international agreement. Subsequently, the Jewish populace multiplied greatly due to immigration. Fatefully, during World War II the gates of the "promised land" had been all but closed to Jews. A mere 73,000 managed to get through. But by 1947 there were some 650,000 Jews in the country. During the three and one-half years following the Proclamation of Independence almost 700,000 more reached Israel.

Most of the immigrants who had previously come were either self-supporting or able to fend for themselves. But now the situation changed dramatically. Hundreds of thousands, including many death camp survivors from Hitler Europe and great numbers of Jews from Asia and Africa, came seeking admission. These were anything but pioneers. They were hapless refugees. As examples, during the 1949–51 period, there entered the country 220,000 survivors of the campaign to destroy Polish and Rumanian Jewry, 45,000 Yemenite Jews (the most oppressed and therefore the most backward of all Arab-dominated Jewish communities), and more than 120,000 Iraqi Jews stripped of their possessions. Large-scale emigration began from such North African countries as Libya, Tunisia, and Morocco. The vast majority of post-1948 newcomers did not come as devotees of Zionism, socialism, or a pioneering ethic.

The new mass immigration brought in hosts of Eastern Jews. Most of these people had never even heard of modern Zionism, much less believed in it (although many of them knew of and clung to the persuasion that God would one day return them to their land). Hitherto, they had been anything but a decisive group in Israel. We have already noted the revolutionary consequence of the change: today the majority of Israeli Jews are Easterners or Eastern in origin.

Fewer than four persons in one hundred had any possessions or any means of sustaining themselves. The transportation and initial support of all the others had to be completely underwritten by the Jewish Agency and the new Government. During the first five years of the State the population increased 125 percent. At one point 1,000 persons were coming in every day. The record year was 1949, with almost 240,000 immigrants. In the beginning there was nowhere to put the immigrants save in tented camps, but by the middle of 1951 no fewer than 400,000 had already been given some kind of permanent housing. After 1951, the number of newcomers lessened, in part because so many of the refugees from Nazi Europe had already been given a home.

Between 1952 and 1966, almost 570,000 persons were admitted, a figure considerably less than the total wanting to come—not because any were excluded but because so many East European states had sealed their borders against Jewish emigration.[4] A bright feature of the new period was that almost all newcomers were now enabled to go directly to permanent homes, although of necessity many of these people were settled in development areas. (See Map Eight on page 90 for sites of development towns.)

Over a period of less than two decades, one and a quarter million persons came to the land to begin their lives over again. Barely half that number were on hand to give the new arrivals succor and to meet the task of their absorption (with more indirect but tremendous aid from Jews in other lands). This meant incredible strains upon housing, employment, food, and services. By 1968, as many as 700,000 Jews fleeing as refugees from Arab countries had been taken into Israel.

We have seen how Israel has moved from a homogeneous, if embryonic, society to a heterogeneous one. Professor Weingrod sums up as follows the radical changes sketched above: "This splitting of society along cultural lines has surely been the most significant social development in Israel's brief history. . . . There are many Israels: there exists in Israel—as in all modern societies—a great range of diversity: Israeli-born and immigrant, immigrants of ten years' standing and those who landed a month ago, the Russian-born élite and the 'outsiders,' Yemenites, and Poles, religious and free-thinker, Jew and Arab, *kibbutz* member and city merchant, wealthy and poverty-stricken. Each of these (and there are many more) is a distinct cultural world. . . ."[5]

Entry Problems

For any human being, other than perhaps a small child, to be an immigrant is hard. The challenge of adjusting to a new life is a most serious one. And the immigrant must in some way prove himself in his own eyes and to his new fellow-citizens.

For the Jew who comes to Israel, common historical memories, a shared Jewishness, and the assurance of having in a real sense reached home offset somewhat the shock of being an immigrant. Yet these things do not entirely remove the shock. As for the need to prove oneself, for many a newcomer to Israel there are happy limitations upon this demand. (The special care given the infirm and the aged is a sublime example.) Nevertheless, as made evident throughout this book, for the great majority of people life in Israel presents peculiar problems. "Imagine the shopkeeper from Baghdad turned stonemason, the Moroccan peddler become farmer, or the Rumanian merchant planting trees in a government afforestation project. These were not voluntary shifts— they were not willing pioneers serving the nation—but were rather entered into since there were no other alternatives."[6]

The varieties of response shown by immigrants range over a broad spectrum. (1) Some develop a love-hate attitude. While rejoicing in their new lives and opportunities, they may at the same time resent the fact that they remain in certain respects at the edge of the national family circle. (2) Some people may feel apathetic or even disaffected. A man may simply accept his lot in a fairly passive way, or he may positively dislike or even reject his new situation. The disillusionment of some people is probably linked to foolish expectations. They had somehow assumed that a Jewish society would guarantee them, as Jews, instant happiness. (3) A great many newcomers affirm the values and viewpoints of Israeli society. They are committed to it and involved in it, and they find personal meaning and satisfaction in its institutions and challenges.

Needless to say, these different responses may be found in a single individual at different times, although the one mentioned last is the most stable and the most enduring.

An obvious and burdensome complication is that the social world to which the newcomer has to make some kind of adjustment is itself complex and changing. Its differing standards and causes vie with each other for recognition. There is the old pioneering, public-spirited ethic; the more and more influential middle-class way of life; and the new and potent tradition of the *sabras*, the children of the soil, those Jews born in Israel.

Socialist, pioneering ideals are still pervasive in the land. They constitute a kind of "public ideology," for the simple reason that until now the men in socio-political control have been proponents of these ideals. Both the school system and the army continue to seek to inculcate pioneering virtues.

Competing with this ethic is a newer creed committed to the furtherance of private goals and interests. A "crisis in pioneering" has been occurring in Israel, involving a tempering of goals of national service and the replacing of many voluntary groups by official institutions. "The pursuit of private interest now animates broad segments of Israeli society. . . . Side by side with the heroic, spartan pioneer there stands the consumption-oriented, middle-class suburban-ite."[7]

The *sabra* tradition is as yet rather inchoate and is accordingly harder to characterize than the others. It appears to contain elements from both the other models, but not without providing its own alterations. Insofar as the native-born Israeli still shows something of the outlook of the pioneer, he is nevertheless not as heroic in his style and he is more pragmatic in his behavior. And insofar as the *sabra* has become "middle class," he remains (in ways not unlike many Americans) quite uncertain that this way of living can actually ensure the good life.

Although there are discrepancies among these three traditions, they also possess much in common. Two shared characteristics singled out by Weingrod are:

these models are emphatically Western in their orientation, and each of them is reformist in outlook; i.e., each one seeks to get people to accept and conform to its standards. The immigrant must somehow come to terms with these different traditions. If, as is most often the case, he is an Easterner, the problem of social integration is made all the more difficult for him.

The fact that Israeli society is undergoing great changes makes the immigrant's entry problem that much more arduous. Where are the certainties to remedy his uncertainties? The older, traditional ways of thinking and behaving are being questioned and replaced by new modes of thought and action. While the power and influence of the State have grown, the social efficacy and importance of other, less impersonal institutions have been challenged.

The Conflicts

The unknowing outsider may have been under the faulty impression that sublime harmony somehow characterizes intergroup relationships in the "Holy Land." A major reason why social integration within Israel has been and continues to be such a formidable task is that the potentialities for group conflict are manifold: immigrants as against the native-born, immigrants as against old-timers, Eastern Jews as against Western Jews, Israeli Jews as against Israeli Arabs, and religious Jews as against nonreligious Jews.

While Israel is largely an immigrant country, immigrants have children and the children have children. At the present writing, already some 44 percent of the Jewish population of Israel is native-born. It is anticipated that native-born Israelis will attain a majority by about 1973. Immigration to a new land is notoriously of divisive influence within families, simply because the children quickly turn to new ways while the senior people tend to cling to the old ways. In Ruth Bondy's words, "as far as Kupat Cholim (Public Health Service) is concerned one is an immigrant for ninety days; for customs officials—12 months; for the Jewish Agency—one year; for one's children—all one's life."[8]

There are also certain relentless facts of competition, real or imagined, and of self-interest. Israel is not the first human habitation where men have been torn between the demand of equal treatment for all, including newcomers to their little domain, and the wish or need to retain a job or a privilege. Human beings everywhere are reluctant to have the tranquility of their lives disturbed by strangers or to be burdened with new obligations to people who require help or friendship.

The old-timer whose life before and after reaching Israel has been a story of hardship can scarcely be expected to exude great sympathy upon hearing what are for him the relatively trivial complaints of the new arrival, especially the one who comes from an affluent country. (For all his insistence that middle-class values are shallow and corrupting, the veteran pioneer may have himself accumulated something of a guilty conscience because of the increasing ease of his own life.) On the other hand, accounts of the sufferings of earlier generations hardly make the emotional and practical difficulties of the newcomer any less real or onerous, nor do they eliminate the restiveness he often feels.

There is something of a conflicting viewpoint between the generations respecting the forces behind the rebirth of Israel. For the old-timer, Theodor Herzl, Chaim Weizmann, and the Balfour Declaration continue to be meaningful symbols. But the young Israeli may incline instead—partly out of lack of knowledge, to be sure—to link the revival and reality of his country exclusively to the frightful wars she has had to wage. For him, even if he is well-informed, the Israeli Defense Forces must receive credit at least equal to that of the "founding fathers" for enabling Israel to live.

Furthermore, the new, native-born generation is notably unenthusiastic over ideology, and that includes Zionist ideology. (As used in this book, "ideology" means the doctrines put forward by any social movement, doctrines reputed to embody "the truth.") The rising generation in Israel tends to identify Zionism with Eastern European Jewry, for whose traditions, values, and concerns (Yiddish literature, ghetto humor, sensitivity to persecution, etc.) young, self-reliant Israelis marshal limited interest. These new people "are Israelis, and Israeliness comprehends Jewishness; they have no 'Jewish problem.' Israel is their ideology; beyond it, they have little need and less patience for any other."[9]

It would be quite inaccurate, however, to conclude that Israel suffers from a huge "generation gap." This problem does not appear to be uniquely severe in Israel. For example, more than one study has indicated that the young and the old are quite close in their political views and moral values. It is nevertheless true that among political activists, the old tend to be more ideological and the young more prudential in their respective orientations.[10]

The old-timer, even if he is not at all religious, covets for Israel a certain moral and even spiritual distinctiveness. One of his laments is that the country is rapidly becoming "the same as any other country." By contrast, the young Israeli either does not find anything wrong in this development or he is quite prepared to make a virtue of the necessity.

Much truth lies beneath Ruth Bondy's exaggerated description of the case of the man who finally opts for life in Israel:

> As long as he makes such statements as "I wish to be useful to the society of Israel" or "I am happy to be living on Israeli soil," as long as his attitude toward the State of Israel is impregnated with emotion, as long as he is able to mention Zionism without smirking, as long as he clings to a folder full of documents and letters attesting to his fruitful activities . . ., as long as he lives in the belief that someone is going to thank him for all these good works—so long will he bear the stamp of the new immigrant. In the eyes of the Israeli a long period of Zionist activity is more suspect than assimilation; the question that comes to mind is: "If you have been such a great Zionist for such a long time, why did you wait so long to come here?"[11]

Eastern Jews and Western Jews

It is well-known that Eastern Jews have a harder time in Israel than do Western Jews.[12] We must keep in mind that they have had a lot farther to go. The Easterners come from much more deprived communities, economically, educationally, and politically. They have not known self-government. Until now, their capacities for leadership and for making a contribution to a democratic society have been little developed. (Ironically, some of these immigrants had at one time attained notable social and economic status in their native countries.) The traditions and style of life of these multitudes of people have been much

nearer to Arabs than to European and American Jews. Their mother tongue
has most often been Arabic. Traditionally, Sephardic (Eastern) Jews retain a
patriarchal and authoritarian family structure. The extended family unit is of
tremendous importance. Comparatively speaking, Easterners are as a group more
tradition-oriented and more religious than Westerners.

On coming to Israel, Eastern Jews meet a totally new world, quite different
in social values, technology, and politics from everything they have known.[13]
They encounter a society replete with modern ways: mechanical-mindedness, calculated efficiency, etc. All in all, the cultural shock that Easterners have experienced upon entering Israel cannot be overestimated—this, in considerable contrast to the fortunes of their Western brothers.

For the most part, Eastern Jews are still outside the mainstream of Israeli
political life. In proportion to their great numbers in the country, they have
as yet only small representation in the Knesset (Parliament) and various other
political institutions. They are, to be sure, making increasing claims to be heard,
and there is much concern among other Israelis, including the political leadership itself, to take these claims seriously and to accept them responsibly.

The economic pressures faced by Eastern Jews have helped to aggravate their
social plight. In Israel as elsewhere, the better a man's education, the higher his
economic and social status. Most school dropouts in Israel come from the Eastern
sector of the population. The need to earn a living or to contribute to family
sustenance means that relatively few Easterners have achieved a secondary education. At the post-primary level, the highest rate of school attendance in the
country is found among Israel-born offspring of Western parents. Israel-born
children of Eastern parents show a considerably lower rate, and Eastern immigrants still lower. The majority of university students in Israel are native-born.
Among the remainder, more than twice as many were born in Europe as were
born in various non-European countries other than Israel, despite the fact that
the latter group constitutes a much larger segment of the college-age population.
And of native-born university students, only a small percentage have Eastern
fathers.

Despite vigorous national efforts to reduce inequality, Western Jews continue
to have considerably higher living standards than Easterners. During the 1950's
the income differential between the two groups widened markedly, and this
trend continued, though to a lesser degree, through the 1960's.[14] (Even where
no disparity of income is present, the fact that Easterners tend to have larger
families makes for greater economic hardship. The crucial consideration is per
capita income.)

Some customs and laws inevitably impress Eastern Jews as inherently discriminatory. For example, there is the issue of polygamy. Due to the influence of the
cultures in which they were reared, some Eastern Jews have remained polyg-
amous. But in Israel polygamy is illegal.[15]

The objection is expressed that Israelization is given undue priority over the
values of pluralism.[16] The suspicion is sometimes found among Eastern Jews
that Israelization means turning them into Westerners. The outlook conveyed
in the public schools is largely Western-oriented. The immigrant who has to
adapt to European ways is thereby being asked to accept in considerable measure
the traditions of the old-timers of Israel. For, as we have noted, the ideals of
the early settlers continue to exert great social and political influence upon the

country. Yet it would hardly be fair to tell a man who is already having great trouble competing with more advantaged fellow-citizens that he ought to "be a pioneer" or practice self-sacrifice.

The seriousness of the Eastern immigrants' problem arises from the fact that these people are asked to assume several heavy burdens. They are faced at one and the same time by the crisis of being immigrants, the crisis of being subjected to conflicting ideologies, the crisis of modernization, and the crisis of how to attain reasonable social status for themselves and their progeny in a new world. Whenever Eastern parents oppose their children for falling into Western ways of thinking and behaving, all the above forms of crisis converge in a poignant and explosive way.

In Israel ethnic separation is very largely sustained by corresponding class separation. This combination comprises the basic obstacle to ultimate social integration. Specifically, Western Jews and Eastern Jews (the latter along with Israeli Arabs) constitute, respectively, the higher and the lower classes—with "class" understood in social, political, and educational terms as well as purely economic terms.

It would be wrong to place the entire blame upon Western Jews for enjoying dominance and advantages. For the most part, their superior status results from the exigencies of history combined with their own contribution. The Israeli orientation to the West is itself largely the consequence of circumstance. The original inspiration and leadership, and the financial and political resources of the new Israel have come from that direction. Arab and Soviet hostility has served to perpetuate and aggravate this Western orientation. Furthermore, it has always been recognized that the survival and prosperity of the young country would be impossible apart from technological achievement, and this had to come from the Westerners.

Once these considerations are granted, the presence of a measure of bitterness and frustration among Eastern Jews remains entirely understandable. At the same time, we must not give any impression that the Easterners as a group are alienated from their new homeland. Nothing would be further from the truth. Vast numbers of Eastern immigrants have readily and happily adjusted to Western technology and social institutions. Fein refers to the results of one important study: "When people were asked to rate their past and present happiness, Easterners were much gloomier than Westerners. But when asked to predict how happy they would be five years hence, it was the Easterners who saw the greatest forward movement, bringing them almost to the level which Westerners predicted for themselves. Whatever it is that troubles the Easterner, it does not appear to be fundamental alienation from the State itself."[17]

Thus, the primary state of affairs is not the rejection of Israeli society, even among those who experience the most difficulties. The real problem for these people is how to gain a vital and creative place within a society that has already become their world. To express this matter in the form of general questions: What has been done and what is being done to help make those "from many lands" into "one people"? What resources have been applied and are being applied to the fostering of socialization and integration within the majority population of Israel? And what fresh problems have thereby been created? These questions take us into our next topic.

8. . . . To One People

THE FORCES that are marshalled to unite a people can sometimes be divisive as well. Accordingly, as we review some of Israel's major resources and strategies for social integration, including the absorption of immigrants, we speak not of ideal solutions but simply of practical endeavors to face up to a massive challenge. Space prohibits an all-inclusive survey. We do not discuss, for example, the role of the youth organizations or, save in passing, that of the Defense Forces.

Plainly, many unintentional factors have exerted a positive effect upon the socialization and integration of Israelis. Not least in importance are the more subtle influences exerted by the noteworthy development, despite burdens of economics and national survival, of an indigenous Israeli culture through drama, art forms, and music. The Israeli theater has the highest per-capita attendance in the world. Much of it is mobile. Art exhibitions are numerous and flourishing, even in small communities. Extra effort is expended to preserve and foster Eastern art forms. The *kibbutz* movement has played a major role in furthering cultural pursuits, particularly folk music, dances, and drama.

Again, it is impossible to exaggerate the contribution to social and national unity that was made by the Six Day War of 1967, at which time the entire nation faced the threat of extinction. On a more sustained basis, the Israeli Defense Forces play a formidable integrative role throughout the land—in large measure through their educational and cultural programs but also through the unique *esprit de corps* they develop. In the Army there is neither East nor West.[1]

As a matter of fact, there is a real sense in which the whole life-direction of Israel fosters the goal of integration. However, we are primarily concerned here with selected contributing factors of a more or less tangible and intentional sort. Many of these factors enter the discussion elsewhere in this book, particularly in Chapter 15 on economic life. For instance, responsible social welfare arrangements help to diminish social discord. In Israel, Eastern workers receive the benefit of specially designed training programs.

Learning's Light

We do not have to belabor the point that in Israel as elsewhere in the modern world the school easily rivals the home and other institutions as a supreme integrative force. There is nothing strange in the fact that almost from the very inception of modern Zionism, many envisioned that a restored Eretz Yisrael would serve as a center of intellectual life. Learning retains its classic status as the instrument *par excellence* of Jewish survival and integrity.

The new State of Israel had been in existence barely one year when free compulsory schooling was instituted for those between the ages of five and fourteen, as well as for those up to eighteen who had not finished their primary education. At the end of 1968 the Government acted to extend the Law gradually to the ninth and tenth grades.[2] The remainder of secondary education is not as yet either free or compulsory. New immigrants are enabled to receive free secondary education within four years of coming to Israel, and free higher education through the Jewish Agency within three years of arrival.[3]

Despite the considerable cost, eight out of ten graduates of elementary schools eventually go on to some kind of secondary schooling.[4] At the present time no less than one-half of the population between fourteen and seventeen is pursuing one or another form of secondary education (general, vocational, or agricultural). Until now, academic high school preparation has been (as in England) the stepping-stone to university education.[5]

As a small country with limited natural resources, Israel has a serious need for scientific education and imagination, and particularly applied research. Institutions for higher education and research include the Hebrew University in Jerusalem, the Institute of Technology in Haifa (the Technion), the Weizmann Institute of Science at Rehovot (significantly, all three of these trace their origins to well before 1948), the University of Tel Aviv, Bar Ilan University at Ramat Gan, the University of Haifa, the University of the Negev at Beersheba, and a number of institutes for pure and applied scientific research.[6] There are in addition some 270 *yeshivot*, private talmudical colleges. (See Map Eight for some of the indications of Israel's development.)

Each year sees over 5,000 additional students in institutions of higher learning. Total enrollment is expected to reach 45,000 by 1975.[7] Increasing numbers of Eastern Jews and Arabs are graduating from these institutions.

In Israel today every third person, whether Jew or Arab, is a pupil or student, from kindergarten to university, a record surpassed by very few countries. Approximately 10 percent of the national budget is allotted to the Ministry of Education and Culture, a proportion exceeded only by the Ministry of Defense.[8]

Many schools in areas attended by immigrant children have not been on a par with the schools of non-immigrant families. But Israel is working to rectify this situation. Eastern children receive special scholarship aid out of proportion to their numbers and qualifications. The argument is that the more disadvantaged a child, the more advantaged should be his opportunities. Accordingly, disadvantaged children are enabled to begin school early (with compulsory kindergarten), and to have an extra-long school day, supplementary lessons, and an extended school year. This applies to all whose backgrounds and home environment constitute handicaps. Special textbooks, audio-visual aids, and methods of teaching

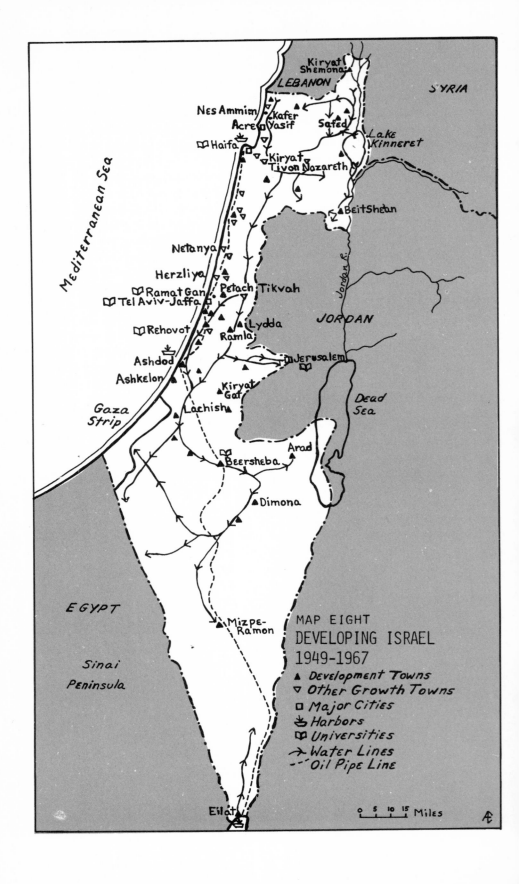

MAP EIGHT
DEVELOPING ISRAEL
1949-1967
▲ Development Towns
▽ Other Growth Towns
□ Major Cities
⚓ Harbors
📖 Universities
→ Water Lines
--- Oil Pipe Line

0 5 10 15 Miles

have been devised. Fees are reduced at the post-primary level for thousands of Eastern students, and entrance requirements for high school have been eased somewhat for them. Tuition is adjusted for needy and gifted students alike.

In Israel, Western Jews formerly comprised the majority of workers; in recent years, the Westerners have been overtaken numerically by Eastern Jews. This could not have occurred without great improvements in the latter group's skills and training.

The peculiarities of the Israeli approach to social integration are in part disclosed by the presence of two quite divergent policies in the domain of education. (1) Connections between the schools and the political parties were prohibited as far back as 1953, thus halting a developing trend toward three major school systems. One was run by the Histadrut (Labor Federation), another by the religious community, and a third by the General Zionist Party. Three different, and in large measure conflicting, ideologies were thus being espoused. The fear of divisiveness was a major factor in the decision to establish a single, comprehensive state school system. (2) The State Education Law of 1953 nevertheless permitted parents to choose between regular state schools and state religious schools for their children. Both kinds are subject to central direction and to minimum educational standards. The reasoning has been that religion is sufficiently important and sufficiently apolitical to justify retaining the religious schools.[9] In other words, religious ideology is not considered as divisive as are other forms of ideology. Surely this is a highly debatable proposition. Opponents of the 1953 law have argued that if religious ideology can be freely taught, why does not the same right extend to, say, socialist ideology? The arguments have been to no avail. The educational system has been depoliticized but it has not been dereligionized.

State primary schools are attended by some 65 percent of Israeli children, state religious schools by about 30 percent.[10] The latter offer state education but are, as the law puts it, "observant of orthodox precepts as to their way of life, curriculum, teachers and inspectors." Greater attention is paid to specifically Jewish studies. However, Bible study occupies a salient place in all public schools. It is at the core of the humanistic curriculum, and serves as a text in history, literature, geography, and language. In the early years of the State, biblical history gained so preemptive a place that knowledge of the remainder of Jewish history was sacrificed, including the history beyond Eretz Yisrael. There is now much more of a balance.

What instrumentality can surpass education as a means of finally overcoming social inequality? That Israel is pledging so much of her wherewithal to equal educational opportunity for everyone constitutes a basic assurance of the coming unity of Israeli society.

An End to Babel

A unique and powerful force in the integration of Israeli life is the Hebrew language. The work of making Hebrew the national tongue of the new State is a marvel of cultural achievement. The decision was not implemented without a tenacious struggle. Israel is the only country in the world where the ancient language of the land has been revived to become the national language of today.

Several generations of scholars have labored long and hard to transform the ancient Hebrew tongue into a contemporary, socially effective instrument.[11] The language lacked any modern vocabulary. Many Orthodox Jews protested that Hebrew ought to be reserved for religious purposes alone, as the language of prayer and study. But the most formidable obstacle lay in the people themselves. Of the hundreds of thousands of Jews who have entered Israel since 1948, few could use the national language at all when they arrived. We must remember that this has been the case with Eastern Jews as well as Western Jews. Immigrant Jewry incorporates a multiplicity of tongues.

The form of pronunciation chosen was that of Sephardic Hebrew, which was used by the Jewish people centuries ago. Significantly, this is the pronunciation that has been retained in Eastern Jewry, in contrast to the Ashkenazic pronunciation employed by European Jews.

Israel's revolution in language has been made possible largely through her famed *ulpanim* or language institutes. In a city *ulpan,* for example, students will live and study together without interruption for as long as six months.[12]

In its favor, Hebrew has always been the language of Jewish faith, and Zionism is not ultimately separable from that faith. Hebrew was a "dead language" only in that it was no longer widely spoken; it had never been given up as the written language of Judaism and it was utilized by poets and scholars.[13] The ability to speak Hebrew was never lost. As an earnest of its recent revival, Jews across the years in different countries who could not comprehend one another's native tongues would resort to Hebrew in order to communicate. Moreover, as far back as 1921, Hebrew had become an official language of Palestine, along with Arabic and English.

Israel's adoption of Hebrew has, nevertheless, created problems. For one thing, there is the issue of isolation and the danger of insularity. Hebrew is the language of no other country. The evidence indicates that Israelis are becoming less bilingual.[14] Again, there is Israel's continuing need for immigrants. Convinced immigrants are, presumably, willing to sacrifice the time and energy demanded to learn the new language. Some of them are already fluent in it. But what about people who are undecided whether to come to Israel? The requirement of mastering the difficult language of Hebrew is undoubtedly a deterrent to some who might otherwise take the affirmative step.[15]

The most serious problem of all has to do with Israel's minorities, and particularly the Israeli Arabs. Weighty and difficult questions are implied here—the nature of Israel as a state, the eventuality of cultural pluralism, etc.—questions considered elsewhere in this volume.

To be sure, certain efforts have been made to recognize and honor the Arabic language. Israeli Arabs are entitled to use their native tongue in all dealings with the Government and in the courts. Arabic is the language of instruction in the Arab schools of Israel, and it is taught as an option in a number of primary and secondary Jewish schools and in the universities. (Arabic is the language of the Druses as well as of Israeli Arabs.) The proceedings of the Knesset are translated into Arabic, and Arab members have the right to address Parliament in their own language. But these points do not really meet the problem. Nor does the opportunity that is afforded Arabs to learn Hebrew.[16]

From the standpoint of cultural pluralism, or at least of minority prerogatives, the right to one's own language and that language alone is no less valid than the right to one's own religion (the latter right being fully respected in Israel). Most Israeli Arabs are still not able to use Hebrew.[17] In the crucial area of language, there remains a wide gulf between many Israeli Arabs and many Israeli Jews.

There is the added complication that the Israeli who knows only Hebrew finds great difficulty in attaining cultural breadth and depth. For example, many university courses rely heavily upon materials published in English. In its completeness, Israeli culture transcends any bounds that the Hebrew language might set for it.[18]

The stubborn truth remains that without competence in Hebrew, no citizen can be fully integrated into Israeli society. Without exaggeration, we may say that the answers to two questions are equally determinative of one's status in Israel: Are you willing to defend this country to the death? Have you made, or are you in the process of making, the Hebrew language part and parcel of your life?

On the credit side of the ledger, the claim can be convincingly made that Israel would never have been reborn without the resolve to make Hebrew *the* language of the land, or, in minimal terms, the language of the Jewish people there. Unity would have been impossible through any other means.

The simplest way to grasp the inevitability of Hebrew as the national language of Israel is to ask: What other tongue could have been chosen? No other language was ever sufficiently in the majority to win the day. And how could Israel ever have become a Jewish state on a different linguistic foundation? Hebrew is the only language possessed in common by Jewry, whether or not individual Jews can actually use it. Insofar as Israel constitutes a genuine rebirth from a long and honored past, the language it chose to embrace could not be alien to that past. Further, on a purely practical level it is very doubtful that Israel will assent to the unconditional use of more than one basic language. The country is far too small to tolerate the burden of multiple languages, a practice that afflicts some other small countries.

All in all, the prevailing Jewishness of Israel makes any alternative arrangement a virtual impossibility. Joseph Kessel has said, "for a writer, three quarters of his motherland is language." Is not this largely the case for most everyone? A people is only as unified as its language. The Hebrew language is among the foremost instruments making the many nations of Israel into one people.

Aliyah *and Absorption: The Need, the Trials, the Ways*

The reception and reasonable assimilation of over a million new citizens by Israel has been a singular moral achievement, quite unparalleled in its intensity, quickness, and variety. And the process goes on. Over 50,000 persons entered Israel in 1969. More than 60,000 were expected in 1970, of whom some 80–85 percent will probably remain as permanent residents.[19] As a tiny nation in a hostile world, Israel has no greater need than that for more and more immigrants.

The word applied to the act of immigration is *aliyah*, which literally means "going up." Here is a striking convergence of religious and extra-religious understanding. The Hebrew Bible speaks of "going up" to the land of promise (for example, Exod. 33:1). In biblical times Jews would make an *aliyah,* a pilgrimage, to the Temple in Jerusalem during certain holy days. Today the new immigrant "goes up" to the homeland of his fathers.

The immigration of any one individual or family is not a simple business. It extends from pre-immigrant orientation and planning, to initial assistance and care upon arrival, to arranging for employment and living quarters. Nor is the immigration process necessarily a happy or successful one. Thus, over the years the great majority of American Jews who came to Israel intending to settle there have returned to the United States. It is hardly realistic or fair to criticize them for deficiency in heroism. To expect that a great many Jews and others will emigrate to Israel merely through appeals to their sense of obligation is quite idealistic. The wise course is to concentrate upon tangible instruments for bringing about a reconciliation between self-interest and a genuine concern to serve. Proper challenges inside Israel include delivering a business man from a bureaucratic maze, aiding a family in need of tolerable housing and proper education for their children of high school age, and giving advice to a young person who is subject to military service.

The Israeli authorities continue to seek energetically to cope with the many problems of immigration by devoting their resources to the resolution of just such tangible difficulties as those mentioned.

The Jewish Agency and the Ministry of Immigration and Absorption now collaborate in providing "absorption centers," of which there are at present thirteen throughout Israel, with a capacity of more than 4,600 persons. Each center offers newcomers to Israel six months of "sheltered settlement" during which time they receive intensive instruction in Hebrew, and are helped with job placement, housing arrangements, and orientation to life in the country. Rental and mortgage loans are available, and also outright subsidies for personal and living expenses.

In its first two years the Haifa Absorption Center, which is specifically designed for people who require training in Hebrew in order to secure employment, welcomed and cared for more than 2,000 immigrants. It is noteworthy that only a handful of these have returned to their countries of origin. Mr. S., an American industrial designer, recently came to Israel with his wife at the Jewish Agency's expense. After six months at the Haifa Center, Mr. S., who happens to be non-Jewish although his wife is Jewish, secured a position in a local electronics firm. They rent an apartment in an Arab-style dwelling in nearby Kiryat Eliezer, with half of the cost paid by the Ministry. Their income is about the same as it was in Chicago. They are glad to be in Israel.[20] Immigrants also receive tax exemptions during their initial years of residence. One advantage to Israel in the character of recent immigration has been the large numbers of academic and professional people as well as skilled craftsmen who have come.

Ever since the 1930's thousands of Jewish children and youth from eighty different countries have been welcomed to the land, rehabilitated, educated, and enabled to take their places in Israeli society. We refer to the celebrated Youth Aliyah, a program supported by several American organizations and by the Jewish Agency. The *kibbutzim* have done much in aid of this program. To date, Youth Aliyah has cared for some 135,000 children and young people, who have in turn labored to establish forty-six new villages.[21]

The different political parties in Israel are at once enabled to serve the nation and to gain adherents through providing advice and help in various immigrant communities.

The very ways and means of *aliyah* and absorption can have a certain therapeutic effect. They direct the attention of natives and newcomers alike to their mutual duties. They galvanize the energies of people, turning them to the building of a future.

Another meliorating factor is that the newcomer to Israel is often given the opportunity to pursue more than one path to social acceptance. Thus, a man may embark upon the "pioneering" course of life in a communal or development village, or he may seek the way of "middle class" recognition in the city. In many other countries, by contrast, the ruling social values have largely foreclosed the first of these routes and left open only the second. It is true that over the years the majority of Israelis have been attracted more to the latter course than to the former. However, we must not forget the solid numbers of Jews, many of them Easterners, who have shunned promises of ease and chosen an arduous and even hazardous way of life.[22]

Of perhaps even greater significance as a policy for meeting the delicate task of absorption is the honoring of ethnic integrity. There can be no genuine integration in any society where ethnic impulses are thwarted. The leaders of Israel have learned this truth from hard experience. Earlier, great energy was expended upon making a given immigrant village into a "melting pot" for newcomers from a number of lands. Soon it was found that this practice often led to friction and unrest, and the departure of many families for the cities. The alternative was introduced of enabling each of many villages to develop from a single ethnic base, although with opportunity for encounters between diverse groups at the village centers. In this way ethnic expression and solidarity have been encouraged.

To honor ethnic integrity is to live with tomorrow. Human collectivities seem to be embarked upon a pluralistic future.[23] Cultural pluralism appears as the fate of more and more nations—yet, hopefully, without the surrender of national distinctiveness. The ideal is a creative tension between homogeneity and heterogeneity.

Paradoxically enough, in Israel ethnic individuality has long since become more meaningful in many respects than was the case in other lands, where Jews were not considered full nationals.[24] Someone has fittingly remarked, "Only in Israel can a Polish Jew be a Pole."

Two fundamental social-psychological findings may not be gainsaid: First, when human beings are deposited in new or strange environments, they require the support and assurance of others possessing the same origins and a common social world. Second, when men are completely forced out of the cultural and spiritual home that has nurtured them they often fall into self-rejection. The Israeli authorities seek to encourage the retention and celebration of older customs and traditions, especially among Jews from Asia and Africa.

In emphasizing the need to respect ethnic integrity, we are aware of the dangers. For example, in Israeli cities there is a certain amount of residential segregation (not sanctioned officially) as between Eastern and Western Jews. Particular ethnic groups will tend to form separate neighborhoods, which tacitly means the exclusion of other groups. The same practice is conspicuous among groups devoted to religious orthodoxy. It is a moot question whether the segregation of such collectivities arises more as a matter of deliberate external pressure, and is therefore suspect, or develops more as a matter of mutual internal preference, and is therefore relatively propitious. Generally speaking, both conditions are usually present in varying degrees.

As the years pass, the demands of social integration within Israel will naturally move more and more away from problems of immigrant absorption and socialization (unless there should occur massive immigration once again). Israel's newer problems of integration will come to bear greater similarity to the corresponding problems found in older countries: the alienation of youth, the conflicts of generations and classes, and economic and political differences.

Significant issues will remain: To what final end is social integration or unity to be fostered? Can the State of Israel be said to possess a unique purpose and meaning in the modern world? What is Israel all about? It is clear that any final answers to these questions lie hidden in the future. Yet we cannot turn our backs upon such questions. They form the basis of many of the reflections offered in Part III of this book.

The Whereabouts of a People

A society's integration is aided—or hindered—through the kinds of communities its people occupy: the locales, the sizes, the styles of living. Despite her smallness, Israel offers great variety here.

Clearly, the resources of Israel's citizens, and especially of newcomers to the land, must be utilized in the national interest. There has been, accordingly, a prevalent tendency to settle immigrants in certain stipulated or advised locales and types of community. Such a policy is understandable and perhaps justifiable. On the other hand, equally indispensable is the effort to enable people to live their own lives where and how they wish. Obviously, no completely happy marriage is possible between these two sets of values.

Of a total Jewish population of some two and one half million, about one-third lives in Israel's three largest cities (Tel Aviv, Jerusalem, and Haifa). One-half lives in seventy-five smaller cities and towns of varying sizes, and of which many are development communities. Some of these towns go back to the biblical period (examples include Beersheba, Tiberias, and Nazareth); others were started as farming villages in the late nineteenth century (examples are Petach Tikva and Rishon le-Zion). One-sixth of the Jewish population lives in some 700 farming villages, most of which have been founded since 1948.

The veteran (pre-1948) groups center in the major cities. Later arrivals live primarily in new communities of the North and South or in areas surrounding the large cities. Broadly speaking, this kind of geographical clustering has tended to sustain the new ethnic diversity of Israel.

One official device for reducing the conflict between national needs and individual and family interests is the granting of subsidies to settlers in development areas. Lower rents, lower taxes, and higher wages help to compensate for the harder life. Businessmen are afforded special concessions and aids. The development areas contain huge immigrant populations. These areas now constitute the primary frontier of Israel's journey toward unity. Here more than in any other places the reborn nation is reaching for maturity.

Israel is concentrating upon regional development. The policy is to orient four or five villages toward a rural center, which contains an elementary school and cultural, health, and farm services. Thus, no village has to fend completely for itself. A number of rural centers are in turn grouped around an administrative "county seat," which offers industries, a secondary school, and social, health, and administrative facilities. For example, the Lachish Region southwest of Jerusalem is one of five major national regions. It is the most advanced of the areas, containing fifty-six villages and the important industrial development town of Kiryat Gat.

A thriving city of 17,000 people, Kiryat Gat was specially designed as a means of integrating immigrants into Israeli life. Its story has been much happier than that of some other towns, which have suffered from great transiency among their populations.[25] Kiryat Gat is one of several instances where a cluster of buildings has become an organism, with a rhythm of its own duplicated nowhere else, "the product of a unique confluence of location, population, resources, and also dreams." Much of Kiryat Gat's considerable success is undoubtedly related to its having been chosen by the Jewish Agency back in 1955 as the planning and administrative headquarters of the Lachish Region. A significant consequence was that by the time the first immigrants came, a nucleus of veterans was already on hand to provide stability and direction.[26]

Kiryat Gat includes, in order of numbers, Eastern Jews (mostly Moroccans), Europeans (mostly Rumanians), and veteran Israelis. The town is large enough to keep ethnic differences from being as divisive as they tend to be in a more confining community. Yet it is worth noting that social relationships among the national groups of Kiryat Gat have remained fairly minimal.

Other examples are pertinent. We select just two. In 1948 Beersheba, where Abraham planted a tamarisk tree (Gen. 21:33), was a small trading post on the edge of the desert; today it is the booming "capital of the Negev" boasting countless trees and a human population of some 72,000. In 1948, Eilat at the southern tip of Israel on the Red Sea consisted of two huts; today it is a year-round resort of 12,000 people with a burgeoning seaport serving as Israel's gateway to the East.[27]

Another option for an Israeli is to take up life within a collectivist settlement (kibbutz) or a cooperative smallholders' settlement (moshav). These communities merit separate consideration.

9. The Communal Settlements

THE PURPOSES of the *kibbutz* and the *moshav* (plurals, *kibbutzim* and *moshavim*) clearly transcend the particular demands of social integration. Yet these communities have made, and continue to make, many contributions to the integrative process. They have done much in the initial absorption and orientation of immigrants.

Certain *kibbutzim* were started by particular bands of immigrants. A goodly number are, however, ethnically diverse. It is true that not many newcomers in recent years have continued to live in the collectivist settlements, although large numbers of immigrants are employed there. Many city children and young people undergo direct experience of *kibbutz* life and work through summer living-in programs.

Return to the Land

For an understanding of the communal settlements, we have to be cognizant of the impulses behind the "return to the land" and the story behind Israeli farming.

One fundamental meaning of the watchword "return to the land" is the reclamation of the soil by committed labor and the development of agriculture. The original Zionist ideal of the unity of labor and soil constituted a conscious moral reaction against the many centuries when, in contrast to biblical times, Jews were largely barred from agricultural pursuits. "Zionism has always had a rural and agricultural mystique. The fertilization of land was only one part of the story. The other part, no less crucial, was the reconstruction of the national personality. The sense of basic creativity, of physical attachment to soil, of remoteness from urban degradations, all came together in the effort to transform the national prototype."[1]

In addition, certain practical requirements lay behind the founding of the communal settlements, such as the severe restrictions upon opportunities for livelihood within conventional agriculture.

In their first twenty-one years the people of the new Israel reclaimed 635,000 acres of arid land. Israeli farmers now provide three quarters of the value of the nation's food together with many exports.

Nine-tenths of the land in Israel is owned by either the State or the Jewish National Fund in approximately equal amounts. This situation results from a combination of socialist ideas, religious influences, and certain events in the story of Zionism. In 1901 the World Zionist Organization created the Jewish National Fund to further the legal purchase of land in Palestine and to aid Jewish farmers. Contributions were received from Jews in various countries. In consequence, the land became the possession not of individuals but in a sense of the Jewish people as a whole.

The Jewish National Fund, which is responsible for land development in Israel, holds the land in trust for the nation, letting it out to collectives and cooperative villages on forty-nine year leases, automatically renewable. This figure accords with the biblical idea of the jubilee year, which taken literally meant periodically leaving the land uncultivated and returning landed property to its original owners. Lands belonging to the State are administered in a similar way.[2] (While Israeli agriculture is prevailingly cooperative in nature, there is a certain amount of private land ownership and cultivation. Ten percent of the land remains the property of individuals, although not all of this is used for farming. Some farmers sell their own produce just as in the United States, although not without supervision by village governing committees.)

The Kibbutz

The beginnings of the *kibbutz* movement date back to the turn of this century. At the forefront were socialist and Zionist revolutionaries and reformers, primarily from Russia and often in rebellion against religion on the ground of its reputedly reactionary and exploitive character. The inspiration behind the *kibbutzim* was more than a matter of ideals, although these were constitutive. A radical pooling of human resources constituted a practical essential for rebuilding the land, providing a sense of community, and fighting off enemies. The *kibbutzim* were a splendidly practical means to these ends—and, in some measure, remain so.

Immovable property and the means of production are owned collectively on the *kibbutzim*. Labor, buying, and selling are organized in a collectivist way. On a given *kibbutz* everyone has the same standard of living. Members do not receive "income" in the ordinary sense. In exchange for their labor, they are provided with food, housing, clothing, and social services. There are individual and family living units but most meals are taken in a central dining hall.

No one on a *kibbutz* need worry about a livelihood for himself or his family. Each community is a miniature welfare state. Infirm and disabled persons are granted total care.[3] *Kibbutz* members are not forced to stay with one type of work; there is provision for rotation in one's vocational responsibilities.

Every *kibbutz* is a self-governing democracy, administered through a general assembly and dedicated to socialist and egalitarian ideals. All members have an equal voice. Membership is not automatic, and there is a probationary period for newcomers. The whole community votes to receive (and sometimes to dismiss) members. Officials are rotated as much as possible in order to prevent the growth of a managerial class. Vigilance is shown against tendencies to social stratification.

Every effort is made to honor and enhance individuality, and to balance personal talents, needs, and rights against community requirements. This applies especially to work assignments. In principle, no type of work is considered inferior to any other. At Kibbutz Dalia in central Israel the noted painter-sculptor Shlomo Meyer works just half-time in the chemical plant so that he may have reasonable opportunity to paint and carve. If the objection is made that this is not enough time for such creative activity, the voluntary character of *kibbutz* membership must be emphasized in reply. Mr. Meyer has chosen his place.

Significantly, the great majority of young people from *kibbutz* families either choose to remain in the community or return there (or settle on another *kibbutz*). On the other hand, after their experience and training in the university or the armed services, some young men and women find that their interests and abilities are no longer satisfied by the routines of the *kibbutz*.

Traditionally, the rearing of *kibbutz* children has been very largely a community responsibility. On the basis of different age groupings, the children spend most of their time in communal quarters apart from their families but under the care of nurses, teachers, and group leaders. However, special periods are set aside every day for parents and children to be together.[4] This arrangement did not first arise out of something in *kibbutz* ideology, although it is generally acknowledged that the original settlers had more or less negative attitudes toward parental roles and were concentrating upon other values and tasks. More positively, the system of communal care and socialization for children was initiated for practical reasons: adverse physical circumstances, security problems of the settlements, and the need for mothers to work. But the system was soon to become fundamental to *kibbutz* teaching and policy.

Protagonists of the traditional system argue that it is a formidable means for removing tensions between the generations; for overcoming the usual causes of conflict between parents and children; for taking away from children the burden of competing with one another for the attention of their parents and other adults; and for enabling the youngsters to develop wholesome relations with their peers as well as personalities that are integrated and other-regarding. The more enthusiastic advocates contend that this method of child rearing can actually help alleviate the stresses that pervade human society as a whole. (In *kibbutz* schools the use of grades and examinations is generally frowned upon.)

Antagonists of the traditional practice claim that *kibbutz* children tend to become unduly "other-directed" at the expense of "inner-directedness," that is, they do not have enough opportunity to develop intimate, person-to-person relationships, and they do not think and act with sufficient independence. Most observers are agreed that the system has not adversely affected the family as an institution, but on the contrary has made for closer and more abiding family relationships.[5]

More than 230 *kibbutzim* are scattered throughout Israel. Over the years these collectives have tended to increase in size. They vary from 50 members to 2,000.

Most of the settlements begun more than twenty years ago number between 300 and 700 members. Additional *kibbutzim* are being established all the time. Much of the manpower for these is provided by graduates of Zionist youth movements inside and beyond Israel. Few are now founded for the traditional reasons; the primary recent incentive has been the need to foster Israel's security in her border areas.

In some measure the *kibbutz* has been impelled to change with the times. The strict rotation in assigned work has been modified to meet the demands of specialization. Increasingly, individuals and families are enabled to own personal possessions secured with funds allocated by vote once community requirements are met.

Today the *kibbutzim* cover the entire spectrum of social and political life. Just about all these communities (as well as the *moshavim*) belong to national federations. Thus, the federation Kibbutz Artzi is Marxist in ideology, while the federation Kibbutz Dati is Orthodox religious. Much attention has been given in the religious *kibbutzim* to developing ways of reconciling biblical teaching with the demands of modern agriculture. Through the federations the *kibbutzim* are affiliated with one or another political party, although some individual settlements remain politically heterogeneous. The *kibbutzim* have been able to exert an influence in politics out of proportion to their relative size in Israeli society. Political action is a basic component of the *kibbutz* outlook. Political representatives who come from *kibbutzim* are aided by the fact that their families can continue to be supported by their communities. Connections of the *kibbutzim* with the Histadrut are also many and varied. The communal settlements have made an immeasurable contribution to the labor movement.

The Moshav

Although the *kibbutzim* are more widely known, the *moshavim,* or cooperative smallholders' settlements, continue to be the dominant form of social organization in Israeli villages. The original goals behind the creation of the *moshav* (the first one was started in 1921) included applying cooperative ideals, fostering economic security, providing permanent homes, absorbing new settlers, contributing to the development of the reviving nation, and, in general, furthering social justice. These purposes remain fundamental.

Morally speaking, one would have to go far to find greater application of the principles of mutual aid and responsibility, within the context of the individual family. For the family constitutes the basic social unit of the *moshav,* in considerable contrast to the *kibbutz.*

Members and their families possess and work their own farms, and accordingly enjoy the fruits of their own labor. However, collective ownership of the means of production and servicing is dominant. Heavy equipment is owned and used jointly. Cooperative institutions are involved in such areas as the purchase of supplies, storage and refrigeration, the sale of produce, transport, irrigation, insurance, and pest control. The *moshavim* are, at once, producer, consumer, and credit cooperatives. They comprise integral, self-governing villages, varying in size from 120 to 150 families.

The life of each *moshav* is guided by a general assembly and a smaller administrative council. As with the *kibbutzim,* inhabitants have equal voices in the governing of the community, and most *moshavim* are attached to regional cooperatives, federations, and political parties. Israel now possesses some 370 of these villages, as against 80 in 1948. New ones continue to be founded. More than 200 are affiliated to the Histadrut.[6]

The spokesman for the *moshavim* emphasizes the ways in which these villages have succeeded in balancing and implementing two values: the need for cooperative agriculture (of the kind that benefits from technological and scientific advance) and the safeguarding of the integrity of the family. (Some new *moshavim* are planned around non-agricultural enterprises, including such undertakings as a school for emotionally disturbed children, a specialized electronics workshop, a swimming pool and resort establishment, and a repertory theater.)

Impact and Role

It is impossible to overestimate the creative role of the collectivist and cooperative settlements in the upbuilding of Israel. They have redeemed the land from the ravages of nature. They have helped to guard Israel from her foes. Their effect upon the national character and upon the shape of Israeli society and culture is immeasurable.

In light of the notoriety and importance of these communities, often people are surprised to learn that today the *kibbutzim* directly involve less than four percent of the population and the *moshavim* less than five percent. It is true that increasingly the communal settlements have been moving away from the center of Israeli social and economic life. Serious challenges have come from more conventional ways of living. Yet the social and moral impact of the settlements has remained out of all proportion to their minority status.

We know that it is anachronistic to identify the Israel of today in exclusively pioneering terms. The word usually translated "pioneers" *(chalutzim)* connotes "self-abnegation, austerity, practical mysticism, and a creative refusal to face uncomfortable facts. The pioneer was totally consecrated to the social and national vision. His satisfactions came not from personal advantage but from the spectacle of growth and expansion of which he was the architect and sometimes the victim."[7] On the other hand, anyone familiar with Israeli life and morality knows that this very understanding of "pioneer" is not without embodiment today. The pioneering vision and pioneering behavior remain very much alive, and the communal movement has been greatly responsible for this fact.

As the times have changed, and as part of the original role of the *kibbutz* has been fulfilled, so too the specific ways in which the *kibbutzim* have come to represent and apply their traditional values have also changed. Their influence today is in the first instance exemplary, but it continues to extend tangibly into political life and to have a place in national defense. There is a consonance of ideals between the *kibbutzim* and the Israeli Defense Forces. For young people in particular, the armed services appear as the most logical place to apply the ideals of *chalutziut* (pioneering) and sacrifice, especially since Israel is constantly faced with threats to her very existence. It is no accident that casualties in the armed forces from among *kibbutz* men have been four times as great as would normally be expected on a population basis. These men volunteer for perilous assignments and serve in hazardous places. They are encouraged to train to become officers, among whom are found disproportionate numbers of casualties. (In the Israeli army tradition, officers lead their troops into battle.[8]) Many *kibbutz* young men and women also join the Nachal, a corps of soldier-farmers serving and working in garrison-settlements in dangerous border areas.

One supporting element in the appeal of *kibbutz* life and values to many youth, from abroad as well as from within Israel, is the contemporary rebellion of young people the world over against values and standards of affluence, materialism, and inhuman competition. When the young are deprived of moral challenges, they either become humorless and fall into premature old age or they go out and make their own challenges. In the latter case, they can continue to laugh, the proper business of youth.

Current Problems

The *kibbutzim* today face the same challenge that all of us meet in a revolutionary time when the validity of traditional values is seriously questioned: What is the meaning and goal of collective responsibility?

More than one observer sees the *kibbutz* of our day struggling with a "crisis of meaning." Some speak of its "growing irrelevance," pointing, for example, to its failure to absorb more Eastern immigrants, and alleging that it has turned into a highly conservative social institution.[9]

The defender of the *kibbutz* stands his ground. For instance, H. E. Retik finds the *kibbutz* "the nearest thing to authentic Communism ever practiced anywhere on earth—with no resemblance, of course, to the tyrannical pseudo-Communism of the Soviet Union or China."[10]

In order to exemplify specifically the relevant controversies of the day, we refer to two themes: the industrialization of the *kibbutz*, and the use of hired labor.

While originally and primarily agricultural in purpose and program, many *kibbutzim* have long since turned as well to industry. As a matter of fact, the major portion of their total income is now non-agricultural.[11] This has created a fundamental problem at once practical and moral: How can the *kibbutz* achieve industrial efficiency and still retain the principle of democratic-collective control?

The issue of hired labor is crucial practically, morally, and also ideologically. Fundamental to *kibbutz* principles (as to *moshav* principles) is opposition to the employment of workers. Hired labor is traditionally associated with exploitive capitalism. Yet due to economic expansion, many of the *kibbutzim* have resorted to wage labor from outside.

Opponents of this trend label it a threat to the fabric of *kibbutz* life. They also envision an increasingly destructive rift between *kibbutz* "managers" and "employers" on the one side and *kibbutz* "employees" on the other. The situation is complicated morally by the fact that those in the former category are most often Western Jews, while the hired workers are most often Eastern Jews. Worst of all, such "profiting from the surplus value of another's labor" is sometimes identified as a betrayal of the very meaning of the *kibbutz* revolution.

Those who sanction the trend to hired help attest that providing employment for those in need, especially recent immigrants, means implementing the ideal of service and contributing to the nation's welfare.

Joel Darom offers a hopeful word:

> Who is to say that [the *kibbutz's* new] "mixed economy" is not the archetype of the society of the future in which the gap between village and city will be bridged? When this comes about, it is theorized, there will no longer be any such thing as a purely agricultural settlement, but rather large communities in predominantly rural settings supporting themselves from an organic integration of factory and farm work, personal labor and sophisticated technological skills, as was prophesied by the founders of socialist thought long ago. . . . All this is only possible, however, if the economic base of the *kibbutz* keeps pace with its population growth. The further industrialization of the *kibbutz,* therefore, is not a possibility which may or may not take place, but a necessity if the *kibbutz* movement is to continue to develop and expand in the future.[12]

The above passage brings to mind a remark made to us by Yehuda Bauer: "The *kibbutz* means living in the twenty-second century." An editorial comment in *The Jerusalem Post* is worth reflection: "The disintegration of the great cities of the affluent countries should be taken for a sign in their favor by the *kibbutzim*—that the future may lie not with the great agglomerations of people and wealth, but with the small groups who can preserve their individuality."[13]

May there finally occur an essential coalescence in social and economic role and identity between the communal settlements and the development areas we referred to in the last chapter? The thought is intriguing.

An interesting innovation is being tried out by American and Canadian immigrants in Carmiel, an "urban *kibbutz.*" It combines the principles of pooled earnings distributed on a basis of need (mainly determined by family size), group planning, shared responsibilities, and communal meals on weekends and holidays, with town living and work. After just one year's experience, the members continued to be excited over this "good way of living" and full of plans for the future. With the enthusiasm of the *chalutzim,* they hope their *kibbutz,* named "Shaal" ("a step"), will be the start of a new form of the collective community.[14]

It is natural that so singular a reality as the collectivist communities should generate argument respecting their overall psychological and social worth. According to at least one authoritative survey, members of *kibbutzim* look upon themselves as significantly more happy than does the rest of the Israeli population.[15] It is very hard to know whether such feelings, highly elusive in themselves, are related to the relatively problem-free character of many aspects of *kibbutz* life, or (just the opposite) to the rigor of that life, especially in hazardous locales, or whether such feelings arise from alternative, perhaps unknown causes. Obviously, the influences will vary from person to person.

There is a genuine sense in which the collectivist settlements will remain morally in advance of the world outside their bounds, certainly in contrast to confessed individualists addicted to the service of the self. For the very meaning of the *kibbutz* movement is to provide "a collective society where each labors for the welfare of the whole" (Eliezer Whartman).

No man who feels himself basically exploited or unwanted is ever truly integrated into a social world. Nor is genuine integration ever possible where the individual has no opportunity to contribute to the welfare of the group. In the *kibbutz* and the *moshav* we find practical implementation of the ideal of each man giving according to his ability and receiving according to his needs. As one young collectivist sees it, "The *kibbutz* is an attempt to deepen human relationships—without any retreat from society as a whole. It is the pioneer of an improved society." It neither turns its back on the world nor falls into utopian abstractions.

10. Jewish Majority and Arab Minority, I

NOT SINCE ANCIENT TIMES has the phrase "Jewish majority" fit. Ironically, it applies today only in a locale where the geopolitics testifies to the fragility of the achievement. Nevertheless, if the Jews of Israel are encompassed by huge Arab majorities outside the land, inside the country the situation is reversed.[1]

It is tempting to say of each of Israel's many fundamental problems: "Here is her most fateful challenge." That impulse is nowhere stronger than when we come to consider the nation's Arab minority. The seriousness of the question is underscored by our allotting two chapters to it. Chaim Weizmann said: "I am certain that the world will judge the Jewish State by what it will do with the Arabs, just as the Jewish people at large will be judged by what we do or fail to do in this State. . . ."

The complexity and the delicacy of the subject are seen in the fact that the Arabs of Israel differ from the Jewish majority in not one but in several major respects. Despite their allegedly common "Semitic" character and a history and tradition containing some shared features, the two peoples diverge ethnically, culturally, linguistically, and religiously. Of greatest seriousness in our day is the conflict in political and national loyalties.

The New Situation

A complicating development, although one that shows a hopeful side, has resulted from the Six Day War of 1967. Over 1,000,000 Arabs, predominantly Muslims, came under Israeli administration. This means that more than one-third of the people within the country's jurisdiction today are Arabs. As we write, the political future of the populations within the administered areas is not predictable.[2] The discussion that follows concentrates upon the original Arab community, the Israeli citizens. Because it is quite possible that the Arabs in the administered regions will remain under Israel's jurisdiction for some time to come, our emphasis upon the smaller grouping may appear somewhat unrealistic. Yet it is improper to treat as a *fait accompli* a highly unsettled state of affairs. Accordingly, references to the administered areas will be limited by their bearing upon the present topic.

The City of Jerusalem is a special case. On June 28, 1967 Israel annulled the Jordanian conquest of East Jerusalem (1948) and incorporated that section into her Jerusalem Municipality. The entire City now stands reunited under Israeli sovereignty. We do not here enter into the merits of this change; we refer to it only in order to make clear that it would be inaccurate to exclude Jerusalem as a whole from a discussion of Jewish-Arab relations in Israel today.[3]

The present Arab population of East Jerusalem numbers some 54,000 Muslims and 12,000 Christians. The population of Jews and Arabs in Jerusalem as a whole is about 275,000.[4]

To turn to the broader picture, somewhat more than 400,000 non-Jews live today in Israel proper, about one for every six Jews. Most of these people are Arabs.[5] This figure is more than three times the number of Jews now living in some thirteen Arab nations—a fact that should be kept in mind when making evaluations. About 74 percent of the Arabs within Israel are Muslims, 18 percent are Christians, and 8 percent are Druses.[6] (The Druse leaders have publicly declared their loyalty to Israel.) The Arab population has greatly enlarged over the past twenty years, due to a very high birth rate and the readmission by Israel of thousands of Arab refugees who had fled with the War for Independence. At present, the numbers of Israeli Arabs are increasing at an average of 75,000 per year. Their population growth has been running more than double that of Jews.[7] Presumably, the Arabs' birth rate will gradually lessen as their living standards continue to rise.

Yesterday and Today: The Arab Plight

Many of the Arab citizens of Israel remain sorely troubled. If the Eastern Jews of Israel have problems, the Arabs have worse problems.

Several hundred years ago Arabs became the majority population in Palestine. As we have seen, in our century they have violently opposed the coming of greater and greater numbers of Jews. To most Arabs, the establishing of a Jewish state was a grave injustice.

Before and after the creation of the new State, the Arabs experienced a great crisis. Their leadership was gone. Most members of the professional class left the country. Many Arabs lost their livelihood. They were humiliated and demoralized. Thousands fled from their homes. A number of their villages were destroyed. In the area that became Israel, their numbers shrank from more than 700,000 to about 160,000. Countless persons were separated from relatives across impassable borders.

Having once been an integral part of the Arab world, the Israeli Arabs became "an isolated enclave with no legitimate communication with its cultural hinterland." Their culture and language were relegated to subordinate status. And with the temporary abatement of armed conflict in 1948 they remained in their plight. Any inclination they might have had at the time to resign themselves to the new situation was obstructed by two circumstances: the continued belligerence of the Arabs states toward Israel (i.e., a virtual state of war still existed, only partially restrained by an armistice) and Israeli security measures against Arabs inside the new country.[8] Furthermore, the Jewish authorities were largely ignorant of how to deal with a minority population.

In the early years the Arabs could not know whether the new State would continue on. They were anxious and unsure about their political and legal status. Many Arabs feared that they would be punished as collaborators by their own kinsmen in the event the Arab armies reappeared. Not until after the Sinai campaign of 1956 did it seem that Israel would endure. And it was not until 1966 that the last vestiges of military supervision of Arabs inside Israel disappeared.[9] However necessary this supervision, and however temperate its actual performance, it had grievous effects upon the outlook and morale of Arabs. They protested that it hindered the growth of legitimate community organization and violated their rights.[10] The security measures also helped to supply raw material to the Arab propaganda machine outside the country.

Perhaps the worst blow of all was the widespread expropriation of the Arabs' land. Included was land of some 25,000 Arab "absentees"—people who fled their homes in 1948 for other parts of Israel—as well as that of refugees. Non-absentee Arabs whose land was deemed essential for "vital development, settlement or security" also found themselves dispossessed. Much of this land was in border areas and was leased to Jewish settlements or farmers as part of frontier defense. It is argued by officials that such settlements redounded to Arab security as much as to that of Jewish citizens.

Arab sources insist that Israeli Arabs have lost 60 percent of their land; other estimates put the total at nearer 40 percent. In response, Jewish spokesmen claim that a large part of the land has been leased back to Arab farmers, not Jews. Since much of it was owned by absentee landlords and worked by sharecroppers, the State's action constituted a needed land reform. Israeli Arab owners were compensated, under law, with cash or other land, though not always to their satisfaction. (Compensation for refugees has been offered but awaits a general settlement of that troublesome issue.) Authorities further point out that despite changes in ownership, Arab farmers have adequate land, especially in view of the rising prices for produce, increased yield (due to irrigation, mechanized equipment, and technological advances), and greater farming efficiency made possible by Government help.

Such explanations convince neither the many Israeli Arabs who have maintained that there was no justification for the confiscation of their property nor the sympathetic Jews who agree with them. Government policy had stopped expropriations by 1965.[11]

New problems in East Jerusalem reopened the question. A typical instance occurred in 1969. After several terrorist bombs tore huge holes in the stone walls of buildings along a narrow and busy route to the Western Wall, the authorities evicted a number of families and billeted soldiers in the homes as a means of protecting visitors to the area. From all the evidence, the dispossessed people were entirely guiltless.

Here was a characteristic dilemma facing the Government. What was it to do? What would the reader have done had he found himself in a place of official responsibility here, charged with the safety and security of all citizens, Arabs and Jews alike, as well as thousands of foreign visitors?

The most that officials can accomplish in expropriation cases is to ease as much as possible the burdens of the people in distress. In this particular case, new housing was secured for the families and they were given a year's rent. They expressed satisfaction with the arrangement.

Nevertheless, the episode "aroused passions throughout the Arab world," especially after it was found that the eviction order extended to a historic Muslim court and mosque. The authorities' rejoinder was that these very buildings command a view of hundreds of worshippers at the Western Wall and hence constitute a security threat.[12] And so the bad feelings live on.

It is important to remember that traditionally the Arabs of Israel, as of Palestine before, have been village-dwelling peasants (together with lesser numbers of townspeople and nomads). Still today, the proportions of Arabs in Israel approximate 80 percent rural and 20 percent urban, almost precisely the reverse of the Jewish population.[13]

The problems of the Arabs have been compounded and aggravated by important social and economic changes within their own society. Before the State of Israel came into being, the social, cultural, and economic world to which the Arabs had clung for centuries had already begun to pass. (There are parallels here to Arab countries beyond the borders of Israel, and indeed to many lands around the world.)

Traditional Arab society is focused in the patriarchal clan (Hamula). Most often, in a given village there are two or more clans, with power and influence divided among them. The smaller family units are also patriarchal. Women are subordinate and the father receives absolute obedience from his sons. Children and wives work the farm; the less labor the father performs, the greater his prestige.

The process of change in the Arab villages presently located in Israel has been accelerated under the new State. Instead of remaining on the farm, many of the young men go off to work in the towns and cities.[14] Many are not able to return each evening. Often they come back only on weekends and sometimes not at all. The result has been a serious weakening of family ties, including an undermining of the father's authority. He becomes the dependent party.

Young Arabs who have taken jobs in the cities have had their own special problems. Most often they do not become part of their new urban environment —usually people just ignore them—and yet they no longer belong to their old village society. They have no moorings. Many times they become embittered. Arab youth who leave home for an education also tend to become estranged from traditional village and family life.

Increased education for the young, including women, itself produces severe challenges to patriarchal power. The development of local self-government—a signal part of Israeli policy among its Arab citizens—and the pull of national and party politics constitute further interferences with traditional clan authority.

Many forces have thus brought about a serious erosion of the old Arab society and its values.[15] The marked prospering of the Arab villages under Israel's governance does not offset this entire development; it may simply contribute to the social disorganization.

At least one further fact must be remembered for even an elementary understanding of the Arab-Jewish situation in Israel: the marked physical and re-

gional separation of the two peoples. Before 1948 there were really two discon-
nected societies. This state of affairs derived primarily from historical and geographical influences, and from different ways of life and interests.[16]

The greatest numbers of Arabs live in the North, many of them in areas that
would have become part of the Arab State of Palestine under the United Nations
Partition Plan. Most Jews live further south and, as we have noted, are predominantly urban. (Haifa and Acre are partial exceptions to the separation of Arabs
and Jews.)

The separation of peoples need not be, in the first resort, a case of "prejudice"
or "discrimination." By and large, the peoples of the Middle East have never
developed the tradition that ethnic or other separation is inherently wrong. A
morally objectionable condition would be present only if the separation were
arbitrarily imposed and enforced by the party possessing dominant power, a state
of affairs productive of invidious comparisons and ghettoization. The alternative
possibility is voluntary separation mutually approved. In large measure the
separation of Arabs and Jews in Israel has exemplified the latter alternative.
Thus, nothing automatically derogatory is suggested by the maintaining of an
"Arab quarter" or a "Jewish quarter" in a particular city.

However, we are quite aware that the acceptability of ethnic separation within
a given society can still entail highly unfortunate consequences, such as lack
of knowledge and understanding of other peoples' problems. We are further
aware that the separation of Jews and Arabs in Israel has been perpetuated by
mutual distrust and antipathy. The struggles between the two peoples before
and during the creation of the State of Israel made the lines even more rigid.
All through the first twenty years of the State nothing substantial occurred to
change the pattern. To the majority of Jews, the Arab was, first and foremost,
a security risk (even though the numbers of security infractions hardly substan-
tiated any such notion). In light of their traumatic experiences and sufferings
at the hands of Arab peoples and others, it is understandable that some Israeli
Jews should fall prey to the unjust generalization that Arabs "cannot be trusted."
This attitude, combined with traditional religious and cultural separatism, ensured that Jews and Arabs would have few associations. The only real exceptions were contacts between Jewish employers and the Arabs who worked for
them, mostly at menial jobs.[17]

Very recent years have witnessed a noticeable change. The separation of Israeli
Jews and Arabs has been considerably offset by the Six Day War and its aftermath, a point to which we shall return. To be sure, there have always been
personal relations and friendships across the lines, and, as we shall note in the
next chapter, currently there are institutional and private efforts to foster contact and understanding.

Toward Equality: The Resolve and the Progress

In the earlier years of the new State very little attention was devoted to the
Arab community. Most Arabs were left to their miseries. Of course, Israel was
fighting to stay alive. Her resources were pitiably overextended. She faced years
of economic distress, of absorbing thousands of refugees and immigrants, and
harassment and attacks from kinsmen of the very people who had remained
within her borders.

Gradually, and despite continuing hardship and danger, the Israelis embarked upon a policy of aid for the Arabs. They gave heed to the voice of their own prophetic conscience. Had not their Proclamation of Independence summoned the nation to implement the ideal of justice and equality for all? The Proclamation declares that the State of Israel "will ensure complete equality of social and political rights to all its inhabitants irrespective of religion, race or sex." It goes on to appeal to the Arab inhabitants "to preserve peace and participate in the upbuilding of the State on the basis of full and equal citizenship and due representation in all its provisional and permanent institutions."

No nation flouts its own interests; neither may we expect it to do so. No responsible Israeli will pretend that equitable treatment of Arabs is not to the long-run advantage of Israel. Concern for one's neighbor is seldom devoid of elements of prudence. Israel will not wittingly provide fuel for the fires of propaganda and hatred kept alight by her enemies. Nor will her politicians close their eyes to the increasing voting strength of Arabs. Again, were Arab workers poorly paid, the labor movement as a whole would be harmed.

Themselves a historic minority, the Jews of Israel know the meaning of oppression. Self-interest and other-regard converge when a nation resolves that it will neither be corrupted nor made cynical by the evil deeds of its detractors and enemies, for to do so would simply give one victory to them. Nations that inflict unjust suffering upon others only degrade themselves. Israel is subject to a command at once moral and theological. That command represents a power able to draw men out of themselves: "If a stranger sojourns with you in your land, do him no wrong. The stranger living with you shall be as one of your own countrymen, and you shall love him as yourself; for you were strangers in the land of Egypt: I am the Lord your God" (Lev. 19:33-34).

In any assessment of the economic, social, and political standing of Israeli Arabs, resort to a single criterion is at once inaccurate and unfair. Equitable judgment demands at least three criteria: comparative conditions among the Arabs in 1948 and today; the relative positions of Israeli Arabs and Israeli Jews; and the comparative status of Arabs in Israel and in Arab lands. The third criterion is particularly important because country or region of residence has become a live option for thousands of Arabs in recent years—despite recurrent wars, persistent enmities, and the attempts of Arab nations to keep frontiers closed.

Israeli Arabs have been enabled to benefit directly and markedly from the country's economic, technological, and social advances.[18] Many efforts have been made to wipe out unfair treatment of Arabs in such crucial matters as housing and employment. Since 1948, Arab social conditions have improved notably and the standard of living has risen greatly. Collectively, these people constitute the most prosperous Arab community in any country.

The social and economic aims pursued by the Government and the Histadrut allow of no distinctions between Arabs and Jews.[19] The goal is full equality for Arab and Jewish workers, with equal pay for equal work and social security benefits. This goal is applied as well to Arab workers who today commute to Israel from the administered areas. In fact, Jews have sometimes grumbled that Arabs compete to the disadvantage of Jewish workers.

In 1961 the Government of Israel inaugurated the first of two five-year plans for developing Arab villages and improving the conditions of Arab life. Provision has been made for schools, housing, roads, public utilities, potable water, and social welfare services. In Arab communities most welfare costs are borne by the Government, in contrast to Jewish communities where local funds predominate.

Special aids are given to Arab farmers (irrigation, land reclamation, and training in modern methods).[20] Agricultural production in the Arab sector has risen markedly, although output per dunam is still far below that in the Jewish sector. The authorities have encouraged small industry and handcrafts, and they have endeavored to establish marketing cooperatives.[21] Some joint Arab-Jewish businesses have been organized.

Governmental agencies expend greater amounts per capita on Arabs than on Jews.[22] Old age and survival insurance carries identical benefits for the two peoples. Health care for Arabs receives special attention. Between 1948 and 1968, the crude death rate among Arabs dropped from 20 per thousand to 5.9, among the lowest in any country.[23] Arabs live longer than in 1948, and longer than their kinsmen in other lands, although their life expectancy is still twenty years below that of Israeli Jews. Israel has carried on a massive campaign to get Arab women to go to hospital when giving birth. The nation now has the lowest Arab infant death rate in the Middle East.

An essential for ensuring Arab-Jewish equality is equality of education, a goal that the authorities are determined to realize. The opportunities for education among Arab Israelis have long since surpassed those for Arabs in other countries. Eventually, Israel will have the first Arab community anywhere in which almost everyone can read and write.

Under the British Mandate, of eligible Arab children between five and fourteen years of age, 65 percent of the boys and 15 percent of the girls went to school.[24] Today the respective percentages are 95 and 75 (the latter figure representing a radical break with tradition).

In educational institutions more stress is being placed upon Arab history and culture. A number of high schools have recently added Arab and Muslim studies. There are *ulpanim* to teach the Arabic language to Jews. Encouragement is given to vocational training among Arab young people, along with Jews. More and more Arab youth are being enabled to attend secondary school and university. There are special scholarship funds for these purposes. A small but increasing number of students from East Jerusalem and the West Bank are enrolled at the Hebrew University.

In Israel there are Arabic newspapers, periodicals, and books, as well as radio and television services. The Arabs themselves deserve much credit for their progress in these and other areas, progress that is revealed as all the more remarkable when we recall that until recently these people had no noticeable place in Israeli cultural life.

Israeli Arabs have infinitely greater freedom of political expression than in Arab states. Infringements upon civil or other rights are barred. In the Seventh Knesset there are six Arab members. (One hears it said by some Arab critics that these officials do not truly represent Arab interests, a judgment not unlike the "Uncle Tom" charge leveled against moderate civil rights leaders among blacks in the U.S.) A Jerusalem Arab editor who is very critical of Israel in his newspaper—he has called for the return of East Jerusalem and the West Bank to

Jordan—readily admits that were he to have said comparable things when Jordan was in control, he would have landed in prison. Already, 35,000 Arabs from East Jerusalem may vote in municipal elections, compared to 3,000 under Jordan, although this group cannot as yet participate in elections to the Knesset (unless they apply for Israeli citizenship). In the elections of October, 1969 about 10,000 of these East Jerusalemites exercised this right—both women and non-property owners for the first time. The surprising turnout, in the face of terrorist threats and a Jordanian radio call for a strike, was considered by some to "mark a turning point in the city's affairs."[25]

A powerful boost to equality for Arab citizens in Israel was the abolition of the Military Administration in 1966. (This was reinstated during the 1967 crisis but very quickly withdrawn again.)

Two developments associated with the Six Day War are of much significance. First, if until 1967 there was much indifference and inattention to Arab-Jewish relations in Israel, the War changed all that. The entire question was forced upon the public conscience, and it became the subject of all kinds of meetings and discussions. With the continuing international crisis, the issue may be expected to remain at the forefront of national attention. Second, the separation of Arabs and Jews has been counteracted. The reunification of Jerusalem has resulted in a commingling of Arabs and Jews on an intensive and continuing basis. Already, more than 25,000 Arabs from East Jerusalem and the administered areas (the West Bank and the Gaza Strip) have taken jobs inside Israel.

The contacts of Jews with Arabs in reunified Jerusalem and the administered areas, and also with visitors from Arab countries, are contributing, at least obliquely, to the lowering of barriers inside Israel proper. The interest of Israelis in the Arab people and their culture and language is being quickened.

Jerusalem's Arabs comprise the largest concentration of these people in any of Israel's cities. As Ernest Stock points out, the significant thing is the circumstances under which the two peoples are meeting. "For the first time, Israelis are face to face with an Arab society whose leadership and structure are intact, self-confident and politically conscious. It has not suffered from 20 years of minority status."[26]

It is sometimes argued that the relations now developing between Jews and Arabs of the administered areas will contribute to a wider framework of cooperation in the future between Israelis and the Arab world. Of course, there are serious doubts that this will happen. After all, from the Arabs' point of view, their overall condition is that of being subjected to occupation by a victorious army. At the same time, we must not underestimate the possibilities of change due to the new and flexible situation. In the specific case of Jerusalem, while mutual distrust between the two populations has by no means disappeared, some progress toward harmony has nevertheless been achieved, especially among workers laboring together.

The services of the Histadrut have been of particular significance for Arab workers in East Jerusalem. At first frightened to join, by May of 1969 some 40 percent of East Jerusalem's laborers had taken membership after the Histadrut helped some hotel workers win the simple right of union membership. Since then the Histadrut has assisted other workers gain not only better pay, shorter hours, and other rights they never had before but also a new sense of dignity.

The most noteworthy factor in this success story is the independence the Arab workers showed in ignoring anti-Histadrut propaganda from Arab sources and in striking against employers of their own nationality with the guidance and help of Israelis.[27]

The knowledge that Israeli Arabs today are gaining of life beyond Israel's borders is just as decisive as the things Arabs from outside are enabled to discover about Israel (usually the exact opposite of what they have been told for over twenty years). For their part many Israeli Arabs have been shocked to behold with their own eyes the conditions that many of their kinsmen on the West Bank had to endure while under Jordanian control, especially the refugees. One such visitor to the area responded: "How could Jordan ever have allowed these people to exist this way for twenty years? One or at the most two years, but not *twenty*."

Deficiencies

If Israel's drive toward equality for her Arab citizens shows great resolve and much progress, the millennium is still far off. There are weighty and lamentable deficiencies.

For understandable reasons, if not necessarily the wisest ones, official Israeli literature directed to the public abroad tends to emphasize the achievements rather than the shortcomings. For example, an oft-cited survey of Nazareth tells that the average annual income of an Arab family there was 7,000 Israeli pounds in 1965, close to that of the average Jewish urban family: 7,360. Yet in point of fact most Arab families do not have advantages comparable to life in Nazareth. For years Jewish farmers have been the benefactors of enormous institutional and private aid from outside Israel. Quite properly, this assistance has been celebrated. But Arab farmers received very little of such help, and yet this lack is not mentioned very often. Again, it is very fine that two high schools in Tel Aviv have made Arabic compulsory. But there remain large numbers of schools where this has not been done.

Israeli schools have not advanced very far in intergroup education. Although exchange visits are paid between Arab and Jewish schools, the contacts tend to be quite formal and lacking in depth. Despite progress, Arab history still receives too little emphasis in the Jewish school system. There are hardly any integrated schools. This latter condition has multiple causes: the societal separatism alluded to earlier, a scarcity of resources, a formidable language barrier, etc. It is important to bear in mind that any campaign for educational integration would encounter as much, if not more, opposition from Arab quarters as from Jewish quarters.

Israel has a long way to go before she offers equality as between Arab schools and Jewish schools. Thus, at the all-important primary level the ratio of teachers to pupils is approximately 1:27 in Arab schools but about 1:17 in Jewish schools.[28]

All too few Arab youth go on to secondary school (some 30 percent of the numbers of Jewish students) and only a very few to university.[29] There remains a dearth of intellectual and professional leadership in the Arab community.

Even in very recent years, positions in the bureaucracy, professions, and business have often been closed to Arabs. Very few Arabs are employed by the Government and there are none in top-ranking posts.

Still today, when unemployment comes Arab workers are often among the first to be furloughed. Too few of these workers are as yet unionized—something over half of the Arab labor force—and this is due only in part to their own reluctance.[30] Manual labor continues to be the lot of hosts of Arabs.

The Six Day War solved some problems and created others. Many jobs became available in West Jerusalem. Israeli Arab students who had run into trouble obtaining housing could now secure accommodations in East Jerusalem. On the other hand, many intellectuals lost their positions when the East Jerusalem municipality was abolished. Many of those who were offered jobs with the unified City declined, either because they refused to recognize Israel's right to annex East Jerusalem, or because they wished to keep themselves uncontaminated in the event that a peace settlement brought Jordan back in some capacity.

Last but not least, the all-pervading assumption that Israel is a Jewish state has had a powerful effect upon the psychology of Jewish-Arab relations. It has influenced some Jews to act as though they were superior to Arabs, and led Arabs to play a correspondingly inferior role. Highly relevant to this state of affairs is Professor Stock's observation that the mass of Jewish immigrants from Arab countries have manifested very little interest in relations with Israeli Arabs, despite their linguistic ties. It is hypothesized that "expressions of hostility by these Jews derive from a desire to demonstrate their superiority to the Arabs of Israel. Incidents resulting in physical violence between Jews and Arabs have usually involved Jews from Oriental countries."[31] We may further hypothesize that the reversal in social position has been an important factor here. In many of the Arab lands, the Jews occupied minority-inferior status and the Arabs the majority-superior role.

Thus we have seen how the story of the Arab community of Israel is one of great advance combined with continuing and serious need. All in all, the Arabs' socio-economic status is still below that of Jews (just as Eastern Jews are below Western Jews). But the future must see greater and greater equality.[32]

11. Jewish Majority and Arab Minority, II

Arab Responses

HOW HAVE THE Arabs of Israel responded to their recent fortunes, particularly to their improved social and economic status and to the increased contacts with Jews? What continuing dilemmas face the country in the realm of Arab-Jewish relations? Are there insurmountable problems? What is being done to foster understanding and friendship? What may the future promise?

The specific experiences of individuals and their families are of enormous influence in the shaping of attitudes.

In Kafer Yasif, a village in the North of Israel, we visited the home of a young Christian Arab. (Arabs everywhere have a marvelous pride in their homes.) This young man's parents, themselves illiterate, had yearned for good educations and careers for their children—the daughters as well as the son. The dream was realized. The son is a teacher, one daughter is a nurse, and the other is a social worker. They do not think of themselves as anything but Israelis. The young teacher said, "I was raised in this village. This is my home. I have no wish to become part of another nation. There is no discrimination against me. I am happy."

By contrast, in Haifa a well-educated young Arab testified that just when advancement seemed assured in the bank where he worked, he was passed over in favor of a Jewish employee with lesser qualifications. This young man finds it very hard to think of himself as an Israeli. He is a Palestinian Arab first and last, and an embittered one.

Variations in religious background must also be kept in mind, not so much for the influence of religious faith *per se* as for certain social and psychological differences that appear. The tensions involved are not primarily Jewish-Muslim or Jewish-Christian but Jewish-Arab, with the religious element a complicating factor.

Christian Arabs in Israel have tended to be better educated than Muslim

Arabs, largely as a result of advantageous training in Christian missionary schools. The greatest numbers of Christian Arabs are found in the cities; Muslim Arabs are most often rural dwellers. A consequence of these factors is that even though Muslims are by far the majority among Arabs, the more articulate and influential spokesmen in the Arab community have often been Christians. This activity has involved *criticism* of Israel easily as much as support of Israel. On the other hand, better education often leads to a better job and greater satisfaction with one's social world.

One reason why the Christian Arabs of East Jerusalem have of late manifested a slight tendency to be drawn to Israel, in contrast to the Muslim Arabs, is that they number less than 20 percent of the total Arab community in that part of the City. In their relations with Muslims, these Christians have been showing somewhat greater self-confidence than when they were surrounded by a Muslim majority.[1] Hence, Israel finds herself cast in a role not unlike that of the parent who imposes a reasonably bearable peace among different sizes of children.

It is further the case that Muslim Arabs in Israel have felt themselves cut off not just ethnically but religiously from the greater Arab world, of which Islam is such a vital component.

None of the above is to insinuate that Muslim Arabs in Israel are as a group more hostile to the State than Christian Arabs; our purpose at the moment is simply to emphasize that the Israeli Arab community is not a monolith.[2] As a matter of fact, the reunification of Jerusalem by Israel has already become a powerful corrective to the feeling of isolation among Muslim Arabs. They have been set free to participate in the great religious life of the Haram esh-Sharif in Jerusalem, an opportunity that had been barred to them by Jordan.

Many Arabs manifest identifiable reactions to Israel and their lot in that country. They may and do respond in varied and even diametrically opposed ways. We have to remember as well that the one individual will respond differently at different times and under different circumstances. Attitudes run the gamut from enthusiastic support to resentful aversion.

In Chapter 7 we alluded to major kinds of response to life in Israel on the part of Jewish immigrants. The Arabs of Israel respond along similar lines: approval, disaffection-apathy, and a love-hate attitude. Of course, the proportions and intensity of each response are not here the same, and we have to allow for the immense differences in the situations of the two groups. Thus, it would be foolish to look for any great measure of disillusionment among Israeli Arabs, as that phenomenon sometimes appears among immigrant Jews. Disillusionment is possible only after great expectations, and few Arabs have ever expected glorious things from Israel.

If the three types of response apply to Arab residents as well as to Jewish newcomers, this is not primarily due to resemblances in the specific conditions of the two groups. The duplication appears simply because we find these different responses in any social milieu where a new or minority group is trying to find its way. To enumerate these reactions is, in other words, simply to offer a sociological truism. However, the content of the responses is another matter; specific Arab reactions have often been surprising, and they are of much significance for the future of majority-minority relations in Israel.

Naturally enough, any unqualified celebration of life in Israel is hardly the strongest attitude among most Arabs. We have to recall that many Jewish citizens have their own lists of Israel's faults. But because the Jews are the majority party, they can be expected to speak out much more readily than the Arabs. Needless to say, even an approving form of behavior may be a mask for unexpressed or unconscious hostility.

Support for Israel

Within the Arab community there is, nevertheless, much more sympathy toward the country and life in it than outsiders often realize—or than paranoiac propagandists in the Arab countries could ever concede. It is, indeed, a great tribute to the independence of mind and heart of Israeli Arabs that so few of them have ever succumbed to the campaign of hate incessantly waged over radio and television from Arab countries. (As a democracy, Israel does not ban the reception of such materials.)

For years, Israeli Arabs have been free to leave the country. *The vast majority of them have elected to stay.* Why is that? Many factors are involved beyond specific attitudes to Israel: economic security, love of village and home, uncertainties respecting life elsewhere—and, perhaps most important of all, the common knowledge that the few who did leave were summarily sent back by authorities in the surrounding Arab countries. Yet surely if animosity to Israel were a compelling force among the nation's Arabs, many of them would have sought to flee anyway or at least have refused to adjust to life in Israel. They have done neither of these things.

In the previous chapter we mentioned in passing Israel's abolition of the Military Administration in 1966. That this decision could be rendered taught at least two lessons: Those Jews were wrong who had warned that the Arabs in Israel could never be trusted to accept the State; and those Arabs were wrong who charged that Jewish officialdom would never cease to regard them as a "fifth column." (This is said in full recognition of the effectiveness of the system of surveillance in preventing and discouraging hostile acts.) It is highly significant that the reinstatement of the Military Administration because of the June War of 1967 was countermanded again after just a few months.

The War itself provided an incomparable test case. Once more, we must not ignore the realities of the situation. Had the Arab countries succeeded in their planned, total extermination of Israel,[3] it is entirely possible that in the frenzy of the slaughter, distinctions would have scarcely been made between Israeli Jews and Israeli Arabs. And some in the Arab community inside Israel doubtless had forebodings of just such a fate. Any Arab who is a citizen of the hated enemy Israel already has a black mark against him. Yet once these facts are taken fully into account—or perhaps we may even say, granted that these facts were a partially motivating factor in the behavior of Israeli Arabs—the War provided a telling demonstration of the solidarity of these people with their country and of their loyalty to it.

True loyalty implies a fulfillment of self-concerns and personal values, not their abnegation. The Arabs of Israel "identified with the State and its predicament to a remarkable degree. The Arab community expressed its solidarity in a variety of ways: statements by notables, blood donations, volunteer work in *kibbutzim* and willingness of young men to enlist for military service. . . . Thus, the fear of Israeli Arabs that they would be the first victims of another war, and the fear of Israeli Jews that a war would turn their Arab fellow-citizens into a security threat, proved equally groundless."[4] The War saw a marked lessening of the stereotype among Israelis that had lumped Arabs into a hostile and even disloyal group.

The War witnessed at least two other accomplishments. It enabled Arabs to see at close hand the prevailing humaneness of Israel: the compassion with which the Defense Forces sought to do their job, the restraint shown toward the foe, the earnest efforts to rehabilitate human lives ravaged by years of hatred.[5] In addition, the new spirit of satisfaction was reinforced by the fact that, as a result of Israel's victory, thousands of Arabs were afforded the joy of visiting and being reunited with their relatives and loved ones. They have been enabled to move freely between the Israel-administered areas and Israel proper.

The entire experience of the War and its aftermath has done much to build mutual confidence between the two communities.[6] Arabs and Jews have been strangers within one country. Now they are beginning to know one another.

For all the problems and the limitations under which they have had to live, the Arabs of Israel express thankfulness for the good life that is theirs—the self-expression, the prosperity, the security. Arab youths have told the present writers of the gratitude they feel for the actions of the authorities in putting to an end blood feuds between families and villages, and to conflicts between Arab and Druse clans. There is safety in moving about the countryside. There is safety in the cities, infinitely more than in American cities today.

Disaffection—Apathy

If it is beyond doubt that most Israeli Arabs are loyal or at least non-rebellious citizens, it hardly follows that they are not at all disaffected. It is virtually impossible to draw dividing lines among loyalty, do-nothingness, and disaffection. We most often assume that people are "loyal citizens" simply on the ground that they do nothing to obstruct the existing order. But to conclude that they are therefore free of discontent with their society would be silly. That almost no Israeli Arabs have taken any action against the State does not in itself testify to enthusiastic support. All sorts of constraining forces can have been involved: fear of punishment, sloth, uncertainty how to proceed, etc. Many Arabs in Israel still possess highly negative attitudes to the country and, more particularly, to the Jews there.

Whenever we consider attitudes, we are dealing with highly elusive and changeable states of mind. Nevertheless, we have no choice but to assume that some kind of positive connection obtains between inner attitudes and overt behavior.

Eighty percent of eligible Arab voters have participated in national elections.[7] What may this signify? Voter participation is usually taken to reflect supportive citizenship. This is often a sensible interpretation but not always. With respect to the general category of "disaffection-apathy," in actual voting disaffection is clearly a greater possibility than apathy. People afflicted with apathy most often stay away from the polls. The act of voting often expresses hope for a change, and it can represent great dissatisfaction. But dissatisfaction need not mean a total lack of supportive citizenship.

Significantly, over 20 percent of the total Israeli Arab vote has gone to Rakah, a communist party. Arabs are normally reputed to be anti-communist. This substantial percentage is probably linked to Rakah's call for an instituting of the U.N. partition frontiers of 1947, involving the restoration of such cities as Nazareth and Acre to the Arabs.[8]

Let us return to an earlier point about the decisiveness of experience. "Experience" can have a broader signification than events occurring to isolated individuals; it can refer to the fortunes of entire groups. For example, we speak of the experience of the "older generation" or that of the "younger generation." As a matter of fact, in Israel there is something of a generation disparity within the Arab community on our very subject. Relatively speaking, the older generation tends to show less dissatisfaction. Most of these people are very conscious of improvements in their living conditions. Younger Arabs, by contrast, tend to be more subject to disaffection, and usually with reasons for which they do not carry the primary blame. They have never known anything but progress, and they most often take it for granted. (Today more than half the Arabs in Israel were born after 1948.) They see nothing but injustice in any discrimination against them; they are, after all, full citizens of the State who pay taxes and look upon themselves as entitled to all rights and services. One of their major reproofs is the gulf that still exists between living standards in Arab villages and Jewish villages.[9] In addition, resentments originating in the older generation are sometimes kept alive through the younger people. Young Arabs cannot always find employment consonant with their training. This is especially hard on those with superior qualifications. Having genuinely desired to contribute to their country's growth, they naturally become embittered.

Some decisions have moved the different generations to respond as one. Rabbi Cohen writes: "When the Israel Government announces that the central Galilee must be populated by Jews in order to counteract the large Arab population there, what can one expect the Arab reaction to be? I do not question the security motives behind such a policy, but how can one reconcile the callousness of its presentation to the public with the appeal to the Arabs to be loyal citizens of the State? Loyalty cannot be turned on and off like a water tap. It can be elicited only in those who feel themselves to be fully accepted."[10]

Problems such as the foregoing bring us to the real focus of apathy among Arabs within Israel. Apathy is born when, after every effort at redress is made, a man still feels that he has been treated unjustly and his dignity has not been honored. It may be agreed in all quarters that when men *feel* basically wronged, there is a thread of communion, however thin, with what is right. It is within this delicate psychological-moral domain that the really heartrending conflicts are found between the Arabs and the Jews of Israel.

Ambivalence

When, as often happens, the response of support for Israel and the response of opposition converge, the result is psychological conflict within the individual or group. A love-hate attitude toward Israel is not uncommon within the Arab community, particularly among reflective Arabs and in leadership and intellectual circles.

We have referred to the gratefulness of Israeli Arabs for the good things provided them. The difficulty is that in any time and among any people, advantageous living conditions do not necessarily create self-identity or overcome estrangement. The Arab may ask himself: "Who am I? What does it mean to be an 'Israeli'? The Israelis are Jews. But I am an Arab. These people all around me and my village, the people that run things, perhaps they mean to be my friends. They have proved themselves to be trustworthy. But, after all, are they not alien to me and mine?"

When all is said and done, the Arab may still feel himself an outsider—in his own country. To furnish Arab villages with electricity, water, and schools is a very fine thing. But it does not go to the heart of the problem. The issue is not one of material welfare; it is one of psychological and spiritual integrity. And yet few Arabs would actually be prepared to throw over the good life that has come to them and their families for the sake of a mere ideal or in exchange for an uncertain existence.

Consider these words: "Do you want me to tell you the truth? I hate you. Yes, I know, before you came I was much worse off. . . . But we hate you all the same. We would rather be oppressed by our own people than live under you, the conquerors." True, this is an extreme confession, and it may not be typical. The man who uttered these words to a Jewish interviewer is a Bedouin from an encampment somewhere south of Hebron (in the administered territories).[11] His background and outlook are far removed from the situation of most Israeli Arabs, who hardly think of themselves as living under "conquerors." Yet there is a haunting note in the man's words. Our point in citing them is simply to suggest that within the unconscious of many an Arab of Israel, at least a trace of this very testimony may be found. If in some way the Jew's perennial fear of extinction is conjured up by the presence of Arabs, so in some way the Arab's separation from his own world is represented to him by Jews.

Hardship amongst one's own people is sometimes more bearable than outward well-being amongst outsiders. So natural and strong is the impulse to national and ethnic belongingness that this drive cannot be condemned out of hand. The State of Israel must live with the fact—she appears increasingly prepared to do so—that some of her most advantaged citizens would nevertheless prefer to live in an Arab state.

We should be the last to imply hypocrisy in the Israeli Arab's professed loyalty to Israel or in his declared wish that the nation survive. There are many Arabs in the land who are happy despite their minority status. We would simply emphasize that the dilemma of the Arab in Israel arises precisely because there are two factors: his good situation and his unavoidable alienation. The presence of both these elements is what makes the conflict so poignant.

The Arab's inner predicament is aggravated by dilemmas of daily life. As Leonard Fein points out, nearly all the symbols that unify Israel's Jews either elicit antagonism or remain meaningless to her Arabs: the Bible, the Hebrew language, Independence Day, the Defense Forces,[12] not to mention the national religious festivals. To expect an Israeli Arab to sing with devotion Hatikvah, the national anthem, is not completely unlike expecting a Jew to recite with dedication the Apostle's Creed.

No problem has been more insurmountable than the nurture of the young. An essential element in any education is the developing of a healthy national consciousness. But under the tragic international conditions of today how can the Arab child be educated to become a proud young Israeli?[13]

The advantages to Arabs of social and economic development are considerably offset by accompanying losses in traditional ways of doing things. Every people requires a certain amount of traditional behavior to retain its integrity. In Israel, provision for local self-government is intended to foster group initiative and pride within the Arab community. Yet against this must be balanced the troublesome obligations thereby visited upon people whose traditions do not accord substantially with this form of democracy. The imposition of "progress" is all right only where the intended beneficiaries come to believe that "progress" is a good thing.

Again, will involvement in politics help a man's career or will it do him and his family harm? It is difficult for the Arab to know. He may recognize that political action is a necessity for aiding his people. But such action also means cooperating with and supporting the Establishment.

A certain conflict of loyalties, however small or inchoate, is inevitable within the soul of the Israeli Arab. He would not be a man otherwise. We would be inhumane if we did not allow for this. But it is most essential to remember that the conflict is a much more complex one than an encounter of Arab and non-Arab elements. The deeper tragedy is that Arabness itself, marked as it is by highly divergent and competing nationalist elements, has not achieved unity. It suffers from inner turmoil and division.

This divisiveness points up one additional aspect of the Israeli Arab's dilemma: his apprehensions respecting the future. What if there should be another full-scale war? Will it not be much more destructive than the last one? What will happen to him and his family? The evidence is that most Arabs in Israel have been disillusioned and repelled by the reprehensible policies and acts of the Arab nations. Yet if the Israeli Arab has been inspired to greater devotion to his country, he knows only too well that the outside Arab leadership will not be content with anything less than the total destruction of Israel. In that grim eventuality, what would be his fate?

The Israeli Dilemma

If the Arabs of Israel suffer from psychological and moral dilemmas, the nation as a whole lives in a serious and lasting predicament respecting its minority population.

Israel's dilemma is woven into her Proclamation of Independence. For side by side with the promise of "complete equality of social and political rights" are the words, "we . . . representatives of the Jewish people of Palestine and the Zionist movement of the world, . . . hereby proclaim the reestablishment of the Jewish State in the Land of Israel, to be known as the State of Israel." Does this not mean that Israel's non-Jewish citizens fall into a special category? For an

Arab to be denied the franchise or to be paid less than a Jew for equal work would be intolerable. But is not Israel entitled, to take a most obvious illustration, to exclude Arabs or other non-Jews from crucial governmental posts, including the Prime Ministry? Is not Israel, after all, a Jewish state?

Professor Fein writes: "The Israel dilemma is that the very powerful ethic of equal opportunity and full political equality must compete against the equally powerful ethic of a Jewish State. It is not a question of simple bigotry. . . . Rather, the notion of an Arab President of Israel is rejected by the Jewish population because of its historic impropriety, because it would introduce fundamental doubts about the reasoning behind Zionism and about the most basic understandings of what Israel and Israeliness mean."[14]

How are we to answer the allegation that the Arabs of Israel are "second-class citizens"? In most respects any such charge is pernicious denial of the truth. The motives behind such judgments are of the utmost relevance. If, as is so often the case, the critic's ulterior purpose is the dissolution of Israel as a Jewish state, he scarcely qualifies as an apostle of human rights. But if the critic is genuinely committed to impartial justice, this is another matter.

The phrase "second-class citizenship" applied to the Arabs of Israel is not totally incorrect, but only when "citizenship" is interpreted in much broader terms than "civil rights," and when, further, it is remembered that the discrepancy in citizenship does not apply exclusively to Arabs but holds for any non-Jew.

There are two quite different considerations here. One has to do with the contemporary state of affairs in the Middle East; the other is not limited in that way.

1. The "idealist" who, in total repudiation of conditions of time and space, demands absolute equality for any group of men is hardly the necessary friend of justice. He may, all unwittingly, only compound injustice. The spectacle of the Israel of today being subjected to internal Arab leadership, with all the national and international pressures and evils this would assure, is too horrible to imagine.

Above all, we must avoid false analogies. In truth, there are no real-life parallels anywhere in the world to the Arab-Jewish situation in Israel. Here is one imagined analogy: Suppose that the largest ethnic minority in the United States consisted of 35 million people who spoke a language other than English, were of a wholly distinct cultural and religious background in contrast to the majority, and boasted 3.8 billion kinsmen as the controlling peoples of Canada, Mexico, and other nearby lands. Imagine further that the latter multitude had not only been nourished from birth to believe that every effort must be made to wipe out the United States and its population of more than 200 millions,[15] but had already made such attempts through harassment and armed invasion for over two decades. It is difficult to think of the American people going out of their way under such circumstances to ensure justice for their ethnic minority. Probably the opposite type of behavior could be expected. It is a moral miracle that despite threats to her very survival, Israel has resolved upon so humane and just a course with her Arab minority, a miracle for which the leaders and people of Israel merit great praise. At the same time it will be understood why this course cannot be pursued without fear and trembling. With the exception of most Jews in other lands, the outside world lacks almost all comprehension of the powerful *minority* feeling that still pervades the psychology of the Jews of Israel, for all their objective majority status, an outlook fatefully imposed upon them by life today within the bounds of a potential death camp of incredible proportions.

In contemporary Israel it is simply impossible to formulate basic policy without resolute attention to national security and survival. This demand influences practical decisions: the assigning of positions of national trust in banks and elsewhere, the present denial of an independent Arab political party, the exclusion of Arabs from military service, etc.[16]

2. The moral problem confronting Israel is an issue of principle as well as the result of a particular set of circumstances. The question of Arab rights dominates the scene today. Yet this need not always be the case. In the event, to return to the category of miracles, that peace were achieved in the Middle East and Israel's right to exist were granted, the problem would be considerably eased. But it would not be resolved. For the challenge Israel faces is not, ultimately, that of reckoning with an *Arab* minority alone. It is a question of relations with *any* minority. We mean to ask: Could the Jews of Israel ever afford to be placed in a position where they no longer possessed the power of majority decision in their country?

Perhaps as outsiders we ought to remain silent at this juncture. But we submit that it is from the prevailing Israeli standpoint itself that the answer will be "no." Yet the justifications of this answer are much more authentic and compelling than the pressures of contemporary self-interest among Israelis. The Israeli standpoint is vindicated by a very long history, which must never be forgotten. Indeed, it is the entire history of the Jewish people that stands forth as the all-decisive judge of whether Israel ought to remain a Jewish state. That history is a story of suffering and death at the hands of cruel nations and men (largely Christians along with not a few Muslims).[17] Here we speak on strictly moral grounds, where people are no longer "outsiders" or "insiders" but only human beings. No question arises here of "prejudice" against the Arabs of Israel. Prejudice becomes a moral issue only when a particular group is a direct or exclusive target of some form of malevolence. This is not the case here. The Arabs are, *as Arabs,* quite irrelevant to this second dimension of our argument.

The two considerations just reviewed are brought together through an affirmation by Rabbi Jack J. Cohen. A great advocate of Arab rights, Rabbi Cohen nevertheless concedes that until antisemitism is rooted out of human consciousness, the Jews have a right to protect Israel as their "one unquestionable sanctuary," and that on this ground, "the Law of Return, which grants preference to Jewish immigration into Israel, is morally justified."[18] We simply comment that were Israel to attain an Arab majority, the Law of Return would quite probably be repealed as discriminatory. Indeed, it is entirely conceivable that ultimately all Jewish immigration into Israel would be forbidden.

In Part III we return to the highly controversial question of whether a people possesses the moral right to guard its own identity, and accordingly to take necessary political measures to that end.

Abiding Problems, Efforts, Hopes

The conflict between Israeli Arabs and Israeli Jews is in certain respects ineradicable—not because hostile acts are inevitable from either side, but because of the psychological, moral, and political conditions described in the two previous sections of this chapter. The pressing obligation, therefore, is to ease the burden as much as possible. The furtherance of social justice for Arabs is so vital precisely because their place in Israel is not ideal.

This demand applies especially to the advancement of Arab culture, and, wherever possible, to the development of Arab autonomy. Despite the fact that a bi-national state is not possible, either politically or morally, there can be many approximations to that design through, for example, an increasingly effective and independent Arab educational system.

There is a double challenge here: to foster Arab culture and to help the Arabs evolve a sympathy for the emerging Israeli culture. A multi-cultural society adds to the richness of life for Jews as well as Arabs. If Israel cannot be a bi-national state, she can still move substantially towards a bi-cultural and bi-ethnic society.

The obligation to respect the interests and ways of Arabs has to be balanced against their objective welfare. How can this be done without creating some opposition and resentment? The Israeli authorities have had to contend with the fact that some Arabs have looked upon aids to their community as a subtle method of undermining its character and independence, with Israelization as the real, ulterior goal. A case in point is education for girls. This is lacking in the Arab tradition, and there are particularly strong feelings against coeducation. In order to avoid giving offense, the authorities have been lenient in enforcing the Compulsory Education Law. Those who have accused Israel of substandard education for Arabs are many times ignorant (or prefer to be ignorant) of the quandaries the authorities face. Outsiders often have little familiarity with the serious factional strife that pervades the Arab community itself—and has done so ever since the time of the Mandate.

Amidst all the obstacles, efforts go on to break down barriers and further conciliation between Arabs and Jews. The names of some committed campaigners stand out: Jack J. Cohen of the Hillel Foundation at the Hebrew University, Nina DiNur, Benjamin Jeremias, Ammon Linn, and Shimon Shereshevsky, among others. A number of private and semipublic institutions are devoted to understanding between the two communities. Examples include the Arab-Jewish Community Center in Haifa, the Israeli section of the Women's International League for Peace and Freedom, the YMCA in Jerusalem, the Jewish-Arab Institute at Giv'at Haviva (run by the political party Mapam), and the Israel League for Friendship and Understanding.[19] A large number of *kibbutzim* have "adopted" nearby Arab and Druse villages, arranging for joint outings and exchange visits of children. Under the aegis of the Office of the Prime Minister, a summer camp is held in Acre each year for Arab and Jewish young people of high school age. The Jews selected are students of Arabic, and that language is used. The campers visit Arab villages, study and engage in sports together. Near Jerusalem 1,400 teenage campers run a month-long Youth City. In the Summer of 1968, 400 East Jerusalem Arab youths participated and helped elect one of their own number Deputy Mayor.

These individual and group efforts appear to have slight social impact. Yet who can gauge the ultimate effect of even the most modest enterprises?

The above reference to the use of Arabic prompts an added citation from Rabbi Cohen: "Of all the mistakes the Israelis have made over the years, it might well be that their failure to make Arabic a compulsory part of the education of all Jews is the most serious. Nothing could give the Israeli Arab a sense of his own worth more than the feeling of at-homeness which he would have if his Jewish neighbors could share his language! For the learning of the language of a neighbor is the clearest indication of the respect in which one holds him."[20]

No instrument for Arab-Jewish harmony in Israel is potentially more powerful than regional autonomy for Arabs. In the foreseeable future there seems no way to consider that option on its own merits. The intransigence of the Arabs outside Israel prevents it. This is another way of saying that the greatest gift the Arabs of Israel could receive is peace in the Middle East.

The future of these people is fatefully linked to the issue of peace. Without international peace, how can they have genuine security or reasonable peace of mind? In the context of the question of peace, Israel's policy toward her Arabs assumes lesser significance, and the policy of the Arab states toward Israel gains first importance. The life that Arabs lead in Israel is not the problem; the problem is their impossible place in the Arab world.

A secure and lasting peace would transform the entire majority-minority situation in Israel. Those on both sides would be freed from fears. They could be themselves, assured that their words and deeds would not be subjected to the distortions of international strife. Considerations of national security would cease to be a source of tension. Erstwhile limitations upon independent Arab political movements would lose their warrant, as would objections to the employment of Arabs in positions of national trust. The Arabs of Israel could very well come into their own as builders of bridges of understanding between their country and their own Arab brothers.

These words are dreams, for the present. Barring a miracle, peace remains extremely remote. It is a sad caprice of our era that Israel's largest minority should come from among peoples who have never accepted that State, and are, indeed, dedicated to her death. Yet the Israelis have little intention of permitting the whims of history to dictate their future. They know that the only release from this particular fate is to fashion justice for their Arab citizens.

A sterling truth remains: In one country of the world Arabs and Jews do live together in peace. That land is Israel. The path to this achievement is not an easy one, but it is marked by purity. It is the way of showing respect for human beings. Probably none of this will make the larger Arab world cease its hatred of Israel. But the lesson is still there for any who are openhearted enough to learn it.

12. Some Issues of Religion, I

THE CHAPTER HEADINGS of this volume do not for the most part seem to suggest religious subject matter. However, in the Jewish tradition (as in much of the Christian tradition) religion has to do with all of life, and all of life is open to the response of faith. From this point of view, none of the topics we are considering can be finally separated from religious faith. The paradox of human affairs, and accordingly of books, is that religion appears everywhere, but sometimes it emerges here more explicitly than there. (We know that the subjection of religion to analysis tends to chill the devout and bore the nonbelieving.)

The Nature and Focus of the Religious Problem

The issue of majority-minority relations in today's Israel extends to the explicitly religious domain, but in a manner quite different from our discussion of the last two chapters. Only in secondary ways does the religious question involve relationships between Jews and non-Jews. The most sensitive and nationally decisive issues concerning religion are focused inside the Jewish community. This will become especially apparent in Chapter 13.

The disposition of religion stands among the thorniest domestic challenges in the country. Harold Fisch of Bar Ilan University goes as far as to say that "next to the problem of survival itself, the question of whether Israel is to be a secular or a religious state is the central issue of all."[1]

The faith-tradition to which most Israelis are heirs is, of course, Judaism. If, as suggested in Chapter 11, the Jews of Israel have a certain moral right to majority status in their land, it follows that Judaism can be expected to remain dominant among the faiths there. But there are serious complications.

Great uncertainty is manifest within Israel over questions of religious faith, a condition that at once causes and results from uncertainty over the meaning of Jewishness. Before the modern period, both these forms of uncertainty were much less profound.

Large numbers of Israeli Jews neither observe Judaism nor claim to "believe" it. To some of these, religion is a foolish waste of everybody's time. Besides, if religion is all that virtuous, why are not its disciples morally superior to non-religious people? Very often, the opposite is the case. Furthermore, so it is argued, religion is quite irrelevant to life, to the problems that count: peace (or war) with the Arabs, the need for immigrants, the development and industrialization of the country. The real purpose and value of the refounding of the State of Israel has been to give Jews their rightful standing as a people, and not to "realize" the teachings of the Torah, whatever that might mean. Many native-born Israelis are very secular-minded, and sympathize with the foregoing argument.

Others are not so aggressive in their reasoning, although the practical effect is the same. Those Israelis who are personally uncertain respecting faith and its truth often end up doing nothing about religion. Many people do not appear to care one way or the other.

In the thinking of a related group, while religious consciousness may once have had a good function—to create Jewish reality—it long ago finished its work. Now, Jews have "come of age" as a nation and regained their political independence and integrity. Peoplehood must take precedence over religiousness. How else may nonreligious Israelis and religious Israelis attain unity?

Opponents of this reasoning are aghast that Jews should ever talk this way. To fail to honor Jewish faith and the God behind that faith is to reveal moral and spiritual bankruptcy. "Israel is a nation only by virtue of its Torah" (Sa'adia Gaon, tenth-century sage). Without the Jewish faith and heritage, where is the justification of the State of Israel? What else can give her unity? What else can keep her from eventually deteriorating into an assemblage of mere Hebrew-speaking gentiles, a nation like unto all other nations?

It is an ill omen, the religionists contend, that some apostles of "Canaanism" have appeared in Israel. This is the view that Israel is an entirely new and unique nation, free of any essential bond with Jews elsewhere, independent of Zionism ("an alien culture of the Diaspora"[2]), and devoid of any connection with Judaism. Some of these people claim that they feel themselves to be "Hebrews" rather than "Jews." Is not all such talk proof, the religionists continue, that in Eretz Yisrael genuinely Jewish peoplehood actually depends for its integrity upon the historic Jewish faith-tradition? When the faith goes, Jewishness deteriorates into a kind of Semitic nationalism. ("Canaanism" is, of course, a minority viewpoint; most Israelis, including youth, think of themselves as Jews.)

The differences of viewpoint just sketched raise the inevitable question: What is to be the future of Judaism in the land of promise? Israel faces the overall, practical problem of a serious lack of any clear consensus on the place religion ought to have in the national consciousness, and a consequent lack of surety respecting the proper relation of religion and the civil order.

Striking similarities are evident here to Arab national consciousness, which is extremely unsure of the role of religion in its social and political world. The religious uniformity that once prevailed in Jewish and Arab society has long since broken down, and, as Rabbi Cohen points out, in neither community has a satisfactory means been found of responding to religious pluralism.[3]

Israel faces the corollary challenge of which version of Judaism, if any, is to be socially authoritative and normative.

The dominant religious viewpoint in the country is Orthodox Judaism. The term is the "modern designation for the strictly traditional section of Jewry." The literal authority of the Torah and the Tradition is advocated. Though Orthodoxy shows wide diversification, Orthodox Jews accept the historical event of divine revelation at Mount Sinai as described in the Torah; the immutability and binding character of the divine Law, in its written and oral forms; and the authority of duly qualified rabbis to interpret and administer the Law.[4] There is conscientious observance of the Sabbath, *kashruth* (the dietary laws), and other requirements.

The view that contrasts in considerable measure with Orthodoxy may be identified as "Liberal Judaism." There are, to be sure, difficulties with this phrase. Many Orthodox do not wish to be known as "illiberal," just as many Liberals do not approve any implication that they have betrayed the values of Orthodoxy.

We do not here use "Liberal Judaism" as a value term. We employ it as a means of representing those Jews who are prepared, in varying degrees, to apply the Tradition in ways that meet demands of morality, reason, experience, and the exigencies of contemporary life. A Liberal watchword is, "Halachah [the Law and Tradition] is not our governance but our guidance." Liberals insist that a given act that may *seem* to go against the Torah does so only for those who have arbitrarily ruled out responsible change. The fulfillment of the Torah lies in faithful adherence to its principles, to spirit over letter. Liberals especially honor the teachings of the biblical prophets. "It is through justice that the Lord of hosts is exalted; the Holy One is sanctified through righteousness" (Isa. 5:16).

Liberals vary in the degree of their observance of the Sabbath, *kashruth,* and other traditions. In general, however, there is much greater observance of Halachah within the tiny Liberal community in Israel than among Liberal Jews in the Diaspora.

Alternative terms for "Liberal" are "Reform" and "Progressive." With some simplification we may say that Conservative Judaism, which is also represented in very modest fashion in Israel, tends to fall to the right within the Liberal arena (or just outside it, depending on one's viewpoint), inasmuch as the Conservative position occupies something of a mediating role between Orthodox and non-Orthodox interpretation and practice.

The Conservative and Reform movements are, of course, major bodies in American Judaism, as is Orthodoxy. As an organized body, Conservative Judaism originated in the United States. In Israel, the Reform and Conservative movements share official nonrecognition. Although Conservative and Reform leadership in the United States and Israel is at present endeavoring to strengthen non-Orthodox Judaism in Israel, only a fraction of the latter country's 6,000 congregations are non-Orthodox.

As with the other topics explored in this study, a comprehension of the religious situation in today's Israel requires some cognizance of ongoing historical influences and traditional arrangements. Two such factors are of crucial importance in the present context: the early and continuing alliance between religious and extra-religious forces; and the relation between the civil order and the religious communities of the land. These factors are considered in the two following sections of the present chapter.

A word of caution is fitting at this juncture. To understand religion in Israel,

Americans must be wary of easy recourse to such expressions as "separation of church and state" and "freedom of religion." Although these and related concepts are not irrelevant to the situation in Israel, they have special meanings there. Americans must also remember that their judgments of what is religiously "right" and "wrong" will not necessarily correspond with Israeli standards. At the same time, they have to avoid the conclusion that Israeli practice must be antithetical to American practice. It is sometimes alleged, for example, that Israel is a "theocracy." In truth, any such description is seriously misrepresentative.

A Polar Alliance

For centuries, Jewry has meant a religious community, an ethnic reality, an entire culture. Because of this breadth and depth, the *laos* (peopleness) of the Jews has been able to endure in defiance of the loss of statehood.

In the modern period the emancipation of Western Jews from the ghettos of Europe contributed to a blurring of laic identity. ("Laic" is here used as the adjectival form of *laos*.[5]) Many Jews came to think of themselves as primarily a religious community, although with a national past. But the Zionist development constituted an opposite movement: emphasis fell upon laic identity, although in a way that obscured its religious component, at least for a time.[6] Most of the pioneers who performed the actual task of restoring the Jewish homeland were freethinkers.

We encounter an odd combination. On the one hand, as previously noted, the religious Jews of Israel are prevailingly Orthodox. And yet, on the other hand, the majority of Israelis are not religious men in the accustomed meanings of "religious." Then we meet the further striking fact that these two disparate groups are heirs of a viable social and political alliance worked out in earlier years. Both sides had to be represented because they were alike constituent to the Zionist cause. They had to cooperate for the sake of the upbuilding of the homeland and, eventually, for the survival of the new State.

Had the religious adherents who early came up to Eretz Yisrael been Jews from countries other than Russia and Eastern Europe—had they been primarily, let us say, Liberal Jews from the United States—the story of religion in the land would have been markedly different.[7] That story would also have been very different had the Russian Jews who stood at the forefront of the reborn Zionist movement not been exposed so tellingly to secular European civilization, and to the intellectual and political agitation that began to loosen the hold of traditional Judaism.[8]

However great the distress among advocates of Orthodoxy over the secular nature of so much Zionism, it was to them providential that the "pure" form of Judaism became foundational in Eretz Yisrael. Some of their opponents answered that not the divine intent, but only the dubious contingencies of life, accounted for Orthodoxy's priority—a diagnosis not dissimilar to the explanation forced upon the Orthodox themselves respecting the assembly of irreligious stalwarts who stood right in the front ranks of Zionist leadership.

We must not forget the religious Jews of such holy cities as Jerusalem, Safed, Tiberias, and Hebron, whose families go back hundreds of years. (Safed has a very special association for the Hasidim.) The spirituality of these people has been a countervailing influence upon secular Zionism.

For various reasons, the new Government in 1948 would not look for political and social support to groups further to the left of its own socialist position or to groups on the right. Ben Gurion and the labor forces turned instead to the religionists to sustain the coalition that was being forged. The invitation served to ensure that the religious bloc would eventually have to be rendered its due (for example, and as we shall discuss, in rabbinical control over Jewish marriage). The religious interests were considerably distant from the secularist orientation of the Government, and infinitely removed from the religious libertarianism of the Gurionites and most of the citizenry. Nevertheless, Ben Gurion preferred this kind of alliance to making concessions in his economic and political objectives.[9] In these latter respects, the religious interests did not offer serious trouble. One important factor making the alliance possible was that the secularist pioneers, for all their anti-religiousness, practiced an austere ethic that was in many ways consonant with the religious tradition.[10]

Today the "curious alliance" continues "between those for whom religion is —theoretically at least—the be-all and the end-all of Jewish life, the *raison d'être* for Israel's existence, and those for whom religion is just one useful element— like the Hebrew language—in defining and preserving national individuality."[11] In the meantime, the Orthodox coloring of Judaism in Israel has been intensified by the great influx of Eastern Jews.

The extra-holy alliance of religious and extra-religious forces has necessitated continuing compromises in political decision-making and in social life, and it has hardly resolved the conflicts between the two sides.

The Religious Communities and the Civil Order

It is impossible to comprehend or to appreciate the religious situation in Israel without being aware of the unique arrangement for the religious communities and how this has come about.

Earlier regimes in Palestine enabled the different religious bodies to conduct their own internal affairs. The tradition is traceable as far back as the sixth century c.e., and remains a very strong one in the Middle East. As long as a particular community possessed official recognition, it could freely administer matters of personal status within its membership.

From the inception of the State of Israel, this practice was retained and given legal sanction. Recognized communities today include the Jews, the Muslims, the Christians, and the Druses. For Jews, official recognition extends only to Orthodox Judaism. Some Jews approve this limitation; many others disapprove it. The point to remember here is its historical and traditional basis.

Israel is the only democratic nation to maintain a cabinet post in religion. Israelis have mixed feelings about this. The Ministry of Religious Affairs through its various departments cooperates with and substantially assists (financially and otherwise) the several religious communities. In the Jewish community, the office of the Chief Rabbinate passes upon the qualifications of local rabbis.[12]

The primary understanding of religious freedom in Israel lies in the institutional and group recognition here outlined. The religious communities oversee their own institutions, worship according to their own customs and beliefs, and maintain their own councils and courts.

For each body of adherents, the religious courts (and not Israel's civil courts) have entire jurisdiction over marriage, divorce, guardianship, adoption, burial, and legacies and wills. In the Jewish community, the jurisdiction of the rabbinical courts extends automatically to issues of marriage and divorce alone. In other matters of the personal status of Jews, the parties involved may choose between a rabbinical court and a civil court. The decisions of religious courts are enforceable through the civil courts.[13] Thus, as with her schools, Israel maintains two types of courts: state and religious.

As we have earlier suggested, it is incorrect to equate the American and Israeli situations. There are, however, limited parallels. Israel, like the United States, is a secular state. But it would be quite wrong to conclude from this fact that Jewishness must be understood in purely secular terms.[14] The latter question is left entirely open. A related condition exists in the United States. Just because that country is officially secular, the Christian identity of the majority of American citizens is not thereby reduced to nonreligious terms.

The basis of the similarity here is that the two nations share a common moral and political assumption, namely, that it is not wrong for the religion of a country's inhabitants to exert influence upon social practice and custom. In the United States, Sunday is the traditional day of rest not because the country is constitutionally Christian—it is not—but because most of its citizens are Christians. In Israel, Saturday is the official day of rest not because the State is officially married to Judaism—it is not—but because the overwhelming numbers of people in Israel are Jews.

While the cessation of public transport on the Israeli Sabbath has strong religious motivations, there is no necessity to view it in exclusively religious terms, any more than one has to do that with the Sunday closing of Government office buildings in Washington, D.C. As a matter of fact, the citizenry of any Israeli municipality possesses the right to vote alternative arrangements. In Haifa, buses run on the Jewish Sabbath.[15]

The foregoing distinction between official secularity and the religious self-identification of citizens is a most essential one. It brings out the all-important difference between theocracy, which in principle forbids change, and democracy, which keeps the way open for change.

> In connection with the function of the Jewish law and the rabbinical courts in the general legal system of the country [of Israel], one often hears the statement that Israel today has theocratic aspects. This involves a misunderstanding of theocracy. In a theocratic society, the religious law is in force inasmuch as it is a Divine law. The principle of its validation is religious. In Israel, however, whatever religious law is in force, derives its validity from the political authority. When the Israeli legislator grants force to the religious law, he does so at his own discretion and for reasons of policy. This should be no source of alarm to the secularist and no cause for encouragement to those who favor a true theocracy.[16]

Whoever charges that Israel is a theocracy is forced into a rather bizarre rendering of the divine will. The Lord appears unable to make up his mind among Jewish, Muslim, Christian, and Druse ways of faith and life.

The religious problem is complicated for Israeli Jews by a combination of four factors: different religious communities have official recognition (unlike the practice in the United States); most Israelis are Jews; the majority of these Jews are not religiously observant; and the only recognized Jewish religious community is Orthodoxy.

All this helps to account for the complaint sometimes voiced by Israeli Jews that they are discriminated against in favor of a minority of non-Jews. An illustration is the observance of weekly rest-days and other holy days. The Jewish Sabbath and festivals are prescribed days of rest throughout Israel (just as are Sunday and Christmas in the United States). But in Israel non-Jews are explicitly given the right to observe their own sabbath and festivals as rest-days. Every employee must be allowed at least thirty-six consecutive hours of leisure per week. However, with Jews this period is normally to coincide with the Jewish Sabbath, while non-Jews have freedom to choose between the Jewish Sabbath and their own rest-day.[17] Again, an Arab shopkeeper may decide to close on either Friday or Saturday (or, if a Christian, on Sunday). The Jewish storekeeper has no such choice. On this particular matter Jews as a group are restricted more than other groups.[18]

Jewish Religious Observance

We come to the question of the extent of religious observance among Jews together with their attitudes on the official support of Judaism.

It is impossible to specify in any scientifically satisfactory way the degree of expressed adherence to Judaism. One can offer impressions. Thus, celebrations of the High Holy Days are nationwide events. During the twenty-four hours of Yom Kippur (Day of Atonement), the most solemn of all days, all services cease save for essential ones. Radio Israel falls silent. In Jerusalem most people spend the day in the synagogues while a minority remains quietly at home. There is no *law* against driving one's car on this day, but very few Israeli Jews seem prepared to do it.

The Israeli Institute of Applied Social Research recently obtained a national sample among sixteen communities on the subject of religious observance. The study revealed that 16 percent of the respondents said that they honored all the traditional religious requirements, such as Sabbath observance and *kashruth*. Another 16 percent reported that they adhered to the commandments "for the most part," and 48 percent said that they observed the traditions "to some extent," but 20 percent indicated that they were not observant at all.

An estimate of 40 percent is generous respecting the numbers of religiously observant Jews in Israel, and this includes many whose connection with the synagogue is tenuous and sporadic. On the other hand, observance in the home, the traditional center of Judaism, appears to be quite widespread.

Difficult as is the estimate of religious observance, the extent of religious belief is much harder to judge. Historically, Judaism has, of course, subordinated doctrine to practice. (For this reason, Orthodoxy should actually be called Orthopraxy.) Yet the very distinction points to one of the limitations in the figures reported above. Religious belief may manifest itself in ways other than ritual observance. It is true that most "believing" Jews in Israel are Orthodox. Nevertheless, while Liberal Jews would tend to appear relatively less observant on the above scale, we are hardly justified in concluding that they are of necessity non-religious.

Most difficult of all is any assessment of the depth and intensity of religious conviction and commitment, which may in some cases transcend ritual observance completely. Furthermore, a number of Israelis confess that they engage in religious observances, not because they are themselves religious and not because the observances are religious, but for such other reasons as identification with family and nation. Sometimes, traditions appear to be observed because this was the way one's parents or grandparents conducted themselves. A desire is present to preserve something from the past. There is also the factor of personal identification with the Tradition during such an event as Passover. That event gained meaning for the most secular Jew in June of 1967, if not before. He was himself delivered from the Egyptians.

Another poll conducted by the Institute of Applied Social Research, earlier than the one reported above, asked whether public life ought to be conducted in accordance with Jewish religious custom. We find that 37 percent of the respondents said "no"; 23 percent answered "definitely yes"; 20 percent, while uncertain, felt that it would "probably" be good to maintain such enforcement; 16 percent acknowledged the Government's right to enforce religious tradition but asserted that the authorities would be unwise to exercise the power; and 4 percent did not answer. Thus, 53 percent opposed governmental enforcement and 43 percent favored it.

When these two studies are compared, we have some evidence that among Israelis the support of religious observance on a personal and family basis is noticeably stronger than their readiness to sanction official enforcement of such observance.[19] Most people in Israel disapprove coercion in religion. Large numbers of Israelis resent the Orthodox religious regulations and demands. Yet many religionists continue to maintain that the State should not only sanction faithful national observance of the Torah but also require it.[20]

The most patent evidence that religious observance is not a *sine qua non* of Jewishness or of loyalty to Israel is that incumbents of high public office are often nonobservant Jews.[21]

The Muslims of Israel

Palestine and Jerusalem have not been of primary importance in the Islamic tradition. The historic center of Islam is, of course, Arabia. Mecca is the Muslim Holy City, with Medina second in rank. As an evident sign of respect for Judaism and Christianity as precursors of the "true faith" of Islam, Muhammad originally enjoined his followers to face toward Jerusalem in their prayers. When the Jews in Medina refused to be converted and to accede to his claim to be the divinely-chosen successor to all their prophets, Muhammad changed his instructions and made Mecca the focal point of worship.

Today, Muslim visitors previously subjected to Arab propaganda are often amazed by the vitality and spirit of the Muslim community in Israel. Large amounts of public funds are expended for the protection, welfare, and improvement of Muslim (and Christian) holy sites and institutions. By law of the land, provision has been made for Muslim religious endowments to be delivered to

Muslim trustees in villages and towns, so that the income might be put to communal, educational, and charitable use.

Services are regularly held in some 90 mosques throughout the country. No Muslim village is without a house of worship. In Nazareth a strikingly modern edifice, the el-Salaam Mosque (Mosque of Peace) has recently been completed, with the Government's aid.

As with the rabbinical judges, the Muslim (and Druse) religious functionaries represent and are paid by the State. There are more than 200 Muslim officials in Israel. In contrast to conditions in certain neighboring Arab countries, there is greater freedom in some respects for the Muslims in Israel. In several other lands, the religious courts have been abolished and their authority transferred to the civil courts. Possessing exclusive jurisdiction over every question of personal status, the Muslim (and Christian) courts in Israel have wider powers than the rabbinical courts.

To the fundamental autonomy of the Muslim community new freedoms have been added since 1967. Israeli Muslims were before that year prevented by Jordan from visiting and utilizing their holy sites in East Jerusalem and elsewhere. This has all been changed. (Muslims and Christians in the administered areas also have complete freedom to go to the holy places in Israel proper.) Although the Israeli Government has tried unceasingly to obtain permission from Jordan and Saudi Arabia for her Muslim citizens to make the all-important pilgrimage to Mecca, this continues to be denied. Only the Muslims of East Jerusalem and the administered territories are enabled to fulfill the obligation.[22]

We select two related subjects of a controversial sort as a means of exemplifying the delicacy of the question of religious freedom and the inevitable link between that right and other rights. The references are to Israel's prohibition of polygamy and the law respecting divorce.

There is no final solution to the time-worn conflict between group autonomy and tradition and the rights of individual human beings. On the one hand, few customs have been more entrenched among Muslim Arab peoples than the right of males to have as many as four spouses at one time. On the other hand, the status of Arab women has been greatly advanced through the abolition of polygamy and child marriage. Hence, the question is not simply one of Muslim morality versus Jewish morality, but one of traditional Arab practice versus the rights of Arab women.

The Supreme Court of Israel has held that the law against polygamy is not a violation of religious freedom, since Islam does not demand polygamy but only permits it. Yet we have to point out that traditional Muslim religious law authorizes virtually unconditional divorce by a husband. He need only assert three times to his wife, before witnesses, "I hereby divorce you." The Israeli law against polygamy also forbids any such unilateral divorce.

There is no way to deny that this latter prohibition constitutes restraint upon religious freedom, from the Muslim standpoint. Yet it is equally essential to observe that the forbidding of unilateral divorce is not determined by any anti-religious bias. The positive rationale for the restraint is the dignity of women.

13. Some Issues of Religion, II

The Christians of Israel

"'Resurrexit sicut dixit' (for He has risen as He said). With these words Easter reached its climax, at the mouth of the Tomb of Christ, in the Basilica of the Holy Sepulcher." Thus began a recent *Jerusalem Post* account of Easter in Israel.

We are occupied with the land where Jesus was born; where he lived, died, and, according to the confession of the Christian faith, was raised from the dead; where the Christian church took its rise; where the church has remained in fundamental historical and geographical continuity with its origins; and whence it has moved out into much of the globe. Thus, there are continuities with Eretz Yisrael, and there are discontinuities. Christianity soon became a prevailingly gentile faith, and most of its centers lie in the gentile world. Nevertheless, that the church is living freely in a Jewish state is testimony, not alone to recognition of a daughter-faith from within Judaism, but also to the Jewish historical and theological foundation of Christianity. (Since the decision of the Holy See permitting vernacular usage, one may hear Christian Mass celebrated in Hebrew, uniquely in Israel.)

Even though the land of Israel possesses infinitely greater spiritual meaning for Christendom than for Islam (although not the ineluctable and catholic meaning that it has for Jews and Judaism), the Christian community is much smaller than the Muslim. It will be recalled that most Israeli Arabs are Muslims. The Christian population in Israel proper is about 72,000, some 12,000 of whom reside in East Jerusalem. Just about all the Christians are Arabic-speaking. Divisions are many and conspicuous. Of the 30 or more communions, the principal ones include Greek Catholics (25,000), Greek Orthodox (22,000), Latins (16,000), Maronites (3,000), and Protestants (2,500).[1]

There are about 2,500 Christian clergy, nuns, and monks. The country contains over 400 churches. One of the largest religious edifices in the Middle East is the recently-completed Roman Catholic Church of the Annunciation in

Nazareth, constructed with considerable financial and other assistance from the Government.[2]

Following upon the June War of 1967, Christians joined Muslims and Jews in being granted unrestricted access to their sacred places in the Old City of Jerusalem, Bethlehem, and elsewhere.[3]

One moral issue in Jewish-Christian relations is that of potential Christian expansion in Israel, including missionary efforts by some Christian groups. As a matter of fact, within certain church bodies in Israel there is increased and serious questioning of, and even opposition to, any attempt to convert Jews to Christianity. This new sentiment has developed, not on latitudinarian grounds, but on Christian theological grounds.[4]

Such opposition to Christian missionary efforts as is found among Jews comes from individuals and private groups, not from official circles or the Government, which stands for tolerance (in contrast to suppression and acts of persecution against Christian communities in such Arab countries as Egypt, Syria, Jordan, and the Sudan).[5]

Even apart from Jewish memories of centuries of Christian antisemitism, Israeli Jews can hardly be expected to look upon Christian missionary endeavors among their people as legitimate religious competition. Religious Jews see those ventures as an affront to the people of God on the part of men whose faith would never have come into being without Judaism. Jews as a whole react to the conversionist attempt as an attack upon their integrity as a people. Both of these responses reflect the inseparability of Jewishness and Judaism.

Let us change the focus of the problem somewhat. Suppose that a formidable immigration of Christians to Israel were to begin to develop—not with any missionary designs but for quite different reasons, perhaps including the wish to be of service to the country. Individual Christians and small groups are, of course, entirely welcome now. In Liberal Jewish circles the weakness of the Christian community in Israel is occasionally lamented. For these Liberals, greater Christian strength is desirable, not alone for the sake of the Christians, but for the worthwhile intellectual and moral challenges the Jewish community would receive. (There are no relationships of any substance between Christian Arabs and other Christians, the latter of whom still constitute to a large extent a series of foreign enclaves in Israel.) It is, nevertheless, hard to imagine that a large movement of Christians into Israel would be generally acceptable. In the Israel of today there is simply no way to separate religious considerations from other values. Nor can any such separation be morally justified, from an Israeli point of view. The preeminent question remains: How are the integrity and the future of Israel as a Jewish state to be insured?

The Jewish Dilemma

We have not yet elaborated upon the special religious-moral-political predicament that besets Israel. A fundamental problem centering entirely within the Jewish community now concerns us.

It is sometimes affirmed that in Israel no religious faith possesses peculiar legal privileges denied to other faiths. If this refers to equality among the recognized religious communities, the statement is correct. But when differences and conflicts *within* a given community are taken into account, the affirmation is brought into question. The fact is that a minority inside a religious community (and, not impossibly, even a majority) can come to a point of view or propose a practice that will nevertheless remain officially forbidden. In this sense, the affirmation referred to at the beginning of this paragraph should be amended to say that in Israel specific legal privileges do extend to those who adhere to the authorized version of a recognized religious faith.

An argument for the political embodiment of religious claims is offered by Dr. I. S. Ben-Meir:

> What collective image shall the Jewish nation establish and maintain in its homeland? What the religious community demands is that the Torah be applied as a sociological doctrine, as a way of life for the Jews in Israel. . . . Without faith a person cannot be asked to fast on Yom Kippur, or attend the synagogue. Commandments relating to the orderly functions of society, on the other hand, such as marriage and divorce, or Sabbath and holiday observances by commerce and industry, involve the nation as a whole. Affected is a way of life which is essential to the nation's unity, to the creation of social and behavioral norms that should distinguish it from other nations, and preserve the Israeli Jews' bonds with their fellow-Jews in the Diaspora. . . .
>
> But it is often argued, all these things belong to the province of education. Actually, the point is not whether a law is coercive—most legislation is of the coercive kind —but whether it is necessary for the public welfare. . . .
>
> It makes no sense to say that the laws may not be adopted because religious people advocate them. One may as well taboo social laws because these are desired by the poor or the working classes. What counts is whether the laws are essential for the benefit of the State or the people.[6]

Israel is a democracy. But its religious arrangement respecting Jews is not necessarily democratic. We say "not necessarily" because much of the problem centers in what is meant by "democracy." The complication in Israel is that while the prevailing religious forces do not represent a majority of the citizenry, they do constitute the overwhelming majority of all practicing religionists, and these forces are able to benefit from available political wherewithal. One of the many paradoxes of public life in Israel is that the religious Establishment draws its power from the dominantly secular character of the nation.[7] Yet the Orthodox can hardly be refuted when they emphasize that those national decisions that support their position have been reached through accepted political behavior. Nevertheless, the moral problem remains: What provisions, if any, are to be made for the rights of the non-Orthodox religious minority?

Some see in this question a challenge to the very meaning of Israel as a state. The argument that the country is a Jewish state may be in some way resorted to in considering relations between Jew and non-Jew. But how could that argument ever be used in relations between Jew and Jew? Any radical equating of "a Jewish state" with "a state for Orthodox Jews" is morally out of the question. The normative Israeli understanding is that "Jewish state" means "a state for *any* Jew." Were this not the case, thousands of Jews would have to be excluded from Israel.

We are met by a most bizarre state of affairs. In the previous chapter we noted how some Israeli Jews feel that they are discriminated against in favor of non-Jews. Now we face the spectacle of some Jews lamenting that they are discriminated against in favor of other Jews—and this in a Jewish state! Liberal religious Jews are heard to protest that they have a harder time in Israel than nonreligious Jews, the latter of whom are seldom much exercised about religious matters anyway.

The problem is such an intractable one because it is moral as well as political. The persuasion is widespread among the Orthodox that Liberalism constitutes a debasing of Judaism into an instrument for the satisfaction of human needs and the enjoyment of human wishes. Through the power of this conviction, the Orthodox are often led to follow an intransigent public policy, which to their opponents sometimes appears as a form of dictatorship.

We must not assume that all Orthodox Jews advocate coercion in matters of religion. Many of them question whether it is the State's province to sponsor and enforce religious legislation. Many observant Jews, themselves entirely Orthodox, are not happy with the present system of official controls in religion. Some of them see no reason why public recognition cannot extend to Liberal rabbis and congregations.[8]

We must not paint a false picture. It is misleading to assert categorically and without qualification or explanation that there is suppression of Liberal Judaism in Israel. On the contrary, Liberal rabbis and congregations have freedom of worship and expression.

Liberal Jews differ somewhat among themselves in assessing the situation. One rabbi writes: "There is as much autonomy and freedom to assemble and to speak and practice in Israel as there is in the United States. . . . No one is laboring under the strain of perpetual disability or constraint, as the popular myth would seem to have it."[9] Another representative of the Liberal position speaks in a rather different vein, in reporting a visit to the Progressive Congregation in Tel Aviv: "That the hall was below street level seemed to me symbolic. The congregation I had joined for the evening was in a way an underground religious sect, unrecognized by the Government, under continuous attack by the rabbinical authorities, unable to pursue its activities under normal, dignified circumstances befitting a religious movement."[10] Liberals have often experienced difficulties in obtaining premises for their meetings, although recently this problem has eased somewhat.

The point to remember is that, rightly or wrongly, Liberal congregations in Israel constitute private religious associations. This entails certain privileges— and certain restrictions.

A major obstacle to the expansion and hence the ultimate recognition of Liberal Jewry is the small number of its declared advocates. Liberal Jews in Israel are like a tiny body of Protestants in a massively Catholic land, or of Catholics in a prevailingly Protestant land. The Liberal predicament today is that on the one hand, religious recognition remains contingent upon the achieving of some kind of political voice, and yet, on the other hand, Israeli religion is greatly in need of liberation from political entanglements. In Liberal religious circles an increasing desire is present to avoid purely ecclesiastical competition in favor of more positive values, including the prophetic criticism and guidance of Israeli life.

Legality and Morality

An important illustration of the dilemmas and conflicts just considered is the national law on the marriage of Jews.

The Jewish religious community retains exclusive jurisdiction over marriage and divorce. (Divorce may be granted when both parties consent.[11]) Marriage registration and services (and burial services) cannot be arranged for a non-Orthodox Jew (Reform, Conservative, or nonreligious) by a non-Orthodox rabbi.[12]

Eliezer Goldman offers one justification for the law of marriage:

> The introduction of civil marriage and divorce in Israel would disrupt the solidarity of Jewry the world over, the nation being divided into two non-intermarrying "castes." . . . Restriction of marriage between religious and non-religious would be unbearable. . . . Many an Israeli of secular view would see nothing wrong in marrying a non-Jew, who would become a Jewish national by accepting Israeli citizenship. But this would set a precedent for the Diaspora, where intermarriage is the gravest danger facing Jewish national existence. Adherence to the Jewish law of marriage and divorce is, thus, dictated by the obligation of Israeli Jews to Jewish survival the world over.[13]

Professor Werblowsky of the Hebrew University, himself a practicing, believing Jew, writes in a diametrically opposite way:

> Since the days of Ezra and the earlier author of Deuteronomy, Jews have been firmly convinced that mixed marriages constitute the greatest threat to Jewish distinctiveness and survival. In fact, Jewish distinctiveness and group survival become invested with the halo of an absolute value, and hence many Jews cheerfully go on believing that the responsibility for Jewish existence and unity requires that the State of Israel offend in the most flagrant fashion against . . . the Universal Declaration of Human Rights of December 10, 1948, according to which people are entitled to marry and to found families irrespective of race, nation, or creed.[14]

Non-Orthodox Jews sometimes contend that the lack of civil marriage in Israel is a device of the religious Establishment to retain a hold upon the life of the nation. Liberals also attest that hundreds of years of experience in the Diaspora disprove the claim that the Jewish community cannot retain its integrity without a unified marriage law.

An additional example of disparity of legal privilege is that Liberal Jews and others pay taxes that serve to support the Orthodox religious Establishment, yet they must independently sustain their own religious institutions.[15] This is not totally unlike the requirement in the United States that Roman Catholics and others pay taxes to support the public schools even though their own schools depend upon them for survival. Furthermore, in Israel the taxes of nonreligious citizens are used to maintain the recognized religious communities, non-Jewish as well as Jewish.

Any resolution of the legal-moral problem of religion in Israel remains extremely difficult. The origin of the difficulty lies in the secular-religious alliance and the accompanying need for compromise that we described in the previous chapter. An abiding consequence of that arrangement is profound uncertainty and inconsistency within official and other circles respecting religious policy. Some statutes reflect the religious interests. One law prohibits the raising of swine except in an enclave around Nazareth populated mainly by Christians. But certain fundamental laws of the land conflict with traditional religious practice. Thus, a provision in the Women's Equal Rights Act (1951) gives married women the right to own and administer their own property, together with the right of inheritance. Women have equal status with men before the law. Again, in 1969 the Israeli cabinet voted to extend state television to seven days a week. Representatives of the National Religious Party became irate, contending that this would mean a desecration of the Sabbath. But the vote stood.[16]

The abiding legal-moral conflict came to a climax in early 1970 in the celebrated Shalit Case and resultant actions by the Government. Binyamin Shalit had sought to register his children as Jews even though his wife is non-Jewish; the children, accordingly, did not meet the traditional religious standard for Jewish identification. The Shalit family professes no religious commitment. By a 5–4 decision in January the Court held that children could be registered as Jewish by nationality rather than by religion. Liberal religious Jews and non-religious Jews welcomed the ruling, while leaders within the religious Establishment and Orthodox Jews everywhere were most upset. Amidst considerable public turmoil the Knesset (Parliament) then passed legislation in March making religious law the criterion in Interior Ministry registrations: "For the purposes of this law, a 'Jew' is one born to a Jewish mother, or converted, who is not of another faith." This new law does not accord with the wishes of vast numbers of Israelis who oppose any strengthening of the grip of the religious law upon the nation's civil law. (In 1958 the Knesset had ratified a Government decision according to which "any person declaring himself a *bona fide* Jew and not a member of another religion is considered a Jew for the purpose of the Law of Return and the Population Registry Law.") However, at the very same time (March, 1970) other legislation was instituted that helped somewhat to conciliate opponents of the new criterion for Interior Ministry registrations. We refer to the change in the 1950 Law of Return (whose terms enable Jews from anywhere in the world to enter Israel). That Law was amended to give full immigration and citizenship privileges to non-Jews related to Jews by marriage or by descent. Hence, the one party could welcome the Government's decision to reject the High Court ruling; the other party could welcome the liberalization of the Law of Return. Yet both sides remain much less than happy, the usual price of compromise.

The Faces of Freedom

One Orthodox rabbi in Israel responded to a question of ours with these words: "There is complete religious freedom in Israel." But a friend in Jerusalem exclaimed, with knowing exaggeration: "Israel is the only country in the world where there is no religious freedom." He was concerned to call attention to the primacy of Orthodox Judaism in the country.

These opposing responses not only reflect fundamental divergence of conviction on the question of religious freedom; they underscore the necessity for clarity in the way the phrase "religious freedom" is employed.

At least three dimensions of religious freedom are germane to our present discussion:

1. The freedom of a particular religious community to foster its own life.

2. The religious acknowledgment that more than a single interpretation of the requirements of religion is justifiable, including the requirements of a single religion.

3. Freedom of religion as extending not just to the right of an individual to practice religion but to his right not to do so—in other words, freedom *from* religion.

As we have seen, in Israel stress falls upon the first of these understandings, the social and communal nature of religious expression. Traditionally, the right of those who desire to practice religion is honored primarily through their relationship to their community. This emphasis contrasts with the predisposition, widespread in the United States, to concentrate upon the third of these understandings, to view religious freedom from the standpoint of conscience.

Even if all parties were to agree that religious freedom is to be identified in communal terms, this would hardly resolve the controversy over the practice of Judaism in Israel. The real question is: What are the bounds of the Jewish religious community?

In July of 1968 representatives of the World Union of Progressive Judaism were prevented by the pressures of Orthodox Jews from conducting worship of men and women together at the Western Wall in Jerusalem. The following are among the conflicting ways of reacting to that event (with religious freedom still being construed as the freedom of a given religious community to foster its own life): (a) The group referred to is not a legitimate entity within the Jewish religious community. It is a collection of traitors to the faith, and is not entitled to freedom. (b) Conjoined worship of men and women is a form of sacrilege. Those who engage in it are foes of religious freedom. (c) The members of the World Union are as legitimate a group as any in Judaism. When they were barred from the Western Wall, the sovereign right of the Jewish community to worship God was trampled upon.

Those Israeli Jews who oppose the policy of privilege for Orthodoxy maintain that there is grave doubt whether official policy in fact represents the will of the majority of Jews in the country.[17] Of even greater importance, say the critics, the principle of group integrity and recognition ought to be applied much more widely and responsibly. The objection to Orthodox privilege is not a wild, individualistic exercise. Those offering the objection are a small group, to be sure, but their existence itself accords with the requirement that religious freedom be comprehended in group terms. (There is a small Israeli Council of Progressive Rabbis.) Liberal spokesmen attest that the restricting of their movement to the category of "private" is an indefensible form of discrimination.

We must emphasize that these criticisms are not provincially "American." They are tendered by Israelis themselves. As a matter of fact, sympathy with the argument is sometimes manifest among Orthodox Jews in Israel.

To exemplify the second of the dimensions of religious freedom previously listed (that varied religious interpretations are justified), let us suppose that a small group of Israeli Jews desires to protest against a particular religious requirement—for example, the rule that Jews in Israel must be married under the aegis of an Orthodox rabbi.[18] Many people in that country (and not only the religiously observant) will assume that the protesters must be opposed to "religion," that they represent an anti-religious, or at least a nonreligious, perspective. Yet in point of truth the critics may be standing up for a positive religious principle. They may look upon the controversy as having to do with rival forms of religion—and, indeed, of just the one religion, Judaism—rather than being an issue of religion versus irreligion. Hence, even though they will probably end up being labeled "irreligious" by Orthodox Jews and others, they are convinced that their own critics are intolerant *of religion*.

Many *sabras* have yet to be brought to see that religious Jewry is a much larger category than Orthodoxy. In this deficiency, a tiny embodiment of nationalism creeps out into the open: non-Orthodox Judaism is treated as a foreign body, and, what is more, as a Western and even American business. (Such an attitude invites derision, since, as Mendel Kohansky points out, Orthodoxy in Israel is in all its shades just as much an imported commodity as is Liberalism.[19])

Consider the third interpretation of religious freedom. Let us imagine a small group of Israeli Jews who express opposition to obligatory *kashruth* in the armed services.[20] The obvious rejoinder to them is that the practice is a justified embodiment of religious freedom. Of course, this is to represent religious freedom only in the initial meaning we have listed. But let us assume that our new protesters speak as avowed foes of Judaism and of all things religious. May their own objection be considered an instance of religious freedom? No, plainly, in the first two interpretations of the term. Yes, in the third way of grasping the concept: freedom *from* religion.

In actuality, this last kind of protest can be supported by something in the Israeli ethos. The State's official position is that the personal observance or nonobservance of the precepts of religion is decided by the individual citizen (another evidence of the inappropriateness of the label "theocracy" for Israel).

However, the thing to note is that in the Israeli outlook there has been until now no real way to associate the nonobservance of religion with a positive religious impulse, much less to think of it as a religious act. By contrast, in the American heritage it was the religious tradition itself that served as a major creator of religious dissent. Accordingly, still today in the United States the criticism of religion can be celebrated as a form of religious witness. While Israeli social morality recognizes the right of individuals to refrain from religion, this has come about largely through secular, rather than religious, influences.

Israel is a Jewish state; it is also a democracy. It may abide as a Jewish democracy through the continuing growth of religious voluntaryism, personal and collective. While religion may flourish in a democracy, democracy is hard put to endure amidst the kind of religious constraint that impedes voluntaryism.

The Israeli Proclamation of Independence lists freedom of religion and freedom of conscience side by side. This suggests one means for nurturing the second and third understandings of religious freedom, without surrendering the initial understanding. The acknowledgment that the requirements of the Jewish religion may be conscientiously interpreted in alternative ways is itself a triumph of conscience, and so is the extension of freedom of religion to freedom from religion. The more catholic the understanding of religious freedom, the more is freedom enabled to nurture faith.

For Reconciliation

Many people feel that Israel's list of worries is already long enough without any outbreak of great and inevitably divisive public conflicts over religion. This attitude merits great sympathy. Yet it has the effect of supporting the Establishment and preserving the *status quo*.

Much of traditional Judaism in today's Israel continues to live in ironic denial of the traditional teaching that faith extends to the whole of life. For the most part, Israeli Judaism has, quite simply, very little to say respecting not only Israel's most fateful moral challenges (such as minority rights), but many of the life-interests of most of her citizens: vocational life, leisure, science, literature, art, politics, etc. To young Israelis, vitally concerned with how a modern, scientific world view can be harmonized with the ancient faith that is their heritage, the religious Establishment offers just about nothing. Israel does not even have a theological seminary to debate intellectually this and other vital issues.

Uncompromising religion and uncompromising secularity have thus far been the prevailing voices in Israel, while those who would reconcile the two sides have been seldom heard.

Religious Zionists have naturally looked to the new State of Israel to resolve problems of faith created for Jews by life in the non-Jewish and often hostile world of the Diaspora. Faith would be reborn and the Torah would "go forth from Zion" (Isa. 2:3). Secular Zionists have also looked to a new Israel to settle problems of faith, but to do so by making traditional Judaism unnecessary in a free and just land for Jews. Between these two parties stand some advocates of Zion who refuse to grant any division between religion and secularity. Do not the twin commandments of love of God and neighbor preclude any such division?

Reconciliation begins in an acknowledgment that the claims and outlook of religionists and secularists are alike going to persevere. Neither side will go away. Differently stated, Israel will neither be transmuted into a theocracy nor converted to sweeping irreligiousness.

Israel's religious challenge lies at a much more serious and decisive level than arguments over whether automatic electric devices in the dairy of a religious *kibbutz* satisfy or compromise the commandment to remember the Sabbath. Such arguments are symptoms of a profounder crisis, a crisis of faith.

The deeper crisis is reflected in an open letter to the Jewish religious community by a member of a left-wing *kibbutz*. She asked: "How do you propose that the faithless should begin to believe?" In seeking to grapple with this poignant question, Professor Fisch contends that many Israelis look upon bearers of the ancestral faith as prisoners of the past. Much more fatefully, Fisch continues, the secular Jew of Israel is himself traumatized by the past, by "the tale of trial and suffering which is Jewish history." This "traumatic fear and hatred gets directed against the religious Jew whose way of life comes to symbolize the intolerable burden of the past." (Can we not add that the religious Jew may direct the same fears against himself and his fellow-religionists?) However, with the Six Day War "Israelis who had never known that they were Jews suddenly awoke to their inheritance." Yet, significantly, they almost monotonously insisted that they were "not religious."[21]

It is impossible to say that the past is dead or can be cast away. It is there. It had been buried alive. The soldiers who shed tears upon reaching Jerusalem's Western Wall were not performing narrowly "religious" acts. They were rediscovering themselves, their entire history as Jews. The same phenomenon occurred amongst Diaspora Jews. "To be a Jew is not so much to believe in certain things, but to be in a certain existential situation: The Jew is that person who is caught in the grip of Jewish history, with its unique traumas, its dangers, and its glories." What, then, distinguishes the religious Jew? He is the one "who acknowledges and accepts that situation as a charge."[22]

The Israeli may be fearful of the past and all its reminders, yet something in that past has a strong appeal for him due to his own life-experiences: the ideal of obligation. Although Rabbi Herbert Wiener speaks as a Liberal, he grants this particular appeal within Orthodoxy. Here "is a faith which offers a 'yoke' rather than the nod of permission. It is a way which loads the individual and community with burdens, tasks, obligations. All of this strikes the Israeli as 'real' for the Israeli has learned that only the readiness to fulfill such demands has enabled him to survive, and not only to survive but to have touched the deepest moments of fulfillment in his national and personal destiny." One Orthodox rabbi in Israel testified that the trouble with Orthodoxy is not that it asks too much of people but that it asks too little. Israelis are not put off by such demands as *kashruth;* what they need and even want is such a commandment as "love thy neighbor as thyself."[23]

The challenge is how to marry the past that lives to the future that is ever being born, how to reconcile the precepts of the Torah with the demands of life in the modern State of Israel. How can we be honestly religious men and honestly secular men at one and the same time? (This fateful question confronts all of us: Jews, Christians, Muslims. It is said that ours is an epoch in which God has hidden himself.)

We cannot foretell the future shape of religion in Israel. There is no basis for predicting either a massive, explicit return to the Tradition or a radical departure from it. There are, however, persistent if unpretentious signs of the reconciliation of faith with secular concerns. There is a groping, a questioning, a hunger.

Secularist Israelis have grown less contemptuous of things religious. Secular *kibbutzim* are experimenting with ritual and observing holy days. Some of them have even constructed synagogues. Inchoately, the Israeli is aware that he cannot very well succeed in identifying himself or his nation apart from the Jewish faith-tradition.

If a new though modest secular turn to spirituality is apparent, a growing concern is evident in religious quarters (Orthodox as well as Liberal) for greater social responsibility and a more humane society. In 1966 a "Movement for Torah Judaism" was initiated among Orthodox Jews. The movement remains fairly small. Its aims include not only the political disestablishment of Orthodoxy, but religious freedom and diversity in Israel, and a responsible application of the Halachah to the pressing economic, social, and political issues of today's world.[24]

The signs of reconciliation must not tempt anyone to expect that unrestricted freedom and recognition of non-Orthodox Judaism is possible in the foreseeable future. The jurisdiction of the rabbinical Establishment over questions of personal status amasses tremendous power. This power will not be surrendered without a great struggle, a struggle for which many Israelis are not prepared. To recognize Liberal rabbis would mean the ultimate collapse of the whole Establishment, and this is why the Establishment fights Liberal Judaism with every possible weapon.[25]

Nevertheless, there is hope. It is within the ancestral land, its own land, that Judaism is struggling, and this is where the hope lies. Elsewhere, the prosperity of faith could always be attributed to self-defensiveness, and its failure charged to adversity. Only in a Jewish land may Judaism be judged on its own terms. Only in Israel may the Jewish faith travel its way either to a natural end or to a natural glory.

14. Politics in Action

For many people, Israel has a near-mythical quality, a surreality which makes of it more mood than Leviathan, more state of mind than State. Perhaps, in some strange way, that perception is not far off the mark. But it would be well to bear in mind that the sovereign State of Israel, whether more or less than myth and mood, is at the very least something else as well. Its soldiers march to real drums, its cannon inflict fatal wounds, it has houses and schools and radio stations and cemeteries and traffic lights and dirt and canned foods and bulldozers and currency and barbers. It is a mystery, as all countries are mysteries, perhaps more mysterious than most, but it is also a country with laws and jails and policemen and all the other accoutrements, the palpable paraphernalia, of nationhood. To understand its politics, one must know the machinery as well as the mood; indeed, the political story is mostly one of inter-action between mood and machinery.[1]

The Working System

The resurrected State of Israel quickly fashioned a stable, democratic political system, in contrast to so much of the long history of Palestine and also to many other new countries today.

Among the assets the early leadership enjoyed was a not inconsiderable political experience in the years before the actual reestablishing of the State. For a time, political development was able to outstrip social and economic development. From among the circumstances that have helped make Israel's political consensus stronger than her social consensus, Professor Fein stresses the relative freedom of the political sphere from the strains pervading the society at large. This freedom has been made possible by (a) the universal awareness that, in the presence of external threats, the country simply could not afford governmental instability, and (b) the heavy investment of the Government in reckoning with social conflict within Israel.[2]

An interesting combination of competing historical influences has contributed to the structuring of the country's national political system. Thus, the very

147

name of, and number of members in, the Knesset, the Parliament of Israel, are traceable to ancient history. In Chapter 2 we alluded to the origin of the Knesset Hag'dolah (Great Synod) in the period of the Second Temple. This central legislative and religious body consisted of 120 members, a number duplicated in today's Knesset.

In the new State the governmental procedures of Europe and of Great Britain have alike been of influence, with Israel's own traditions as an added factor, including the old Zionist congresses with their multiplicity of interest groups. Many European peoples are accustomed to a multi-party system (or lack of system) in government. Most of the Jews who have shaped Israeli politics came from Eastern Europe. Indeed, it was only after the Soviet Union turned against the young State that the leaders of Israel were impelled toward a Western political orientation.[3]

When the American citizen goes to the polls he gives primary attention to the identity of individual candidates. Also, geographical or regional considerations are many times decisive. Let us picture, by contrast, a national election in Israel. The time of year is the same: Autumn. But in Israel all citizens over the age of eighteen are entitled to vote. Furthermore, and as the most significant difference, the party slate alone counts. People vote not for individuals but only for the party of their choice. In addition, the entire nation is treated as a single constituency. A proportional allocation of seats in the Knesset is then made.

Suppose that Party Aleph receives 40 percent of the total votes cast. That party will choose from its own list 48 names (40 percent of 120) using whatever order of priority it has already fixed. Each of these persons becomes an "M.K." (Member of the Knesset) or is reelected. Under the assumption that this particular party has received a plurality of the votes, the party must then obtain from another party or other parties a promise of 13 votes at the very least if it is to succeed in forming a government (since a minimum of 61 votes is needed to secure a bare majority in the Knesset). Of course, an effectual government requires more votes than the minimum.

Once sufficient support is garnered, the President of the State calls upon the leader of the dominant party in the Knesset to form a government. This entails the choice of a cabinet of ministers for conducting the country's affairs. In sum, experience down to the present has called for the setting up of a coalition government.[4]

Seats of Power

Israel is hardly unique in possessing several centers of political power. The uniqueness lies in the special complexities of Israeli politics, and more especially the crucial role of her political parties.

Part of the complexity is linked with uncertain attitudes among Israelis toward governmental authority. On the one hand, while the citizenry may rail at the bureaucracy, and resent the press of the Government upon their daily lives, the fear of government as such is a lot weaker in Israel than has been the case in the United States. The American tradition has sought to observe careful lines between society and government. But among Israelis the persuasion is strong that the society men desire and need is to be nurtured and sustained with the aid of governmental effort, and indeed, that all social problems are automatically and properly governmental concerns. The hope is also pervasive that a government *of* Jews will be a government *for* Jews. Furthermore, in some contrast to the American historical consensus, few Israelis look upon the diverting of political power into several different centers as in itself desirable or necessary.

On the other hand, however—and now the paradox becomes clear—the equally strong persuasion is present in Israel that government is not the most reliable source of authority. The historic oppression of Jews by hostile political forces in Europe has doubtless been of influence here.

At least two added complications have to be remembered. First, many of those Israelis who question the reliability of governmental authority do not speak from a neutral standpoint. They are themselves representative of alternative centers of influence (as examples, the Jewish Agency, the labor movement, or one or another political party not in control). Second, a number of the specific powers that are at issue have never been definitely assigned to the Government, and hence are not the Government's to dispense.[5] This latter state of affairs helps to intensify the whole argument over political authority. It is interesting that in Israel, unlike the United States, a citizen may sue the Government without its permission.

Let us inspect more closely the seats of political power.

The outsider may incline to attribute more power to the Knesset than the facts warrant. He may allege, for example, that since Israel lacks a written constitution, the Knesset can pass any law it wishes. This is so only in a completely hypothetical sense. The fact is that the Knesset does not possess primary control over legislation. To be sure, that body fills many important functions and possesses great institutional significance. It is a source of information and judgment for the people; it can act to modify and improve legislation; it subjects cabinet ministers to questioning and conducts legislative hearings; it legitimates governmental decisions; and its members act to meet the queries and complaints of individual citizens.[6]

The truth remains that the Parliament is not in and of itself the real center of political power in Israel. We understand this once we become aware of where dominant power actually lies. That power has two foci: the Government and the political parties, with the latter comprising the major focus.

The parties involved make the Government possible, since the members of the Government are the leaders of the politically successful parties. Further, the Knesset members are primarily judged, not as individuals, but in terms of their relation to their parties. Stated baldly, "the Knesset is less significant an institution—in power and control—than the Government," while within the Government, it is the ministers of the prevailing party, and particularly the Prime Minister, who have the major voice.[7]

Paradoxically enough, the secret of the Prime Minister's power lies in the fact that he is able, by resigning, to bring down the whole Government. He is, after all, the leader of his party. Should he resign, his party is forced into a choice. It can either accede to his demands (in which case the Government is re-formed under his direction) or have to face a national election as a divided party.[8]

Two additional factors help us to apprehend the dominant place of the political parties: The country's heritage of ideology has contributed greatly to the power and significance of Israeli parties. The parties are much more than that; they constitute entire social movements.

Ideological elements are still to be found within American political parties. But in the United States particular ideological claims and policies are in large measure subordinated to a kind of national consensus and also to the prudential business of winning elections. While a certain pragmatic outlook is inevitable in the politics of Israel, and is in fact growing more and more conspicuous, special ideological influences continue to play an important role within that country. Among the historical and psychological factors that have contributed to this political atmosphere are: the residue from the volatile character of the old politics in Eastern Europe; a strong propensity within those parties currently deprived of power and responsibility to exhibit ideal visions of themselves; emotional and political substitutes for erstwhile religious commitments; and a felt need within the many political factions to retain their moral identity. Further, the traditional demand that political argument be couched in ideological terms has itself tended to color the debate: "The White Knight and the Black Knight tilt, in full regalia, in defense of Virtue, where the real issue is an increment in the cost of living allowance provided government clerks; Gog and Magog meet in cataclysmic battle over a decision by the Minister of Agriculture to change the government subsidies for various breeds of tomato." The point is that the presence of ideology, or at least of a ritual of ideology, exerts a certain influence upon the substance of the political encounter and helps to condition the nature of the compromises finally reached.[9]

We mentioned that the political parties of Israel are not only that but are also social movements. What this means is, on the one hand, that ideology is an inevitable component of their behavior and, on the other hand, that their efforts extend far beyond the strictly political domain. The parties are dedicated to winning converts to their point of view. Furthermore, the parties play a great role in the daily lives of their members. "The ideal movement member lives in party housing (or in an agricultural settlement affiliated with the party), reads the party newspaper, handles his financial transactions through the party's financial institutions, attends seminars at party schools, reads books published by the party, belongs to his local party club and participates in its weekly or biweekly meetings, sends his children to the party's youth movement, and, perhaps most important of all, believes in the party's ideology as a comprehensive statement of political truth." As a matter of fact, in Israel most newspapers, youth and athletic organizations, and collective and cooperative agricultural settlements are affiliated with the parties.[10]

That the political groupings in Israel are social and ideological movements as well as parties coveting election helps us to understand an added paradox: the lack of seriousness with which politics is taken in Israel; and the great seriousness with which it is taken. For large numbers of citizens, political matters are merely at the periphery of their interests—this, despite the truth that the Government is so potent a force within the personal lives of Israelis. Even among party members there is often no vital connection between personal beliefs and party ideology. And yet, one also encounters intense political consciousness in

Israel. The smallness of the country is probably of relevance here; however, countries equally small often manifest much less concern with politics. More than 80 percent of the people of Israel honor their right to vote in national elections, among the highest percentages in the free world. Many immigrants to the country have never had this right before and, accordingly, are eager to implement it.

One key to the puzzle at first seems to be anything but that. Studies have shown that those people who fall among the most politically-minded and democracy-supporting segments of the Israeli population nevertheless look upon themselves as exerting very little influence upon the nation's political decisions. When the entire population is taken into account, this personal feeling of having no real influence upon politics is of course even stronger. Furthermore, in sharp contrast to the American ethos, the notion that every citizen has a duty to make known his political views is almost totally lacking in Israel.

The prevailing feeling among Israelis of having no real political say must signify something quite different from what it means in a country where politics plays no vital role. An answer to the puzzle, as suggested by Professor Fein, is that the intense political participation of Israelis does not represent the hope that they will exert substantial influence upon the Government. May not the political world furnish important rewards other than those of immediate political power? Fein offers the fitting analogy of New York's famous Tammany Hall: "immigrants traded votes for services, not for a voice in shaping public policy."[11]

We may sum up the matter this way: The social and ideological world tells the Israeli citizen that he ought to be a politically involved person and that his actions can really have positive consequences for the political domain. That so many people vote in the country shows that these political ideals are taken seriously. At the same time, other interests powerfully compete for the citizen's major attention. Fortunately for his conscience, the society's demand that he be politically involved can be met, or at least tempered, through the effective activities of his party, partly as a political force but also as an important social institution. The citizen may be quite aware that he pulls little political weight, yet he remains assured that he is doing his part. And he is meeting his obligations while being rewarded in a variety of ways. The party is both a social home and a socio-political force for good.

The above interpretation also helps to explain why many of the Israeli political parties that can offer no real chance of positive political triumph in the foreseeable future nevertheless persist in attracting sizable numbers of votes.

When to the influential ideological role of the parties and to their functions as social movements is added the decisive place of the Israeli electoral arrangement, we begin to understand the uniqueness of Israeli politics. That uniqueness lies in the decisive centering of political and social power around the party system.[12]

Party Identities, Party Trends

The Israeli scene has been witnessing a strong trend toward the consolidation of political parties. As time goes by, the distinctive characteristics and ideologies of each party will probably be much less marked.

A most significant development was the conditional merger early in 1968 of three major groups representative of labor (Mapai, Ahduth Avodah, and Rafi) into the Israel Labor Party. This grouping was thereby enabled to command a near-majority in the Knesset and to constitute the most powerful political force attained to that time in Israel.[13] The Six Day War of 1967 and the renewed Arab threat to Israel's existence helped facilitate this achievement. The late Prime Minister Eshkol's call for a broadly-based government of national unity was sustained in succeeding months by, among other things, the absence of any international peace settlement. The National Unity Coalition was looked upon as offering a united front in the presence of Israel's foes.

The power achieved by the party merger was strengthened all the more in late 1968 through an alignment agreed to by the Israel Labor Party and the United Workers' Party (Mapam).[14] The consequence was a clear majority in the Knesset, a majority that did not, however, survive the 1969 elections. (We should be the last to suggest that these decisions constitute ideal attainments forgetful of all group interests. In Israel, as elsewhere, politics is politics.[15])

The trend to party consolidations has been hailed as marking "the political emergence of Israel as a nation" in its own land, boasting a "normal party" broadly representative of worker interests in contradistinction to diverse pre-state "movements."[16] Needless to say, those parties to the right and to the left of the broad labor coalition have been less than enthusiastic over recent developments.[17]

Ervin Birnbaum speaks of a promise and a threat in the original merger of the three labor parties. The promise is the establishing of a stable, effective, and fully accountable single-party government for the first time in Israel's history, in contrast to governments dependent upon the tenuous agreements of factions. Any party to a coalition is easily tempted by irresponsibility. It can plead that an alleged failure to make good an election promise was "their" fault and not "ours." The threat referred to by Birnbaum is that a continued lack of success amongst the unhappy opposition may cause it to shrivel away. No democracy can endure where the government in power is not confronted by a free and operative opposition.[18] Without opposition, essential stability and accountability are absent. Lea Ben Dor writes that if there is any threat to democracy in today's Israel it is not because Labor is powerful but because there is no strong opposition program. Only when Labor will have become a truly majority party, with total political responsibility, can any other party have a chance of dislodging it if it loses touch with the citizenry.[19]

It is too early to say whether the broad political alliance of labor interests in Israel will endure. In their brief history, Israeli political factions have fallen into almost as many divorces as marriages. More fundamentally, it is impossible to know as yet whether the country will retain a multiple-party arrangement (which keeps demanding some form of coalition or alignment) or will move finally to the practice of a two-party system with a one-party government. We must not forget that a faction completely inside a party can often attain a strength beyond its numbers just as effectively as can an outside party, at least where such a faction is enabled to collaborate with an independent bloc. (Witness the Southern bloc of the Democratic Party in the United States and that bloc's traditional collaboration with conservative elements in the Republican Party.) Further, there is always a possibility that people who vote for erstwhile smaller parties ill not go along with a large, united party. As Birnbaum says, political wholes not always prove as large as the sum of their parts.[20]

Of peculiar import within the Israeli political scene is the presence of religious parties representative of varying degrees of theocratic wish. There are three of these groups: the National Religious Party, Agudat Yisrael, and Poalei Agudat Yisrael.[21] The religious parties have exerted an influence beyond their numbers (in the history of the modern Knesset they have never occupied more than eighteen seats) and there has been a degree of dependence upon these parties in the national coalitions. The National Religious Party has been a member of every governmental coalition. On the other hand, the consolidation of the labor forces has served to moderate the independent political influence of the religious parties. Not only are there conflicts inside the religious bloc; these parties simply do not have enough strength to mount a successful opposition. The only way the religious bloc could ever effectively oppose the Israel Labor Party would be through securing almost total support from every other non-labor group in the Knesset, an eventuality that is hardly possible. (In the eventh Knesset elected in October, 1969 the strength of the Labor-Mapam alignment fell to 56 seats from the 63 seats it could boast in the Sixth Knesset. Nevertheless, the Government that subsequently took office was, through the coalition arrangement, able to control 98 of the 120 votes in the Knesset.)

We do not contend that the consolidation of the labor parties will hasten the end of the religious Establishment in Israel. It is relevant to mention, however, that many of Israel's religiously observant people do not vote for the religious parties. While these parties average some 15 percent of the Knesset seats, the numbers of religiously observant citizens are proportionately higher than that, as we have noted. Of further relevance is the large immigrant population in Israel. Ernest Stock points out that immigrants show a strong tendency to identify themselves with the party in power and hence not to vote for opposition parties.[22] Of course, once a newcomer ceases to think of himself as an immigrant, or once an immigrant generation is succeeded by the native born, voting patterns change.

The System: Pro and Con

One advantage of the present electoral arrangement is that every party is represented in exact ratio to its strength and hence to the presumed state of opinion in the country. No minority party can possibly capture a majority of parliamentary seats.

However, the electoral system contains a number of drawbacks. Some have doubted whether a really responsible and effective "loyal opposition" can be developed in the Knesset until the system is changed. The representative character of the Knesset is severely limited. The parties have tremendous power. And yet, ordinary party members have very little say in the drawing up of lists of candidates. The members of Parliament are not directly accountable to popular constituencies. The parties devote much more attention to electing their national lists than to local politics. It is argued that direct elections would make the individual candidate less a creature of his party and give him freedom from endorsing national policies that lack relevance to local problems.[23]

It is further contended that no completely democratic system can be achieved in Israel as long as personalized regional elections are lacking. Again, the criticism is made that Israel's powerful tradition of ideology induces the governmental authorities to pay comparatively little heed to public opinion. From this standpoint, what "the man on the street" happens to think or feel may be far removed from "correct doctrine," and may therefore be safely discounted. However, considerable evidence is at hand that ideology is waning in Israel. One consequence is that the political leadership is tending to become more conscious of, and amenable to, public opinion, including the demand for electoral reform.[24]

As evidence of national concern with ways in which voters may participate more directly and democratically in the political process, a modification of the proportional representation system was urged in June, 1969 by a panel appointed as part of the merger agreement between Rafi and Mapai a year earlier. On the new plan, 30 constituencies of roughly the same population would be formed throughout the country, each of which would elect 3 members to Parliament. The remaining 30 representatives would be elected separately under the traditional system. On the basis of experience in past elections, the party in power would have a majority in the Knesset.[25]

The Israeli political structure does provide for a measure of checks and balances, with a separation of powers between the executive and legislative branches of government. Somewhat reminiscent of the Scandinavian institution of the ombudsman[26] is the office of the State Comptroller, who is accountable to the Knesset. The Comptroller is responsible for exercising a check upon both the Administration and the local authorities in such areas as budgetary accounting, the deportment of public servants, and possible waste arising from inefficiency or incompetence. Any citizen has the right to file a complaint against public servants through the State Comptroller.

Citizens have a similar right of complaint to the Supreme Court of Israel. The courts and the judiciary are totally independent at all levels. Judges answer to no authority save that of the law. The Supreme Court is completely above party politics. And it has not hesitated to criticize the acts of public officials.[27]

However, on the other side of the ledger, and in contrast to the system in the United States, there is no judicial or other immediate appeal from the decisions or laws of the Knesset. The only ultimate check upon such acts lies in a new national election.[28]

Obviously, the political system of any country is a crucial determinant of success or failure in coping with immediate and long-range problems of national life and in implementing national goals. Israel is now facing a necessary transition from a monopoly of political leadership by the "founding fathers" to direction and control by a newer generation. No internal challenge is more serious for Israel today than that of finding and agreeing upon legitimate sources of leadership and power (including coping with the growing presence of economic and political "experts" and of a scientific-managerial elite). But so far, the period of transition has not produced any fateful tumult.

Israel is one of the few countries in the Middle East to provide free elections, and the first state where Arab women were enfranchised. It is the only nation

n the region where communist parties are permitted to exist; such parties are
utlawed in Egypt, Iraq, Jordan, Lebanon, and Syria. This situation compounds
he absurdity of the charge by Communists and devotees of the "New Left"
hat Israel is an "imperialist tool" encroaching upon the "progressive" Arab
peoples.

On balance, if the overall system in Israel is not perfect, it does work and it
works well. In Professor Fein's words, "Israel's position as a new nation, as a
nation of immigrants, and as an embattled nation, deprives its leaders of much
of the agenda-making authority which is, in many ways, the real key to power.
. . . The most impressive fact of Israeli political life is that Government has
managed to survive at all amidst awesome burdens. That it has not only survived, but managed to do reasonably well in the business of social management,
is an achievement of heroic proportion."[29]

15. Ways and Means

AS WE MOVE to the domain of economics, it is with the awareness that no major area of Israeli life (social, religious, political, or economic) can be separated from the others. While this is the case in every modern society, the ties are especially strong in Israel. Not only does the Israeli Government exercise very great influence within the economy; the Government is also engaged in such social matters as the integration and housing of immigrants, the relations of different ethnic groups, and the development of new settlements. The economic and social sectors of Israeli life are substantially influenced by the political sector.

Economic Challenges

We consider some of the major difficulties and opportunities presented by the Israeli economy.

One concentration of assets of which the new State became custodian was the property and incomes made available through the departure of many Palestinians in 1948.[1] It must be pointed out, however, that much of that property is still subject to compensatory claims contingent upon an Arab-Israeli peace settlement. One interesting and relevant case is that the City of Jerusalem is today granting assistance to Arab families whose property claims against Israel go back more than twenty years.[2] Furthermore, the resources mentioned were offset by the thousands of Jewish refugees (largely from Arab countries) who have come to Israel penniless and in dire need of all kinds of social services. As emphasized in earlier pages, the absorption of newcomers created massive social, economic, and psychological problems.

Israel's efforts to establish a firm economy have encountered tremendous obstacles. Much of the land was at the beginning unfit for farming due to centuries of noncultivation, misuse, and erosion. The early pioneers faced the hard tasks of draining swamps, creating new soil, nurturing the land, and finding water resources. Limited rainfall, particularly in the South, is a continuing en-

156

cumbrance in Israel. The country as a whole is woefully deficient in natural resources. There is neither coal nor iron, and only very limited oil.[3] Two out of three people in Israel have had to learn a new trade at some point in their lives.

The establishing of markets in their natural locale—neighboring countries— remains for the most part an impossibility for Israel. With enemies on three sides, she is forced to deal with more distant buyers and sellers.

The most serious economic handicap faced by Israel has been the continuing excess of imports over exports. True, great improvement has been made. The unfavorable balance of trade has been notably lessened over the years, although it is still very large. In 1949, exports comprised only 11 percent of imports (not including services); by 1966, the figure had risen to 59 percent. In 1967 it jumped to 70 percent but in 1968 it fell back to 57 percent, despite the fact that in the latter year exports increased by 28 percent over goods sold abroad in 1967. Exports rose by 14 percent in 1969 while a rise of 12 percent was expected for 1970.

Because of Israel's huge expenditures for arms, her trade deficit has soared and her foreign currency reserves have been shrinking rapidly. The trade deficit grew from $445-million in 1966 to $930-million in 1969. Israel's unfavorable balance of trade has also been closely tied to her huge growth and development campaign.[4] At the end of 1969, due largely to increased consumer expenditures, the nation's per-capita debt was $1,400, the highest in the world.

The most decisive fact about the economy of Israel over the years has been the availability of outside capital in amounts that more than offset her huge import surplus.[5] But the country's economic growth has meant strong pressure for increased imports and a corresponding reduction in the expansion of exports.[6] Growth necessitates capital, and to the extent that capital must come from outside, Israel's economic independence is thereby postponed.

Such serious problems as the foregoing together with the presence of foes bent upon Israel's extermination have hardly expedited the achievement of an ideal socio-economic order. Defense expenditures have about doubled since the Six Day War of 1967. For the fiscal year beginning in April, 1970 direct expenditures for defense consumed almost 38 percent of the total national budget. (In the same fiscal year enormous sums had to be set aside for the more than 60,000 immigrants that were expected. It is estimated that at least this same number of newcomers will enter Israel per year, on the average, through 1975.) At present, Israel is expending more than 20 percent of her gross national product on defense. Military costs take 80 percent of income from taxes. These rising costs continue to hamper the nation's efforts to fight poverty, expand education, and achieve economic independence. "Only sustained economic growth and stability achieved by a careful balancing of priorities and continued outside aid at a high level [will] make it possible for Israel to carry the heavy weight of defense costs in the uncertain years ahead without severely disrupting economic progress."[7]

The country's urgent needs today include increased exploitation of raw materials, improved industrial know-how, enlarged marketing facilities and foreign marketing outlets, further dispersal of industry (which will help to spread the population), greater managerial and marketing competence, more intense utilization of assets, and enhancement of productivity, including larger units of production.

An Economic Mixture

The nation's overall policy for grappling with these and other needs has been and continues to be the fashioning of a mixed economy. Israel's rough balance between collectivism and private initiative is sometimes placed among the achievements of the recent governmental coalition. There are, in fact, deeper and longer-lived reasons for the economic mixture. It has been made possible and even necessitated by certain historical and human circumstances.

The pioneering Zionism that came out of Russian Jewry proclaimed ideal, classless collectivism. But the ideal society has never come off in Israel (or anywhere else). As a practical substitute for revolutionary hopes and designs there has developed in Israel, as in many other countries, a tension between various forces of self-interest. An amalgam of competing socio-economic devices and programs has resulted. Which emphasis ought to receive priority, socialist development or economic development? Israeli leadership ranges itself on different sides of this issue. Nowadays the balance is tilting toward economic development.[8]

It is contended that even if Israel had been left alone to manage her own destiny, the pioneering vision would not have endured. What we have instead is a welfare state that falls somewhere between collectivist aspirations and traditional capitalism. More than competing ideologies have had the say. There are also the relentless socio-economic demands of today's world: "The idyllic image of a nation of educated pioneers, plow in one hand, book in the other, could hardly sustain a modern, differentiated economy. The doctrinaire aversion to the 'middleman' neglected the hard requirements of complex societies." This is not to suggest that the Israeli compromise—a social-service state involving a "thorough consensus on the propriety of welfare and of investment in human resources"[9]—must last forever in its present form. We simply point out that Israel has long since passed "the revolution" by.

Lea Ben Dor goes so far as to contend that "the concepts of Socialism of 50 years ago are unrecognizable today, and the ideals that were cherished then have been so far outdistanced by reality as to seem a touching relic of utopian aspirations."[10] Yet it would be quite unfair to conclude that collectivist economic institutions and socialist expectations in Israel are no more than mere vestiges of abandoned dreams. On the contrary, the presence of these institutions and policies demonstrates the abiding impact upon the country of socialist ideas and goals.

At the same time, we are confronted by a dynamic social and economic order where opposition to socialism can be as freely expressed as can its support. Today, majority public opinion in Israel simply does not advocate the collectivization of the means of production. Most of the citizenry seem to be attached to private enterprise and to competition. Vast numbers of recent immigrants (in contrast to the original pioneers with their socialist egalitarianism) possess neither knowledge of nor interest in collectivist ideals.

A ready illustration of the practical tension between collectivism and individualism is wage policy in Israel. The nation still maintains a highly egalitarian wage structure. This is in harmony with two main factors: the continuing influence of the socialist pioneering outlook, and certain contemporary economic circumstances, such as the large number of investments handled by public institutions and the youth of the economy. Since the resurrection of the State in

1948, however, increasing gaps have appeared between the wages of different income groups. Poorer urban wage and salary earners are receiving a noticeably smaller percentage of the total income available to such workers, while the wealthier group has gained a larger percentage. And the average real income of the poorer group has been getting smaller as compared with that of the wealthier group. However, there are relatively few wealthy people in Israel, and relatively few poor people; hence we must be careful not to exaggerate these differences.

We have here "a direct confrontation between the older egalitarian and the new economics." Pressure continues in behalf of greater differentiation between the wages of skilled and unskilled workers, and between professionals and clerks.[11] Georges Friedmann asserts: "The economic importance of specialized training and knowledge and technical expertise is universally admitted, and failure to recognize it is going against the facts. The principle of equal pay for equal work is a Utopia that fails to take psychological and social realities into account."[12] The fundamental socialist tenet of wage equality has fallen upon harder and harder times, though it has by no means been completely betrayed.

The overall outcome of Israeli historical experience is that public, cooperative, and private enterprise are all permitted to vie reputably with one another in the land. However, until now the public sector has remained the dominant one. The economy is still heavily regulated by the Government. In fact, the major employers are public agencies.[13] There is government ownership of radio, television, the telephone system, and electric power.

One distinctive policy of the Government is to initiate businesses that are vital to the economy but that in the nature of the case must run initially at a deficit. If they make good, they may be sold to private investors; the proceeds are then applied by the Government to the initiating of similar difficult ventures. Many small businesses are privately owned, and each year several hundred private enterprises are inaugurated. For all the public control of the economy, Israeli socialism is flexible and open enough to permit the operation of private enterprise.[14]

A number of the large industrial concerns are financed through both private and cooperative investments. There are relatively few large corporations in Israel. Hence, there is no possibility (in contrast to the experience of certain other countries) that one or another industrial giant will determine for a time the fate of the nation.

Cooperative enterprise remains prominent. Important segments of industry, trading, and services are run by cooperatives, as is almost all road transportation and of course most of the country's agriculture.

The Israeli practice of national land ownership, together with the placing of development funds under state control, is naturally subject to severe criticism by apostles of free enterprise. Whatever the drawbacks or potential evils in the system, it does open the way for comprehensive, long-range planning. It also serves to prevent speculation and, ideally, the misuse of land, including the irresponsible scarring of the countryside by commercial enterprise. Curiously enough, in Israel only agriculture has thus far undergone careful planning. One of the ironies of Israeli life is that governmental control is so appreciable and long-range economic planning is as yet so inappreciable.[15]

The State of Labor

Labor has very great influence and power in Israel. Generally speaking, Israeli workers are harder to discharge and more protected in their places of employment than their American opposite numbers.[16]

Nine out of ten Israelis who work for wages or a salary are represented by the powerful General Federation of Labor, the Histadrut (Hebrew for "organization"). Including the families of members, no less than three quarters of the Jewish population are involved in the Histadrut, plus some 50,000 Arabs and Druses.[17] The Federation owns or controls fully half the industry of Israel and the preponderance of her transport. The greater number of the almost 2,000 cooperatives in Israel are affiliated with the General Federation of Labor, as are the overwhelming majority of the *kibbutzim* and the *moshavim*.

The Histadrut is much more than another labor union. As a matter of fact, on occasion it has been known to oppose wage increases for its members on the ground that the welfare of the country would not thereby be served. Politically and administratively speaking, the Federation has been compared to the middle layer of a three-layer cake. In the United States the political realm is divided into local, state, and national layers; in Israel, the Histadrut takes the place, functionally speaking, of the states.[18] However, many of its operations would elsewhere be conducted by a national government, and it carries on many functions not filled by American state governments.

The Histadrut engages in no fewer than four types of activity: (1) A trade-union function. (2) An economic function, involving the control, ownership, and management of a great variety of productive enterprises whose value amounts to millions of dollars. (3) A monopoly or near-monopoly function in the fields of social security and medical care. (4) A cultural function including adult education.[19]

It is not strange that, whether with affection or apprehension or both, the Histadrut headquarters in Tel Aviv are popularly known as "the White Kremlin." Accused as it has often been of undue centralization and bureaucracy, and with being an agent (witting or unwitting) of the Government, the organization has had a hard task. It has had to deal with small tradesmen and artisans who, together with Arabs, are unused to the whole idea of unionization; with immigrants many of whom are far from integrated into the nation and look down upon manual labor; and with individualists who identify arbitration with tyranny and desire total liberty of action—many times to the detriment of their own long-run interests. Defenders of the Histadrut are careful to emphasize that adverse opinions of it expressed in employer circles help to prove the validity and efficacy of its representation of labor.[20]

The dominant place of the Histadrut can be understood historically and in terms of the organization's original goals. The decision at a Haifa convention back in 1920 to form a labor federation answered a serious need to organize workers in the Jewish national home. The Histadrut has numbered among its responsibilities the accelerating of the country's economic growth, the providing of employment for Jewish immigrants and Arabs, and, probably most important to its leaders, the reinforcing and extending of the economy's collective sector. In that sector the workers' organization owns the means of production and runs the management.[21]

That the Histadrut should at once prevail as *the* representative of the workers and operate as the nation's largest single employer of the very same workers constitutes a most peculiar aspect of the Israeli socio-economic scene. Needless to say, this arrangement has also made for controversy. Histadrut protection ideally extends to workers in the public and private sectors of the economy as well as within its own domain. But can we expect that an employer will automatically ensure the best interests of the workers? Georges Friedmann, a French authority on the sociology of labor, is extremely skeptical of any affirmative reply. He insists that one can hardly take seriously the claim that in Histadrut factories there is no real opposition of interests between labor and management. Such a claim is somewhat reminiscent of earlier propaganda from the Soviet Union which asserted that, since workers were "the masters now," no conflicts or human problems could possibly arise for Russian labor.

The validity of Friedmann's skepticism is borne out by the occurrence of strikes in Histadrut factories.[22] It is perfectly true that some disputes are settled in the workers' favor. But when, as often happens, trade union headquarters refuse to back a strike, the workers' morale is affected adversely and their cause receives a substantial blow.

Friedmann sees the center of the issue in these terms:

> At what point can labor claims be considered "undue" from the point of view of the Histadrut, a socialist entity in a mixed economy in which it has to succeed if it wishes to establish itself or even simply survive? The borderline is hard to define, and that is the root of the problem. It is here that conflicts arise, and here that the sharpest criticisms in Israel itself of this great trade-union federation's role as employer of a substantial proportion of the working population have their source.[23]

Toward Economic Welfare and Independence

Despite imperfections in the system, and in the presence of great adversity, Israeli accomplishments in the economic sphere have been prodigious—and all within less than a generation.

Since 1955, production has increased more than threefold. The value of agricultural output has multiplied sixfold since the reestablishment of the State.[24] Over the period since 1950 the gross national product has risen an average of over 9 percent per year, an international record.[25] This achievement, together with a continued increase in the national income,[26] has meant an impressive advance in the standard of living, in spite of burgeoning defense needs and the great increase in the population. During the period from 1950 through 1967, the standard-of-living average almost doubled. Israeli workers have recently attained a per capita income of something over $1,100 per year, approximately the level of workers in the Netherlands and Italy.[27]

Israel maintains compulsory, comprehensive programs of old-age and maternity insurance and workman's compensation. She provides special benefits for those with large families. More than 80 percent of the people are protected by health insurance while 60 percent of the work force is covered by pension programs. It is most noteworthy that welfare goals are never debated; "the society is unquestioningly committed to a full-scale welfare system, closest to the Scandinavian model. Given the costs involved, and the sense that welfare is only an intimation

of social justice, the fact of the commitment is significant. It is based, fundamentally, on a non-economic understanding of social responsibility, which, in-
cidentally, makes demonstrably good sense as investment policy."[28]

The area of cultivation has more than doubled since 1950, and the land under
irrigation has multiplied more than fivefold.[29] Fifty million trees have been
planted since 1948.

Investors who build plants in development areas, and agree to export a minimum of 50 percent of their output, receive substantial loans and tax relief.

Israel is earnestly seeking to encourage foreign investment and private business
and industry. Victor M. Carter, an American business leader, was recently asked
about the attractions the country offers to foreign investors. He answered:

> Basically—100 per cent literacy in the labor force; highly skilled and dedicated labor
> at Western European wages; a great reservoir of superbly educated and trained
> scientists and engineers, many temporarily working in other countries (four or five
> thousand in the United States); great financial inducements to investors; a stable,
> highly cooperative, democratic government; easy access to European, Asian and African
> markets; manufacturing costs low enough to support one hundred million dollars'
> worth of exports to the United States in 1967 and that will triple by 1970.[30]

As we have seen, Israel's continuing need for outside capital to sustain reasonable economic growth and to offset her serious trade imbalance remains a decisive
impediment to the nation's goal of economic independence.[31] It is nevertheless the
case that philanthropy is being increasingly supplemented by investment from
outside, by a "strictly business" partnership grounded in the assumption that one
foremost way in which outsiders can help Israel is by making money there.

This changed state of affairs was at once exemplified and furthered by the
1968 and 1969 Israel Economic Conferences, pioneer meetings in Jerusalem of
business men and financiers from various parts of the world. The decisions
adopted by the delegates and approved by the Government in 1968 called for a
wide range of efforts to ensure "price stability, rising productivity, changes in
wage rates related to productivity, incentives for private investment and greater
efficiency, improved Government management, an increasingly favorable private
investment environment, lower interest rates. . . ." The delegates insisted that
the only acceptable basis for such investment will be "solid financial and economic criteria"—in a word, profit—in contrast to the motivations that immediately govern philanthropic decisions.[32]

As a consequence of the 1968 Conference, a large investment holding company
was founded, with 20 percent of its shares to be taken up by Israelis, a company
expected to concentrate upon the development of the country's chemical and
aircraft industries. By 1969 several joint Israeli-foreign firms were created in
such diverse areas as development of a magnesia plant and of a computer "soft-
wear" export industry (preparation and evaluation of computer data). Several of
the new industries are geared especially to utilize highly-trained Israelis now
abroad who may be encouraged to return to Israel.

The year between the two Conferences saw the passage of a series of laws creating a favorable climate for industrial investment, either with independent
Israeli firms or with the Government. Considerable inducement is being offered
through tax concessions on reinvested profits, tax holidays for approved invest-

ments, tax incentives for mergers of small companies, and Government subsidies on salaries of technical people working on approved research projects. Government loans for investments in the West Bank (carrying insurance of 100 percent against political contingencies) are especially designed to provide employment for Arabs within their own area. Of special interest to manufacturers engaged in African and Asian trade is the free-port area to be developed near Haifa. Parts will be assembled by Israeli workers and then shipped duty-free to these markets.[33]

One way to understand these Economic Conferences is to see them against the background of competition between private enterprise on the one side and State and Histadrut companies on the other. The continuing ideal involves a humane avoidance of the extremes of collectivism and disorganization. Aharon Katzir sounds a wise warning: "Modern Israel strives after a Jewish socialism that is a blend of old prophetic humanism with modern rationalist analysis of society. It is inconceivable that the Jewish welfare State, born of so much struggle and hardship by the early pioneers, should be handed over to wealthy monopolists, who know how to make a profit, how to extract economic benefits from scientific advancement, but who have little or no regard for practical humanism."[34]

Israel has taken many steps toward the goal of economic independence. Thus, by 1967 she succeeded in covering over ninety percent of her public and private needs from out of her own resources. Although the balance of under 10 percent was derived from external sources other than exports, less than 5 percent of the latter amount came from outright gifts. The rest was taken care of through bonds and loans, all of which get repaid on time and with interest. A four-year plan for 1968–71 envisaged a reduction in the import surplus to $400-million in 1971, with exports expected to cover almost 80 percent of imports. A longer-range forecast reduces the import surplus to $200-million in 1978, with exports covering over 95 percent of imports.[35]

The Government applies foreign gifts strictly to humanitarian work and to development programs, not to currently essential internal needs. (An unavoidable consequence is that Israelis pay extraordinarily high taxes.) Israel will not put herself in a position where her survival could be threatened by a withdrawal of grants or an embargo on financial or material aid.[36]

The hopeful expectations recounted above have been seriously threatened by the recent sharp rise in necessary defense expenditures. These huge costs together with rising consumption, rapid development, and heavy public spending are, at the present writing, putting a very serious strain on the country's economy. The welcome news that $1-billion in exports were anticipated for 1970 was offset by the grim expectation that the same year would see imports rising to $2.4 million.

Before she can ever complete her avowed aim of economic self-sufficiency, Israel must at least double her exports, a most formidable task. And she must continue to have enormous amounts of capital in order to produce more and more goods in a commercially-oriented and commercially-dependent world. The type of sophisticated industry that Israel hopes to utilize in surmounting her trade imbalance will necessitate great investment in, and expansion of, educational facilities to provide skilled and technically qualified personnel.

Much of the culpability for Israel's continued need of aid from outside the Middle East falls upon the Arab states, barring as they do all direct trade with

Israel and retaining their infamous boycott of firms that do business with her. Granted the pressures of this state of affairs, part of Israel's problem remains an internal one. The difficulty is how to secure the investment capital that has to come from vastly increased domestic savings, when the only way to amass these savings is through reduced spending and reduced consumption.[37] Such reductions are not easy to bring off, and they carry their own price.

A final word is appropriate respecting the goal of economic independence. A certain term was coined in the Jewish ghetto: *shnorrerei*. It means strident beggary. Yitzhak Tishler refers to the relation between that word and *tzedakah*. Although the latter term does not exclude charity, it means much more than that. Charity can become mere benevolence, lacking any attempt to remove the injustices that require the giving. *Tzedakah* means justice, mercy, righteousness. It is best practiced discreetly and with careful attention to the future.

Tzedakah and *shnorrerei* cannot be entirely separated, and it is hard to draw a line between them. Thus, the Jews in Palestine before 1948 could never have survived without *shnorrerei*. For that reason, it was right to look upon *shnorrerei* as a real means of implementing *tzedakah,* righteousness, on the part of those outside the country who were ardently concerned with the welfare of the Palestinian Jews. But times have changed. The goals of the Israel Economic Conferences imply an end to *shnorrerei* and, at least indirectly, a means to the triumph of *tzedakah*. There is no *shnorrerei* where the "giver's" self-interest is being served. *Tzedakah* is fostered when there is equality on both sides. "A historic turning point has been reached where *tzedakah* must take the outward form of a big business partnership between Israel and world Jewry, a partnership which will be morally meritorious only if it is materially profitable to all involved." This truth is being given recognition through the Economic Conferences.[38]

The people of Israel are quite sensitive about the entire issue of *shnorrerei*. They are striving for the dignity that is made possible only by independence. They are against beggary. Some detractors of Israel wish to identify the country as a parasite upon others' philanthropy. These detractors conspire to portray the Israelis as creatures of *shnorrerei*. But the movement of the people of Israel toward economic emancipation is increasingly giving the lie to such accusations.

By failing to include among Israel's goals her serious quest for economic independence and her efforts for peace, Yusif Sayigh comes to the gratuitous and unfair conclusion that Israel must create continuing crises in the Middle East "because tranquillity is not the appropriate climate for obtaining generous financial assistance from without."[39] On Sayigh's reasoning, the Arab states ought to be the ones to foster tranquillity as a decisive means of helping to destroy Israel economically. In truth, there is no sign of any such effort, and Sayigh does not appear to recommend it. Furthermore, as an economist he ought to be aware that foreign investments are only discouraged when the country in need of them is not at peace.

To the extent that Israel's detractors have neither knowledge of nor sympathy with actual economic and social developments in the land, perhaps the reason is that they themselves have not grasped the meaning of the search for *tzedakah,* justice.

16. Israel and the Arab World, I

OVER THE COURSE of our study of life in Israel we have called attention to major problems confronting the nation. In these two final chapters of the present section we are brought to perhaps the most crucial challenge of all: Israel's relations with her Arab neighbors. The problems we have so far discussed are essentially internal to Israel, and are thus largely accessible to her initiative and treatment. But the resolution of this further issue has defied the Israelis' every effort. Among the reasons for this, an overwhelming one has been the hostile position of the Arab nations.

A Resolve for Peace and Cooperation

A continuing drive for peaceful coexistence and mutual good neighborliness has marked Israel's policy toward the surrounding Arab states. Her attempts to negotiate troublesome issues and her offers of concessions have been many and varied. Her proposals for pacific relations have been phrased and rephrased in every possible way.

Across the years, Israel has put forward broad, regional programs to benefit all the people of the area. She has advocated regional arms limitations and even disarmament. She has urged the advantages of area-wide development of transportation, communication, natural resources, and health programs. She expressed to Jordan a readiness to accept for herself a lesser share of the waters of the Jordan River, to grant a free zone in the port of Haifa with transit rights across Israel, and to make border adjustments that would benefit Jordan's West Bank villagers. She was prepared to set aside a corridor across the southern Negev in order to satisfy Egypt's request for a land link with Jordan. She offered economic and political assistance to the Egyptian revolutionary regime that was instituted in 1952, and she volunteered to honor Egyptian rights in the Gaza Strip if the new regime wished to withdraw its troops. She propounded a common-market scheme to the Lebanese and Jordanians. She has made many suggestions and offers respecting the Palestinian refugees. She proposed, and has since been enabled to implement, a plan providing special status for the holy places in Jerusalem, placing them under the jurisdiction and responsibility of those who hold them in reverence.[1]

All that Israel has asked in return for these not inconsequential offers is recognition and peace. Rather than pay that price, the Arab nations have preferred to reject the advantages. Still Israelis remain committed to a lasting peace. They know that the search must be "constant, unremitting, resilient and above all sincere."[2] In that spirit they have, whenever possible, initiated positive actions to break down barriers.

In general, Israel's policies have been highly praiseworthy. We do not mean to suggest, however, that her behavior has been free of all fault or blemish. For example, in 1950 she evicted a number of Bedouin near the Sinai border and destroyed their property. Particularly in 1953–54, her campaign of retaliation against villages in Jordan as a means of forcing the authorities to stop terrorist incursions was extreme and too often directed against civilian centers.[3] Though it succeeded in bringing infiltration under control, this action greatly increased fears and hostility in Jordan and made the Jordanian Government more intractable. In recent years, Israel's increasing mastery and use of modern weapons (especially aircraft and sometimes including napalm) has inevitably led to some civilian suffering and death, despite her attempts ever since 1954 to avoid this. (In view of the flagrant and deliberate attacks upon Israeli civilians by Arab terrorists and armies, Arabs are hardly in a moral position to accuse Israel of bringing harm to civilians. For months before Jordan announced, in April 1970, that she would no longer "observe" the 1967 cease-fire agreement, Jordanian army units regularly shelled settlements within Israel proper in addition to attacking settlements in the administered territories. Moreover, by using villages as their bases, Arab terrorists make civilian casualties inevitable.)

An Israeli decision in the spring of 1970 that may and probably will be questioned is the granting of permission for the settling of an estimated 1,000 Jews in the West Bank city of Hebron, which has a population of some 38,000 Arabs. True, the original Jewish community there is traceable to the end of the Babylonian Exile in the sixth century B.C.E., and Hebron has stood as one of the four holy cities of Jewish Palestine. However, critics of the decision argue that Israel is not treating as negotiable such a place as this one. The reply of Government spokesmen to this charge is that the settling of people in particular areas (Arabs as well as Jews) is not a genuine obstacle to an overall peace settlement.

Yesterday's Springs of Hope

It is perhaps natural to assume that the violence and tensions in the Middle East with which we have become so familiar over the past several years have existed without change since Israel's rebirth. This is not entirely the case. Earlier there seemed to be grounds for optimism.

In the beginning there was the miracle of Israel's survival despite thirteen grueling months of the War for Independence. This in itself gave infinite encouragement to the Israelis. They looked forward to the end of the fighting and to the establishing, so they hoped, of new and tranquil relations with their erstwhile foes.

In this hope they seemed to be supported by the prodigy of the armistice meetings and the agreements produced. Dr. Ralph Bunche, acting for the United Nations, succeeded where other mediators had failed and would fail. He brought the authorized representatives together at the negotiating table. Each Arab state hammered out its terms with Israel. Egypt's representative signed first (February 24, 1949). Lebanon followed on March 23, Jordan on April 3, and Syria on July 29 (the last, a delay caused by internal troubles). The agreements were comprehensive documents establishing temporary armistice lines (see Map Seven, page 69), demilitarized zones, organizational machinery, procedural steps for dealing with problems or emergencies, and basic rules of behavior. All parties agreed to refrain from using or sanctioning force, aggressive acts, or even threats against the other party, to respect each other's security needs, and to see to it that no warlike or hostile acts were initiated from their territory. The governments further contracted to proceed to the next step: a peace settlement. The most striking feature of the agreements was the stipulation that the terms of the armistice would still remain in effect *after* a final peace was negotiated.

Dr. Bunche fully expected a permanent settlement within six months after the armistice agreements were signed. A Conciliation Commission was appointed by the United Nations to aid in negotiating that peace settlement. The Commission's bungling and onesidedness (to be discussed later in this chapter) did not immediately undermine the seeming readiness of single Arab governments to come to some kind of terms with Israel. When the Commission sessions began in April of 1949, most of the Arab delegations held secret meetings individually with the Israelis and showed a certain willingness to ignore the obduracy of the Arab League's leadership. At the July meetings there were occasional rays of hope that agreement might still be reached on fundamental issues.

For a short period of time Arab and Israeli officers worked together very effectively along the armistice lines as members of the Mixed Armistice Commissions. As long as some form of agreement was anticipated, their work and recommendations received cooperative support from governments on both sides.

In July of 1952 Israeli optimism was renewed by the overthrow in Egypt of the corrupt regime of King Farouk at the hands of a young, revolutionary committee. A new and evidently responsible government gained control. Concerned as the new leaders were with domestic reforms and modernization, they could also be counted upon, so the Israelis hoped, to establish relations with their neighbor to the East, especially since Israel was offering both technical aid and political support. There seemed to be no fundamental conflict between Egypt and Israel. The Egyptians' initial response to the Israelis' overtures of friendship appeared most promising.

To the other side of Israel, King Abdullah of Jordan also showed concern for a final peace settlement. Abdullah was well aware that his country's self-interest pointed in that direction. In this way, Jordan's extensive and valuable acquisitions of land, people, and especially the Old City of Jerusalem could be made secure.[4] By August of 1955 a plan for joint development of the Jordan River was all but accepted. It was finally held up only by Arab League members who did not stand to profit.

Lebanon, with her unusual mixture of Christians, Muslims, and Druses, appeared to be benefiting from the presence of Israel as a kind of buffer against a totally Muslim world.

Israel's Sinai campaign of 1956 (to be considered later) appeared to give further ground for hope. Terrorist raids halted almost completely, a condition that lasted from 1956 until late 1964. The Israelis could stop living under constant fear and tension. Of additional importance, the Gulf of Aqaba was opened to Israeli trade with the Far East and East Africa.

Disunity in the Arab world, including especially Arab fears of Egyptian imperialism,[5] seemed to offer further protection for Israel and to suggest an eventual break in the front united against her. The unified military command of the Arabs, established first in 1956 and then again in 1964, proved a farce: On the first occasion, Jordan and Syria remained totally inactive in the 1956 conflict; on the second, Jordan and Syria refused to permit Egyptian troops on their soil, and Syria and Lebanon even rejected Egyptian military advisors.

Thus, periodically, the years before 1967 seemed to give some promise of a brighter future in Arab-Israeli relations. For a time, Israelis, together with Jews of the Diaspora, felt that the world would never again condone the crime of genocide. There were interludes when some people in Israel could be persuaded that the Arab leaders and propagandists did not really mean it when they talked of driving the Israelis into the sea, that such extravagances of language were simply "the Arab way" of speaking. And at certain intervals Israel's reliance upon the United Nations, upon the friendship of other countries, and upon world opinion did not seem foolhardy.

After 1968 it became much more difficult to find springs of hope. Yet human beings always seek reassurance. Many Israelis have hoped that coexistence in the administered territories might help to foster a wider realization that Jews and Arabs can live together in harmony and cooperation. Some West Bank Arabs and Israelis have argued that the resolution of the "Palestinian problem" through a "small peace" can pave the way for a larger peace. The Israeli Government has hoped that the thousands of Arabs who experience Israel and her people at first hand through specially arranged programs of family visits—as many as 16,000 visitors in one month alone—might eventually help to change Arab attitudes.[6] Most Israelis have felt, however, that short of a firm peace settlement, their primary reliance must be on Israel's Defense Forces. Israelis have been aware that this way of realizing minimal security is a negative one and that it cannot serve forever. Many of them believe that Israel must never lose faith that one day her Arab neighbors will become partners with her.

The Hard Facts

Each of the earlier hopes we have noted proved ephemeral. Israelis have had to live with a continuing series of disappointments.

Because in 1949 there seemed sound reasons to believe that the long-sought resolution of Arab-Jewish difficulties could be achieved, the failure of the Conciliation Commission assumes tragic proportions. The Commissioners (representatives of France, Turkey, and the United States) fell into the trap that has ensnared so many: the belief that they could satisfy Arab demands, and thereby win favor with the Arabs for their own nations, without totally sacrificing Israel. They failed to put the real needs of the Middle Eastern nations first. The American delegation, which should have provided strong and disinterested leadership, was particularly at fault in this regard. Against every expert's advice, the Commission brought together at a preliminary session in March 1949 the four Arab delegations. By treating them as a bloc, the Commission members weakened the position of the moderates and separatists and allowed the intransigents who represented the Arab League's view to gain control. Then the Commission, under the influence of the U.S. State Department, compounded its mistake by quite illegitimately accepting the terms for negotiation stipulated by the Arab League: agreement by Israel to the repatriation of a large number of refugees before any other issues would be considered; no direct or separate negotiations with Israel; and boundary discussions based on the Partition Plan rather than the armistice agreements. Ralph Bunche had successfully rejected similar Arab League demands.

Because of having already committed itself to the League's position, the Commission saw fit to reject an Israeli proposal reflecting United Nations ideals: agreement by all delegations at the start upon a desire to end the conflict in keeping with the U.N. Charter, willingness to use peaceful, direct negotiations to settle disagreements, and—most significant—submission of unresolved points to third-party arbitration. The Commissioners further strengthened the Arab extremists by refusing to pass on to the Arabs an Israeli offer to repatriate 100,000 refugees, prejudging it as inadequate.

Trygve Lie, Secretary-General of the United Nations, was severely critical of the Commission's mishandling of this crucial mission, and especially of its failure to establish direct negotiations.

Another fateful and indefensible blunder of the Commission was its failure to grant a meaningful role to the Palestinian Arab delegation. These men, elected by the refugees to represent their cause, asked to be the party with whom Israel should negotiate. They denied the right of the Arab governments either to speak for them or to annex parts of Palestine; they wanted to establish the independent state that had already been conceived by the United Nations.[7] Israel's delegates met with the Palestinians, and then suggested a plebiscite among all the Palestinian Arabs. The Commission ignored this recommendation, and the Arab nations refused to recognize the Palestinian delegation. The reason for such refusal soon became clear when these states presented their own proposal for a settlement (in October, 1950): Israel was to be reduced in size from the 7,992 square miles she controlled under the armistice terms to a mere 2,000 square miles, and the remainder of Palestine was to be divided among Egypt, Jordan, Syria, and Lebanon.[8] There would be no state for the Palestinians!

By September of 1951 the peace talks had collapsed. A most promising opportunity for a peace settlement in the Middle East had thus been lost. By this time the Arab states had already redirected their policies toward the elimination of Israel. Between 1950 and 1956 they tested and put into effect the various techniques they have used since that time: economic and political boycott, blockade, non-cooperation at the armistice lines, murder and sabotage, and military excursions short of all-out conflict. If necessary, total war would be resorted to for the death blow.

The Arab nations made ineffective the Mixed Armistice Commissions by with-drawing support and thereby increasing border troubles. No especial care had been taken in drawing the Israeli-Jordanian armistice line because it was intend-ed to be only temporary. Many villagers in Jordan were separated from their fields, orchards, or wells. Yet when Israel suggested exchanges of land to ease these hardships and reduce conflict, Jordan refused.

Innocent passage across the lines tapered off and was succeeded by terrorist attacks, which inflicted murderous damage inside Israel. Agricultural production was seriously hurt, adding to an already acute food shortage. Worse was the psychological effect. Since no place was safe from the terrorists, fear covered the whole country. From 1954 to 1956 alone Israel suffered thousands of incidents of sabotage and theft, and over 650 casualties, most of whom were civilians.

Aloneness

In 1953 Abba Eban graphically described his country's plight before the Se-curity Council: "We are besieged, . . . blockaded, abused, threatened, encircled, ambushed, harried, and subjected to murderous onslaught at every turn . . . there is no parallel for this situation in the life of any other nation."[9] Yet Israel's appeals for remedial action under the armistice agreements went un-answered.

For a while it looked as though the Arab boycott and blockade would bring about a collapse of Israel's already strained economy. Not only was all Arab business with Israel forbidden by the Arab League, but foreign firms were threatened with a loss of their entire Arab market if they engaged in the smallest trade with Israel. The blockade, enforced by Egypt, closed the Suez Canal and the Gulf of Aqaba to Israeli ships and inflicted damaging and retaliatory action on ships of other nations carrying goods to or from Israel or even touching at her ports.

These actions brought grave harm to Israel's trade with a large part of the world, greatly increased her carrying charges, and cost her untold loss of revenue at the port of Haifa.[10] Egypt's refusal to lift the blockade was to be one of the major factors leading to Israel's decision to invade the Sinai in 1956.

On top of all this Israel felt a growing sense of betrayal and isolation, at least partly as a result of Arab political pressures. Promises made in 1950 by France, Great Britain, and the United States to prevent the use of force in the area seemed worthless. The Administration in Washington appeared indifferent to Israel's fate. The Soviet Union abruptly ended its brief friendship with Israel, launched an intensive anti-Zionist and anti-Israel campaign, and broke diplo-matic relations. The culmination came in 1955 when Israel's only friend in the Middle East, Turkey, signed a defense pact with Iraq.

The worst blow to Israel's declining hopes had occurred one year before when Egypt's revolutionary regime decided against a reconciliation. After that, there was nothing to counteract the demoralizing effect of Arab threats and actions. Egypt underwrote terrorism from Gaza. Her radio[11] and newspapers assaulted Israel daily. Units of her army clashed frequently (over 1,300 times) with Israeli forces. In 1955, Egypt concluded an agreement with the Soviet Union (disguised as an arrangement with Czechoslovakia) for huge arms shipments, thus upsetting the rough balance of power and arms control the Western nations had managed to preserve in the area. Syria contracted for Russian equipment. Great Britain stepped up arms shipments to Iraq.

Israel's Defense Forces were underequipped and most of her weapons were outmoded. Her Government was forced to enter an expensive arms race in which only France would meet her major needs. A sense of impending catastrophe hung over Israel, the same feeling her people would experience again in May of 1967.

Because of the surety that Egypt would strike whenever her forces were ready, and that no political body would deter her, Israel decided to seize the initiative before the Egyptian arsenal could reach full strength. A first strike seemed the only self-defense. The length and indefensibility of her borders, the vulnerability of her population centers, the lack of space into which to withdraw, and the possibility of total encirclement all made an offensive defense an absolute necessity. When a newly-elected pro-Nasser government in Jordan signed a military pact with Egypt on October 23, 1956, any hesitancy Israel may have had vanished. On October 29 she invaded the Sinai. Her forces overran the Gaza Strip and most of the Peninsula, including Sharm el-Sheikh, the fortified position that was closing off the Gulf of Aqaba.

The French and British Governments, incensed at Nasser's actions against their various allies and interests in the Middle East and Africa, had made plans with Israel coordinating their own invasion of the Canal zone with her Sinai campaign. However, though their aircraft began attacking Egyptian airfields and military installations near Cairo and the Canal on October 31, none of their forces attempted a landing until the eighth day. Israel had already attained her objectives. By then, Soviet forces (which had been occupied with the Hungarian revolt) began to arrive in Syria and posed the threat of Russian involvement. The British Parliament was in rebellion against its Government's actions. The American Government warned its NATO allies and Israel that they risked loss of all American support if they did not recall their forces. Israel finally bowed to international pressures, but only on condition that U.N. forces would be stationed at Sharm el-Sheikh and in Gaza.

Under the influence of idealism, Israel made only moderate territorial claims. From 1948 to 1967, she put up with severely restricted boundaries. Yet it was this very moderation, in view of Arab hostility, that actually made war more probable during those years. As Professor AlRoy notes, the circumstances drew so heavily on the Israelis' psychological reserves that their level of tolerance toward crisis was greatly reduced.[12]

The United Nations' insistence that Israel withdraw from the Sinai in 1957 without any basic resolution of the Arab-Israeli conflict simply perpetuated the unstable state of affairs and paved the way for 1967. President Eisenhower assured Israel that she would have no reason to regret her withdrawal. Unfortunately, the assurance was not realized. The firm stipulations Secretary-General Hammarskjold made with President Nasser regarding the presence of United Nations forces at Sharm el-Sheikh were to be totally ignored in 1967 by another Secretary-General, U Thant, who evacuated the troops without consulting anyone.

Again in 1967 the United Nations was to intercede in an open conflict, after failing to prevent its outbreak, saving Arab leaders from having to sue for peace and thus greatly reducing the chances of a negotiated settlement.

Israel's persistent drive for negotiated peace treaties centers around the "effect on Arab ideologies . . . more decisive than Arab facts. The form and content of the peace must be such as would require Egyptian and Jordanian leaders . . . to begin the long, hard process of detoxification. They would have to tell their people that a great historic conflict is now resolved. . . ."[13] Indirect promises made to a third party would not carry this imperative.

Professor Safran writes: "A settlement consecrated in a peace treaty would legally close the conflict and encourage outside powers to deal with Israel and treat with it on that basis without being inhibited by possible Arab reactions. A settlement by some other method, on the other hand, may legally outlaw belligerence and recognize frontiers, but it would permit the conflict to be carried on by political means and would thus leave the Palestine issue open and inhibit dealings by third parties with Israel."[14]

The Arab nations have not believed that Israel is sincere in her protestations of peaceful intent. They have insisted that her ultimate aim is to dominate the Middle East and destroy Arab society. They have interpreted her every action and her every utterance in the light of this conviction.

Every Israeli proposal has been dashed on the same rock: the Arab dictum that Israel's very existence constitutes aggression, prevents the realization of Arab destiny, and therefore must be condemned. The Arab leadership and masses have been consumed by the poisonous ideology that equates Jews, Israel, and her people with the power of evil in the world.[15] This censurious position toward Israel has been a formidable barrier to a freely negotiated peace and to normal relationships between the Arab states and Israel.

In the Arab world it has been dangerous to be considered a moderate regarding Israel. The great numbers of Arabs assassinated by their own terrorists or imprisoned or executed by their own governments for "collaborating" with Jews or Israelis are a tragic reminder of the dominant role that Arab extremists have played in Jewish-Arab relations throughout the twentieth century.[16]

The pattern of hostility the Arab states established between 1951 and 1956 has been hard to break. Thus, an Arab League resolution adopted at its first Khartoum conference in September, 1967 reiterated: no recognition, no negotiation, and no peace with Israel. Leaders continued to call for a holy war against those who would "corrupt" the "Arab Middle East." Many Arabs are convinced they will succeed eventually, and they say they are willing to make any sacrifices to that end.

Two Bands of Refugees

The Arab-Israeli War of 1948 uprooted over a million people from their homes in the Arab world and Israel. Two bands of refugees—Jews and Arabs—comprised the human wreckage.

The Jewish refugees, never supported by anyone but their own people, long ago ceased to be a "problem." They are assimilated, respected, and productive members of Israeli society. In sharp contrast, the Arab refugees are still a very visible and pitiable people, a "problem" that should long ago have been resolved by their acceptance and absorption into Arab society. After almost a quarter of a century, rather than having decreased in number, they are more numerous. Second and even third generations are still listed as "refugees," as if "once a refugee, always a refugee" were some kind of rule. Such listing is often retained even when the refugee has become self-supporting. Financial advantages (such as the avoiding of taxes) and political factors are alike involved. The refugees have become, in effect, permanent wards of UNRWA, which, ironically, was created to resolve the whole problem by aiding in the resettlement and rehabilitation of these people.

Because Arab leaders have not only insisted on the right of "all" Arab refugees to "return" to their former homes, but have made that right rest on the alleged fact of Israeli responsibility, we must look back to 1948.

Basically, it was the Arabs' refusal to accept the partition of Palestine and the establishment of Israel, and subsequent Arab aggression, that produced both bands of refugees.

The first victims, though not the first refugees, were Jews. Not only in Palestine but all over the Arab world, Jews felt the collective wrath of the Arab community. Mobs attacked Jewish quarters. In Arab countries government statements and decrees made life ever more difficult for Jews and ensured further outrages. Some Jews took considerable risks to escape during the War for Independence. But most of the mass exodus that was to bring to Israel 700,000 Jewish refugees from Arab states occurred after 1949. Like the Arab refugees, these people were frightened, bewildered, and destitute. The first Jewish refugees of the War itself were survivors of villages and collectives in eastern Palestine that fell to Arab conquerors after stubborn but unavailing defense.[17] At least eleven such Jewish centers had to be abandoned in the first half of 1948 and the people resettled elsewhere.

Why should so many Arabs (some 560,000) have fled from homes and land in areas heavily populated by their own people? No one planned or anticipated such an extensive flight. Though the Arab League members assumed that there would be some temporary displacement of Palestinian Arabs during hostilities, they did not foresee either the massive numbers or a displacement made permanent by defeat. Certainly the Jews had no reason to expect this outcome. Initially, the Jewish leaders tried to stop the flight. To them, it meant a denial of the ideals of harmonious coexistence they were determined to demonstrate.

With respect to the Arab refugees themselves, the major promptings were fear, and the traditional Arab way of responding to approaching trouble. The second of these needs a little explanation. Centuries of cumulative experience with invading desert tribes and rapacious armies of Mongols, Turks, and others had taught Arabs of different regions the wisdom of flight. After the invaders retired with their booty, as usually happened, or order was restored, the people normally returned.[18] That this practice has continued into the present century is demonstrated by the actions of some 40,000 Arabs who left Palestine during the Arab rebellion of 1936–39, the majority coming back after the trouble was over. Similarly, since 1967 Arab farmers have several times abandoned and returned to their land in the Gilead hills, depending on whether or not the terrorist bands were making the area a battleground.

Contrary to the customary pattern, Jews in 1948 had no intention of retiring once the fighting was over, and the conditions of the War and the post-war years were not such as to make them open the borders to a flood of Arab returnees.

The flight was set in motion by educated, middle-class and wealthy Arabs who, realizing a fierce struggle was in the offing, began to leave as soon as the U.N. voted partition. By the end of April, 1948 some 150,000 Arabs had abandoned their homes. Thirty villages stood empty. Arab leaders of Haifa, Safed, and the Sharon Valley decided to evacuate their people—apparently to cause disruption and confusion for the benefit of Arab armies—despite pleas of Jewish leaders that the people remain. They left by the busload, some 56,000 from Haifa alone.

Fear of Jewish reprisals, based on awareness of Arab atrocities against Jews, was intensified by knowledge of Jewish extremists' actions against the British forces, and a few instances of apparently wanton killing of some Arab villagers. Arab propagandists sought to rouse the populace to a frenzy of hatred and vengeance by spreading stories of Jewish atrocities (some of which were believed by Jews also).[19] The attempts backfired. The stridency of these stories and their exaggerated character, aided and abetted by rumor (the most common news medium of the Arab masses), failed to incite them to violence. Instead, the people were simply terrorized, and there was a panic-stricken rout. The flight tended to create its own momentum.

After Israel's forces were able to assume the offensive, Arab multitudes fled before them. The Jewish authorities ceased trying to stop the movement. Although unanticipated, the flight was perceived, in Weingrod's words as, "a quick way to 'solve the Arab question'."[20] Some Israeli troops and commanders changed their behavior at this stage, making more deliberate efforts to get Arabs to leave. Some used purely psychological scare tactics, some resorted to physical eviction. The extent of such harassment is impossible to determine. Yet there was never an overall plan of any kind to expel the Arabs.

The major handicap of these people was a shortage of resolute leadership. Wherever a strong leader held his people together, as at Nazareth, there was no retreat and no expulsion. Many villages in Galilee were also preserved by this kind of steadfastness.

It is widely believed that the vast majority of Arab refugees had centuries-deep roots in Palestine. This is a considerable exaggeration. Until after World War I, Palestine was essentially a land of emigration. It has been estimated that by 1939 one-third of the Arab populace were newcomers, mostly from Syria and Transjordan. During World War II, there was additional Arab immigration into Palestine. The incentives were work opportunities, good wage levels, and improved living conditions. Many of these recent immigrants became Palestinian refugees in 1948 simply by declaring a residency in Palestine of two years and a loss of home and means of support. We are not suggesting that they were not entitled to claim refugee status. Nor are we forgetting that some of the Arabs did in fact represent families who had lived in the land for perhaps a thousand years or more. But the numbers of such people were limited.

For experts on refugee peoples, the confused 1948 state of affairs is irrelevant to the major problems. Repatriation has not been, and certainly in this explosive situation cannot be, the best solution.[21] Resettlement and absorption by related peoples is the most humanitarian and effective answer for all parties, as has been shown ever since World War II in the treatment of millions of other refugees in many parts of the world.

Refugee experts have long been aware that Arab leaders turned a resolvable problem into a political and propaganda weapon against Israel (and a most effective one). These leaders rejected every offer of international aid that aimed at resettling and integrating the refugees into Arab society. Only Jordan granted them citizenship or permanent rights of resettlement.

Many Arab leaders admit that their stand on the Palestinian refugees has been aimed specifically at Israel's extermination. President Nasser has said, if the refugees return to Israel, "Israel will cease to exist." Other spokesmen have expanded on this theme endlessly.[22]

In the face of this Arab position, how much could Israel do for the refugees? In 1949 she began readmitting some of the 60,000 who ultimately came back, most under a family reunion program. She also offered to repatriate 100,000, or to absorb all 270,000 Arabs (refugees and residents) in the Gaza Strip if the land were ceded to her.[23]

At a time in the early 1950's when Israel's financial condition was extremely grave, she released all refugee bank funds (some $10-million) and contents of safety deposit boxes. No reciprocal action was forthcoming from Arab governments. Israel also offered to set up a fund to aid in resettlement.

Israeli leaders and people have always granted the right of refugees to receive compensation for their property, even though Arab leaders have not admitted a similar right for Jewish property. As a matter of fact, since 1948 Arab League governments have confiscated or sequestered liquid assets and properties of their Jewish citizens valued at one-and-a-half times the value of assets left behind by Palestinian refugees. There has never been any public recognition or even discussion of compensation or repatriation for the hundreds of thousands of Jewish refugees from Arab lands. In contrast, by the mid-1960's a United Nations agency completed a thorough evaluation of Arab claims, and implementation has only awaited Arab arbitration of the refugee question.

In the face of continuing rejections of her various offers, Israel has been forced to conclude that nothing she could safely grant would be acceptable to her antagonists. She finally decided to rest her case on the truth that an approximately equal exchange of populations had taken place between herself and the Arab countries.

17. Israel and the Arab World, II

The Six Day War

Between 1957 and 1967 Arab words and deeds continued to aim at the liquidation of the "gangster state" of Israel. However, the 1956 victory had strengthened the self-assurance of the Israelis and allowed them to turn their attention and energies to a wide range of constructive and innovative undertakings. Israel learned to live with the inflammatory tirades streaming from Arab capitals. No hostile deed—the shelling of northern *kibbutzim*, the firing upon fishing vessels on Lake Kinneret (the Sea of Galilee), months of renewed terrorist acts—succeeded in altering this outlook. Furthermore, the counterstrikes of the Defense Forces were able to contain Arab violence reasonably well. Nevertheless, the constancy and the seriousness of the Arab threat were having their inevitable effects, as shown by the unified reaction of the Israelis to the sudden new crisis of May, 1967.

The crisis actually caught the Israelis by surprise. They knew very well that the U.S.S.R. had provided the Arab armies with huge supplies of sophisticated weapons.[1] Yet there seemed no particular reason for the Arabs suddenly to take a war stance. In fact, indications early in the year had led Israel and the United States to believe that Jordan, Lebanon, and Egypt each had its own reasons for not wanting an open conflict with Israel for the time being.

Syria alone became noticeably more aggressive late in 1966, stepping up terrorist raids through Jordan. Israel responded with an air attack on Al Fatah, a "liberation" organization, at Samu (West Bank), Jordan, and with a stern notice that Syria could expect punitive action if the raids were not stopped. Neither step was different from other anti-terrorist warnings.

Arabs have always maintained that Israel was (and still is) only waiting for the opportune moment to enlarge her territory. In early April of 1967 a serious Syrian-Israeli air battle took place. In May, the U.S.S.R. declared that Israel was mobilizing troops on the Syrian border. Did the Arabs believe that an Israeli assault was being readied? The Soviet Union refused Israel's invitation to send a representative to the area to investigate the alleged movement of troops, and U.N. observers' reports were ignored. It was a Russian lie that occasioned the Six Day War.

Syria called for Egyptian action under a mutual defense pact. Nasser began building up his forces in the Sinai, even withdrawing troops from Yemen. Commanders of U.N. forces were told to withdraw their men from Gaza and Sharm el-Sheikh. Nasser then closed the Straits of Tiran, a clear act of aggression. He argued that such action was justified because a state of war already existed between the two countries. Yet he then proceeded to contradict himself by accusing Israel of being the assailant on June 5. During states of war, attacks by one side upon the other are hardly open to objection. (Nasser's deviousness paralleled the stratagem in the 1950's when Egypt claimed the right to close the Suez Canal to Israel because of a state of war, openly nullified the armistice agreement by mobilizing terrorists in Gaza, but then blamed Israel for breaking the armistice by her invasion of the Sinai.)

The blockade of the Straits in 1967 cancelled Israel's only remaining benefit from the earlier Sinai campaign. She was suddenly faced with almost the identical set of circumstances that threatened her in 1956: the same vulnerable borders, the danger of strangulation, a hostile foe massed in strength on her very doorstep, and a wavering international community that showed no inclination to resist Arab aggression. (In contrast to 1956, the French and British were now urging, even insisting, that Israel take no action.)

For three weeks after May 15, the date when large numbers of Egyptian troops were moved into the Sinai, the Israeli Government waited out the growing crisis while various diplomats did what they could to end the blockade and avert war. Tension and then rising anger gripped Israel as one erstwhile supporter after another deserted her. The waiting period did serve to demonstrate that no political or diplomatic means that anyone was *willing* to pursue could move an uncompromising *provocateur*.

The Arabs argue that the measures Nasser took were demanded in order to forestall an Israeli invasion. They say that, having achieved a position of strength at last, he was trying to de-escalate the tension and was preparing to negotiate.[2] (This claim is hard to reconcile with the mob hysteria in Arab cities roused by official speeches and parades at that very time.)

The Israelis could find absolutely no evidence of de-escalation. On the contrary, Arab pronouncements indicated a steady move toward the "total war" that Nasser proclaimed would "destroy Israel" (May 26 and 28). Jordan and Iraq signed military pacts with Egypt, while Kuwait, Morocco, and Algeria promised to send reinforcements. A ring of steel enclosed Israel, and her vital port of Eilat, through which she receives almost all her oil, remained sealed off. The general feeling was that the Arabs had committed themselves to war, whether or not this had been Nasser's original intent[3] and that by waiting, Israel was giving the enemy all the advantage.

Nasser was entrapped by his own words and deeds. Behind them lay years of inciting mobs to lust for Israel's destruction. From Gaza, Egypt's mortars fired intermittently, while her planes overflew Israel's airfields almost daily during the first week of June. Captured army documents prove that the Jordanian forces had been ordered to take designated villages and kill all the inhabitants.[4]

Israelis (and people around the world) were amply justified in believing that the Arabs were preparing to commit mass murder. As James Michener testified on the basis of personal experiences in Israel, Jordan, and the United Arab Republic (Egypt), "If ever a nation was forewarned by word and act and specified promises of annihilation, it was Israel."[5] A European clergyman in Tiberias told us of having had no illusion that he would be spared from the massacre had the Syrians broken through in the North.

Reluctantly, the Israeli Cabinet decided that nothing would come of peaceful efforts to end the aggression already committed against the country, and that further waiting was simply tempting fate. (A century ago the French historian Taine said, "The aggressor is he who makes war inevitable.") Yaël Dayan asks: "Did it really matter who fired the first shot? . . . Too much was at stake for us— everything. If being the first to shoot gained us an advantage, let us be condemned for it; life here matters more than some petty formality." "We, in the front, had no doubt as to the inevitability of war. We also knew we were going to win it. We were not going to win because we were more numerous, more battle-happy, or more ambitious. We were going to win, at whatever cost, because losing meant extermination. . . . On June 5, 1967, we risked all we had. We crossed into the Sinai while many in the world were composing our epitaphs, and with the determination and courage of a man about to be strangled to death we . . . won the war."[6]

Israel went to war on June 5 not for aggression or territorial acquisitiveness, but for sheer survival. One may disagree with the Israelis' interpretation of the facts confronting them (though to do so is, to our minds, unrealistic). But to say, in the hindsight of their victory, that they had no reason to fear annihilation is to fail to put oneself in the situation of other human beings. It is a failure of empathy.

Amos Kenan writes: "Who will believe us today, that what guided us in the awful days of May 1967 was the oath to the six million? Who will believe we triumphed because we had no alternative? . . . on that bitter day when we felt that everything had closed around us, we knew that what happened once, what had always happened, must never happen again. We decided to resist."[7]

Beyond the military training and the well-coordinated and carefully planned tactics for just such an emergency loomed "the dedication of the Jews, forged in thousands of years of dispersions and persecutions, their inviolable determination to ensure modern Israel's survival as a nation. 'Everybody fought for something that is a combination of love, belief and country,' said Moshe Dayan . . . 'If I may say so, we felt we were fighting to prevent the fall of the Third Temple.' "[8]

The Israelis' success reached beyond all normal expectations (see Map Nine). The Golan Heights, the Gaza Strip, and the Sinai Peninsula including Sharm el-Sheikh were essential objectives because they were the places of greatest enemy threat to Israel. Because the Israelis believed that at the last minute Jordan would stay out of the conflict, they did not expect to find themselves in the West Bank or East Jerusalem.

In six days of war Israel suffered more casualties (some 800 killed and 3,000 wounded) in proportion to its population than the United States lost in fifteen years of warfare in Korea and Vietnam.

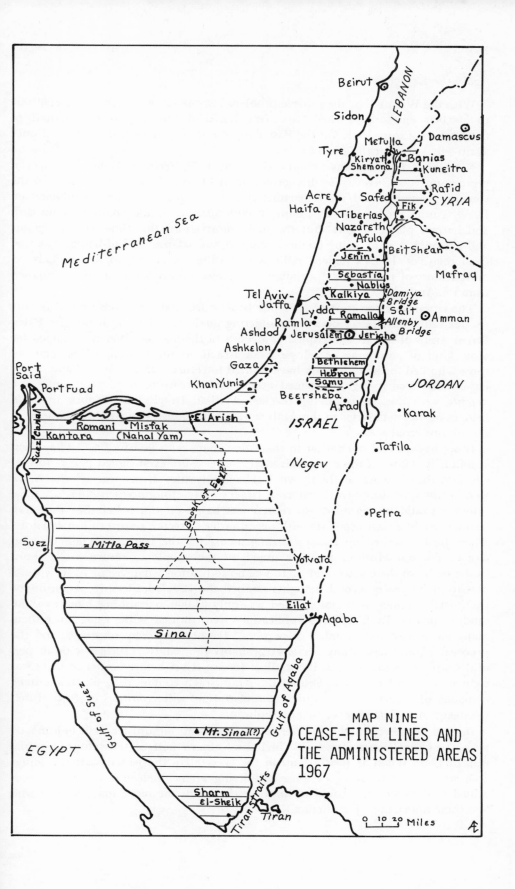

Beirut

Sidon

Tyre

LEBANON

Damascus

Metulla

Kiryat
Shemona

Banias

Kuneitra

Acre

Safed

Rafid

Haifa

Tiberias

Fik

SYRIA

Nazareth

Afula

BeitShe'an

Jenin

Mafraq

Sebastia

Nablus

Tel Aviv-
Jaffa

Kalkiya

Damiya
Bridge

Lydda

Ramallah

Salt

Amman

Ramla

Allenby
Bridge

Ashdod

Jerusalem

Jericho

Ashkelon

Bethlehem

Gaza

Hebron

JORDAN

KhanYunis

Samu

Port
Said

Beersheba

Port Fuad

Arad

Karak

Romani

Misfak

El Arish

ISRAEL

Kantara

(Nahal Yam)

Tafila

Mediterranean Sea

Brook of Egypt

Negev

Suez Canal

Suez

= Mitla Pass

Petra

Yotvata

Gulf of Suez

Sinai

Eilat

Aqaba

Gulf of Aqaba

EGYPT

Mt. Sinai(?)

MAP NINE
CEASE-FIRE LINES AND
THE ADMINISTERED AREAS
1967

Sharm
El-Sheik

Tiran Straits

Tiran

0   10 20 Miles

Æ

Again the Refugees

With the War of 1967 the refugee problem became more complex. Some 200,000 to 300,000 Palestinians[9] fled the West Bank of the Jordan, about half of them refugees from 1948. On the East Bank the misery of 1948 was repeated once again—by some, for the second time.[10]

Nils-Goran Gussing was designated by the U.N. Secretary-General as special representative to investigate this second flight of Palestinians. He testified to the General Assembly that the departure of these people could not be blamed on Israel. Panic, brought on by almost twenty years of indoctrination in untruth and hatred, played a part. But the main motivations this time were economic and personal: fear of losing financial support and savings, and of being separated from relatives. Israel's lenient policies regarding travel and money quickly removed most of these fears,[11] although some restrictions continue to be imposed from the Arab side.

The situation after June of 1967 put Israel once again in a position of having to make difficult choices between conflicting goals. On the one hand, the Palestinian Arabs of the areas occupied as a result of the Six Day War have hoped for some kind of autonomy or release from Israeli administration, while many of those who fled to the East Bank have wanted to return. On the other hand, Israel has needed security against armed attack and terrorism, until such time as a *détente* with the Arabs can be reached. Withal, Israelis have hoped to build bridges of understanding to the Arab world, as demonstrated by their policies in the administered areas.

Israel has no real obligation to the Palestinians who fled in 1967. They went voluntarily. Many of those who left after the cease-fire even signed papers to that effect in the presence of their own local officials after Israel learned the Arabs were again spreading atrocity stories. Israel's early announcement that all these refugees would be permitted to return was based on the belief that the Arab nations would at last negotiate with her in order to secure return of lost territory. Then Jordan stalled on making arrangements for the transfer. When the Jordanian Foreign Minister publicly urged all the people to return as "a thorn in the flesh" of the enemy, and there was no indication whatever of Arab willingness to make peace, second thoughts assailed the Israeli leadership. Accordingly, the initial number of permits issued was only 21,000, a crushing blow to thousands of people. Even so, 7,000 applications went unused at the time. Since then, many more than that number of permits have been used by returnees, and the processing continues. Many persons (probably thousands) returned without permits simply by wading across the shallow Jordan River before border security was tightened against terrorists. Should the Arab-Israeli conflict drag on indefinitely, demands of security and a quiet administration will continue to force Israel to engage in a selective screening of applicants.

Despite the second flight, the territories Israel now administers still hold 55–60 percent of the Palestinian Arabs, including almost half of the refugee population of 1948. When at Jericho and in the Gaza Strip the Israelis saw the miserable state in which refugees were still living after nineteen years, they determined to do what they could to improve the lot of the more than 500,000 who had come under their jurisdiction.[12]

In addition to her own aid programs, which run into tens of millions of dollars, Israel in one year alone contributed over $3.7 million to UNRWA for the aid of Arab refugees in the administered territories (budgetary year ending in June, 1969). Electricity, water, sanitation facilities, and access roads have been provided for camps lacking such necessities. Between 1967 and 1969, Israel constructed more homes in Gaza than were built in all the years of Egyptian administration. For the first time since 1949 the people of Gaza were granted freedom to move or travel outside the Strip. About 15,000 moved to the East Bank[13] before Jordan acted to stop additional moves. Between the work program Israel sponsors and the extension of private industry (in the West Bank especially), more refugees are working than ever before, some for the first time since 1948. Though underemployment still afflicts some areas, new ventures have been proposed to alleviate the situation. In February, 1970 Israel announced further plans to resettle permanently outside the camps refugees who give their consent. Greater provision is to be made for schools and industrial and crafts centers near the settlements, together with improved working conditions.

Outside Jericho and the Gaza Strip Israel found that many refugees located in the West Bank had been enabled to better their own living conditions, although numbers complained of social discrimination at the hands of permanent Arab residents. It is all but impossible to separate the problems of the refugees in the territories from those of the general populace. From the Israeli Government's point of view, both groups must receive equal treatment and be integrated.

The Gaza Strip presents unusual complexities. The refugee masses crowded there have lacked almost any local means of employment. Years of stagnation have bred a population in which bitterness, hatred, terrorism, and rebelliousness abound. Huge caches of arms left by the Egyptians greatly magnify security problems. The terrorism inflicts many casualties on the Arabs. Despite Israeli attempts to provide people with productive work, outbreaks of violence increased during 1969-70. In March, 1970 alone, grenade attacks killed 27 persons and injured 132 others, all but a small number Arabs. Yet a large segment of the population wants to benefit from opportunities for a better life that Israel is seeking to provide. In the Spring of 1970, some 10,000 Gaza residents, half of them refugees, were commuting to work in Israel, although by April this number had dropped markedly due to terrorist threats against these Arabs and their families. Much of the terrorist activity in Gaza has been directed against any normalization of life in accommodation with Israel. Similarly, terrorists on the West Bank have "executed," wounded, kidnapped, and threatened those Arabs they consider "collaborators" with the enemy. In many cases, this simply means that the local leaders have taken some initiative in dealing with Israeli officials on behalf of their people.

As in the past, Israel's concern over the refugees' plight extends to those beyond her jurisdiction. In October, 1968 her Foreign Minister made yet another proposal for resolving the problem. He advocated before the United Nations that Israel, the Arab states, and other countries contributing to UNRWA devise a five-year plan for the rehabilitation and integration of refugees into productive life. He emphasized that the implementation of the plan need not wait upon peace negotiations. As with earlier proposals, Israel's humanitarian plan was denounced by the Arab representatives.

However unfortunate the condition of new and old refugees, there is no comparison with the pitiable state of Jews in most Arab countries. The Six Day War unleashed a new wave of violence and persecution against them. Once again hate-filled mobs assaulted Jewish quarters. Libyan Jews were allowed the luxury of flight, but those of Syria and Iraq, and for at least three years those of Egypt were denied this least act of humanity. These people remain hostages of malignity, of Arab defeat and crushed pride. They have been thrown out of work, their businesses closed down, their personal movements tightly restricted, and their assets frozen. Heads of families are imprisoned (and frequently subjected to inhumane treatment) while their dependents are denied help from or contact with charitable organizations. The Jews of Syria and Iraq are in grave danger of perishing.

Israelis can only agonize over the destiny of these unfortunates and their own inability to give them succor. They cannot help but wonder why the world community should spend hundreds of millions of dollars on, and show great sympathy for, the Palestinian refugees, and yet not find a way to aid these suffering people or, at least, express concern for their fate. When Israelis are admonished again and again to consider the misery of the displaced Arabs, they must only stand aghast at the blindness that refuses to see the injustice being perpetuated against their own kinsmen who would give their all for the privilege of becoming displaced persons.

The issue of the refugees cannot be divorced from the overall political state of affairs in the Middle East. The Arab nations today repeat their earlier mistakes and sins. They demand that Israel readmit all refugees. Yet their very next words and actions convince Israel that she would be foolhardy to take the risk. Their demand remains essentially unjust. As a recent American interdenominational statement says: "Israel would clearly be unable now to absorb anything approaching" 1.3 million Palestinians. Nor can she assume "the risk of subjecting her economy (and her polity) to intolerable strains . . . on the basis of an uncertain assumption" that most refugees would choose compensation instead of repatriation if given the choice.[14]

The Fedayeen *and the Nameless War*

The *fedayeen*[15] are among the grim reminders of an unyielding Arab determination to deny coexistence.

These men (some of them, Palestinian nationalists; some, Israeli-haters; others, mercenaries[16]) wreak vengeance upon Israel because she commits the sin of existing. They purposefully strike at civilians whenever possible in order to spread fear and to undermine morale. Explosive devices are hidden in a supermarket, a crowded city street, a university cafeteria, a bus station. Mines are planted on farmland and along roads. In the night, artillery barrages from across the lines strike people in their homes and force children in frontier *kibbutzim* and villages to sleep underground. From miles away pre-set rocket launchers aim at the heart of a city. Israeli citizens are not even free from terrorist savagery when traveling far from their country, and neither are citizens of other lands. Between July, 1968 and February, 1970 there were ten Arab terrorist attacks upon international aircraft and airline offices, inflicting fifty-one deaths.

No act is more satanic than the murder of children. On May 22, 1970 terrorists of the Popular Front for the Liberation of Palestine attacked—with American-made weapons—an Israeli school bus from less than twenty yards away. They murdered eight children and four adults, and wounded twenty others. It is murderers such as these who claim to represent "justice" for their people!

Arab practitioners of terrorism try to dress it in the cloak of a "liberation" movement, a just means employed by desperate men to rid "their homeland" of an "alien" people who "stole" it from them. This ploy has won the *fedayeen* widespread sympathy, despite their announced intention to massacre Jews, and their readiness to strike equally at tourists and travelers. The terrorists inject themselves with the drug of hatred[17] and fancy themselves expanding into "resistance" fighters. However, many members of World War II resistance groups are scandalized when today's *fedayeen* are identified with them. They point out that the resistance fought against armies, not civilians. They speak of Arab terrorism as cowardice.[18]

Despite the upsurge in terrorist acts since June, 1967, Israelis have not given way to the terror that gripped them in the mid-1950's. The people have not surrendered to mass hysteria; they stubbornly refuse to succumb to fear. Moreover, Israeli security forces have become increasingly effective in discovering terrorist cells and infiltrators. Constant alertness to potential dangers, and the use of specialized devices to detect bombs and mines have greatly reassured residents and visitors alike. (Most of the risks today are along the frontiers.) Yet, despite the fact that the ratio of infiltrators killed or captured is extremely high,[19] Israelis also are killed and wounded in the process. The cost of security is great.

Professor AlRoy reminds us that *fedayeen* warfare comes quite naturally to Arab society and therefore is easy to institute and maintain. It requires little organized discipline (even though abject submission to the group's code is part of the accepted pattern), and it appeals to a culture "based on the ideals of male vanity."[20] For some months after the Six Day War, terrorism was the one remaining means available to those Arabs who wanted to continue the fight. The *fedayeen* were given a free hand by Jordan, Egypt, and Syria,[21] as well as equipment and verbal and moral support. They were acclaimed as heroes, and temporarily assuaged Arab frustrations. They rapidly grew in numbers. (In March 1970 it was estimated that perhaps 50,000 were in varied stages of training or preparedness.[22])

The proclaimed strategy of the *fedayeen* is to provoke ever greater Israeli counterattacks in order to lose Israel international support, and to entice the Arab governments into ever more hostile acts against Israel. (The strategy has had marked success.) These men hope that Israel will eventually be goaded into extending herself beyond the erstwhile cease-fire lines, and that she can then be strangled by the large numbers of enemy Arabs inside her bounds. "As Napoleon and Hitler were drowned in the snows of Russia, the sands of our deserts will swallow the Israelis."[23] In more grandiose fashion, the terrorists occasionally dream that eventually their forces will be powerful enough to overwhelm an encircled Israel. By refusing to abandon the fight, they anticipate winning ever-wider international support for their claim that the State of Israel is an unjust intruder into the Middle East that must be eliminated.

Meanwhile, the terrorists hope to damage Israel's growth and economy by frightening off immigrants, investors, and tourists. (Their expectations have not been fulfilled; all three groups have steadily increased.) The deaths of Arab civilians through Israeli retaliation are, in the words of one terrorist leader, "exactly what we want . . . it angers the people and diminishes chances for a peaceful solution which we cannot accept."[24] On this view human life loses all sanctity.

Such an outlook is not alien to Arab governments, or even to many Arab people. A study committee from the American Professors for Peace in the Middle East was told by official Arab spokesmen that they were quite prepared to accept mass destruction of their population centers as long as they could do the same to Israel, because they could survive such devastation while Israel could not.[25] The present writers were assured by assorted persons—the manager of a hotel in Amman, an official of UNRWA in Jordan, a clergyman's wife in Beirut, et al.—that Arabs will "fight to the death" to destroy "those arrogant Jews."

Israel steadfastly refuses to engage in counter-terror, despite the fact that she could easily and effectively do so. Israelis long ago regretted and abandoned the limited terrorist measures they used. Most Jews *never* sanctioned terrorism.

Israelis express concern over the eventual effect the terrorist campaign may have upon their feelings toward Arabs. "How long shall we be able to maintain such an amount of self-restraint?" asks an Israeli friend who holds strong religious and humanitarian convictions. Following terrorist murders of two young teachers as they were carrying books into a newly renovated Arab school, our friend admits: "I myself begin to feel sometimes an alarming hardening in my attitudes. I am afraid that I shall become 'hawkish,' and that will be the real victory of Arab terrorism." (The contrast between this expression of moral concern and the Arabs' glorification of terrorist acts is most striking.)

When Arab governments enter into compacts with guerrilla and terrorist groups, these latter become, in effect, an arm of these governments. The governments must therefore be held entirely responsible for the behavior of the groups. International law is on the side of Israel's policy of self-protection. The governments involved are obligated to neutralize guerrillas and terrorists, and to prevent them from carrying out hostile actions from their territory, unless, of course, they themselves wish to be held responsible for waging open war. Failure to prevent these actions justifies the threatened or victimized nation in invading the neighboring country to disarm the bands. Attempts by the latter country's armed forces to protect or help the marauders make the government involved an accessory to the crime.[26]

If the world community does nothing to implement international law against terrorism, the mere fact of international law gives no solace to the victims. Ever since the early years, Israel has been forced into taking remedial measures of her own. Because it is impossible completely to stop terrorist depredations at cease-fire lines, Israel must strike at the sources inside the Arab countries. Yet there is great difficulty in permanently putting out of action small, mobile *fedayeen* units.

For her acts of self-defense Israel has been frequently condemned by self-righteous nations (including the United States) that are free of terrorist threats to their own citizens. These condemnations are not balanced by any denunciations of the terrorist organizations or the governments that support them. Thus have the terrorists been encouraged to engage in further acts of murder.

Israel has emphasized that at least since 1954 the Arab governments have been able to control the *fedayeen* whenever it suited their policies. The best evidence for this is the almost total lack of terrorist activity from 1957 until 1965, even though bands were trained and ready during that time. Even as late as the summer of 1969 King Hussein maintained a six-week truce arranged with Israel through American officials. Sabotage activity across the Jordan River ceased completely while the East Ghor irrigation canal was being repaired.[27] Once the work was completed, both terrorist and Jordanian army attacks resumed. It is evident that the Arab governments have wanted the *fedayeen* to inflict as much damage on Israel as possible while they themselves escape the consequences of all-out war. Arab leaders have acted to sustain and strengthen the terrorists' campaign against Israel. In March of 1969 President Nasser promised: "We will give our total support by every means to the Palestinian organizations." In November, 1969 he declared: "The commandos will stay until the Palestinian nation is established." In February, 1970 King Hussein affirmed: "Jordan backs the commando action with all its resources."

If the *fedayeen* become strong enough to dictate to, or overthrow, one or more of the Arab regimes, those governments will have brought about their own downfall by not subduing or disbanding the terrorist organizations in their formative stages.

Even as the terrorists have stepped up their activities against Israel and against Israeli firms and government offices abroad, the Arab states have waged their own nameless war without reprimand from the world of nations.[28]

Soon after the end of the Six Day War and continuing into 1970, the Soviet Union moved to replace and to multiply armaments for the Arabs. The United States and Great Britain supplied arms to Jordan.[29] Egypt and Jordan broke the cease-fire they agreed to in 1967—thus, in effect, reopening the war. These acts received no censure at all from the international community. Due to President Nasser's announcement in the Spring of 1969 of a new "war of attrition" against Israel, together with attacks from Jordan and Syria, Israel was once again forced to take measures to protect herself. Nasser's renewal of hostilities brought an alarming increase in Israeli fatalities in the Suez Canal area. By her destruction of Egyptian artillery through air strikes across the Canal in 1969 and 1970, Israel succeeded for a time in reducing these casualties. However, by May, 1970 the Soviet Union had supplied Egypt with SA-3 missiles, and had raised the numbers of Russian military personnel in Egypt to 16,000. Beginning in mid-April, 1970 Soviet pilots based on Egyptian airfields were carrying out combat missions against Israeli aircraft. Both these moves were offensive acts against Israel, since they enabled Egypt to escalate her war of attrition and markedly to increase Israeli casualties once again.

Despite Israel's acts of defense, the toll of deaths from terrorism and the nameless war continued to be exacted. From the cease-fire of 1967 to the end of January, 1970, Israel suffered 513 military fatalities and over 1,800 other casualties—more than half the number that had been sustained in the Six Day War. Comparable figures for the United States would come to 190,000. One Israeli soldier killed and 15 wounded in one day at the "cease-fire" lines corresponds to 82 American soldiers killed and 1,230 wounded. Twelve people killed and 52 injured by a terrorist-planted explosive in a Jerusalem market is the same as 984 killed and 4,264 hurt at a public gathering in Washington, D.C. In a nation of only 2.5 million people, every person must count. Quite apart from this, in the

Jewish tradition every human life is precious. Existence is a treasure. But freedom and safety are also treasures. How can all three be secured?

The nameless war has afflicted Israel with many more difficulties than it has the Arab countries. A highly organized and industrialized country such as Israel is far more disrupted by permanent mobilization of large segments of an already limited population than are less industrialized societies. To man her Defense Forces Israel must rely heavily on reservists, while the Arab states boast an abundance of unemployed or surplus labor that can be utilized in standing armies. Furthermore, Israel must pay for all her arms, which she has very great difficulty in obtaining. Her neighbors are subsidized by oil-rich Arab countries and by the U.S.S.R., and can readily purchase weapons from Western nations.

In the new-type war the problem of countermeasures is as delicate as it is acute. The challenge for Israel is to attain effective self-defense short of full-scale hostilities, and with as little endangering of Arab civilians as possible. Granted that such self-defense is entirely legitimate, nevertheless it is inevitable that innocent people will be harmed in the process. The deaths of Arab civilians are no less deplorable than the deaths of Israeli civilians, and the same is the case with soldiers. Yet we may not permit this judgment to obscure the essential moral distinction between a policy of deliberate terror against civilians and the accidental killing of civilians. Early in 1970, 80 Egyptian workers were killed and 50 wounded when, due to an electronic error, a metal works was bombed by Israeli aircraft instead of a military installation. Despite the great tragedy of this event, there is no comparison here with the calculated Arab murder of civilians.[30] For example, in April, 1970 on the Golan Heights, Syrian soldiers deliberately ambushed two automobiles filled with tourists from Israel, killing two persons and wounding five.

In the spring of 1970 Arab spokesmen took special refuge in one of their traditional propaganda devices: the charge that Israeli forces willfully attack and kill civilians. In point of fact, Israel does no such thing.[31] Imagine the hue and cry that would be raised around the world if Israel were to resort to *one* act of terrorism.

It is ironical that the Arabs' total rejection of Israel, their attempts to obliterate and isolate her have all combined to help create the Israel of today. Without Arab rejection of the U.N. Partition Plan and without the armed aggression that followed and was repeated throughout the years, Israel would be confined within a much smaller and much less viable territory. Without the economic boycott, Israel's agriculture in support of her people and her technology in competition for markets would quite possibly not have attained their present sophisticated levels. Without Arab persecutions, Israel's Jewish population would today be much smaller. Without the political boycott, Israel's program of international aid and development outside the Middle East would probably have been reduced due to the assistance she would have felt it a duty to render the Arab countries. Without international insecurity, her own diverse population would probably not have attained so great a degree of unity in so brief a time. Without the constant threat to her life, the ties that bind Israel and Diaspora Jewry would have been less strong.

Such are the strange ways in which the enemies of Israel have betrayed their own purposes and, ultimately, their own self-interest.

n Search of the Seventh Day

"The Israeli army of 1967 was the saddest victorious army in history" (Golda Meir). A paratrooper who fought in the Old City of Jerusalem, where Israeli roops were outnumbered three to one, confessed that he "came back without any joy. The victory didn't mean anything to me. None of us could even smile, hough the people were cheering us . . . the battle was: murder and fear, murder and fear. We had enough, enough. We had to do it. . . . But it must never, never happen again. If it doesn't then perhaps it will have been worthwhile. But only f it never happens again."[32]

Arabs in the administered areas were totally unnerved. Israel had to ensure he resumption of everyday activities at once in order to prevent hunger, disease, and disorder. Life could not wait for lengthy negotiations or high-level discussions. The Israeli Defense Forces tackled all kinds of nonmilitary tasks, especially helping farmers to save and market their crops. With Jordanian cooperation, commercial traffic between the West and East Banks was resumed. Work for the jobless received prompt attention. Medical and welfare personnel went to work to assist Arab colleagues who had stayed on.

Israel committed herself to establishing normal relations with the people, giving them opportunities not only to maintain their traditional ways of doing things as Arabs but also to better their social and economic situation. By Israeli standards such a policy is a moral requirement, not a matter of political expediency. Mayors, police, and teachers were asked to resume their duties. Owners of workshops and factories were encouraged to reopen. Israel provided a ready market for much of their output while advocating the maintenance of traditional outlets on the East Bank.

Agricultural programs that assist farmers to increase their yield and income are extremely important for the West Bank. More than 50 percent of the people there depend on agriculture. Previously we mentioned opportunities Arabs have for working in Israel, and the improvement in wage levels, as well as work projects Israel has established in the administered territories themselves. Vocational training has been instituted for both men and women. The Arab response to all these programs has been enthusiastic.

Rapidly rising bank deposits in the West Bank also reflect the success of these various efforts. That region's economy has not merely recovered; it has greatly improved. By early 1970 unemployment was reduced to as low as 6 percent. The Arabs of the territories are learning that coexistence is not only possible but can be profitable as well, however much they may resent the Israelis' presence.

The Defense Ministry's overall plan for the areas is one of security and "non-administration," which means that security forces are on hand but are little in evidence. The Arabs administer their own affairs as long as this does not jeopardize Israel's safety or disrupt their own life. For example, when teachers went on strike in September of 1967 because textbooks containing hard-core antisemitism and anti-Israel sentiments had been replaced, a town mayor asked a local Israeli commander to use a show of force to end the strike. The commander surprisingly refused, remarking that it was the parents' business whether they wanted their children educated or not. In a short time the schools reopened.[33]

The Israelis have used substantially less force in the West Bank than that resorted to by King Hussein. And the Gaza Strip, despite all its unrest, has been no more disturbed than it was under Egyptian occupation.

Since (at this writing) the future of the territories remains unsettled, Israel's policy has not been designed to tie them irrevocably to her either politically or economically, despite the increase of *de facto* integration. But the Israelis hope that the normal relations built up among people working together in various ways will persist whatever the future political arrangements, and that meanwhile Israel's search for concord will exert a redeeming influence.

As we read in the ancient tractate, *Ethics of the Fathers,* a hero is one who can conquer his impulses and turn his enemies into friends. These are the great challenges Israel faced in the past and still faces today. Israelis are more keenly aware of them than are any outsiders. Seldom in history do national desires coincide with what is morally right, especially in terms of a nation's own religious faith. But now in Israel that situation does exist. The national yearning for peace coincides with both the universal idea that peace is a positive good and the Jewish imperative for peace.

Israelis do not relish the role of an occupying power. They fear the corrupting influence that any occupation, no matter how humane, can visit upon vanquished and victor alike. They can sympathize with the feelings of the Arabs. Nevertheless, Israel has been forced to administer areas taken in a war she did not want. Were there any positive prospect that the withdrawal of Israel from the administered territories would produce an end to Arab belligerency and the recognition of Israel, she would be the first to take such action.

The evidence does not suggest that Israelis are becoming aggressive militarists, or arrogant conquerors. It was General (now Ambassador) Yitzhak Rabin who first designated the 1967 conflict as the "Six Day War" because the phrase implies that a seventh day is still to come, a day of rest and peace. Here is epitomized the outlook of Israelis. They possess a deep revulsion for war and all its horrible destruction, a feeling that is naturally strong among a people dedicated to brotherliness and constructive endeavors. In 1970 the popular "Song to Peace" could readily exalt love among men in contrast to military triumph. Significantly, the song was introduced to the Israeli public through Army entertainment groups performing before soldier audiences.

Israelis show great concern over the possible effects upon themselves of the constant need to be ready for war and of the repetition of war itself. Under such awful circumstances, can they maintain their moral values, their reverence for every human life? Will their children grow up to be cynics, or Arab-haters, or militarists? These are tormenting questions. Yet Israelis asking them inevitably return to the agonizing query: What is the alternative? Despite their commitment to peace, they simply cannot afford the luxury of pacifism. To do so would mean the sacrificial offering of all their people. Still, this does not relieve the individual of a feeling of aversion, and perhaps of shame or guilt, over what he has done and may have to do again. Golda Meir has said: "We can forgive the Arabs for killing our sons, but we shall never forgive them for forcing our sons to kill them."

The people again and again probe and dissect their emotional responses to war, terrorism, and continuing casualties. Generally speaking, Israelis have not succumbed to hatred for those who hate them. In one discussion a young *kibbutz* member said he found he could not hate the enemy, even in battle. "Actually it's an absurd situation: to be surrounded by enemies and at the same time not to hate them; to plead for peace, and at the same time to recognize that peace is unattainable in the foreseeable future."[34]

Another *kibbutz* member readily admitted to feeling hatred during the fighting of 1967, when friends were falling. He thought of what might happen to his people if the enemy got through. Yet when it was all over, he suddenly saw the Arab soldier as a man with a family just like himself.

Israelis felt an overwhelming response of pity for the dazed, numb fugitives on the road who were silently pleading for bread and water. A soldier wrote home: "This isn't something we've been trained to cope with. . . . It doesn't become us, we a people who ourselves trudged for years in long columns from town to town. . . ."[35]

At the same time, the Israelis are realists. They have felt Arab hatred in the administered areas, a hatred that defies good treatment by Israel during and since the War. An officer serving in the administered territories remarked: "You sense their hatred. It's like an emanation."[36] Will the daily, ordinary contacts in the West Bank, Jerusalem, Gaza, and Israel proper lessen the hatreds and erase the fears that decades of indoctrination have imbedded so deeply? There are some hopeful, if limited, signs.

After 1967 the Arab states refused every Israeli offer to negotiate questions of boundaries and refugees as a way of reaching a peaceable and honorable settlement for all parties. Will continuing Arab intransigence force Israel to make the present "cease-fire" lines into her virtual boundaries as the only available means of survival? Or will the stalemate be broken? In August 1970, Egypt, Jordan, and Israel accepted an American proposal for a three-month cease-fire and a renewal of the Jarring U.N. mission. The cease-fire was rejected by the Palestine Liberation Organization (embracing eleven terrorist groups), a rejection that was supported by Syria, Iraq, Algeria, and Red China. As this volume went to press, there appeared small hope of any kind of settlement.

During a recent meeting held in East Jerusalem with leading Israelis and outstanding Arabs of the West Bank, a Knesset member spoke for his kinsmen: "I think our Arab brothers here will have gained the conviction that the Israelis, coming as we do from different walks of life, from different backgrounds and from different political camps, all share a common desire, a deep desire for peace, and feel a natural affinity for the Arabs, despite all that has happened . . . [we] yearn for a peaceful, a warm relationship. . . ." Similar desires for friendship free of all hatred are expressed in discussions in every part of the Israeli community. "We Israelis don't want war. I don't think there's a nation on earth more eager for peace than we are. Not because we are more angelic. But because we are tired of war. . . ."[37]

The last statement is characteristically Israeli in its self-effacement. For all their seemingly hard-shelled and pragmatic approach, Israelis are highly imbued with idealism. Without it, they either would have given up the struggle by now, or would have succumbed to a thoroughgoing militarism. Neither has happened.

Israel continues to search for the seventh day.

PART III
The Affirmation of Israel

18. For Truth and Justice, I

WE HAVE CONSIDERED some of the main historical roots of Israel. We have surveyed certain salient features of the life of her people. The moral and religious affirmation of Israel—our concluding responsibility—involves bringing out some of the major implications of our study thus far, analyzing more intensively a number of issues that we have referred to only briefly, and offering some personal judgments on the challenge of Israel today.

Because the two final chapters in the division of the book just concluded deal with Israel and the Arab peoples, we shall for the sake of congruence discuss several crucial moral, political, and psychological issues that have an intimate bearing upon that subject, and then return more directly to the theme of Israel as such, with special attention to moral and theological questions.

Moral Obligation

Decision-making is a process of accumulating friends and enemies, at least where the issues in question are life-and-death concerns that arouse passion. Most readers of this volume will have already developed either hostility or benevolence (or ambivalence) in conjunction with the materials before them, and not least respecting the authors. Few will have felt pure indifference.

On the basis of our conversations and research in the Middle East and elsewhere, we have been forced to the sad conclusion as writers that quite literally, no way was in fact open for us to prepare a study that would be considered fair-minded by the opponents of Israel. When we started out, we had a few dreams of the alternative possibility. The awakening soon came. We have retained our present pessimistic viewpoint for some months, and have been given no reason to change. The basis for speaking this way is that the people we have in mind (many of them are Christians) are convinced that the reality and the cause of Israel are unjust—not merely particular acts of Israel, but *Israel* as such. No book we could write would change their belief that we too participate in the injustice. We have failed to find any way to be received by the enemies of Israel other than as adversaries. In sum, while we have sought to be fair, we know that those who oppose us will think of our work as unfair.

In the Arab-Israeli conflict, the moral issue for third parties is not primarily one of choosing the lesser of two evils. Nor is it a question of absolute right versus absolute wrong. Instead, the poignancy of the moral problem for any third party arises from the fact that one of the two main antagonists denies that the cause of the other antagonist can make any essential claim to justice. This state of affairs confronts us with a peculiar moral dilemma: We are forced into making a categorical moral judgment in a situation where there are, objectively speaking, only relative rights and wrongs. That is to say, we are compelled to choose between the parties *as if* one were entirely in the right and the other were entirely in the wrong, even though this is not the case. In other words, we are at once prevented from being neutral and from offering any sort of compromise. A nation either has a right to sovereign existence or it does not. There is no such thing as a partial right to exist.

Accordingly, we who believe that Israel does possess the right to exist are compelled *at this one crucial point* to oppose any Arab denial of that right, even though we find much that is of value in the Arab cause. Here we are in the same predicament as those who deny the right of Israel to exist as a sovereign nation, even though they may find something of value in the Israeli cause. We and our opponents are alike confronted by an either-or decision. However, there remains all the difference in the world between the two decisions. In committing themselves to the abolition of Israel, those in the one group maximize, in effect, violence and bloodshed. Those committed to the preservation of Israel work to minimize, and even to annul, violence and bloodshed. The one group is forced to favor war; the other group bespeaks negotiation and peace.

Even though the antagonist of Israel and the supporter of Israel may not be able to change the contrary party, both parties are bound by certain standards as they seek to influence the attitudes of still other people. The decision to support one side in an intergroup conflict is morally authentic only when it is sustained by painstaking and objective assessment of the truth—which means, unavoidably, the truth as an investigator apprehends it. Moral decisions invariably outrun the totality of facts, simply because all the facts are never "in." But to the extent that such decisions are grounded in convincing historical and contemporary evidence, to that extent they help to counteract the prejudices from which none of us is wholly free.

The canons of objectivity also require us to assess the reliability of different literature and other data, and to give greater weight to materials that, according to all available evidence, are the more trustworthy.

At the last, opposing parties must equally concede the possibility that they can be mistaken or even deceived in their overall commitments and judgments about truth. No absolute certainty is guaranteed in any of our moral decisions. Decision-making is a risk. Nevertheless, moral obligation demands that we take such risks, and stand up for what we believe to be true and good. The alternative would be irresponsibility.

Here is an account by a well-known Israeli writer:

During the Six-Day War, in June 1967, the battalion I serve in was ordered to supervise the demolition of four Arab villages. I considered it my duty to desert from my unit, to write a report of this action, and to send the copies to the General Staff of the Army, to members of the Government and to Knesset members. This report has been translated and circulated to the world as a proof of Israel's crimes.

But permit me to conclude the story. The action I undertook was in flagrant violation of any military law. According to military regulations I should have been court-martialed. . . .

After returning to my unit, I was ordered to present myself—I, a private in rank—before the General commanding all the divisions on that front. He told me that he had read my report and considered it his duty to inform me that what had occurred was a regrettable error which will not recur.

Deep in my heart I disbelieved his statement that this was only a mistake. I was convinced that whoever ordered such an action did not expect such resistance from within—the men of my battalion refused to carry out the order—and was alarmed at the impression such an action might create abroad. But I was glad that he found it necessary to announce that this was only an error. I asked him how he intends to ensure that the "error" will never recur. On the spot he signed an order permitting me free movement in all occupied territories so that I could see with my own eyes that such an action had not recurred.

But since then, in all the peace-papers in the world, my report about the destruction of villages is being reprinted over and over again, as if it happened only yesterday, as if it happened again and again, as if it is happening all the time. And this is a lie. It is like writing that witches have been burnt at the stake in England—omitting the date.

I hereby request all those who believed me when I reported a criminal act, to believe me now, too. And those who do not believe me now, I hereby request to disbelieve my former report too, and not to believe me selectively, according to their convenience. I should also add that the town of Kalkiliya, which began to be demolished during the writing of my report, is now in the process of being rebuilt, after the expelled inhabitants have been brought back.[1]

In the final resort we have to ask ourselves: Who is behaving humanely? And whom does experience lead us to trust?

Immorality, Psychopathology, Sacrilege

The principles suggested in the previous section may be applied more concretely and intensively to wider moral questions of Arab-Israeli relationships.

What are investigators to do if an honest study of the evidence leads them to adjudge that Arab charges against Israel tend to contain many falsehoods, while Israeli counterclaims do not? They hardly do their job responsibly if they attribute equal credence to both sides. Our own experience, and it is not inconsiderable, has taught us that Israeli testimony is so much more trustworthy than Arab testimony that comparisons are very often ludicrous.

As a matter of fact, Israel's enemies resort to the Lie quite unreservedly and unhesitatingly. It is employed as a fundamental instrument of national policy. This practice is not an accident in cases where hatred is also central to policy. Hatred is itself "the expression of a falsification, of a lie" resorted to as a means of covering up awareness of one's own guilt.[2]

It was widely alleged in the Arab press that the assassination of Senator Robert Kennedy was a secret Zionist plot to arouse hostility toward Arabs. In complete opposition to this charge, the inhabitants of Sirhan Sirhan's birth-place in Jordan, in a telegram to King Hussein appealing to him to intercede for the condemned man, said that Sirhan "has done his best to serve the Arab cause and to turn his trial into a trial of Zionism."[3] At the same time these people were being quite representative of Arab psychopathology concerning the Jews and Israel: Anyone who expresses any sympathy for the Israelis is as bad as the Jews, even if he is not himself Jewish. He may lose the right to live.[4]

Of great aid to Arab governments in their use of falsehood is the subjection of communications media to official control. Thus, Radio Cairo told the Egyptian people on July 6, 1969 that "the Israeli authorities have today cut off all water supplies to the Arab residents of Jerusalem in retribution for the Security Council Resolution of July 3 [concerning Jerusalem]. The aim is to compel the thirsty people to flee the City." How could the ordinary Egyptain know that this was a complete lie? It is a notorious fact that whenever Middle Eastern Arabs have the competence or incentive to seek to ascertain what is actually going on in the world they shut off local propaganda channels and turn to Israeli and other sources that can be trusted. Yet the tragedy remains that in most Arab countries, where illiteracy, ignorance, and superstition are regnant, most people are simply barred from finding out the truth about Israel.

Americans may tend to assume that when someone like President Nasser or King Hussein is interviewed in such publications as *The New York Times, Time,* and *Newsweek,* the statements that are made somehow constitute information that becomes available to the Arab populace, or indeed that those interviewed are somehow speaking truthfully or representing their people. These are gratuitous assumptions. The text of every Nasser interview is subjected to intensive editing and censorship before being released to the Egyptian press. Thus, there is double lying: Foreigners are misled into thinking, or at least hoping, that Egypt may have become a little reasonable; and the Egyptian public is given doctored versions. In the same way, King Hussein's speeches and statements during his visit to the United States in 1969 were changed and slanted for home consumption.

After the Six Day War, Nasser and Hussein were forced to admit to the outside world that their conspiracy charging that the British and American air forces took part in the conflict was a complete fabrication.[5] (This episode is particularly revealing in view of the fact that Hussein has succeeded in devising a reputation for courage and veracity in Western circles.) Ominously, inside Egypt and much of the Arab and Communist world, the people have never been told the truth. There is in fact a growing Arab literature to "prove" the Anglo-American intervention, even to the extent presently of claiming that "thousands of American and other troops" fought for Israel. Not only are Egyptians given to understand that the real victors in the War were the United States and Great Britain rather than Israel, but in October, 1969 they were fed the new lie that Americans were piloting the Israeli planes that were attacking Egyptian forces along the Canal.

Such charges have caused broken diplomatic relations and widespread hostility to the United States. Here is the real evil in such organized lying: it prevents any possibility of mutual understanding. It only guarantees a climate of hatred, suspicion, and strife.

One of the most infamous and incredible tales of recent years grew out of a fire in the Mosque of el-Aqsa in the Old City of Jerusalem on August 21, 1969. We devote extra space to this episode because of its twofold significance. On the one hand, the fire represented a frightening convergence of immorality and psychopathology among the foes of Israel. On the other hand, it embodied the prostitution of religion to extra-religious purposes.

The Jordanian state radio and television declared that "the Government of Israel held a special session and after detailed discussion decided to burn down the el-Aqsa Mosque." The Foreign Minister of Jordan cabled the President of the U.N. Security Council that Israel was guilty of the "horror crime" of starting the fire. The Premier of Lebanon spoke of putting an end "to this fiction of a state with its barbaric methods." Syria announced that "the fire was planned by the occupation authorities who aim to wipe out Arab sites in order to make Jerusalem a wholly Jewish city." Even the King of Morocco saw in the fire "Israel's barbarity." Radio Cairo found a chance to put the responsibility on the United States because she had failed to prevent "Israel's previous crimes against the Arabs."

All these accusers fell into a single pattern of fantasy in a way directly opposite to the facts of the el-Aqsa fire. In truth, Israeli had nothing to do with the fire, and neither did a single Israeli. Thanks to prompt and effective work by Arab and Jewish fire brigades, the actual blaze was confined to the roof and an outside wall. The main structure of the huge Mosque, including its famed silver dome, was preserved. Normal prayers and services were quickly resumed. Regrettably, a valuable and beautiful twelfth-century pulpit was ruined, and a number of costly rugs were badly damaged.

Fantastically, a mob of Arabs beat and stoned the firefighters and prevented them from putting out the blaze more rapidly,[6] thus helping to make hollow any claim that these people had a pious interest in preserving a holy place. Evidently, they would have preferred to see it burn to the ground than permit it to be saved by Israelis. In this connection, it is worth noting that one of the heinous charges leveled against Israel was that she was preparing the way to build the Third Temple on this site. Apart from the truth that the Israelis have no wish to do any such thing—the most Orthodox among them insist that there are absolute objections, grounded in the Halachah, to reconstituting the Temple and its rituals—the Arabs who sought to fight off the firemen almost seemed to be saying, "You must not interfere with the Israeli plot."

There were immediate and somber calls by the leaders of the Arab world for Arab and Islamic "summit conferences" to deal with this "monstrous" manifestation of Jewish "evil." Were it not for the diabolical character of these summonses, they—together with all the accusations—could have been put down as an exercise in high or pitiful comedy (depending upon one's theory of comedy). Unhappily, ludicrous events such as these are closely tied to tragedy. Ultimately speaking, comedy is not very funny.

Almost unnoticed in the uproar, and in fact vehemently denied or at least labeled as irrelevant by Arabs with eyes tightly shut to reality, was the confession by an itinerant Australian Christian of having set the fire. An independent commission of inquiry immediately established by Israel, and including distinguished Arabs, was made slightly superfluous by the efficiency of the authorities in apprehending the culprit.

It is important to remember that the administration and security of the Mosque is the direct responsibility of the official Muslim authority, the WAQF Organization, reflecting a general policy that antedated 1967. As we have seen, with respect to the holy places Israel provides full freedom to, and supervision by, the various religious communities. Thus, any culpability beyond that of the arsonist would fall upon the Muslim overseers. (The commission of inquiry concluded that there had been negligence on the part of the guards and administrators of the Mosque.[7]) The Government of Israel had previously offered to place security police in the vicinity of the Mosque, but the WAQF rejected the offer. Nevertheless, immediately after the fire the Government volunteered full technical and material assistance in making repairs.

Among the noteworthy aspects of the case, and one of its few sanguine elements, was the interest in justice and truth shown by Muslim authorities in Israel proper, and the contrast between their spirit of cooperativeness and concern, and the behavior of other Arabs. Entirely on their own volition, Muslim trustees of WAQF properties in several Israeli cities denounced the attempt to blame Israel for the blaze, and spoke disparagingly of "the rumors spread by Arab countries." It is also significant that a Muslim guard at the Mosque and other members of the Muslim community in the Old City supplied the Israeli police with the fundamental information that helped in the apprehension of the arsonist.[8]

This event is highly representative of the Arab fantasy-world and of the kind of behavior that Arabs visit again and again upon the people of Israel—and inflict upon themselves, to their own grave spiritual and moral hurt. Needless to say, the leadership of the Arab states has done absolutely nothing to correct the original charges against Israel or to alter the false claims impressed upon the masses.

The reaction to the el-Aqsa fire constituted, in addition, a horrendous example of the traditional device of inflaming religious passions and hatreds for political and antisemitic ends. We alluded in Chapter 4 to the use of this weapon in the Arab riots and massacres of Jews in 1929.

With the fire of 1969, there were immediate calls for a *jihad* (holy war) against Israel. King Feisal of Saudi Arabia issued such a summons to the world's six hundred million Muslims. In a message to the armed forces of *all* Arab countries, President Nasser declared that it was now their sacred duty to go to war against Israel. He said: "In the coming battle, the Arab soldiers will not be soldiers of the Arab nations alone but soldiers of God and protectors of His religions, houses of worship and holy books." Then Nasser continued: "We have left no stone unturned [in the search for peace], but *the enemy of God* and our enemy has foiled all efforts and obstructed all means, *revealing to the world his hidden nature and designs.*"[9]

Nasser's use of the plural terms, "religions" and "holy books," is most revealing. Muslim calls to holy wars, of which there have been very many, are by all traditional rights supposed to concentrate upon the threat to the "one true faith" of Islam. Clearly, Nasser was here resorting to a time-dishonored antisemitic nstrument employed by non-Christians: to seek to inflame the Christian world against Jews.

The same device was given even more transparent form in the demagoguery of the terrorist Palestine Liberation Organization: "What are you doing while the Mosque burns? Tomorrow it will be the Church of the Holy Sepulcher and the Church of the Nativity."

As Abba Eban declared, the el-Aqsa fire entailed two crimes: the simple crime of an individual, and an infinitely more serious international crime committed by Arab governments and spokesmen, who sought "to extract political advantage by a campaign with very few parallels in the history of our age." We witnessed "very deep, submerged instincts bursting out of the depths of history." We witnessed as well President Nasser's " 'enlightened' reaction that the only answer is force, bloodshed and bombardment, in his words, in order to purify the land of Israel." Eban added: "You don't need much research to find out where that particular language comes from."[10]

It is sad that these words had to be uttered by an Israeli official. By their silence, world leaders allowed the purveyors of lying and hatred to hold center stage.

Significantly, there had been fires in the Church of the Holy Sepulcher in 1949 and in the Mosque of el-Aqsa in 1964. These conflagrations were accepted by the Arab world without any disturbance or outcry for a simple reason: the Old City was then under Arab control.

The piety of the Muslim Arab leaders was conquered by their obsessional hatred of Israel. In non-Arab Islamic countries, as elsewhere in the world and particularly in Israel, the concern and regret were concentrated on the damage to the Mosque, and many offers of aid were forthcoming. By contrast, the Muslim Arab leaders pounced with glee on the news of the damage to their "supposedly treasured holy site."[11]

With the el-Aqsa fire, the cesspool of contemporary Arab antisemitism overflowed. The identical methods were utilized that have characterized "classical" antisemitism for centuries, and that included, ultimately, the charge of a "Jewish conspiracy" and the interchanging of truth and falsehood. In the episode of el-Aqsa there was, finally, a reincarnation of traditional religious antisemitism: the identification of Jews as enemies of God. (We return to this matter of antisemitism in Chapter 20.)

Politicide and Genocide

A common bias is the assumption that the Middle East has one problem: Israel. As a matter of fact, inter-Arab conflicts and the conflicts of Arabs with other non-Jewish minorities and the wider world have been easily as intense as, and far more prolonged than, the Arab-Israeli struggle. It has been well said that "the Arab world's internal problems are so mountainous that its leaders can only scream about the enemy outside." The entire region is still racked by political instability and rivalries, the exploitation of the poor, the perpetuation of human misery, and social and economic backwardness. Rather than typifying these evils, Israel provides answers to them. And through the Arabs' shared enmity toward her, she fills the strange and thankless role of helping to prevent these people from fighting with and destroying one another. (Any attempt by one or more of the Arab nations to break this united hostility can easily end the inter-Arab truce.)

In contrast to the above complexities, the Arab-Israeli problem is morally simple—not, obviously, in the sense of being soluble (it may well be the opposite of that) but in the sense that it focuses in a single moral issue: Ought the Arab world be enabled to plan and to carry out politicide against Israel?

Is politicide a lesser crime than genocide? Politicide is the destruction of a state and its people; genocide is the destruction of a *laos,* a people, without special attention to statehood. Qualitatively speaking, politicide *is* genocide: the persecution and/or murder of all "available" persons. The only variation is that in politicide the carrying out of total destruction may be inhibited by certain factors beyond the annihilators' control such as national boundaries or the possibility of intervention by third parties. In contrast, "ideal" genocide is the type that can be visited upon a defenseless *laos* trapped within the boundaries of the destroyers' sovereign state, or within a conquered state or states, as happened to Jews and Gypsies under the Nazis. The genocidal representatives are then enabled to consummate their task of total annihilation smoothly and without interference. Death is one and the same phenomenon, whether we speak of politicide or of genocide. (Genocide need not occur overnight or even within a brief span of years. It can be a drawn-out process, as exemplified in the ongoing persecution of Jews in the Soviet Union and a number of Arab countries.)

It is often alleged that Arab promises to obliterate Israel are "exaggerations." People who react in this idealistic way tend to fit one or another of the following categories: those who cannot bear the reality of human sin in all its ugliness and, accordingly, are unable to face up to the inevitable consequence of the Arab threat; those who secretly desire Israel's death, and employ as a trick the protestation that this will not really happen; and those who inhabit a psychological and moral world so far removed from the Middle East that they lack any real comprehension of the historical background and the actual state of affairs there today.

The truth of the matter is quite different. Adolf Hitler never exaggerated and never kept silent concerning his intentions. Neither do the present heirs of his gospel. The very words they use comprise a fearsome repetition of history. Countless Arabs have proclaimed countless times that Israel is "a cancerous growth" within "their" body. The growth must be cut away before it brings death to the whole Arab world. And these are not just words. Year upon year, Arab deeds have been suited to the threats. Threat and deed have vied in their viciousness. Had the Israelis ever fallen prey to the myth that Arabs did not mean what they said, the entire country of Israel would have long since become a huge death camp. There would be no Jewish refugee camps.

On June 5, 1967 Radio Cairo besought the Arab armies: "Destroy, ruin, liberate. Woe to Israel, your hour has arrived . . . this is your end. . . . We shall drive out of existence the shame of Zionism. . . . There is no room for Israel in Palestine. This is your responsibility, Arab soldiers! Israel, taste death!" At the same time, in a military order King Hussein said to his men: "Go out and kill Jews. Kill them wherever you find them. Kill them with your nails and with your teeth."

The military success of Israel in 1967 was nothing more than an averted pogrom, a pogrom that would have been exceeded in its vastness only by the Nazi inferno. This is what accounts for the fact that the victory produced only fleeting elation in Israel. On the Arab side, fury against Israel increased enormously after 1967, due to the "shame" of a defeat instead of a triumph that was to have solved "the problem of the Jews" for all time.

The campaign for exterminating Israel has utilized a familiar double strategy: intensification of military and terrorist actions, and political and propaganda efforts at the international level. The first involves what President Nasser has identified as the *war of attrition* against Israel, gradually to wear down her will to resist and her defenses through unrelenting terrorism, bombardments, and casualties Israel cannot bear forever. Al Fatah leader Yasser Arafat has called the struggle "the war of the long breath." After visiting the United States in April of 1969, Jordan's King Hussein assured Arab terrorists that they are a completely legitimate movement, possessing the right to throw off the Jewish "aggression" that robbed them of their "land, resources, and property."[12] In early September of 1969 a "summit meeting" involving Egypt, Jordan, Syria, Iraq, and the Sudan once again called upon all Arab states to prepare for the coming battle with Israel. Two months later President Nasser proclaimed that a path of "fire and blood" and "the battle of destiny" will be the inevitable culmination.[13]

To entertain the idea of a military defeat of Israel followed by occupation and then peace terms for the nation is to fall into utopian dreams. No such luxury would ever be allowed to Israel. The Israelis are given only two alternatives: independent survival, or total destruction.

The political and propaganda dimensions of recent Arab strategy to ensure the final dismemberment of Israel have entailed keeping at the fore a demand for Israeli withdrawal from "occupied Arab lands." The Arab stratagem has involved dropping a hint now and then that once Israeli withdrawal were accomplished, "concessions" just might be forthcoming, and the way opened to nonbelligerency.

Such a diversionary tactic is a prescription not for peace, but for renewal of war and slaughter. Nonbelligerency is not peace. Until the present time, no major Arab leader in the Middle East has taken a firm stand on behalf of final peace with Israel. There is no reliable evidence as yet that the Israeli-administered areas, once restored to Arab control, would become anything but launching pads for an intensified onslaught upon Israel. As a matter of fact, this position was exemplified by President Nasser on February 1, 1969: "There is one cardinal truth about the Middle East situation—*the need to restore every last step of the sanctified soil.*"[14]

On March 27, 1969 Nasser asserted: "The Palestinian soil is not subject for discussion. . . . We have declared our principles—no negotiations, no peace, *no relinquishing one inch of Arab land,* and no bargaining over Palestinian rights."[15] On February 9, 1970 the Cairo Conference of Arab states issued a communiqué containing these words: "Israel has violated the whole of Palestine."

Arab policy toward Israel has been a politicidal one ever since the early days. Its consistent foundation has been the total extinction of Israel. The point of view as late as mid-1970 was identical with Nasser's avowal of May 29, 1967:

"There is no doubt that God will help us and enable us to return the situation to what it was *before 1948*" (italics added). This same position had already been expressed by an Egyptian Foreign Minister in 1954: "The truth is that we will by no means be satisfied by the implementation of the United Nations Resolutions. . . . The Arab peoples . . . will not be satisfied by anything less than the obliteration of Israel from the map of the Middle East."[16]

The hope of politicide-genocide as the deserved fate of the Jews of Israel is most conspicuously found today in the so-called liberation organizations. Those in this camp sometimes resort to inoffensive language in order to camouflage their real designs. They speak of establishing a new "pluralist, non-sectarian, democratic state" for Arabs and Jews in replacement of Israel. Israel is to be "dezionized" for the "benefit" of all, including Jews. It is significant that within the past three years, apostles of "dezionization" have become much less pleasant-sounding and much more radical. This development is typified in the revised Palestinian National Covenant adopted at the fourth meeting of the 100-member Palestinian National Council in Cairo, July 10–17, 1968. The Council is comprised of representatives of almost all Palestinian "resistance" groups existing within Arab countries. It is at present dominated by Al Fatah. In significant contrast to the 1964 Covenant, which implied that Jews living in Palestine from before 1947 would be allowed to stay, the newer Covenant emphasizes that only Jews "living permanently in Palestine" before "the beginning of the Zionist invasion" would be permitted to remain. At the same meeting the Council adopted resolutions explicitly stating that the "Zionist invasion" refers to the date of the Balfour Declaration: 1917. According to the Covenant, the way that "dezionization" is to be consummated is by war: "Armed struggle is the only way to liberate Palestine. . . ."

The vast majority of Jews in Israel were either born after 1917 or came there after that date. Only a tiny minority would be allowed to remain, while almost everyone (assuming that any would still be alive) would have to leave. But, of course, very few would have anywhere to go. The story of the Nazi period would be repeated. The "dezionization of Israel" is a euphemism for the annihilation of most of the 2.5 million Jews of Israel.[17] The annihilationists know as well as anyone that the Jews will resist to the death any and every attempt to obliterate the State of Israel. The one effective protection an oppressed people can have against those who would destroy them is sovereignty and the political and military power that accompanies sovereignty. The only way to translate "dezionization" and the "liberation of Palestine" is: death to the Jews. (Since the meeting reported above, Yasser Arafat has come increasingly under the influence of Maoism. Communist China has never acknowledged the reality of Israel but it accepts a diplomatic envoy from Al Fatah. At this writing, Arafat has ceased all mention of a pluralist Arab-Jewish state.[18])

Even where the advocacy of "dezionization" contains an element of sincerity, it remains fraught with irony. "Dezionization" is no more than a guarantee of war and bloodshed, and of the hostilities and barriers among peoples that war creates. The promise of a more open society within erstwhile Palestine (especially the Arab part) cannot be fulfilled until the Arab peoples are ready to recognize by deeds the legitimacy of Israel's existence.

In its essence, the Arab-Israeli conflict has little to do with boundary lines or with any similar, tangible question. There is only one issue: As long as Israel occupies *any* "sacred" Palestinian soil, to the Arabs she bears infinite "guilt." Israel could partially withdraw from the areas administered at present, she could withdraw to the pre-1967 armistice lines, she could withdraw to the 1947 partition lines, she could withdraw to the boundaries proposed in the Peel Report, and she could withdraw to a single beachhead on the Mediterranean Sea. In each and every case she would remain as "guilty" as she is now. No matter how far she shrank, this would make no difference in the eyes of her enemies—until and unless she shrank out of existence.

Whenever outsiders today tolerate or sanction the charge that the reestablishing of the State of Israel constituted a basic injustice, they help to compound immorality by giving aid and comfort to those who are dedicated to committing politicide against Israel.

Thus are we brought back to the issue of moral neutrality. If party A intends to destroy party B, the option of neutrality is closed to party C. He either consents to the intended destruction or he opposes it. Any third choice is not open to him. However, this need not mean that he is opposing the welfare of party A. Genuine concern for the moral and spiritual well-being of Arabs requires that we do whatever we can to turn them away from politicide.

19. For Truth and Justice, II

The Sin of Double Standards

A major impetus that has enabled the Arab states to persevere in their political campaign against Israel has been the indifference and immorality of much of the world, especially its repeated application of one set of moral standards to Israelis and a quite different set to Arabs.

Chief among the transgressors has been the United Nations. One influential case of U.N. bias is the acclaimed Security Council Resolution of November 22, 1967. Bernard Lewis points out that while the Resolution requires concessions from both sides, it does so in a one-sided and unfair way. The concession demanded of Israel is territorial and strategic. Should the necessity of reversing the concession arise, this could only be accomplished by a resort to force (with the inevitable charges that would be forthcoming of Israeli "aggression"). By contrast, the concession (reputedly) demanded of the Arabs is strictly diplomatic: it can be "reversed by a simple declaration."[1]

We are obliged to point out that the only real concession explicitly demanded of any party is the one applied to Israel ("withdrawal of Israeli armed forces from territories of recent conflict"). Only Israel is mentioned by name. Unbelievably, no tangible concession is in fact required of the Arabs, i.e., of *specific* Arab nations. The device used is the omitting of any reference to a single Arab state by name. Apart from the insistent identification of Israel, resort is made to the artful abstraction "Middle East." In a word, everyone's duty readily becomes no one's duty. Only Israel is seized by a concrete duty. The all-important consideration to remember here is that for the Arabs, Israel is not a genuine state. It is a bastard pretender born of an infamous union of Jewish evil and Western sin. Accordingly, the Arab nations have an easy escape from the wording, "respect for and acknowledgment of the sovereignty, territorial integrity and political independence of every state in the area. . . ." Since when does Israel qualify as a state?

204

The foregoing analysis helps to explain how several Arab governments have been able to contend that they fully accept the U.N. Resolution, and at the same time have shown no intention of permitting the document to alter their position respecting Israel.

In the councils of the United Nations a certain pattern of behavior became conspicuous during 1969: An Arab country, through either terrorist or regular military forces would engage in an unprovoked raid, or series of raids, upon an Israeli community. Israel would act to defend her people by firing upon or bombing terrorist or military bases. One or another Arab state (usually Jordan, Lebanon, or Syria) would call for an "urgent" meeting of the U.N. Security Council, which would then dutifully move to condemn Israel for her "aggression." For example, 21 times during a 30-day period in July-August, 1969 terrorist bands based in Lebanon shelled Israeli border settlements and crossed the armistice line to plant mines. Israeli planes responded by attacking seven terrorist encampments. The Council unanimously—which means with American complicity—then condemned Israel for her "premeditated air attack" upon Lebanese villages.

One cannot escape the uneasy feeling of having been carried away to a world of make-believe: the assaults upon Israel are waved off the stage of history, as though by some master magician. The real aggressors are safe from decisive rebukes. At the most, vague phrasings have been included suggesting that it would be well if "all parties" were to behave themselves. The resolution referred to above only "deplored" other "violent incidents" in violation of the cease-fire, and, significantly, mentioned no names. Neither was there as much as a hint that these Lebanese villages had been converted into terrorist bases for launching raids against Israel. It is noteworthy that, at Arab insistence, any direct or explicit call by the Security Council to all parties to honor the cease-fire was excluded.[2]

In another flagrant application of a double standard, the Security Council ignored an attempt at Athens by terrorists who had come from Lebanon to kill all the occupants of an El Al airliner. (The terrorists succeeded in murdering one Israeli.) Yet when, in an effort to demonstrate to the Lebanese Government that failure to restrain terrorism would not go unpunished, Israel destroyed a number of empty aircraft at Beirut in December of 1968, the Security Council unanimously condemned her. Thus were we instructed by an international body reputedly devoted to justice, as well as by representatives of the United States, that a human life is of less value than material objects—at least when it is a Jewish life. Ambassador Tekoah of Israel spoke for all Israelis in identifying the U.N. censure as proof of "the moral, political and juridical bankruptcy of the Council regarding the Middle East situation."[3]

One consequence of this utilization of a double standard was encouragement of greater and greater aggression. Thus, in a single week in December, 1969 there were 120 attacks from Jordan upon Israeli villages.

The same dreary pattern continued into the following year. For example, following a series of intensive attacks from Lebanon in April and May of 1970, causing a number of deaths, Israel struck back in force at the terrorist bases. On May 12, in an "emergency" meeting, the U.N. Security Council unanimously demanded the withdrawal of Israeli forces, but, in complete accordance with that body's past record, it refused to censure those responsible for the reign of terror from Lebanon. On May 19 the Council voted 11-0, with four abstentions, to "condemn" Israel for the raid, after having defeated an effort to refer to terrorist provocations in the resolution. Thus, incredibly, the Council continued to act as if the terrorists did not exist, and thereby tried to deny Israel the right to protect her people.

As a Mauldin cartoon portrays the matter, an Israeli soldier stands before the bar of the United Nations and is admonished, "You must give up this vicious habit of committing self-defense."

Secretary-General U Thant's bias against Israel has been saddening. An example in 1969 was Thant's implied equating of Israeli and Egyptian responsibility for cease-fire violations and for attacks on U.N. observers at the Suez Canal, in clear contradiction of the unimpeachable evidence of Egypt's guilt as testified to by the observers themselves. As Ya'acov Ben-Israel writes, while the Israelis have learned to live with Thant's "particular notion of even-handedness," even Israeli patience has its limits. On this specific occasion, Israel's U.N. Mission protested Thant's behavior.[4]

The U.N. has not been the only practitioner of double standards respecting Israel. Elements in the Christian church have vied for the same dubious honor. A sorry case of this occurred in conjunction with Israel's raid on the Beirut Airport mentioned above. So unjust was the response in official Christian circles that the American Jewish Congress was moved to issue the following statement, through President Arthur J. Lelyveld:

> The apparently automatic reaction by the Christian world to violence against Israel, including the murder of innocent women and children, is one of disregard and silence.
>
> So it was in June of 1967 when the Arab world mobilized to fulfill its boast that it would butcher the people of Israel. So it was last month when a bomb exploded in a Jerusalem marketplace and killed a number of Israel's citizens. So it was a few weeks ago when Arab terrorists in Athens, avowedly bent upon the destruction of a planeload of passengers aboard an Israeli civil aircraft, succeeded in killing one person and wounding two others.
>
> But this indifference is dramatically transformed into deep concern and active sympathy when Arab property is damaged or Arab prestige impaired. So it has been on each occasion when Israel has sought to defend its citizens and its territory from repeated terrorist incursion. So it was on that day when Israel destroyed 13 Arab-owned aircraft at the Beirut airport, with meticulous care to avoid taking any life or inflicting any injury.
>
> Suddenly the palpable silence that had surrounded the murder in Athens was broken. Highminded declarations of Christian morality began to issue from all sides. In Rome, the Pope found occasion to express sympathy to the President of Lebanon while referring curiously to Israel as "Palestine."[5] In our own country, the president of the National Council of Churches went out of his way to commend Administration policy "especially for Ambassador Wiggins' reported condemnation of the Israeli attack on the Beirut airport."[6]
>
> Not a word about Athens. Not a hint about the losses of life in Israel. Not a thought about the unremitting determination of the Arab nations, broadcast daily over their State radios and drummed repeatedly into the Arab mind, that Israel must be destroyed.

This lack of balance, this moral fuzziness is the inevitable result of turning a face to the Middle East that is blind in one eye and deaf in one ear.

Men of all religious beliefs equally deplore violence and the taking of human life. But ultimate moral blame belongs on the heads of those who make such actions inescapable and unavoidable. Every one of the eruptions in the Middle East is attributable directly to the obsessive refusal of the Arab governments to consider peace on any terms except the demise of Israel.

We respectfully suggest that our Christian friends address themselves to this root cause of the Middle East tragedy.[7]

A more recent manifestation of adherence to a double standard on the part of a religious body is "An Approach to Peace in the Middle East," a study document issued on April 25, 1970 through the American Friends Service Committee, in conjunction with Quakers from other countries. The Quaker statement strongly supports the U.N. Resolution of November, 1967. The Friends demand that, on the basis of *the manner of her creation in the Middle East,* Israel take the "first step" toward peace by pledging to withdraw from "occupied" Arab territories. By contrast, the Quakers only ask the Arabs to respond to the Israeli move by declaring their acceptance of Israel's existence and "a willingness to live, *on however distant terms,* in a condition of non-belligerency with Israel" (our italics). The framers of the Quaker document are under the illusion that the Arab nations are prepared to make peace with Israel, a claim that is highly questionable. Unfortunately, the Arabs are not Quakers.

There is a recurring pattern in pronouncements such as the one by the Friends: By assigning an inferior degree of legitimacy to Israel ("the manner of her creation in the Middle East") in contrast to other states (in point of truth such nations as Jordan and Lebanon were "created" in very similar ways),[8] church spokesmen and others fancy that they have a right to tell Israel to *do* something, while they need only advise the Arab states to *say* something. Specifically, Israel is told to engage in an act that would leave her no less vulnerable to aggression than she was in 1967, and with no allowance at all for the suffering and loss of lives she sustained as the direct consequence of that vulnerability. All the Arabs are asked is to offer promises—which, as in the past, can be easily negated whenever the time seems advantageous.

In the same vein, the Quaker document proposes, fully and carefully, ways for repatriating or compensating all Arab refugees since 1947, in accordance with U.N. resolutions, but then it makes only passing reference to "attention" to be given Jewish refugees.[9]

The fact that Arab demands for the withdrawal of Israeli forces have been echoed again and again within pronouncements by the U.N., by American Church bodies,[10] and by various governments provides Arab aims with witting or unwitting support. If aggressor nations are to be handed back land lost in fighting, all aggressors are thereby encouraged. They receive the assurance that they need run no territorial risks.

There could not be a much lower form of immorality than the way Israel was forced into continuing military acts as the only possible means of defending herself, and was then charged with being guilty of "aggression" and "expansionism."

It is almost as though the ulterior purpose of shared world policy has been to marshal all available energy to turn the Israelis into cruel people, into unqualified chauvinists, so that their detractors may return to the scene of what is in fact their own crime, and gloat: "We told you so!"

Many people shamefully avoid the question of exactly what Israel is supposed to do. Evidently, she is expected to surrender and die. Yet who dares to apply that reasoning to other countries or to their own?

Condemnations of Israel's conduct have stood in woeful contrast to the atmosphere of forgiveness and toleration of the Arabs' illegal and vicious acts, including terrorism. One of the more repugnant deceits is to drag up monotonously from the past the relatively few cases of Jewish terrorism before and during the War for Independence, as though yesterday's wrongs can justify today's. Previous terrorist acts by Jews have been dwelt upon and exaggerated preposterously; and, as in the past, deliberately employed to develop bitterness and hatred toward Jews. The recent Arab effort, aided and abetted by U.N. "investigating committees," to invent contemporary Israeli atrocities is so far removed from reality that it does not merit reasoned analysis. Israel and the administered territories are quite open to study by outsiders. For example, Curtis A. Chambers, Editor of the United Methodist publication *Together,* has described his recent visit with other church editors to the military prison at Nablus, where prisoners made clear to him that they are treated humanely.[11] We are entirely aware, however, that no refutation of Arab accusations could either change those who want to believe them or prevent the fabrication of fresh atrocity stories. This state of affairs in itself makes fruitless any detailed discussion of such charges.

Israeli spokesmen described as "a new low of irresponsibility and irrelevance" a Muslim-sponsored Security Council Resolution of September 16, 1969, which craftily linked the el-Aqsa fire to the status of Jerusalem. The Resolution said that "the execrable act of desecration and profanation" of the Mosque "emphasizes the immediate necessity" for Israel to rescind "all measures and actions taken by it designed to alter the status of Jerusalem." The Resolution referred to "encouragement of, or connivance at," any act of destruction of holy places and religious buildings in Jerusalem, contending that any such act "may seriously endanger international peace and security"—wording that could have no purpose other than anti-Israeli incitement. Israel correctly identified the Resolution "as intended to deceive and cast aspersions" by fabricating a libelous charge of arson against her and seeking to further the political and warlike designs of the Arabs under the guise of a holy war. She officially protested Great Britain's special backing of the Resolution.[12]

The most shocking and at the same time historically portentous aspect of this particular case was that Britain should be joined by France and the Soviet Union in supporting the Resolution, and that the United States should abstain rather than have the moral integrity to veto the unconscionable Resolution. These are the four powers that have appointed themselves "arbiters" of the Middle East conflict—as if their quest for a settlement could or would represent impartial justice.

Were further proof needed of the perfidy of the United Nations, as well as of the bias that has pervaded the major parties working for a settlement, this

Resolution would readily provide it. As we have seen, Israel was totally innocent of the slightest act of malfeasance or even negligence in the el-Aqsa affair.

During her twenty-year control of East Jerusalem, Jordan could desecrate and completely demolish all but one of thirty-five synagogues, burn innumerable Torah scrolls and holy books, pillage academies of learning, and utilize Jewish gravestones in the construction of army latrines. These officially sanctioned acts were perfectly acceptable, according to the world's standards as reflected in its silent consent. But when a psychotic Christian from abroad tries unsuccessfully to burn down a mosque in the same city, this becomes a heinous crime on *Israel's* part, for which she must be chastised before the world by the United Nations Security Council.

Another Arab nation—Syria—could openly flout international law by imprisoning two Israeli civilians abducted from a hijacked American airliner and then be elected by the U.N. General Assembly to the Security Council (in October, 1969).

The United Nations Charter bespeaks "sovereign equality" of all members, and the need for all members to refrain from "the threat or use of force against the territorial integrity or political independence of any state." Yet the Security Council has not once condemned Egypt, Jordan, or Lebanon for thousands of cease-fire violations against Israel. And there is little hope that the Council will behave any differently. Israel has been forced to abandon any and all requests for U.N. censure of Arab terrorist acts and other aggression. Only those resolutions sanctioned by Arabs can ever be passed. Almost half of the Council's fifteen members do not even maintain relations with Israel, yet are free to condemn her. And the Arabs can always rely upon the Soviet veto (in contrast to the lack of any such assurance for Israel on the part of the United States). Only the Israeli delegation is left to speak for Israel. She stands bereft of any reliable international support or protection. She is forced to fend for herself. Not without reason, "United Nations" has become a derisive phrase throughout Israel. For Israelis, the so-called Security Council is in fact the "Insecurity Council" (Professor AlRoy).

Big Power Politics

The periodic interference of the major powers, either singly or jointly, in affairs of the Middle East has almost without exception made things worse. Professor Nadav Safran of Harvard University observes that the Arab-Israeli conflict was the first international conflict in which the notion "no-war, no-peace" was established. "Had the big powers not interposed their protection—thus taking pressure off the Arabs in 1949—peace would have been concluded" years ago.[13]

Have not these major powers repeated the same mistake? The U.N.-arranged cease-fire in June, 1967 saved the Arab nations from having to deal directly with Israel. Then the diplomats devised a formula whereby the Arab governments (those who provoked and then lost the war) could be satisfied and their losses restored. Many nations tried to reenact the 1957 affair, but this time the United States did not support a resolution that demanded Israel's withdrawal from territory without any provision for future security.[14]

When Gunnar V. Jarring's first attempts to foster negotiations under the "ac-

210 THE AFFIRMATION OF ISRAEL

cepted" U.N. Resolution failed, President de Gaulle and the Soviet leaders proposed that the so-called Big Four should pool their wisdom and authority, and
draw up a plan for resolving the conflict. President Nixon consented, despite
most strenuous objections from the Israeli Government. (The Johnson Administration had steadfastly refused to involve the U.S. in such discussions.) Israel
submitted an official protest to the United Nations, claiming that the Soviet
Government had disqualified itself from any mediating role because of its "un-
reserved identification with Arab aggression." (Though France was not singled
out for denunciation, de Gaulle had already forbidden the delivery of fifty
Mirage jets to Israel as a way of trying to force her to withdraw from the administered areas—hardly the act of an impartial mediator.) After the start of the
talks, Great Britain moved further into the Arab camp through her policy
of arms sales.

Israel has emphasized that she "is prepared to conclude at any time peace
agreements with each of the Arab states."[15] No intermediate political scheme
will be accepted by Israel "because any such arrangement is not a lasting settlement of peace. It is a mere breathing spell for the next war."[16]

Critics of big power intervention add that such effort can only serve to keep
the antagonists from accepting full responsibility for the consequences of their
own behavior. The one decision of the major powers that could benefit the Middle East would be an agreement not to interfere. Such a decision is, of course,
hardly likely. Yet the fact remains that the more the powers interfere, the less
will the rights and interests of the people in the Middle East be fostered. The
real tragedy to date is that these people have neither been granted the opportunity to resolve their own differences nor required to do so.

The behavior of the big powers has been an aggravating force not only when
they act in concert but when they act individually. We shall limit the latter kind
of discussion to two countries, the Soviet Union and the United States.

Russia is the most shameless advocate and ally of the Arab cause. The powerful support by the U.S.S.R. of Egypt and other Arab states has gravely altered
the whole character of the Arab-Israeli relationship. Russia has invested a minimum of $5-billion in military and economic aid to the Arabs.

The policy of the Soviet Union in the Middle East has been: no war and
no peace. The total obliteration of Israel and the achieving of a peace settlement
have both been opposed by the U.S.S.R. In either eventuality, Arab reliance upon
the Soviets would largely vanish. Without that reliance the current Russian
effort to dominate the Middle East would receive a severe setback. Russia has
openly committed herself to helping the Arabs eliminate the territorial changes
"due to Israeli aggression." The great danger is that such a commitment may lead
the Soviet Union into a full-scale partnership in the larger Arab goal: Israel's
extermination. Even prior to Russian offensive moves in Egypt there were huge
disparities in the size and resources of the original antagonists. Today, these disparities are gravely intensified.

Where does the United States fit into the picture?

Overall American policy and behavior have been divided and irresolute, as we
have more than hinted in earlier pages. Yet Arab propaganda has been successful
at a most crucial point: in getting many Americans to accept the myth that the
U.S. is the intimate friend and protector of Israel and that she is anti-Arab. The

facts show this to be a vast oversimplification. It is as easy or easier to argue in exactly the opposite way. Despite his own favoring of an even more pro-Arab foreign policy, Professor John Badeau nevertheless insists that the idea of the United States being pro-Israel is a false impression that overshadows the record of American behavior.[17]

The premise from which Arab propaganda operates, and the delusion it falls into, is its equating of a political acceptance of the existence of Israel with enmity to the Arab cause. The Arabs have succeeded in confusing the entire issue. In effect, they demand absolute loyalty from other nations. Any nation failing to agree that the State of Israel ought to be brought to an end is inherently suspect.[18] (It is significant that the Arabs have been prepared to exclude Russia from this latter judgment. One does not bite the hand that feeds him.) Because the American Government has not consented to the scheme to destroy Israel, at least not yet, the United States has become, in Arab polemic, an accursed, "vile and treacherous" nation, "an unconcealed enemy waging an overt war" against the Arab people. "The U.S. is Israel and Israel is the U.S.," shouts The Popular Front for the Liberation of Palestine. American "imperialism" is utilizing Israeli "imperialism."

This Arab charge is false. The United States has neither given Israel unqualified support nor shown any favoritism toward Israel.

More than once the U.S. has capitulated to the Arabs and joined the U.N. chorus denouncing Israel. Not a single time has the American delegation ever exercised its veto in the Security Council to prevent action against Israel. More serious is the recent American move breaking with Israel and siding with the Soviet-Arab bloc on the question of big-power intervention in the Middle East crisis. A very live temptation for the United States today (not unlike temptations to which she in fact succumbed in the past) is to become a tacit ally of the enemies of Israel by enabling the Arab states to escape coming to direct terms with Israel, to continue to avoid acknowledging Israel's reality.

Over the years American policy on the sale of arms to Israel has been quite unpredictable, along with that of the French and the British. At times no sales at all have been permitted. Not until the end of 1963 did the U.S. furnish Israel any substantial quantities of weapons, and then only in response to an extensive arms deal between Egypt and the U.S.S.R. At other times delays or limitations have been imposed, and refusals have been forthcoming, as in the denial in March, 1970 of an Israeli request for additional jet aircraft. Furthermore, it is misrepresentative to speak of American military "aid" to Israel. The term is a misnomer. Israel pays for every weapon.

In addition, the United States continues to furnish arms to the other side. When Arab terrorists hijacked a TWA jet in August of 1969, and blew it up at the Damascus Airport, the terrorists announced that they were "punishing" the U.S. for selling aircraft to Israel.[19] By the same reasoning, the terrorists were implicitly advising the Israelis to seize an American aircraft in retaliation for American sales of jets to Jordan. Since 1957, the United States has been a major supplier of Jordanian arms. For some time the U.S. has been training several hundred Arab pilots at American Air Force centers, a fact that was withheld from the public until it was revealed by several U.S. congressmen.

Between 1946 and 1968 the United States provided $3,762,700,000 in aid and development programs to the Arab states while granting only $770,600,000 to Israel.[20] Much additional financial and technological assistance has been offered to the Arabs—and rejected!—for projects to help settle refugees and provide jobs for them.

Frequently, American decisions seem to be based on restricting Israeli power in order to avoid arousing "undue" Arab or Russian wrath, and to guard Israel from the temptation of "aggression," a moralistic posture hardly justifiable before the fact of Israel's peril. In view of the unlimited supplies of arms available to the Arab states from their supporters, the West's limitations and embargoes on armaments sales to Israel are one-sided and unjust. The moralism and imperialism of the United States, by which that country arrogates to herself the right to make decisions for Israel respecting the latter's defense needs, circumscribes Israel's freedom to make her own decisions, and is indeed an infringement upon her sovereignty. Such limitations only contribute to the probability of another war, through tempting the Arabs to believe that "this time" their preponderant weaponry will successfully crush Israel.

The peculiar brand of "evenhandedness" represented by the United States was illustrated in the call by Secretary of State William P. Rogers in December of 1969 for the withdrawal of Israeli forces from territories "occupied" in 1967, in return for an Arab "agreement" to "accept a permanent peace." Revealingly, Mr. Rogers asserted: "We do not support expansionism." He further declared that the United States "will not shrink from advocating necessary compromises,"[21] as if a proposal that fosters Israeli strategic vulnerability in exchange for mere paper guarantees from the Arabs can somehow qualify as a "compromise." Perhaps most ominous of all is that, for the first time, an American statement should omit the rejection of an imposed settlement, and advocate instead "necessary compromises." Prime Minister Meir quite properly reacted to the American proposals by seeing in them a threat to both the sovereignty and the security of Israel.

We would be omitting pertinent data if we did not refer to the weighty influence of pro-Arab interests upon the United States. American churches and educational institutions with long-standing connections among Arab peoples exert great pressures upon American opinion and political leadership. The oil companies, with their vast investments and profits tied to the Arab states, are probably the most potent of the forces. Through Middle Eastern oil investments alone, there are profit transfers representing a $2.5 billion annual contribution to the American balance of payments. The oil interests receive huge tax write-offs and have made funds available to Arab terrorists. Some of these corporations have helped finance Arab propaganda campaigns in the United States and Europe. The oil lobby exerts marked influence within the State Department, as exemplified in various inter-Arab struggles as well as in the Arab-Israeli conflict.

A U.S. State Department official recently asked: "When is Israel going to learn that it cannot shoot its way to peace?" So nonsensical a question could be uttered only by someone who has not bothered to learn or to remember all the other methods Israel has tried in order to achieve peace, or who has not faced up to the reality that the only other possibility is for Israel to be shot into the grave. On February 12, 1970 a representative of the State Department "deplored" the bombing of an Egyptian factory, and in the very next sentence "deplored" terrorist attacks upon civilians at an airport. The latter was a reference to the terrorist killing of one Israeli and wounding of eleven others at Munich. This instance of American "evenhandedness" comes down to either of two possible judgments. Either murder is put on the same moral level as deaths through an electronic error, or Israel is accused of a falsehood in asserting that the bombing involved an error. Such "evenhandedness" in the State Department stands in sharp relief to a declaration signed by members of the United States Congress calling for "direct unhampered negotiations" between the Arabs and Israel, and affirming that "the deterrent strength of Israel must not be impaired." By the end of March 1970, 70 senators had signed the declaration, and 280 representatives had signed a similar one.

The State Department has long sought to make it appear that American vital interests depend on maintaining the friendship of all the Arab world, and that the Arabs can use their oil as an ultimate weapon. The latter myth has long since been exposed.[22] Revealingly, President Nasser once remarked, "After all, they can't drink it." He was referring to a possible failure of the oil states to sell their product. Oil needs markets. Due to recent discoveries of oil in many places other than the Middle East, a buyer's market is developing more and more. An embargo on Middle Eastern oil would be a highly effective weapon against Arab intransigence. At present Jordan and the U.A.R. are being kept from financial collapse largely through grants from oil-rich Saudi Arabia, Kuwait, and Libya. (The terrorist organizations receive much of their support from these same sources.[23]) That the weapon of an oil embargo has not been used is partly indicative of the entrenched power of the oil interests, involving a partnership of Western oil companies (especially American ones) with the Arabs.

It has been well said that the oil companies, the U.S. State Department, and Arab-orientated American churches comprise a formidable triumvirate in the development of anti-Israeli pressures and sentiment in the United States.

The overall American position on the Middle East has involved the identical blunder and fault that afflicted British policy under the Mandate: the notion that by being "nice" to the Arabs and not too "nice" to the Jews, Arab hostility would be overcome. President Nixon has declared that the United States is committed to maintaining "friendly relations with the people of Israel and, indeed, with all the nations of the Middle East."[24] The second part of this avowal is easily as crucial as the first. The real moral question for Americans is whether it is right that their country remain friendly to nations committed to politicide against another nation.

What would a more just American policy be like? It would see American representatives denouncing peoples that support and use terrorism. It would mean voting against unjust U.N. censures or resolutions, and desisting from resort to a double standard in the Middle East. A new policy would see increased, unrestricted support for Israel as a means of counterbalancing benefits now granted to Arab nations, and of offsetting the powerful Russian political, economic, and military alliance with the Arabs. The United States would take necessary measures to annul Soviet participation in the Arab aggression against Israel. The American Government would insist in the end that the parties to the conflict in the Middle East meet in concert to resolve their own problems, free from outside interference.

A final matter for the present section is the Arab charge that only the Israeli-Jewish side of the story is heard in the United States. In actuality, press, radio, and television give as much space and time to the Arab side as to the other side, and perhaps even more.[25] The *fedayeen*, Arab refugees, and Arab leaders receive a great deal of attention. News reports stress much more Israeli counter-attacks and "retaliations," in contrast to the acts of aggression that make these responses morally and strategically necessary. U.N. sessions with all their vituperation against Israel, and the anti-Israeli resolutions promulgated by U.N. bodies have received national coverage. The news media exhibit a widespread tendency to equate the basic attitudes ("hatreds," "intransigence," etc.) of Israelis and Arabs. Israel has often been accused of undue harshness and militancy. Falsehoods created by Arab propagandists are circulated (such as grossly exaggerated figures for the numbers of refugees). The distortions of Arab government releases are reported as fact, with little effort at verification or correction. To publish side by side Arab and Israeli claims as if they possessed equal truth is a violation of objectivity.

Thus is the Arab charge of one-sidedness revealed as a myth.

A special word is in order concerning religious media. American religious publications are noticeably weighted on the side of the Arabs. Although Christians and Muslims in the Arab world have complained to us that American churches are pro-Israel, we have searched American denominational and other religious publications only to find that materials sympathetic to Israel are extremely rare. The Reverend Karl Baehr has pointed out that it is very difficult for Israeli points of view even to get a hearing in these Christian media. By contrast, presentations sympathetic to the Arab side are legion. In innumerable articles by Christians, emphasis falls, revealingly, upon alleged Israeli culpability and particularly upon factors over which Israel can exert some measure of control, but not upon corresponding Arab obligations or responsibility. The moral demands are unbalanced. The Israelis, but not the Arabs, are supposed to change their behavior.[26]

We have been analyzing a pattern of behavior that utterly disillusions the people of Israel. They have grown sick of the world's hypocrisies. They have been pushed into that total reliance upon themselves which becomes, in effect, their only hope for staying alive.

One of the more reprehensible of the wars against Israel has been the one waged by the outside world, with its insufferable self-righteous demands for Israeli "patience," "moderation," and "generosity," only to be closely followed by its own indignation, condemnations, and acts of outright prejudice. "Friends" of Israel keep preaching to her that war, force, retaliation, etc., are not the ways to deal with the Arabs. These "friends" are addressing the wrong party. Their advice ought to be directed to Cairo, Damascus, Amman, and Beirut. When under heaven will demands begin to be made of the Arabs?

Maurice Carr speaks of "Great Power antisemitism rationalized as politics." The phenomenon appears in varying degrees and different guises, whether we are dealing with the United Nations, the Soviet Union, France, Great Britain, or the United States. Many nations share an impulse to persecute Israel. We consider the question of the deeper reasons for this in our later discussion of anti-semitism.

Jerusalem, Jerusalem

A special and vital case of injustice in the halls of nations is manifest in the controversy over the disposition of Jerusalem.

Several points are essential to remember.

First, had the Arab world agreed, as did the Zionist leadership, to the U.N. Partition Plan of 1947, Jerusalem in its entirety would today be an internationalized city administered by the United Nations inside the boundaries of the Arab State of Palestine. Demonstration was here given of the Zionists' and Israelis' readiness to accept compromises, even at the cost, in this case, of their ancient capital and spiritual center, with all the attachments to it they had retained through the centuries. But compromise would not satisfy the absolute demands of the Arabs. While the British Mandate was still, in force, Arabs attacked Jewish sections of Jerusalem. Among other areas, Transjordan's Arab Legion finally conquered East Jerusalem (which includes the Old City). Against bitter opposition from all other Arab states as well as from many Palestinian Arabs, Transjordan annexed this part of the City.

Second, Jerusalem has never been the national capital of any people but the Jews. It is misleading to identify East Jerusalem as "Arab Jerusalem." Prior to 1948 all of Jerusalem was a heterogeneous city comprised of a number of national and religious quarters. On the ground of both historical tradition and historical fact, it must be stressed that Jerusalem (which, until the late nineteenth century, meant essentially the Old City) is very much more a Jewish city than an Arab city. During the century that culminated in the reestablishment of Israel, Jews were the largest community in Jerusalem, according to official censuses. At the very time of its enforced division, Jerusalem had 100,000 Jews to 65,000 non-Jews. In the fight for Jerusalem in 1948, the Jordanians decimated the Jewish Quarter of the Old City, killing many of its inhabitants (mainly religious Jews). The rest were evicted when the Quarter surrendered.

For political purposes, Muslim Arabs have sought increasingly in recent years to emphasize the Islamic "sacredness" of Jerusalem. Objectively speaking, there is no comparison respecting Jerusalem's importance as between Jews and Muslims. For Muslims, Jerusalem is only the third most holy city. For Jews, Jerusalem is the "historic cradle of the nation, the focus of its longings,"[27] which makes all the more remarkable Jewish readiness in 1947 to accept international status for it.

Third, East Jerusalem would be in the hands of Jordan on this very day had that country accepted Israel's guarantee of nonbelligerency in 1967 and refrained from hostilities. Jordan's response was an artillery bombardment directed against synagogues and churches, hospitals, centers of learning and residential areas. Dozens of Jerusalemites were killed and hundreds wounded. Israel had no choice but to fight back.

We have already noted Israel's decision, after gaining East Jerusalem, to annul the Jordanian conquest and to reunite the entire City under her own sovereignty.

Morally speaking, Jordan had disqualified herself from trusteeship of the City by her many acts of desecration, her abrogation of signed agreements regarding Jerusalem, and the random shootings of Israeli civilians by Jordanian soldiers posted on or above the walls of the Old City. The same disqualification applies to the United Nations. According to a General Assembly Resolution of November 29, 1947, the U.N. was charged with ensuring that "order and peace, and especially religious peace, reign in Jerusalem." The U.N. did nothing either to ensure the internationalization of the City or to enforce the later Armistice Agreement. And it did nothing to protest the Jordanian desecrations.

It is interesting to ponder how the nations that have castigated Israel for reunifying Jerusalem would respond to an enforced division across the center of their own national capitals, with sovereignty totally denied to them in the one half. Most of them would doubtless fight rather than permit any such condition. In 1967, Israel had only two choices: to move unilaterally to restore to unity the most holy city of the Jewish people, or to allow its rupture to be perpetuated for an indefinite future. The second eventuality would have meant not alone giving assent to Jordan's original seizure of East Jerusalem, but also capitulating to Jordan's act of war against Israel in 1967, despite the latter's guarantee of peace, and in contradiction of Israel's subsequent defeat of Jordan. That Israel followed the first course represents a convergence of international law, moral principle, practical necessity, and national self-interest.

Those persons who maintained silence in face of the original Jordanian invasion, conquest, and acts of destruction and noncooperation within East Jerusalem, and who have now criticized Israel for her reunification of the City, are guilty of hypocrisy. That most of the Christian world remained unperturbed by Jordanian behavior in Jerusalem, and then quickly protested against Jewish "occupation" and "annexation," speaks volumes about the spiritual and moral plight of Christendom. Professor Benjamin Halpern's comment, in response to a public communication from an American church official on the recent decision to beautify and restore Jerusalem, ought to induce some humility in Christian circles: "The Romans attempted to keep Jews out by sowing the land with salt, the Christian Crusaders by bloodshed, the Muslims by burying Jewish shrines in dung. Only when the Jews plan to restore space and beauty to the holy places does the Christian conscience of the American churchman rebel."[28]

We leave it to the reader to decide whether the U.N. General Assembly's vote (July 4, 1967) opposing Israel's unification of Jerusalem, together with the Security Council's subsequent reaffirmation of resolutions barring a change in the status of the city, were just or unjust acts.

20. From Antisemitism to Acceptance

WE DISCERN A CLEAR, if morally intolerable, reason for the pro-Arab bias of the world community: there are many, many more Arabs than there are Israelis. Such elements of the nations' self-interest as international trade and balance of power come inescapably to mind. However, if we are to comprehend the force of the world's iniquitous treatment of Israel, its persistent hostility toward her and her people, together with the palpable resort to double standards, we have to probe beneath external behavior and surface policy. The question of antisemitism imposes itself upon us.

The Face of Antisemitism

We are forbidden to insinuate that every individual or group that is critical of Israel must therefore be antisemitic. This would put a considerable number of Israeli and other Jews within the antisemitic camp. We the authors of this volume could also be labeled as antisemites, since we hardly approve or agree with every act of Israel or every policy of Zionist bodies. Yet it is just as essential to remember that an anti-Israeli expression of opinion may be a mask for antisemitism. The only way to tell is to probe more deeply and to ascertain how far the critic is prepared to carry his opposition.

One criterion of whether antisemitism is present in negative attitudes to Israel is suggested by this question: Do you accept the independent reality of the State of Israel?

This is by no means to identify as antisemitism "anything short of total commitment to the rightness of Israel's cause."[1] With respect to specific claims and values, there will always be debate. But we must make a distinction between such arguable points and the basic question of Israel's existence. On this latter there can be no degrees of rightness; either Israel lives or she is to be destroyed. If the distinction mentioned is not grasped, the basic Arab point of view is not understood fully, for it is the *existence* of Israel that has been there opposed.

Even if it were possible in some earlier time to speak against the existence of

217

a Jewish state in Palestine without being subject to a charge of antisemitism, this is no longer the case. Now that the State of Israel is a reality, to plead for its destruction is to give evidence of antisemitism. The only possible exception to this conclusion would be the critic who does not single out Israel but includes other states as rightfully deserving of abolition. Perhaps he is against the whole institution of statehood for any people. If, on the other hand, the critic argues for Israel's destruction alone, while insisting that Lebanon and Jordan (two states established about the time of Israel) and various other states all have a perfect right to exist, we are left with no choice but to adjudge that antisemitism is present. There is no way to call for the abolition of Israel without at the same time calling for harm to be done to more than 2.5 million people, most of whom are Jews. (We do not imply that everyone who supports the independence of the State of Israel is therefore entirely free of antisemitism.)

Apart from antisemitism, there appears no convincing way to account for the ferocity of today's politicidal and genocidal attitude toward Israel within and beyond the Arab world. At the same time, exploration of the ultimate roots of antisemitism, while never wholly avoidable, would take us beyond our present scope.[2]

We cannot enter fully into such issues as the relation between religious and extra-religious incitements to antisemitism, and the extent to which the hatred of Jews within one culture infects another culture. Our attention has to be limited for the most part to the reservoir of antisemitism, to the waters that rise from the springs (or, perhaps better, the sewer) of antisemitism and pollute the world through varied hostile acts toward Jews. Nevertheless, since the symptoms and manifestations of antisemitism within diverse environments are so similar, and often identical, it would be unreasonable not to discern connections among them.

Arabs often protest that they cannot be antisemites because they are themselves Semites. This is a semantic maneuver. Antisemitism on the part of Arabs is not lessened or robbed of its fury by playing games with words. "Antisemite" has only one meaning: a person who is hostile to Jews. Arabs who are antisemites are no less that for being Semites.

We do not include the subject of antisemitism among Arabs with any intention of arousing enmity or hatred toward any people. We do so only in the search for a more thorough understanding of the passions directed against Israel. Only when an illness has been fully diagnosed can effective treatment be applied.

Arabs insist that they do not oppose or hate Jews as Jews. Some of them speak almost rapturously of the wonderful, brotherly relations they "always had" with Jews, and indeed of their great goodness toward Jews—until the State of Israel came between them. Doubtless many Arabs have been taken in by this myth of Arab-Jewish amity prior to the Palestine/Israel problem, and hence honestly believe that Zionism is the root cause of all the bitterness and strife.[3] Nevertheless, the overall protestation will not stand. It is decisively refuted by the truth that those Jews who even now suffer under persecution in Arab countries are hardly Israelis. Many of them are not even Zionists. For centuries these people have lived and regarded themselves as Iraqis, Syrians, Egyptians, Algerians. Yet the some 75,000 Jews that still remain in Arab countries, after the flight of thousands of others, have been confronted by an increasingly harsh existence.[4] Most

Jews were prevented from leaving such oppressive lands as Yemen and Libya before 1948 by restrictions or by lack of resources due to the penury to which so many had been reduced.

Contrary to what Arabs would have the world believe, their mistreatment of Jews antedates the State of Israel by many centuries. Further, modern Arab denigration of the Jewish people and discriminatory legislation against them are much more than an accompaniment or consequence of the establishing of Israel, although these attitudes and this behavior have been, of course, aggravated by the coming of the new State.

Many of the most severe laws directed against Jews have their roots in medieval edicts and codes (which applied also, to be sure, to Christians). Studies of Arabic literature from the Middle Ages show that the only ingredient of modern anti-semitism lacking at that time was the charge of a Jewish world conspiracy.[5] Since then, Arab antisemitic materials have plentifully made up for the lack. True, through the years Arabs have learned some antisemitic ideas and devices from the West (plenty of these were waiting to be appropriated) just as in our own day they have learned directly from the Nazis. Nevertheless, a great deal of Arab per-secution and degradation of Jews has always been independent of outside in-fluence. Thus, the very requirement in medieval Christendom and then in twentieth-century Nazism that Jews wear a distinctive garment or identifying badge originated in Islam.

The currently revived Muslim Arab accusation that the Jews debased and falsified the Torah goes all the way back to Muhammad's time. Attempts are now being made to furnish a Muslim religious base for antisemitism by recalling to memory the feud between Muhammad and the Jewish tribes of Arabia. Legends of Jewish efforts to poison Muhammad have also been resurrected.[6]

It is impossible to separate Arab anti-Israelism and anti-Zionism from anti-semitism. They are mutually reenforcing. The conflict of Jews and Arabs over the past fifty years, culminating in the warfare of almost a quarter of a century between the Arab nations and the State of Israel, has brought into being an ex-tensive literature condemning, not just Zionism, but the Jews and Judaism. From the Arab point of view, so evil a state as Israel could only have been created by a wholly "noxious" people, a people given over to stealth, domination, and expansion, a people who are a threat to the whole world. Thus it is that the con-demning of Israel can be nourished by the historic condemnation of Jews as Jews.

The call for the wholesale destruction of Israel is made possible *by* antisem-itism, and it is at the same time a contributor *to* antisemitism.

Historically, Muslims did not, in contrast to Christians, single out Jews as "deicides" or devil's advocates. The significant thing today is that Muslim Arabs are utilizing for their own purposes Christian literature defamatory of Jews. Thus, with the highest support, a campaign is being waged to show that Israel is the enemy, not only of Arabs, but of Christians, Muslims, and indeed the whole world.[7] An Egyptian Army indoctrination booklet declares, "We are fighting for God; Jews are fighting for the devil."[8]

An Egyptian professor asserts that the conflict between Israel and the Arabs is just one part of the centuries-old "holy war for the sake of the humanity of man." Arabs are carrying on "the struggle to save mankind from the curse [of] the Jewish race."[9]

Unlike the case in the United States or Great Britain, but like the situation in Nazi Germany and the Soviet Union, antisemitic literature in Arab countries is not the work of a "lunatic fringe." It is official, literary, government-sponsored, and government-formulated. The amount and the vehemence of such literature coming from Arab sources is unparalleled since World War II.[10] As the world's centers of the most virulent forms of antisemitism since Nazism, the Arab countries have as major contemporary competitors only the U.S.S.R. and Poland. The assorted techniques and lies of historic Christian antisemitism and Nazi antisemitism[11] are incorporated into officially-sponsored materials. Nazi propagandists living and working in Egypt ever since World War II serve among the chief architects of Arab propaganda against Jews and Israel.[12] That propaganda also utilizes hate materials from the Soviet Union that concentrate upon the "Zionist, imperialist Jews."

For final "proof" of the Jewish-Zionist "plot," Arab antisemites make climactic reference to the *Protocols of the Elders of Zion.* This "document" is in fact a notorious forgery that "describes" an organized campaign by Jewry to seize world power. According to the *Protocols,* Jewish leaders from different countries hold periodic meetings to decide the fate of the world: which economic crisis should be caused next, which regime is to be overthrown, where another war is to break out, etc. Ever since its fabrication near the close of the nineteenth century, the *Protocols* has been among the big guns of the antisemitic arsenal. Today the forgery is available under Egyptian government imprint, in Arabic and in foreign languages—along with Hitler's *Mein Kampf*—throughout Arab countries. In July, 1968 alone 600,000 copies were published in Beirut. Of this number, 200,000 were in French, for distribution in French-speaking North Africa and other areas, while English, Spanish, Italian, and Arabic editions ran to 100,000 each. The contents of the libel are cited over the radio and in school books. Copies have been found in U.N.-operated refugee schools. President Nasser and other Arab leaders have cited the *Protocols* in official speeches. It has been appealed to from the rostrum of the United Nations.

Medieval ritual murder slanders, in which Jews are accused of requiring the blood of non-Jews, and especially children, for use in their rituals, are to be found in popular Egyptian publications. In these same works, Hitler's extermination of the Jews is applauded, and Adolf Eichmann is called a martyr *(shaheed).*[13]

School books published between 1963 and 1967 by several ministries of education in Arab countries have been surveyed. Here are examples of the official effort to instill hatred of Jews among Arab children: "The Jews, more than others, incline to rebellion and disobedience. These verses warn you against the Jews" (*Religious Teaching,* Egypt). "The Jews in Europe were persecuted and despised because of their corruption, meanness and treachery" (*Modern World History,* Jordan). "The Jews are scattered to the ends of the earth, where they lived exiled and despised, since by their nature they are vile, greedy and enemies of mankind, by their nature they were tempted to steal a land as asylum for their disgrace" (*The Religious Ordinances Reader,* Syria).[14]

In the fantasy-world of antisemitism, the Zionist movement becomes the contemporary method *par excellence* for insuring the success of the age-old Jewish conspiracy to seize effective control of the world. Zionism becomes a conspiratorial instrument for humiliating Arabs and for subjugating the great Arab culture and nation, denying it the recognition and respect it merits in the world community.

Cairo's leading editor and, since April of 1970, Egypt's Minister of National Guidance, Muhammad Hassanein Heykal, recently expanded on the theme of a world-wide Jewish conspiracy. According to him, American Zionist organizations have succeeded "in naming Jews to one out of every five major State Department positions."[15]

At the time of the Second Vatican Council, great Muslim pressure, both official and private, was brought to bear upon the Vatican to prevent any declaration being made that would "exonerate" the Jews from responsibility for Jesus' death—this in face of the fact that the Koran denies that the Jews crucified Christ! The argument used with the Vatican was that the issue is not at all religious or theological, but involves a Zionist political plot.[16]

Arab nationalists and intellectuals see the emerging "Arab Nation" struggling against a conspiracy of gigantic proportions—not only Zionism, but Zionism backed by imperialism in the form of the United States, Great Britain, and Western Germany.[17]

Rationally and historically speaking, it may seem difficult to account for the Arabs' conviction of a Jewish conspiracy against them. However, Arabs and Muslims have a long tradition of seeing a conspiracy behind everything bad that happens. (Christians have had related notions of sinister plots in the world.) Anti-Zionism is a powerful mechanism for preserving and carrying forward the conspiratorial tradition.

In the Spring of 1968 the Government of Saudi Arabia refused to accept the appointment of Sir Horace Phillips as British Ambassador because of the disclosure that he was of Jewish background. Sir Horace is a distinguished Arabist, is not a Zionist, and does not even consider himself a Jew.[18] But to the Arab antisemitic mind, a Jew is a Jew. He need not be an Israeli, and he need not have the slightest interest in Zionism.

Arabs have even endeavored to apply their notorious boycott to foreign firms that employ Jews, *even firms that do no business at all with Israel.* In both these cases we are provided with evidence that Arab antisemitism is in some respects much closer to Nazi antisemitism than to mere anti-Zionism. Sometimes it even bears little direct relation to the Zionist or Israeli questions. Thus is the lie given again and again to the protestation that the Arab nations only abhor Israel but have nothing against Jews.

The Confederates of Antisemitism

Our analysis thus far has hinted at multiple responsibility for the antisemitism that Israeli and other Jews have suffered. This point requires additional attention.

Arabs are fond of complaining that the outside world carries the blame for "inflicting" Jews upon them. To be sure, antisemitism (including the Western and Christian species) embraces a readiness to "get rid" of Jews. But the Arab accusation is not convincing. As elaborated on elsewhere in this study, the Jewish people are in erstwhile Palestine by historical and moral right and in no way by the sufferance, or even the complicity, of anyone else. The Arab charge, through its own insinuations about Jews, is seen to be itself antisemitic.

Within the Middle East it is not only Muslim Arabs who resort to antisemitic behavior. In August, 1969 a group of Catholic and Protestant editors from the United States participated in a fact-finding tour of the Middle East under the auspices of the United Church of Christ. In Cairo and Amman they were addressed by high-ranking Arab Christian prelates who utilized the charge of deicide and the theme of God's alleged rejection of the Jews as part of the grounds for their public attack upon Jews, Judaism, and Israel.

Are we suggesting that the outside world is not among the confederates of antisemitism, that it is free of blame? Not at all. But its culpability is of an entirely different kind from the accusation made by Arabs. The outside world is guilty of having helped immensely to create an atmosphere in which antisemitic attitudes and behavior are accepted. It is guilty as well of having done little or nothing to counteract Arab efforts to harass and destroy Jews. The current anti-Israeli-antisemitic endeavor of Arabs could not be successful without international complicity in the denigrating of Jewish people.

Just as medieval Christendom convinced itself that the Jews were seeking to destroy the church and Christian society,[19] and just as the Nazis proclaimed that Jews would destroy the entire German people unless "stopped," so Arab antisemites now bring the accusation down to date: History "has not known a movement more criminal than the Zionist movement"; its aim is "the extermination of the Arab race."[20]

Edward H. Flannery combines ethical reflection with psychological analysis in a penetrating essay on "Anti-Zionism and the Christian Psyche." Father Flannery is Executive Secretary of the American Bishops' Secretariat for Catholic-Jewish Relations. He emphasizes the marked similarities of response within Christendom to the Nazi Holocaust and to the re-creation of the State of Israel. These are symptomatic "of determinative unconscious forces, specifically, of an unrecognized antipathy against the Jewish people." After all, the two events are at opposite poles in Jewish experience and as history: the one represents Israel prostrate; the other, Israel triumphant. And yet, while the stimuli are poles apart, the response in our Christian world to the Jewish situation has been the same: indifference-hostility, often accompanied by passionate denials that we are antisemitic.

This similarity of reaction to such different realities has to be more than coincidental. It points to the presence of irrational forces within us. In his judgments respecting the Christian community, Father Flannery is cautious but candid. He reasons that the multiplicity of the indictments of "Zionism" by Christians, in the very times of Israel's greatest peril, may well conceal unrecognized and unconscious motivations. "A certain vague uneasiness attends the idea of Jews restored to Palestine, and to Jerusalem in particular. This uneasiness *may* serve as the subliminal foundation for a Christian anti-Zionism and as the dynamics [behind] the various 'reasons' supplied for disfavoring the State of Israel. . . ."[21] In anti-Zionism and anti-Israelism, the death wish that far too many Christians have for Jews is carried forward.

For hundreds of years the Christian church has been telling the world and itself that by "rejecting" Christ, the Jews lost the divinely-given right to sovereign identity, as a people and also as a faith. Pope Pius X followed this theology when he informed Theodor Herzl that as long as Jews refused to accept Christ, the church could not recognize the Jewish people or condone their repossessing the Holy Land.[22] From this same theological viewpoint, the church has replaced original Israel as the people of God. The church is the "true Israel."[23]

This traditional Christian ideological scheme continues to exert a powerful influence. It not only conditions our attitudes through our collective unconscious but elicits positive responses at the conscious level. The Scriptures and historic teachings of the church thereby become weapons directed against political independence for Jews. Accordingly, a contemporary Protestant writer argues that Zionism constitutes "a rebirth of the spirit against which Amos and Jeremiah and others were fighting."[24]

The questions will not leave us: Who but the Jewish people are subjected to moral standards that no human group can possibly realize? Why should Israel be singled out for denunciation when other nations, with no fear of reproach, can invade neighboring countries or wage war on people inside their own borders? Why should Israel alone have to practice no end of *havlagah* (self-restraint), when the countries all around are exempt from such demands? Why is it that Arabs are "entitled" to their homelands, but not Jews? What is the possible ethical basis for allowing and encouraging the "dignity" of "face-saving" among Arabs, while never suggesting that Israel is owed a comparable right? Why is Israel alone deprived of what Marie Syrkin calls "the right to be ordinary"?

The anti-Zionist and anti-Israeli policies of so many nations and peoples are most difficult to account for apart from the influence of the antisemitism and the anti-Judaism that have afflicted Western and Eastern Christendom for centuries. How else are we to make sense of pervasive Christian silence amidst the continuing Arab campaign to destroy Israel, and of Christian denunciations of Israel when she manages to gain respite from her foes? What other explanation is there for the deliberate efforts of large numbers of clergy and laymen to help the Arabs "regain Palestine" when such an eventuality would mean certain death and suffering for countless Israeli Jews (not to mention Arabs on both sides)?

Just as in the 1930's Christians in more than one land could find in the Nazis unwitting instruments of divine punishment of Jews, so in the 1960's and 1970's a potent ideological affinity can appear between Christian attitudes toward Jews and Arab annihilationist designs. The churches do not act effectively or courageously to oppose today's politicidal campaign against Israel because their own repressed enmity toward the Jewish people is too powerful an inhibiting force.

The Arab world today suffers from a double malady: its own heritage of antisemitism, and the heritage of Christendom, whose antisemitism helped to condition and to make possible Nazism, and also contributed greatly to the antisemitism of the Soviet Union.

At the time of the Arab defeat in 1967, M. T. Mehdi, Secretary-General of the Action Committee on American-Arab Relations, made this prediction: "The United Nations will force Israel back to her 1948 boundaries, after which all Arab nations will unite in a war to exterminate her, *because this is going to be just like the Crusades.* For two hundred years, the Arabs will continue their fight and in the end they'll do exactly what they've said. Push Israel into the sea."[25]

Here is a shift in roles as significant as it is curious. The Islamic Arabs take over the function of the Christian Crusades: "freeing" the "Holy Land" from the "infidel." Of course, the Crusades were originally directed against Muslims as the alleged "infidel"—although not without accident the Crusaders also took time to massacre Jews. Recent Muslim calls for a holy war to rid the "sacred soil" of Jews strangely echo the summonses of long-dead Christian popes and bishops.

The historic Christian stand respecting Jews has been that they should convert or leave or die. Although Muslims today appear to have little desire for the conversion of Jews, a certain related demand is nevertheless present: the conversion to statelessness. The Jews are to accept politicide as their proper destiny. And they can leave "our land," or stay to fight and die.

Adolf Hitler followed his Christian forebears in promising to purify Germany of the Jews. Gamal Abdel Nasser has promised to purify the land that Israel has "usurped." Here are two "deliverers," called to cleanse the world of Jewish perfidy and sin. The mantle of executioner of Jews, worn for so many years by Christendom, has been taken up by the Arabs.

However, a strange new fact has also been introduced, a fact that can only confound the despisers and murderers of Jews. In principle, everything has changed. Yesterday only Jews were to do the suffering; their destroyers could go free. Today, the victim is not a victim in the traditional sense; he has been empowered, in the providence of history, to face up to the enemy. Shortly after the Six Day War, Dr. Otto Frank, father of Anne, said: The State of Israel teaches that there will be no more Anne Franks. There will be dead heroes, if need be, but no more martyrs.

The god of Jewish pariahs is dead. He received mortal blows in Dachau and Belsen and Auschwitz. And he breathed his last when the Proclamation of Israeli Independence was issued. The pattern of centuries has been altered: Jewish lives are no longer cheap. Humankind must now pay Jews for its crimes against them. This is the totally new state of affairs initiated in 1948.

Elusive Peace

Peace in the Middle East is elusive because so many forces are present to make for war. Not least of these is antisemitism. Whether hatred for Jews will ever be overcome is highly problematic. This does not excuse us from utilizing every possible method for its effective control.

The drive in much of the world to demand the very most of Israel and the Jewish people, and to expect the very least of them—to require that they be saints and to insinuate that they will be devils—points to an aberration that is at once a psycho-pathological problem and a moral problem. When Jews are weak, they are condemned for that; when they are strong, they are condemned for that. These facts remind us that we are dealing with a disease that, ultimately speaking, has nothing to do with the way Jews behave or do not behave. The disease is within the minds and hearts of antisemites. To the extent that the disease is controlled, Jews begin to be treated as human beings, from whom other men normally expect neither too much nor too little. When this changed attitude is extended to the state, Israel is at last accepted as a nation among other nations.

The psychoanalyst Otto Fenichel speaks of antisemitism as "more a conflict within a person than between persons." When this insight is applied at the collective level, we may say that antisemitism is more a conflict within a nation than between nations. In the Middle East today the Arab nations are riddled with antisemitism. What Israel does or fails to do is not the real problem. The challenge is to find the means to help Arabs change their attitudes and behavior.

The Arabs' hatred of Jews makes it almost impossible for them to recognize the absence of hatred among Israelis and to comprehend Israel's desire for concord and friendship. The Israelis are not angels. But they do not ideologize and institutionalize the hatred of Arabs. When, as occasionally happens, an Arab succeeds in admitting that some Israelis may desire peace, he usually claims that such people are powerless to influence the militaristic regime that controls them. The pity and the irony here is that the Arab is actually reflecting and portraying the situation in which he and his own people are caught.

Furthermore, the very admission that some people in Israel would like to be friends compounds the pathological and moral plight of Arabs. The self-accusations that must finally plague the Arab conscience (what other effect could result from an obsession with exterminating other human beings?) force these people to play out their own self-hatred by means of greater aggression. Aggression and hatred reinforce each other. Excessive aggression itself leads to hatred, and such hatred adds to the already existing burden of unconscious guilt and self-hatred. The hater is driven to ever-greater frenzies of hatred and aggression.[26] His very self-interest is betrayed.

The essence of antisemitism involves an irrational flouting of one's own true and legitimate rights to life and well-being. Through the obsessional goal of purifying the world of Jewish "corruption," the antisemite only succeeds in destroying himself. These Arabs are prisoners of hatred. Lamentably, awareness of this self-imposed captivity is not enough. Several Palestinian Christians confessed to us that they *knew* that they ought not hate Jews, and yet they felt powerless to cast off the shackles of hatred.

The degree of one's optimism or pessimism concerning the Arab-Israeli conflict will depend upon where he stands on this question: To what extent can political and other concrete programs resolve problems that are in essence psychological and moral? Psychological analysis or insight is not able of itself to keep the drive toward politicide from fulfilling itself. Yet the knowledge gained from studies of hatred should make us aware that to appease the one who hates by sacrificing the innocent does not serve peace; instead, it enormously strengthens the hatred and leads inevitably to dreadful results.[27] Today deadly impulses are manifest, straining to repeat the history of the 1930's and 1940's. The madness will have to be stopped through specific measures before it is too late—for the sake of the Jewish people, for the sake of humankind, and not least for the sake of the Arabs. Disaster awaits a world ruled by cowardice and injustice.

The politicidal impulse can be brought under control only through momentous and revolutionary changes in thought and behavior patterns. The chance that this may occur in the Arab world is in considerable measure contingent upon the eventuality of equally revolutionary changes taking place in the conscience and conduct of the world outside. The question remains: Will politicidal behavior be tolerated?

Hopefully, when aggression (physical or even verbal) is estopped, the feelings of hatred may be given a chance to subside and even die, the erstwhile hater can start to live with and accept himself, and there can be the beginning of inter-group peace.

Recently, a Jerusalem-born Arab, who fought with the Syrian Army in 1948 and became an official in the Jordanian Government, volunteered this refreshing testimony: "Straight after the Six Day War I began very enthusiastically to study the possibility of a bi-national State [as a solution to our problems]. Now I have given that up . . . out of respect for the Israelis and the Jews, whom I have since got to know more intimately. . . . I learned there was a very genuine motive in the heart of every Jew for preserving his identity. . . . Now I believe that the Jewish people are entitled to self-realization. . . ." Perhaps the best prescription for Arab-Israeli relationships is "good neighborliness."

On the same occasion an Israeli asserted: "Two nations have their claims on this country . . . the key to peace is the mutual recognition of the national rights of both peoples. . . . I won't accept any solution that does not recognize and secure the rights of the Palestinian Arabs as a people. . . ."[28]

The first statement hopefully represents a growing, though largely unexpressed, willingness by West Bank Arabs to accept Israel as a permanent neighbor. The second statement reflects a widespread Israeli sympathy for the national aspirations of Arab people and a concern over the homelessness of many Palestinian Arabs. Israelis recall their own homelessness as a people.

Sometimes the Israelis go so far as to try to excuse, or at least explain, Arab belligerency and hatred. It is strange but true that in certain respects some Israelis feel closer to their Arab enemies than to detractors of Israel in the wider world, whose intransigence is not tempered at all by the sufferings and frustrations the Arabs have had to endure. Outside hostility to Israel is less honest than a lot of Arab hostility. It does not challenge Israel on the battlefield but hides behind safety, security, and well-being. The Arab foes of Israel's existence and the Israeli adversaries of the Arab design to destroy Israel are linked in a kind of tragic unity by the unhappy but stubborn fact that tomorrow, if not the next day, neither antagonist will have gone away. The two sides are bound together by the terrible companionship of suffering.[29]

The Israelis have learned once and for all that military withdrawal without an overall peace settlement and tangible, locally enforceable guarantees would be a giant step toward extinction. They have hoped that the policy accompanying this realization—non-acceptance of any half-way measures—would be an aid to future peace, because of what is at stake for their foes. Regrettably, it remains highly questionable whether Arab governments will finally agree to a reasonable and just settlement. Though the extension of Israel's authority over former Arab-administered areas was forced on her by the belligerence and intransigence of her enemies, she yet acknowledges tacitly the negotiability of large parts of the areas if only the Arab nations will come to terms with her.

Here is a place where a magnanimity seldom seen in international affairs comes together with national interest. It is not in Israel's interest to retain all the administered areas. Israelis have no wish to become a minority people within an Arab majority, a result that would be their eventual fate were they to engage in the "expansionism" their foes have invented as Israel's aims.

Although the "Land of Israel" movement inside Israel has called for the re-

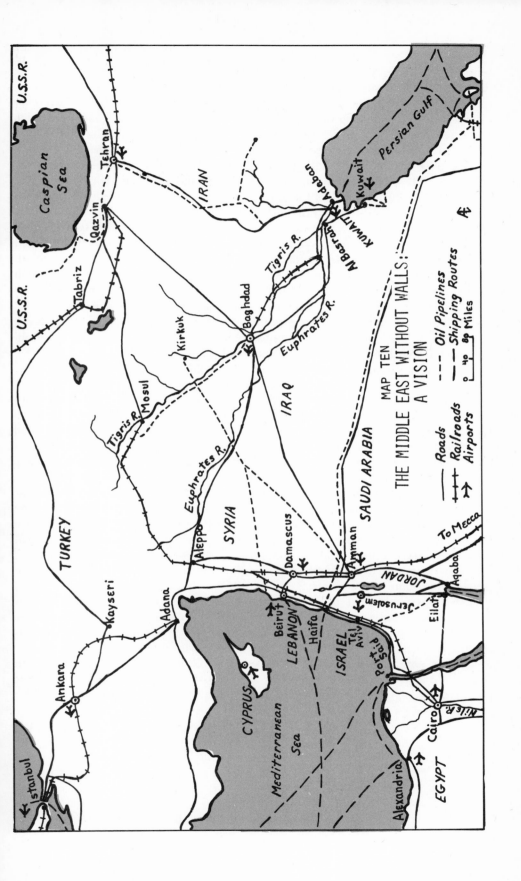

MAP TEN

THE MIDDLE EAST WITHOUT WALLS:
A VISION

Roads ———
Railroads +++++
Airports ⬆

Oil Pipelines ---
Shipping Routes ---

0   40   80 Miles

tention of all the territories on combined religious and security grounds, the movement is relatively small and is fractured by divergent ideologies. Most Israelis talk much more pragmatically and responsibly, emphasizing such considerations as the demographic problem, the need to keep the way open to a peace settlement, and justice for Arabs. Yet it must be granted that the longer the situation remains unsettled and Israel's security continues to be endangered, the more possibility there will be of a change in Israeli attitudes toward the territories.[30] It must be remembered that Israel and her neighbors have never had final and mutual borders but only armistice and cease-fire lines. Almost all national boundaries in the Middle East are of recent origin.

Only a full peace settlement can open for Arabs as much as Israelis an honorable path away from tragedy. We the authors of this book are as much concerned for the well-being of Arabs as for that of Israelis. How can the legitimate interests of the Arab peoples and nations possibly be served insofar as they retain a fixation on the abolition of Israel? We are persuaded that the most pro-Arab affirmation anyone can make is to stand for peace between the Arabs and Israel. The most anti-Arab course is the one that cares so little for Arab well-being that it fails to fight against obsessional antisemitism and anti-Israelism, and instead simply encourages traditional Arab policy and behavior.

The Israelis cannot and will not agree to anything less than peace with their neighbors. No wish is more fervent among the people of Israel and their leaders. Prime Minister Golda Meir has expressed every parent's feeling: "We didn't raise our sons to kill and be killed. There is more glory in wanting peace than in wanting war."[31] As Israelis say, we could win a hundred wars and still lack security; the other side needs only to win one war. Yet the wish for peace can and ought to dominate Arab thinking as well, for the well-being of Arabs everywhere.

Psychology and morality come together in the truth that we do not fully accept ourselves until we fully accept other human beings. There is more than one aid to the acceptance that is needed. The practical measures of conciliation are those that mankind has found effective and necessary elsewhere: mutual political power and recognition, legal agreements and compromises, justice for workers, better standards of living, international trade and travel, educational exchanges, freedom of communication, etc.

Such steps could lead ultimately to a Middle East without walls: an open region of connecting air, land, and water routes that would make it a crossroads of trade, transportation, and travel (see Map Ten); a community of nations coordinating agricultural, economic, and scientific development that would "redesign the environment" for all the people's welfare; an inter-cultural milieu that might spark another Renaissance. The possibilities are limitless.[32] There is one absolute prerequisite: the moral resolve to live and let live.

21. Every People's Right, This People's Right

ONE NECESSARY and important means of affirming the integrity and dignity of Israel involves turning away for a time from a direct encounter with that land, and speaking instead of the integrity and dignity of any and every nation. The mere fact that numbers of Jews claim Israel for their own hardly justifies that claim. Unless Israel possesses a right-to-be that is held in common with other nations, any affirmation of Israel becomes mere special pleading. To be sure, there are unique elements in the reality we call "Israel." But these cannot be used to justify the right she shares with any nation.

The Dignity of Any Nation

We speak here of laic freedom. This is freedom "of the people," the right of a people to be itself politically, socially, culturally, religiously—in every way. This right is closely related to civil freedom; indeed, it is no more than the collective counterpart of the right of the person to be himself.

The individual's right to life and freedom is not contingent upon his achievements (although that right may be annulled or circumscribed if he behaves destructively). A human being takes up space and consumes natural resources; these acts do not call into question his right to live. That right is grounded in the fact that he is already alive. The same is the case with a nation. Particular men or groups may have certain expectations for a nation: that it be "religious" or "scientific" or "cultured." But should a nation fail to realize any specific hope for it, it does not lose the right to live. That right arises solely out of the fact that the nation is already possessed of the gift of life.

Ideally, every nation has sovereignty. Sovereignty is to the nation as freedom is to the individual. A man can exist without freedom, but then we say that he is "not really living." Nations can exist without freedom, but then they are being deprived of their birthright.

Some men have questioned the moral legitimacy of the nation and the nation-state. They link nation and state to a host of evils. They argue that humankind will never achieve universal justice until the nation is abolished. In part, this sentiment is a reaction against the historical degeneration of national integrity into aggressive nationalism, where one nation serves itself at the expense of others. However, this fault does not justify bringing the nation to an end. To argue that it does is like saying that family aggression against another family requires the end of the family as an institution, or that the rising individual crime rate demands restrictions on the freedom of every individual. When nations fall into evil ways, the need for national moral integrity simply becomes that much greater.

The legitimacy of the nation has a solid foundation in the Western religious tradition. The nation may be characterized, along with the family, as one of the "orders of preservation." Far from being an anachronism in the contemporary age, the nation-state continues on, not as an end in itself, but as a means to the fulfillment of human needs, the nurture of human creativity, and the protection of human beings in an unredeemed world. Not until recent times has the integrity of the nation received full acknowledgment—through the international attestation that politicide and genocide are crimes against humanity.

The state is an essential structure for the realization and preservation of the nation. It constitutes the power framework that makes possible the life of a people in its fullness. It can provide insurance against exploitation from within and without, though it may of course fail in either direction. No American who assents to and benefits from the reality of his own nation-state is in a position to deny that same opportunity to other men. From this point of view, there is no need here for a lengthy apologia in behalf of national sovereignty.

Is the right of sovereignty absolute? Are nations entitled to act completely as they wish? Once again, the analogy with the individual is of help. An individual cannot behave just as he wants merely because he exists. Personal freedom is not an absolute right. If a man uses his freedom—or, we ought to say, misuses it—to destroy other human beings, that freedom will probably be curtailed and his life may even be taken. In the same way, if a nation applies its sovereignty to an effort to abolish other nations, its own rights may be restricted and it may even be destroyed in the process. To speak this way is not at all to question the right of sovereignty. It is, on the contrary, a way of giving honor to sovereignty.

Sovereignty is a relative or limited right, just as is the individual's right to freedom. To argue otherwise is to succumb to fascism, for the root of fascism is the romantic notion that the nation-state is an indestructible organism possessed of absolute rights.

Sovereignty is the prerequisite of compromise; it can never be the price of compromise. Were sovereignty ever offered as the price of compromise, the freedom of the nation would be desecrated, and overlordship would reign in its place.

All individual human beings are equal. That is to say, they possess, in principle, the identical right of life. So, too, all nations are equal, no matter how they may differ in size or power.

Israel's Right to Life

Nations do not live out in space—not yet. They live upon this planet's soil, within particular geopolitical areas locatable on the map. It is one thing to agree with the principle that nations have a right to exist; it is something else to adjudge that *this* nation-state possesses the right to live *here,* in this place.

Of course, the right to live and the right to live in a particular place cannot be separated. Fortunate is the people that possesses a home of its own. A people without a land or a state must endure a deprived existence. The Jews of ancient and medieval times had a strong sense of peopleness even while lacking national sovereignty. Jewry has lived without Israel as a state, and could, if tragically necessary, do so again. But then the peopleness of Jews would remain assailed and incomplete.

To contend that Jews have a right to exist as an ethnic group and/or a religious community within someone else's sovereignty, but not as a sovereign nation themselves, is an example of antisemitism. The reason we make this harsh judgment is that such a viewpoint imposes on Jews other men's conceptions of Jewish identity, rather than accepting Jews on their own terms. Only if these terms implied the destruction of, or illicit interference with, another people would it be legitimate to challenge Jewish self-understanding. As long as the sovereignty of other peoples is acknowledged on all sides, we cannot deny that identical right to the Jews of Israel.

The very title of the present section of this chapter is a reminder of human sin. It is like the phrase, "the rights of black men," a phrase made inevitable only by the presence of those who mistreat blacks. We do not have to talk about "the rights of white men." In the same way, no one seems to argue over France's right to life or Brazil's—or Jordan's (despite the fact that Jordan was not even accepted as a member of the United Nations until well after Israel's admission).

Israel asks nothing for herself that is not granted to Egypt or Japan or India—or the United States. *Before the bar of humanity, only historical reasons can be called upon to authenticate a people's right to a particular territory.* (As we have stated, immorality can result in a loss of this right.)

The historical-moral validation of Israel as a state within the Middle East has come forward in much of the discussion in earlier pages. Few people have as compelling a right to their soil as Israel possesses. Frederick C. Grant, the New Testament scholar and historian, has observed that "no nation has a historical claim to the land of Israel that can even be compared with that of modern Israel."[1]

The right of the Jewish people to Palestine antedates by hundreds of years that of any surviving people. As James Parkes expresses the matter, the real title deeds to the land are an enduring, continuous Jewish community. Ever since biblical times, including the period after 70 C.E. and well before Arab and Islamic times, Palestine has had a Jewish population. That population "has always been as large as could find the humblest means of existence" in the land.[2] Any reductions in the size of the community came only as a result of wars, deportations, persecutions, or economic difficulties. Unlike other nations that have passed into obscurity with the loss of political and communal structures, the Jewish people in dispersion retained their identity. They never surrendered the claim to their ancestral home, and they never ceased to look upon it as Eretz Hemdah, the land for which one yearns. They continued to sustain the Yishuv (the indigenous Jewish community) by immigration and contributions. Significantly, the Jewish people never attempted to take or claim another land for themselves, in contrast to other displaced or migrating peoples.

This unique set of circumstances—continuity of residence and claim, immigration, and fidelity to the nation's past as well as to its anticipated future in the one land—is the essence of the Jewish people's case for their historical rights in Eretz Yisrael. (The special connection of Jews to the land was recognized by every Muslim ruler until the end of the nineteenth century.)[3]

Once historical right to a given portion of land is used as a means of defending residence there, one is obliged to be thoroughgoing and consistent. It is forbidden to bend the history to special interests. Thus, when some Arabs today assert that the Jews have taken away "our land," they fly in the face of the truth that Jewish residence preceded by centuries Arab residence, and never ceased. Hence, the Arab claimant is forced either to abandon the charge of theft and to rest his case somewhere else, or to acknowledge the validity of the Jewish claim precisely on the basis of the standard that he has himself introduced. (Later in this chapter we discuss the validity of the Palestinian Arabs' claim.)

A nation is born from within. It is not called into being by external fiat. Neither the nation of Israel nor any other nation has been created by the United Nations. In a very real sense, Israel already existed before U.N. recognition became a fact. Nevertheless, it is not without significance that the world community, first through the League of Nations and then through the United Nations, has fully recognized the independent rights of the Jewish people in Palestine.

Fortunately for the freedom and dignity of Israel, the U.N. is not a sovereign body but is only a collection of sovereign states, among which Israel has the same rights as any other state. John Badeau, former American Ambassador to Egypt, interprets the U.N. decision of 1947 as a recognition of Jewish corporate political and social identity, an act acknowledging Israel's right to develop freely without external restraints.[4]

In light of the Soviet Union's recent formidable support of the Arab states against Israel, it is of the utmost relevance to note that the Russians have not once questioned Jewish rights in Palestine or Israel's sovereignty. On November 26, 1947, just before the vote for partition, the Soviet delegate Andrei Gromyko declared before the General Assembly: "The representatives of the Arab states claim that the partition of Palestine would be a historic injustice. But this view of the case is unacceptable, if only because, after all, the Jewish people has been closely linked with Palestine for a considerable period of history. . . . [Partition] is in keeping with the principle of the national self-determination of peoples . . . [and] will meet the legitimate demands of the Jewish people. . . ." When the Arab countries subsequently rejected partition and invaded Israel, the Soviet Union expressed "surprise" at the Arabs' repudiation of the Jewish "national liberation movement" in Palestine.[5] Russia was indignant at the "act of aggression" of the Arab League against Israel and demanded that the aggression cease. Shortly after the June War of 1967, Premier Kosygin, in the very course of a bitterly anti-Israel speech, reminded the United Nations of the Soviet Union's original vote in support of independent Jewish and Arab states in Palestine.

Some further words of James Parkes are most relevant on the question of Israel's historic right to life: "It is quite superficial to argue, as some do, that 'Israel exists and the Arabs must be realistic enough to see that this is a fact which cannot be changed.' Human nature is to this extent the same everywhere, that a sense of injustice can rankle for centuries. . . . [If] the presence of Jewry as an equal partner in middle eastern life cannot be shown to be just, then no solution imposed either by Israel or by the United Nations can be of any permanent value."[6]

The affirmation of Israel's integrity moves upwards from the foundation of historic right to the level of moral right, which we consider next.

Brothers

Were it the case that in our time Jews took over Palestine from a sovereign nation, or stole the land away from its inhabitants, such behavior would be on the face of it indefensible. However, these allegations, favorites among Arab propagandists, constitute a grave sin against the facts of history. No sovereign nation possessed the land. Only under the Jewish people has there ever been an independent state within Palestine. During the formative years of the twentieth century only the Jews created responsible, self-governing bodies capable of carrying on the life of a nation, and voluntarily taxed themselves to meet community needs.

Fayez A. Sayegh seeks to tell us that the Zionist movement is the new face of Western imperialism and a new variety of racist colonialism.[7] A major part of the complete falsehood of this charge is its ignoring of the many positive affinities between Zionism and the modern nationalist movement among peoples in the Middle East and elsewhere. Zionism is one of the oldest of all modern liberation movements. As with the Arab nationalist enterprise, the Zionist movement has sought to re-create an ancient past, to give dignity to a people long repressed. Both movements combine religious, ethnic, linguistic, and cultural elements. Yet, whereas Zionism developed an idealism that looked forward to a harmonious bi-national state, the Arab nationalist movement remained rigidly exclusivist.

Certain "New Leftists" are fond of trying to link the new Israel with "Western" interests. The truth is infinitely more in the other direction. The main opposition to Zionism in the mandatory period came from those who feared that its success would help spread socialism and communism. The conservative Arab leadership worried about the example of social progress the Jewish agricultural and town workers were setting for the Arab masses. The Zionist settlers, having experienced repression in Eastern Europe not unlike that of natives under colonial rule, were determined to avoid creating another exploitive society. Jean-Paul Sartre characterizes colonialists as men who never work with their own hands. Joseph Neyer points out that in "mixing their labor with the soil and basing their economy on agrarian socialism," the Zionists were actually in the forefront of the revolution against colonialism.[8] As we have learned, Israel increasingly warrants identification as a modern Eastern state, devoted to an order of social justice that surmounts many of the evils of capitalism. Were devotees of the "New Left" not so blindly prejudiced against Israel they could learn much from her that would benefit their own cause.

It is important for Americans to remember that laic freedom may assume different forms in different lands. For many peoples, the ideology that commends a pluralistic or non-particularistic society is quite a foreign idea. In contrast to much Western thinking and practice, intimate and distinctive bonds are often found among culture, religion, ethnic character, and the other aspects of national life. Such is the case in the Middle East.

We have emphasized the injustice of applying to Israel a standard different from that applied to other states and peoples. John Davis, former Commissioner General of UNRWA, recently demanded that Israel be forced by outside powers to become a "conventional" national state.[9] The question arises of whether Davis is prepared to apply his demand to other Middle Eastern states or whether he is simply to be numbered among the many devotees of a double standard. Perhaps "outside powers" might decide that Iraq and Egypt must cease to be Islamic Arab nations and become pluralistic, secular states. Thus, on Davis' reasoning, Iraq would be required to take back all Jews who had fled, and to restore all their property. All Islamic characteristics would be removed. Iraqi Arabs might face the possibility of becoming a minority, once the Kurds, Jews, and other groups were to receive completely equal status.

Can Israel withstand deceitful or unthinking pressures to make her into a pluralistic non-Jewish state? Only the future will tell. However, one important ground for a hopeful answer is, strangely enough, Israel's very location in the Middle East. Israel is by no means alone in her self-identification as a laic state. Thus, in the foreseeable future the public leaders of Egypt will be Egyptian Arabs. It is inconceivable that a Jew would be given opportunity to become even a minor official of that country.

A repeated charge against Israel in Arab circles is that as a Jewish state, she is guilty of "racism." A curious aspect of this charge is that many of the accusers represent highly particularistic Muslim Arab states whose polities bear some resemblances to that of Israel. Along the same line, if we are to speak of real racism, it can be readily found in the unrelenting persecution of Jews in these very states, in contrast to justice and civil equality for Arabs in Israel.

A major moral challenge in relatively "closed" societies is the treatment of minorities. This is in no way to imply that pluralistic societies necessarily treat their minorities with any greater justice. The pluralistic social world is subject to the same divisive intergroup conflicts that beset any kind of human society. The fact remains that as a Middle Eastern, Jewish state, but a democratic one, Israel has embarked upon a unique and pioneering role in the area of intergroup relations.

Any consideration of Israel's moral right to life would be incomplete without reference to the costs that have been paid. Beyond the huge funds expended in purchasing land is the human price of suffering and sacrifice. Many of the early settlers, seeking to raise the soil from the dead, died themselves from malaria and other hardships. We know of a man who walked to Israel—from Rumania. His story is not an exception; there have been countless acts of that sort. In the Six Day War Israeli soldiers were shot by enemy snipers while carrying aged or infirm Arabs away from danger. In the battle for Jerusalem, an unnecessarily large number of Jewish soldiers lost their lives solely because of the Israeli refusal to resort to heavy weapons and air strikes that would have killed many civilians and demolished shrines revered by Christians and Muslims. (No important Jewish structures were left to save except the Wall, which had been permitted to stand because it was an intrinsic part of the Muslim Haram esh-Sharif.) The order calling for hand-to-hand combat was adhered to despite the fact that the Jordanians had carefully placed their own artillery pieces in and near the holy places.

When people pay for something with their blood, for something that has been unjustly seized by their foes, where is the justice in the demand that it be "given back"?

In our relations with the people of Israel we are forbidden to require anything of them that we do not expect of other men or of ourselves. At the same time we are assured that the Israelis themselves seek to honor the highest moral standards in their daily and national life. The key to understanding Israel is the nation's commitment to the ideal of social justice. This is so whether the issue is relations between Jews, between Jews and non-Jews in Israel, between Israelis and Arabs, or between Israel and other nations, particularly the developing nations and even including enemy nations. For example, Dr. Kalman Mann, director-general of the Hadassah Medical Organization in Israel, recently stated that if only Arab authorities would permit Israeli health officials to enter their lands, "the Arabs' general level of health could be raised to standards prevailing in Israel."[10]

The Israeli outlook here tends, characteristically, to combine pragmatism and self-effacement. Injustice to other men only redounds to one's own hurt; justice to others gives a man happiness. To observe the biblical commandment, "Thou shalt love thy neighbor as thyself" (Lev. 19:18), is to foster mutual enrichment. More important, the commandment helps to make possible human reconciliation.

In her short history the new Israel has already proven herself more deserving of sovereignty than many nations whose sovereign freedom has not once been challenged by the outside world. The record in the earlier chapters of this book largely speaks for itself. Our attention has been directed to the nation's drive for social integration, social welfare, and social equality; justice for minorities and workers; provisions for religious nurture and freedom; Israel's stewardship of the soil and of her natural resources; her educational, cultural, scientific, and technological development; achievements in democratic institutions and defense; financial stability and great strides toward economic self-sufficiency; active participation in all international organizations; efforts for peace and international justice; and aid to other developing nations.

A special word is in order respecting the last item on the above list.

When the Congo achieved independence in 1960 and almost all foreign doctors left the country, fourteen million people were left without medical care. Israel, answering a request from the United Nations, sent in teams of doctors and nurses to reopen the hospitals, and to provide medical and sanitation services. The Congo was saved from pestilence. In Burma there are villages modeled upon *kibbutzim* and *moshavim*. In Nepal there are cooperative bus lines and banks organized by Israelis. In Tanzania a labor federation modeled after the Histadrut protects the workers and develops natural resources. In India scholars apply "Zionist" methods in order to advance Hindi as the common language for the whole country.

At the invitation of other governments or under U.N. auspices, Israeli teachers, advisors, and survey teams have been sent out to different lands. Between 1958 and 1968 more than 2,500 experts from Israel served in some 60 countries. During the same decade, approximately 10,500 trainees from more than eighty countries in Africa, Asia, Latin America, and the Mediterranean world took part in some 800 courses and study missions in Israel, always at the initiative and with the support of the participants' governments. Free scholarships are granted foreign students by the Government of Israel and by Israeli and Zionist organizations. Proportionately, more young people from the new nations go to Israel to study than participate in student exchange programs in the United States.

Primarily in Africa and Asia, Israel has organized hospitals and clinics, built water and sanitation systems, constructed dams, roads, and hotels, and taught modern methods of farming, manufacturing, mining, fishing, and food packaging. Joint companies for construction, water supplies, shipping, and foreign trade have been established in various lands, with the local governments or companies owning major shares in the enterprises, and the Israeli partners transferring their holdings to local ownership once the projects are proved viable. The countries and their citizens become the sole owners.

In Laos today a team of Israeli farmers is helping Laotian farmers to multiply their rice yield. The Israelis have formed the first cooperatives in Laos. At present, more than 800 specialists from Israel are "on loan" to foreign nations. As we would expect, a disproportionately large number of participants in development projects abroad come from *kibbutzim*. In sum, Israel serves as a model for undeveloped nations who share the same goal of entering fully into the modern world.[11] David Ben Gurion has said that Israeli aid to other nations rests upon ideals expressed in several passages in the Book of Isaiah. One of them reads: "I have given you as a covenant to the people, a light to the nations" (42:6).

In any discussion of the historical and moral rights of the Israelis, the question arises: What is to be said for the claims of the Palestinian Arabs? This question requires special consideration.

The Claims of the Palestinian Arabs

More than 2,000,000 Palestinian Arabs are living in various regions, some 50 to 60 percent still within former Palestine (primarily the West Bank and the Gaza Strip) and the remainder in Arab countries. These figures do not include the many Arabs who chose to become Israeli citizens and were fully accepted as such.

If a nation actually exists in some sense prior to the honoring of that existence by other peoples, is there convincing evidence that the Palestinians now comprise such a nation? Do they in fact constitute a *laos* comparable to the Jews of Israel, or to the Egyptians or Syrians?

Prime Minister Meir recently insisted that there is no such thing as a Palestinian entity.

Now those Palestinians who remained in the West Bank [after the 1948 War]. Why did they not set up a Palestinian state? After a while, since they didn't do it, King

Abdullah went and annexed the West Bank. The U.N. didn't decide on that. Only two countries ever recognized it, Britain and Pakistan. Abdullah gave them Jordanian citizenship. They voted for the Jordanian Parliament, some were elected to Parliament, and some were members of the Government.

From then until 1967 nobody heard of a Palestinian entity. Where were they? What makes them now more Palestinian than they were until 1967? What happened to Jordan? It wasn't a viable state. What made it viable were the Palestinians who became Jordanian. What should really be Palestine is Jordan. They could call it Palestine.[12]

Arie Eliav, recently elected Secretary General of the Israel Labor Party, has spoken in quite a different vein: "The first thing we have to do is to recognize that the Palestinian Arabs exist as an infant nation. It is there. We have to recognize them. The sooner we do it, the better it will be for us, for them, for eventual peace."[13] The Israeli political party Mapam has offered as its fundamental position that "the territory of Palestine, on both banks of the Jordan, constitutes a common homeland for the two peoples who are actually there—the Jews who returned there and the Palestinians who have been living on the land. Both have the right to nationhood within the framework of two independent states."[14]

There are historical and contemporary factors that make the problem of the unhappy Palestinians more complicated than is allowed by either of the above positions, taken in themselves.

Until recent times, the Palestinian Arabs have been identified by their respective religious affiliations rather than by either ancestry or geographical location. It is still largely correct to speak of them as two groups, Muslim Palestinians and Christian Palestinians, possessed of quite distinctive life styles, institutions, and convictions, and manifesting considerably hostile attitudes toward each other. Their tendency in the present century to identify themselves as Arabs has dulled these mutual suspicions, but it has not eradicated them. The differing religious traditions prevented the development of any rudimentary sense of a common history until into the twentieth century. Even then, the aspirations of the Palestinians were largely oriented toward pan-Arab unity rather than to a national entity of their own. They have not shared, nor do they yet share, common institutions that can actualize their oneness or provide the required nucleus of a self-governing state.

Our study has revealed the great falsity of the charge that Palestine is solely an Arab land from which the Jews dispossessed the rightful inhabitants. There is, indeed, some force in the contention that the Palestinians have lost their moral right to the land—at least those who actively and fanatically oppose the Jewish claim. Such opposition stands in direct contrast to the readiness of many Israelis to compromise and to acknowledge Palestinian rights. We have ourselves stressed that the collective rights of any people are not absolute but are contingent upon behavior. Much in the national consciousness that is being claimed for the Palestinians is not a positive reality but a negative one: antagonism toward Israel. Professor Harkabi writes: "In the usage current among Arabs, 'a just solution of the problem of the Palestinians' is actually a euphemism for the destruction of Israel. The existence of Israel and a just solution of the problem of the Palestinians, as the Palestinians and Arabs define it, are thus incompatible." Harkabi goes so far as to claim, we believe debatably, that the Palestinians are not hostile to Israel because of the hostility of the Arab states; rather, the Palestinians, as the chief inciters against Israel, are largely the cause of the Arab states' hostility to Israel.[15]

In addition, we cannot ignore the objective disparity between the situation of the Jews and that of the Palestinian Arabs. Thousands of Jews have come to Eretz Yisrael as the only refuge from persecution and death, the one place where they can be themselves, without fear or aggravated self-consciousness. Vast numbers of Israelis have, literally, nowhere else they can go. If forced to flee, only Arab lands await them, where they would face almost certain liquidation. The Palestinian Arabs are in no such condition, and they have never been.

How much the identity of the Palestinians arises from within and how much their common outlook derives from their unfortunate conditions as human beings (particularly the refugee status of so many) remains a moot question. Arab continuity of residence in Palestine goes back many centuries, even if not to the exaggerated degree often alleged. Many Arabs look to no homeland but Palestine. They take great pride in their Palestinian culture, and are among the best educated of the Middle Eastern Arabs. They have a strong attachment to the land, including the local holy places of their respective faiths (Christianity or Islam). Indicatively, few West Bank Arabs have ever looked upon themselves as Jordanians. Many Palestinians feel almost like total strangers in different Arab countries.

Significantly, every commission that ever studied the Palestine situation agreed that Arabs and Jews together have rights in the land. Yet, regretfully, no real effort was ever made by any responsible authority to educate the Palestinians to see that a shared right is present, rather than an exclusive right for them alone.

Together with large numbers of Israelis, we believe that the claims of the Palestinian Arabs must be taken seriously. Many of the arguments advanced for Jewish rights to the land can be presented in behalf of the Palestinians. We must try our best to understand their anger, frustration, and longings.

Many Israelis give evidence of certain feelings of guilt respecting these Arabs, despite the strong justification they can themselves advance for their own presence in the land. It is not strange that ever since the Six Day War the possibility of a Palestinian Arab state should be an especially live topic within Israel. Israelis passionately discuss such questions as these: Is the West Bank again to become subject to an existing Arab power, or is it to be granted some form of independence? Will the Palestinians be able to find and develop the leadership from within their own ranks that they so desperately need? What are the wisest and most practical political and economic arrangements for securing maximum cooperation between Palestinian Arabs and Israel?[16]

Once again the irony of the Middle East manifests itself. Had the Arab nations peaceably accepted the interlocking Israeli-Arab states of Palestine, bound together by economic union, the final result might well have been a genuine bi-national, Palestinian entity—in fact even if not in name. The goals and aspirations of Arabs and Jews alike would have been satisfied without the terrible sufferings both have endured and without the wasteful destruction.

The Palestinian Arabs have long been aware of their insignificance in the eyes of Arab leaders of such states as Egypt, Syria, Iraq, and even Jordan. True, no decisive rift between Palestinian and non-Palestinian Arabs can be found before 1948. However, the first Arab-Israeli war, the creation of the refugees, and the division of Palestinian land led to the forming of a temporary organization of Palestinians, who, as we have noted, asked for, but were denied, recognition by other Arabs at the futile post-armistice talks of 1949–50. Over the past two decades and more, the split between Palestinian and non-Palestinian Arabs has grown much deeper.

Lamentably, there is simply no evidence in past or current history to support the hope that the Palestinians will be treated other than as pawns by the various Arab states or that their interests will cease to be entirely ignored by outside powers. Though the subject of many touching speeches and countless promises, these people remain the stepchildren of the Arab world. (The U.N. Resolution of November 22, 1967, earlier discussed, perpetuates this general condition by failing to allow any change in the political status of the Palestinians.)

This unpardonable state of affairs is fully understood among the members of the so-called Palestinian liberation organizations. But, of course, the only way the *fedayeen* cause could "advance," even temporarily, would be through efforts to destroy Israel. This aim is the single thing the *fedayeen* and the larger Arab world have shared. Yet even if—God forbid—this intention were realized, the plight of the Palestinians would probably not be eased at all. If anything, they would be worse off. For, if history is any guide, they would simply be caught once more in the clash of Arab nations battling each other for the control of former Palestine. In all likelihood, the Palestinians would again emerge the losers.

The Jews of Israel have never held that the validity of their national claim nullifies the rights of the Arabs. In partial contrast to the political slant of Prime Minister Meir's statement quoted above, Israel long ago implied the reality of a Palestinian entity. Of all the peoples in the region, only the people of the nascent State of Israel were ready to honor Palestinian rights. (This was an Israel with an even more impossible geography than she subsequently managed to hold on to in the face of Arab invasions.) Israel accepted the U.N. Partition Plan of 1947 and the establishment of a Palestinian Arab state. No other nation has been prepared to treat the Palestinians with equity. As we have learned, inside Israel Arabs have been enabled to make notable progress. The same is increasingly the case in the administered areas. Were peace ever permitted in the Middle East, there is every reason to believe that Israel would fully accept the sovereignty of Arabs within some mutually negotiated portion of former Palestine. The one locus of hope for the Palestinians remains Israel.

Regrettably, the above hope has been devastated by two conditions: an obsessional hatred of Israel among the Palestinians (although many of these people, especially in the West Bank, remain eager for peace and friendship with Israel); and the fact that Israel's hands have been tied by Arab behavior everywhere, as well as by the absence of United Nations' effort in behalf of Palestinian sovereignty.

The tragedy remains: Zionist and Israeli support of a Palestinian Arab state has been effectively blocked by the Arab world. As one Israeli diplomat comments, Palestinian Arabs "had a right to statehood; they were denied statehood by their fellow Arabs. . . . They will have to claim it back from the Arabs, they cannot claim it from us."[17]

It is foolhardy to expect that apart from a strange miracle, Israel can be of positive aid in assuring independence for the Palestinians. Sadly, the question has become a strictly Arab one. This is another way of saying that for the present, the Palestinian cause seems almost hopeless. Thus, any possible settlement with Israel on the part of West Bank Palestinians would brand them as traitors to the Arab world, and make them more liable to terrorist vengeance than is presently the case. (More Arabs, including women and children, have been killed by terrorist attacks than have Israelis.) Even more serious is their fear of being cut off, as a penalty, from their families and relatives in Arab countries. These are among the decisive reasons why so few Palestinians have ventured to support publicly a state of their own.[18]

There is no possibility that the present Jordanian regime will voluntarily restore to the Palestinians what is rightfully theirs and has been forcibly taken away. The only eventuality of independence for the Palestinians appears to lie in political changes within Jordan (apart from a possible military defeat of Israel). But even if substantial changes within Jordan do occur, the chance that such a happening will aid the Palestinians is itself highly unlikely. (At this writing, Al Fatah is threatening the political stability of Jordan.) While a Palestinian revolution within Jordan could conceivably be acceptable to Egypt, it would very likely encounter opposition from Saudi Arabia (like Jordan, a monarchy) and produce unpredictable results in Iraq and Syria. Such a revolution might simply set off a scramble for Jordanian territory by Arab neighbors.

Any revolutionary overthrow of an Arab government that would benefit the Israeli cause would be totally unacceptable to the larger Arab world. Further, there is no ground for anticipating that a Palestinian-dominated regime in Jordan would be less hostile to Israel than is the present belligerent regime there. Its enmity toward Israel would probably be even greater, and its willingness to negotiate a mutually advantageous settlement would be hardly likely.

We have cited Arie Eliav's affirmation of the infant nationhood of the Palestinian Arabs. The decisive norm for assessing that affirmation is revealed in this question: Is Palestinian identity today founded primarily upon the wish to commit politicide against Israel, or can it boast independent integrity? To the extent that Palestinians acknowledge the sovereignty of Israel, their cause gains infinite moral force and their political claims become worthy of acceptance within and beyond the Arab world. Such an acknowledgment and such acceptance remain, alas, far from reality.

22. People—Faith—Land

THE FOUNDATION of Israel is historical right, which is vindicated in turn by the Israelis' moral and political contributions. Where, then, does the Jewish faith fit into the picture? As outsiders to both Judaism and to Israel, we are hardly capable of presenting an authoritative reply to this question. We venture to point up the major issues.

A Critique of Territorial Fundamentalism

For some, the possession of Eretz Yisrael is by divine assignment. Although this is a minority view in Israel today, it directs us to a most crucial problem: Is there any validity in territorial fundamentalism? We refer to the belief that an unconditional title to land can be awarded by divine fiat. When this form of fundamentalism is rejected, as it is by most people, must the rejection imply that the Jewish faith is deprived of positive significance in the triad people-faith-land? In the present section of this chapter we offer several preliminary suggestions.

1. Customarily, those who oppose territorial fundamentalism insist that the divine will must never be equated with the partisan designs of men. Who could disagree with the need for this distinction? However, in fairness we have to add that the distinction carries a two-edged blade. True, no human being could know for certain that God has willed to the Jewish people an irrevocable title deed to Eretz Yisrael. Yet any categorical assertion that God has not so willed is equally forbidden. The reason is the same in both cases: the gulf between human truth and divine truth. Our own denial of territorial fundamentalism involves in this respect as much of a moral venture and risk as does the opposite position.

2. If the opponents of territorial fundamentalism are taking a risk, they are at least in good company.

Soldiers and leaders of Israel's enemies have unabashedly called upon the name of Allah for victory in a "holy" war. Such behavior throws into sharp relief the notable caution of Israelis. Naturally, religious Israelis *hope* that they are somehow honoring God's will for them—everywhere men of faith have a similar hope —but (from the experiences we have had of Israelis) they are most wary of making absolute religious claims. Any disposition to exalt Israel under the guise of divine favor, or to make Israeli successes a proof of the divine presence in contrast to the "judgment" of God upon one's "foes" is a most minor strain in Israeli life today, including its religious life.

William Holladay is entirely right in his critique of the kind of biblical literalism that seeks to give Israel absolute rights to the land. Unfortunately, he fails to recognize the pervasiveness of agreement with his viewpoint within the State of Israel itself. His allegation that the people of Israel refuse to be subject to a God who judges them, or refuse to consider their successes gifts of grace, could only be made by someone grieviously unfamiliar with Israeli spirituality and morality.[1]

Israeli religious restraint has deep roots in the Jewish tradition. It is related to the fear of idolatry, the worship of false gods. Idolatry also extends to the effort to subject the divine will to the interests of men. Unqualified devotion to anything less than God himself is inherently idolatrous. And so is any absolute human claim. (Christian opposition to idolatry is part of the great inheritance bequeathed to the church by Judaism.)

Among the reasons for Israeli religious diffidence and humility, an eminently realistic one stands out: the insuperable moral difficulty in any effort to equate the less-than-ideal acts of men with the purity of God. Israel is not a device for advancing some *égoisme à deux* between the Lord and his people. Deep within the conscience of Israelis, as of Jewish people everywhere, is avoidance of the sin of manipulating God. We are convinced that this is one major reason why so many Israelis are extremely wary of religious claims, and why such a large number identify themselves as nonreligious.

We remember the Torah's witness that all land remains the possession of God. Men are never more than his stewards: "The land shall not be sold in perpetuity, for the land is mine; for you are strangers and sojourners with me" (Lev. 25:23). Any blind, unqualified devotion to the earthly reality of Israel is contradicted by something within the Jewish tradition itself: an opposition to idolatry that is the very ground of the assertion that all human rights are conditional. God is not the servant of geopolitics.

3. In both the Jewish and the Christian traditions, the presence of God is glimpsed by a practical test: the presence of justice, peace, and happiness for human beings.

As in stories of unnumbered human migrations, the original entry of the Hebrew people into the "promised land" involved overcoming native populations. In the same way, the reestablishment of the State of Israel in 1948 led, however unintentionally, to the displacing of many inhabitants. There have been several wars and much suffering. We know that the rebirth of Israel has produced many good things, and we know too that Israel is free of guilt for a great deal of the evil. Yet the point stands: No man's hands are so clean that he can say without any reservation, Here is the will of God.

Following upon the Six Day War, a noted American scholar provided an Israeli audience with a ringing religio-patriotic message praising the Israeli victory as, in effect, a divine triumph. He was interrupted by an Israeli soldier who stood up and cried out: "These hands of mine are drenched in blood. With them I have killed many human beings. How can you talk that way?"

4. We have to be on the watch or we will usher absolute claims out through the front door only to permit their entry through the rear, in the person of Israel's enemies. The theological testimony that no people possesses an unconditional right to land has to be handled with great care, lest it be disavowed in the very act of approving it.

Either we support Israel's rights or, in practical effect, we absolutize the claims of her foes. The right of a nation to exist does have, in a sense, an absolute or unconditional side to it. That is to say, a nation ought to be enabled to endure unless or until compelling moral reasons can be marshalled for its abolition.

5. The only sure safeguard against the temptation to equate our perceptions of what God wills with what he really wills is to stop fancying that we are somehow his special agents. The wise and responsible course is to temper our theological convictions with historical and political considerations, and most especially to be vigilant against the evil of judging the State of Israel with a different standard from standards we use in assessing other nations. Particularly objectionable is the idea of some kind of theological trial, the notion that if the Israelis do not behave in ways that appeal to us, they have to fall under the divine judgment and perhaps even lose their right to life.

Professor Werblowsky of the Hebrew University reminds us that the "biblical view of history is extremely naive: if thou shalt hearken unto the voice of the Lord then success, health and blessing are assured, whilst disobedience will be punished by famine, pestilence, defeat and exile." (The prophet Jeremiah may be permitted to interject: "Amend your ways and your doings, and I will let you dwell in this place" [7:3].) However, as Werblowsky goes on to say, even though the biblical account of history is inadequate, it nevertheless provides indispensable testimony: our historical experience is to be linked to the divine ground of history and of all life.[2] In sum, while the biblical rendering of the historical pilgrimage of Israel cannot be taken literally or in any absolutist way, we are still obligated to take the biblical account and symbolism seriously.[3] The answer to territorial fundamentalism is hardly to take flight into timeless truths removed from political or other controversy. There is just one equitable alternative to fundamentalism as a means of supporting human claims to land: historical and moral right. The truth that no people has any absolute right to territory does not at all warrant the conclusion that nations are without *relative* rights. Such a conclusion would be at once frivolous and irresponsible.

The Gifts of Faith

In the section just concluded, faith appears to play a largely critical and negative role. Does not Judaism also possess positive, creative relevance to the reality of Israel?

The testimony of faith enters the picture both *before* and *after* an assertion of the political and moral rights of a people. By "before" we mean that the very ground of any declaration of such rights is the divine gift of life itself. By "after" we mean that faith takes us beyond the purely political domain—without annulling that domain or its values. While the justification of Israel for what she shares with other nations must be strictly historical and moral, the spiritual affirmation of the *laos* of Israel means honoring her in and for her uniqueness.

Spirituality means the offering of thanksgiving and the celebrating of new opportunities. Men may not find in their faith irrefutable, scientific validation of every one of their specific rights and claims. But they may turn to faith in order to honor divine gifts and divine responsibilities.

It is understandable that numbers of Jews (and some non-Jews) should identify in religious terms Israel's place among the nations. Judaism, after all, bears the most intimate relationship to history as to morality. For many Jews, not alone Israelis but those in the Diaspora, Israel's spiritual quality constitutes her very uniqueness, a quality perhaps clothed in mystery, but nonetheless real. The religious Jew is moved to apply to Israel the biblical injunction, "you shall be to me a kingdom of priests and a holy nation" (Exod. 19:6). He emphasizes that Israel is the one place in the world where the life of Judaism is blessed by a Jewish national milieu. He testifies that if Israel were to become a conventional state cut off from the Jewish tradition, her whole *raison d'être* would vanish.

Some Israelis go further: Apart from explicit faith in the God of Israel, where is the nation's uniqueness? Where is its peculiar meaning and contribution? All peoples have histories. History is not enough. But there is sacred history, and this is more than just history. Without the God of Abraham, Isaac, and Jacob, Eretz Yisrael finally becomes merely another piece of land. This nation that outwardly seems like other nations is inwardly a peculiar nation, a nation called to witness to the Lord of all things.

There are no proofs. But perhaps there may be a few signs, a few tiny points of light. Rabbi Abraham J. Heschel testifies that it would be sacrilegious to treat Israel either as a compensation or as an atonement. Yet "the existence of Israel reborn makes life less unendurable. It is a slight hinderer of hindrances to believing in God."[4]

We may venture still further. Perhaps Israel is a response to an unbroken trust. "Pagans have idols, Israel has a promise. We have no image, all we have is hope. Israel reborn is a verification of the promise." Is there a relation between Auschwitz and the State of Israel? We must be mad to ask this: "There is no answer to Auschwitz. . . . To try to answer is to commit a supreme blasphemy." And yet: "Israel enables us to bear the agony of Auschwitz without radical despair, to sense a ray of God's radiance in the jungles of history." Here we may offer a response—not a resolution of mysteries, but the response of our own lives: "Israel reborn is an answer to the Lord of history who demands hope as well as action, who expects tenacity as well as imagination."[5]

We are commenting theologically here, and not for the sake of some kind of demonstration. Events, even those that impress us as wonderful, do not prove the truth of faith—not unless we are prepared to concede that events impressing us as evil or satanic go to disprove the truth of faith. The double standard is a temptation not alone in our assessment of nations; it invades religious thinking as well. No one is entitled to find an element of divine judgment in the historic dispersion of Jewry who does not also find an element of divine support in the rebirth of Eretz Yisrael. Any who argue for "the rod of God's anger" in the one case and against the saving presence of God in the other case need to have both their logic and their morals inspected.

In Israel the ancient spiritual covenant may be reborn and realized in a unique way: in the life of a free people. But cannot Israel erect obstacles to the divine-human covenant? Of course. Faith may be subjected to national interests, and even to the idolatry of the state. How easy it is for national prestige and power to be confused with the will of God.

If freedom did not entail temptation, it would not be freedom. The unique opportunity for Jewish faith within Israel may be accepted and fulfilled, and it may be denied. This is precisely why the religious Jew may not draw any theological conclusion that Eretz Yisrael means unconditional rights. Were Israel ever to convey such rights, it would constitute an insult to the humanity of the Jewish people. It would violate the dignity of men created in the image of God. To be a man is to work, to strive. "Choose this day whom you will serve" (Josh. 24:15). Men make choices. If they "choose the Lord," it has to be their decision.

Israel is like a wife or husband. Neither wife nor husband is owned by the partner. Each partner is a gift, offering meaning to the other's life. The proper attitude to one's marriage partner is thanksgiving and celebration. A husband or wife is the steward, the trustee of the other.

Faith bestows meaning upon Israel, by giving special meaning to the lives of the people involved. In the eyes of faith, Israel is a gift. Or perhaps we ought to say, Israel is a loan. (The Lord said: "The land is mine.") The people of the land are the stewards, the trustees who celebrate and are thankful for Israel. *From the standpoint of faith, Israel is not primarily a claim. She is a responsibility.* No longer is Israel looked upon as simply one nation alongside others. She is "our" nation. Conjugal life and the life of Israel are alike confirmed only through love, honor, and obedience.

Ideally, the gift of a marriage partner does not mean the disparagement of other marriages. So too the trusteeship of the Israelis can be neither narrow nor exclusivist. Ideally, Israel is "a light to the nations."

Israel guarantees nothing. She is a chance.

A word of warning must be interposed. There is only one thing worse than trying to change an opportunity into a guarantee: the insinuation that unless Israel acts in such-and-such a way religiously, she forfeits the right to life. At once, Israel is *this* nation and she is one nation among many nations. *No outsider has any right to demand that "this nation" behave in superhuman fashion.* If the Israelis choose to commit themselves to uniquely creative causes, that is their business and their honor. The outsider has only one right: to rejoice, whenever rejoicing is called for.

Nevertheless, for the religious Israeli, strictly human wishes ought not determine the survival or the eclipse of Israel or the Jewish people. The counterpoise of human freedom is objective duty. The covenant means obligation, the commandment to testify by word and act to the Lord's love, to his faithfulness, righteousness, and power. It is a bad thing to preach the kind of religion that merely bathes human self-interest in an aura of sanctity. It is a good thing to stand for a prophetic faith that subjects all human behavior to standards of justice.[6] How infinite the difference between those who think they have appropriated the will of God and those who, without illusions about themselves, trust and pray.

Faith is of unlimited relevance to every bit of life in the State of Israel. It means, or it can mean, fresh wars upon the idolatries that beset the human family, openness to the future, hope for tomorrow, humility, courage to choose, zeal for justice and peace, steadfastness, sharing, thanksgiving. The greatest of these is thanksgiving.

How, then, are we to cope with the painful truth that so many people in today's Israel appear to have no regard for Jewish faith? For an answer we must probe more deeply into the reality of Jewish peopleness.

The Meaning of Jewish Peopleness

When in preparing for this book we asked a friend in our local church which issues she felt needed exploration, she replied with a question: "Isn't the revival of the State of Israel a political affair rather than a religious one?" By contrast, one often hears outsiders to Israel, and especially Christians, insisting that the Israelis ought to fashion a "spiritual" kind of life instead of a "materialistic" one.

The above outlooks have one thing in common: they are equally far from the Jewish point of view. Within Jewish self-awareness, the secular and the religious domains are wedded, and they cannot be divorced. Any dualism of "politics" versus "religion," or of "matter" versus "spirit," is fundamentally alien to the Jewish tradition. It is no accident that Zionism in its totality is neither a purely secular-political phenomenon nor a purely religious one.

How can Jewish "religious ideals" ever be realized in the modern State of Israel? The question reveals considerable ignorance. The ancient covenant involves a *people*. There is nothing of abstract idealism in it. The Jewish faith centers in the life of this people. Its principles apply to national life as much as anywhere. The State of Israel constitutes one direct fulfillment of the Jewish tradition.

Here is a hard but necessary lesson for non-Jews and particularly for American Christians: Jewishness is not this, that, or the other single thing; it is an indivisible unity of historical memory, spirituality, moral and social principles, community existence, culture, and intellectuality.

There is no way to understand Israel, or the wider Jewish point of view, without sympathetic awareness of the unity of people-faith-land.

We observe the contrast between Jewry and the Christian community. Those in different nations who are members of the church, "the body of Christ," are united by their faith (including the history and traditions of that faith). Those who stop adhering to the faith thereby act to place themselves outside the Christian community. By contrast, while there can be ethnic differences among Jews, and while many Jews do accept a common faith, behind and beyond these things stands a fundamental *laos* sustained by a much broader history than a religious one. If we must use the term "Judaism," we have to make entirely clear that we mean the religion of a particular people.

The inseparability of Jewish peopleness and Jewish faith is demonstrated in Israel by a certain social policy. Jews who become Christians or Muslims can expect a certain amount of ostracism or social disability, including those very Jews who satisfy the traditional requirement of Jewishness: to have a Jewish mother.[7] Superficially, this situation might seem to imply that Jewishness and Judaism are reducible to religiousness. That conclusion is unwarranted. It is contradicted by another fact: Israeli and other Jews can be completely nonreligious and even antireligious, and yet be fully accepted as Jews. Were religiousness the deciding mark of Jewishness, this could not happen.

We reach this great paradox: religion is not an absolute requirement for Jews, but Jewishness is bound to the Jewish faith, which is in turn bound to the land. Jews are a "natural community" (James Parkes). One is a Jew simply by living. The Jew who converts to a different faith is as a man who has disowned his family.[8] The secularized, nonobservant Israeli finds an equivalent of religious fulfillment through identification with the life and future of his people and the land. He can follow a course that is not open in quite the same way to his like-minded brother abroad. The Israeli may attest that he is fully a Jew simply by being in the land. The Tosefta, a rabbinic work probably from the third century C.E., says: "Living in Israel is the equivalent of fulfilling all the commandments in the Torah."

Jews could not have become an integral people without the land. Even the "Canaanite" Israeli,[9] by his very presence in the land of his ancestors, testifies to the historic link with Palestine. Without Zion, the Jewish faith would be a different faith. (Christianity, which arose out of Judaism, would be quite different as well—or, perhaps we should say, it would be nonexistent.)

Jewish faith and Jewish peopleness developed as one; it is out of the question to say that the one preceded or caused the other. There is a saying in the Talmud: "Your father is the Almighty; your mother is the congregation of Israel." Historically speaking, the most we can say is that the people Israel were born out of the faith, and the faith was born out of the people Israel.

However, it is still possible, and indeed necessary, to assign priority as between faith and people. We cannot accomplish this through a search for historical cause and effect. What we must do is to turn to classical Jewish experience. The crucial point for an understanding of Jewish history is not whether the Jewish people were created by means of faith, but instead (in Werblowsky's words) "the undeniable fact that since biblical times this was precisely the way in which the Jews saw themselves and experienced their existence." It is on this decisive ground that we find Judaism to be linked to the Jewish people much more exclusively and intimately than the Christian church is associated with, say, Western civilization, or Islam with the Arabs. From this perspective, we can recognize Judaism as "the fountainhead and the purpose of Israel's existence."[10] For it was by faith that the people endured, by the faith that God had summoned them to be a people within the land. This faith, as recounted and reenforced in the Torah, molded the Jewish people just as surely as did the land.

A most significant aspect of the inheritance of a common history among Israelis is the appropriation of that history by religious and nonreligious people together, as well as by the many who fall somewhere in the middle. On first consideration, a quite different state of affairs might be expected: Just because Israel's history is so permeated by religious elements, one might anticipate that the great numbers of nonreligious Israelis, and especially the many antireligious people among them, would wish to dissociate themselves from the history and oppose its dominant place in the body social. This has not happened.

A contrast with the American situation may help to bring out the point. Consider the conflict in the United States over the place of the Bible in public education. Bible instruction, and even brief Bible readings, are criticized and opposed by many secular and religious people alike, although not always on the same ground. The major basis for such protests within both groups is that the use of the Bible violates the separation of church and state. Other criticisms put forward include the following: Such use of the Bible is a return to superstition; it is "out of place"; religious instruction is best handled in religious institutions or in the home. In Israel, by contrast, instruction in Bible is, as we noted in Chapter 8, an essential part of the curriculum in all public schools. There is little objection to this and it is widely supported.

Why is there such a difference between the two countries? The reason is simple. In Israel the Bible is a component part of the living history of the nation. (This can hardly be said of the United States.) Thus, Abraham is much more than a religious figure; he is the "father of our people." The parallel in the United States is much more George Washington than Jesus of Nazareth. A Jew can ignore Abraham religiously without at all forfeiting him as a special ancestor, whereas the Christian who turns from Jesus religiously loses him in other decisive ways.

In the stories of Hebrew Scripture the secularized Israeli is somehow confronted by the story of his own life. In Israel, among the most serious students of the Bible and supporters of biblical study in education are people who could not care less about "religion" as such. It is relevant to note that an Israeli telephone directory reads like a roll call of biblical heroes; also, that the periodic national and international Bible contests in Israel are famous events, followed almost as eagerly by the nonreligious as by the religious.

The religious camp in Israel is drawn into the common outlook by the influence of a salient truth: Jewish faith is itself grounded in certain historical events, which are in large measure the very foundation-acts of Israel, and not least of the State of Israel. Indeed, for Judaism "all religion is history" (Martin Buber).

For many Israelis, particularly the native-born, biblical history remains more alive than the history of Jews in the intervening centuries. This is quite understandable, since so much of Jewish history after Roman times has taken place in other lands, and has been marked by much suffering and grief devoid of the consolation of Eretz Yisrael. In the land, by contrast, the link with the Bible is direct, resting securely upon common geography and common language, and pointing back to days of valor, or at least of solace, in the land.

Of course, any attempt to remove or discount the religious dimensions of the Bible and to have very much left is impossible, objectively speaking. But to concentrate exclusively upon this objection is largely to miss the point. Instead of reading biblical history through the eyes of faith, as the religious man would do, the nonreligious Israeli reads the faith through the eyes of history, the history of his people and in a real sense, therefore, of himself. He effectively demythologizes Scripture, almost without being aware of it and certainly not as a calculated policy.

The religious man repeats, "He brought us forth from Egypt." The secularist proclaims, "Masada shall not fall again." Each man can appropriate the other man's event. The nonreligious individual celebrates the biblical Exodus from Egypt, and the religious person celebrates the transreligious, post-biblical epic of Masada. Existentially speaking, the two are sharing one experience.

Again, religious and secular Israelis alike can find in the rebirth of their country immediately following the Nazi Inferno sublime realization of Ezekiel's vision of dry bones gathered together, covered by flesh, and the spark of life breathed into them. "Behold, I will open your graves, and raise you from your graves, O my people; and I will bring you home into the land of Israel" (Ezek. 37:1-14). Perhaps only the Jew feels the full power of these words. Yet can we not identify with him?

In our discussion of religious issues in Chapters 12 and 13, we saw that there are plenty of conflicts over religion in Israel. Here we underscore the truth that Israeli Jews on opposing sides of the religion question are nevertheless bound by a common heritage and destiny. The sharing tempers the wrath that so often accompanies controversy over religion.

Religious Israelis, in enumerating the challenges that confront Israel, yearn to know and to do the will of God. Secular Israelis speak differently: How can justice and human welfare be achieved among us? There is more to unite these advocates than to separate them, especially when we remember that the will of God and justice for men are inseparable in the historic Jewish consciousness. The outcome is a single question: What is our moral calling as a people?

Each element in the triad is nourished by the other two: Without people and faith, the land is not the same. Without faith and land, the people are not the same. Without land and people, the faith is not the same.

In one and only one respect the people and the faith are more indispensable to Jewish reality than is the land. The people and the faith can survive, and have survived, apart from the land—although never without remembering the land, and never without the hope of restoration to it.

The capacity to survive beyond the land suggests our next theme: the relation between the Jews of Israel and the Jews of the Diaspora. What may the Diaspora mean for Israeli Jews? What may the State of Israel mean for Jews who remain outside Israel?

Israeli Jews and Diaspora Jews

This topic lies strictly within the family of Jews. The decisions must be made and will be made by Jews. Yet we include the subject for the benefit of non-Jewish readers, and perhaps a few Jewish readers, who may desire greater acquaintance with the main issues.

Within the Jewish community as a whole, there are three points of view.

The one view is "anti-Zionism"—more accurately, anti-Israelism. This is very much of a minority position. One form of reasoning leading to such a stance is the idea that Israel and Zionism have no intrinsic relation to Judaism. This interpretation came into Jewish thinking largely under the influence of nineteenth-century German Protestant denominationalism. From this viewpoint, Jewishness stands for nothing more than a religion; it is not a matter of *laos*, peopleness. The bitterly "anti-Zionist" American Council for Judaism argues this way. But the Council is a minuscule and unrepresentative (though loquacious) group among Jews in the United States. It finds its most ardent publicizers among pro-Arab Christians and Arab propagandists. The Council, which might more appropriately be called the "American Council Against Judaism," has been repudiated by every major agency of Judaism in the United States.

History has left the "anti-Zionists" as rebels without a cause—unless they are prepared to join with would-be politicides. Today the only surviving way to express "anti-Zionism" is through anti-Israelism, which is steadfastly opposed by the overwhelming majority of Jews in the Diaspora.

The second viewpoint is an anti-Diaspora one. Only too often, personal and family suffering has made this outlook inevitable and deserving of anguished sympathy. A woman from Hungary said: "When I recall that my homecoming started on a death march, I've only three words to say to the Jews in the Diaspora: 'Jews, go home!' " Other expressions of an anti-Diaspora position either derive from Israel's great needs or arise as a matter of principle. David Ben Gurion has repeatedly asserted that all Jews ought to come up to Israel.

A less aggressive version of the second outlook, perhaps better identified as "non-Diaspora" rather than "anti-Diaspora," is fairly widespread within Israel. As Leonard Fein points out, "it is no longer clear what being a Jew means that being an Israeli does not." The young in Israel are more and more socialized to statehood rather than to a wider Jewishness.[11]

The unwitting or witting consequence of the second point of view is to seek to contain Jewishness within nationality, to transform it into a special political reality. (However, a parallel anti-Diaspora view may arise out of a religious notion that only in Eretz Yisrael can the Jewish faith be correctly practiced.) Apart from practical obstacles within the second position, most Jews, including a number within Israel, simply do not accept the opinion that Jewishness can be restricted to Israelness.

The trouble with the first two views, as suggested in the previous section of this chapter, is that they fail to honor the Jewish tradition in all its breadth and depth. Jewishness equally transcends pure religiousness and pure nationality, and it even transcends any combination of those two realities.

Thus are we brought to the third viewpoint, which assumes the authenticity of Jewish life both in Eretz Yisrael and in the Diaspora.

A singular paradox within the Jewish *laos* is the ability of Jews to live beyond Eretz Yisrael at the same time that their bond with that place gives them essential nourishment. To approach the matter from the opposite direction, Jews within Israel retain a kind of dual citizenship. As Israelis they are citizens of a particular nation. Yet as Jews they are more than mere inhabitants of a given country. Tellingly, many Jews, even a number who do not look upon themselves as religious, recognize instinctively that there is much more to Jewishness than its ethnic-national side.[12] Christians ought to find a certain kinship here, for they too are citizens of various nations and yet members of the world-wide community of the church, called out of all nations.[13] Even if Christians were totally absent from the land of their faith's origin, Christianity would not be gravely wounded. As a matter of fact, more than once the Christian movement has put forth a negative view of spatial ties. The heavenly Jerusalem has taken precedence over the earthly Jerusalem—and even over Rome or Geneva. With respect to Islam, the link to Palestine is, as we indicated in Chapter 12, secondary in objective importance, in contrast to Arabia.

Unnumbered Jews of Israel recognize the authenticity and the unique contributions of Jewish life in the Diaspora. Yigal Allon, Deputy Prime Minister of Israel, has pointed out that the ties of Israel with the Diaspora can help the younger generation of Israelis to identify with the fate of Jews everywhere, and thereby to avoid the pitfalls of isolationism and introversion. On the other side, the refusal of Israel to dissociate herself from Jews in different lands is one preventive of their assimilation.[14]

It is not necessary to provide lengthy documentation of support for Israel on the part of Jews of the Diaspora. Their dedication is well-known. Eretz Yisrael has endured, it is true, by virtue of an unbroken Jewish community there. By inner power, Zion has fought off total destruction. Yet it is equally true that a free Israel could not have been reestablished in our time without the heroic efforts of Diaspora Jewry, especially Jews from Eastern Europe.[15] The vital interest of American and other Jews in the survival and future of today's Israel reveals an existential solidarity that is not narrowly "religious." Neither is it narrowly "national," for as citizens in various countries Jews of the Diaspora also contribute fully to the life and welfare of their own nations. In the United States the concern of Jews for Israel unites them with millions of other Americans who have meaningful ties with another country.

The difficult issue remains of the meaning of the Diaspora both for Jews who live there and in its independent relation to Israel.

"Diaspora" is a uniquely Jewish concept and reality, sustained by centuries of life beyond the land. Many have argued that the Diaspora is as much a fulfillment of the Jewish tradition as is Israel. Jewishness is open upon the world. Not only is the God of Jewish faith the creator of heaven and earth, and the maker and redeemer of men; the Jewish ethic is one of universal justice, righteousness, and peace.

Nevertheless, from a Jewish point of view, it was perhaps inevitable that the great fact of Israel's rebirth in our time would pose questions about the rationale of Jewish life outside Israel. The fear is often expressed within Israel that the country cannot survive without greatly increased numbers of immigrants. Certain Israelis seem to have the idea that the Diaspora is made up of second-class Jews, who are on the way to oblivion through social and cultural assimilation. (Some Israelis have little conception of the vigor of Diaspora Jewry in the United States and elsewhere.)

We are faced with what seem to be two irreconcilable persuasions. On the one hand, the Diaspora is designated as *galut* (exile). Accordingly, the homecoming of Jews to Israel is called *kibbutz galuyot,* the ingathering of the exiles. On the other hand, thousands of Jews in the free world, including great numbers of American Jews, do not feel that they are living lives of exile. Are these people wrong?

Only one way is open for their testimony to be other than a case of self-justification. We must ask: Is there within the very reality of a sovereign Israel something to vindicate the life of the Diaspora?

With the original loss of Jewish sovereignty, the movement of Jews into the world lost its voluntary character. Diaspora became the enforced and unmitigated evil of exile. Under conditions of duress and of sufferance, rather than those of right, Israel beyond Eretz Yisrael was, in the words of Rabbi David Polish, "no longer a continuum of the universal vision of prophecy. It was no more a messenger of [moral and spiritual] universalism than a prisoner is a monastic." During the long and impatient years from the Romans until our time, the sovereign reality of Israel was only a memory and a hope. Then came 1948. *"Coercion makes the difference. . . . Israel, once sovereign and dispersed, then homeless and exiled, is now again both a State and a world community, both a political entity and a universal reality with which every one must reckon and which no one can define."*[16]

A most sublime fact in the reestablishment of Israel is that instead of cutting the ground from under Diaspora life, the rebirth has contributed to the opposite result: it has given meaning and authenticity to the Diaspora. True, Jews who are *compelled* to remain beyond Eretz Yisrael live in unrelieved exile. But of those who can *freely choose,* and who choose to live in another land, we may apply the term "Diaspora." It is the State of Israel that makes their choice possible. Without Israel, there is no such freedom, and every Jew is in exile. (The fact of a free Diaspora means that there is no guarantee against the assimilation of some Jews into non-Jewish culture. Assimilation need not mean the end of a Jewish contribution; many assimilated Jews have had a significant leavening influence upon non-Jewish society. Nevertheless, *as a policy* assimilationism contradicts all the values of Jewish survival.

It is the law of the land that Jews from anywhere in the world have the right to come up to Israel. This law has various implications. We refer to it here only for its powerful and liberating effect upon the psychology and spirituality of Jews in the Diaspora. Suppose that the menace of antisemitism is actualized. I, an American or South American or French Jew, can go to Israel tomorrow and be welcomed home—unconditionally. No prodigy is more conclusive than this in showing that the exilic aspect of the Diaspora is no longer unrelieved. The Jew who today lives beyond the borders of Israel has Israel as his portable homeland, accompanying him at all times and in all places.

The Christian can be "at home" in the United States as long as (assuming his faith is operating) he is part of the life of the Christian community and can live in hope of the final coming of the Kingdom of God. (Exile can be a present reality for the Christian in the sense that his earthly life differs from eternal life with God. Many religious Jews share this conviction.) Yet, distinctively, the Jewish community can be "at home" in the United States only as long as Israel is more than a memory or a hope.

Are we to conclude that nothing of exile remains in Diaspora life? Unhappily, no. Before mid-1967, many Jews would have answered "yes." But then came the total threat to Israel. We reported above the attestation of Rabbi Polish that a free Israel gives relief to exile. That testimony was made before the Six Day War. After the War, Dr. Polish wrote in different vein, and spoke for countless Jews of the Diaspora: The difference between us and the Jews of the Soviet Union and Poland is that they are in captivity. Yet we are still in exile. *Galut* is characterized by the uncertainty of existence, and this is what we experienced when the world turned cold in May of 1967. We felt alone and abandoned. "Suddenly we found ourselves emotionally and spiritually uprooted, and our entire beings, which until then we were capable of sharing with generous capacity both with Israel and with our own Western society, were violently torn from their moorings."

Rabbi Polish then asks the inevitable, agonizing question: Are Jews to withdraw? Are they to abandon the prophetic struggle? His answer is possessed of great courage. It is the courage to look into the very face of evil and still say: We are responsible men. Israel does more than give relief to exile; she offers meaning for all exiles. Israel gives the courage to act *despite* the reign of devilish powers. For that is what Israel is all about. Israel provides "the mandate to the Jew to assume his responsibility for redemption. . . ." The only way that Jewish existence outside Israel can be justified is through the release of the Jewish ethic into the world, just as Zionism released that ethic into Eretz Yisrael—*despite* the powers of evil. The sovereignty of Israel has hardly vanquished the evil powers. Yet, in spite of them, Israel steadfastly pursues the course of justice and freedom.

There is one reservation: "If the world closes in upon us too much, we will be too embattled for any concern except for our survival. The Jews of every generation who would march to Utopia on the trampled bodies of the Jewish people expose the lie of their cause, since, in the name of a new life, they would deny life to this people; in the name of freedom, would enslave this people; in the name of redemption of every group, would thwart the redemption of this group."

Why must this reservation be made? Because the Jewish people have a duty to survive. The "faith of the Jewish people is the most authentic test yet devised of the world's integrity. *The truth of every cause is validated or found fraudulent in the way in which it confronts the Jewish people. . . .*" What other people, destroyed and exiled for almost two thousand years, has ever been reborn? The wise men "who measure the life and death of every civilization, who predict the decline and fall of every living society"—what do they have to say about Israel? "To have crawled out of the sewers of Warsaw, the barracks of Auschwitz, the forests of Poland, and to give birth to a people again is a marvel that no deterministic interpretation of history, no economic dialectics can possibly cope with. *This* is the moment from which Jewish theology and a theology of consolation for men everywhere arises. And this is the saving event which rescues the Jewish people from ultimate terror and despair."

The event rescues all men: "The capacity of a people to face the demonic in man and to overwhelm its own fate is a vindication not only of this people, Israel, but of the spirit of man, flickering desperately in the dark night of human anguish." Because of Israel, Jews in the Diaspora-exile may stand erect—and so may every man.

The Jewish people do not accept the idea of fate. Dr. Polish concludes: "Even in the midst of a world caught in nationalist frenzy, the possibilities of community beyond national idolatry are beginning to emerge. Can it be that this people, rooted in soil and drifting in the world at the same time, can show a new way—a love of land and a kinship with mankind, an attachment to home modified by an openness to the world? The *Galut* says to the State: 'Remember, you were born for prophecy and for messianism.' The State says to the *Galut*: 'Remember, you have gone forth into the world to live and not to die.' Let the world, which is also in *Galut,* learn this lesson of the two-fold existence."[17]

The autonomy and relative separation of the Diaspora and Israel are justified. The justification arises out of an obligation that transcends both the Diaspora and the State of Israel. Were the world redeemed, antisemitism would be at an end, and we would be free to reason differently, were reasoning required under such blessed circumstances. The hope of Zion as a refuge from harm has had infinite meaning at different times in Jewish history, and never more than with the

Nazi Inferno. Yet at other times, and never more than today, Eretz Yisrael has not been enabled to provide a guarantee of safety. Israel is always a sanctuary, but often in the original meaning of that word: a place of holiness, and hence a place of challenge, of destiny. All who hold the conviction that Jews are possessed of a transcendent duty to survive as a people will plead and work both for a strong Israel and for a strong Diaspora in many lands. In an unredeemed, genocidal world, it is at once irresponsible and foolhardy to commend the gathering together of the Jewish people in any single home.

Where the Jewish *laos* makes its unique and indispensable contribution to the human family is through the persuasion (in opposition to all forms of otherworldliness) that prophetic spirituality and morality demand rootage in "ordinary" space and time. The very essence of Israel lies in her relating of the great heritage of the Jewish people and Judaism to normal political and social life. Without universal demands and responsibilities, particular human communities become self-centered, exclusivist, and subject to the corruptions of power. But without any application to concrete human problems, universal principles remain empty dreams.

Particularity is the home that keeps universality from flying away into abstract ideals; universality is the adventure that judges particularity and lures it away from self-concentration.

We must not overstate these differences. In one major respect Israel can be more effectively universalistic than the Diaspora: through her sovereign participation in the international community, through her right "to speak with dignity in the council chambers of the world."[18] By contrast, the international-mindedness of Diaspora Jews will, in the foreseeable future, naturally give prime attention to the security of Israel.

It is possible that the Jewry of Israel and the Jewry of the Diaspora will one day experience a kind of separation. Such an eventuality need not be the result of conflict. It can be a matter of coming of age, of the development of relative self-sufficiency. (The presence or absence of peace in the Middle East is the greatest single determining factor here.) After a time, parents and children cease to be one household. It is better if both have their own homes. This does not mean a severing of relations or the end of mutual helpfulness and concern. To the extent that separation reflects autonomy and maturity, it is to be welcomed.

Finally, there is between the Diaspora and Israel a certain relative difference in emphasis. Inevitably, religious forms of Jewish self-expression will tend to predominate within the Diaspora. There are special lessons for Israel deriving from Jewish religious experience within pluralistic, non-Jewish societies. Within Israel, political and social forms of self-expression will be accentuated. However, advocates of a wider Zionism see Israel as increasingly the center, not alone of scientific, educational and cultural achievement, but also of Jewish spirituality. There is no ultimate conflict or division here. It is a question of distinctive vocational contributions within the one Jewish *laos*.

23. From Penitence to Reconciliation

THE AFFIRMATION of Israel has taken us through several levels. At the foundation is the right to life that every people must have if the Jewish people are to share in it. From this foundation arises a specific right created by history, the right of Jews to a certain place once known as Palestine. This, too, is a shared right, shared with Palestinian Arabs. Next above is moral right, made peculiarly authentic by Zionist and Israeli stewardship. Finally, there is the capstone of faith, in no way an argument for someone's rights but instead a gift. Israel is received with the kind of thanksgiving that seeks out duties.

May others share in the thankfulness and the celebration? Here is the last of our many questions. In most of this volume we have sought to fill a surrogate role in behalf of the people of Israel. Now we speak at once more personally and more representatively of certain testimony beyond, but not in separation from, the Jewish community.

In the Beginning, Shame

How can we enter the sanctuary for a celebration if we do not have clean hands and a pure heart, if we have lifted up our souls to what is false, if we have sworn deceitfully?

There can be no human fellowship without mutual acceptance. Still today in the churches many have not really accepted the right to life of the Jewish community in Israel and the world. There is no way the Christian world can be healed of its transgressions against the Jewish people without acknowledging and repenting of its evil.

Is the world Christian community ready to consent to another Holocaust as it did to the first one? Recently, a New York City rabbi could almost routinely entitle a Sabbath sermon, "Preparing for a Second Holocaust: The Christian Response to the Middle East Crisis"—the routinization adding to, rather than detracting from, the horror.

It is odd that Jews have anything to do with us. It is unbelievable. There must be a miracle of grace here. Jews ought to be most suspicious of Christians. They have little, if any, reason to trust us, or to expect that Christians are going to respect them and their faith. They cannot readily forget, nor ought they, the unending years when the church has said (it still says): "You are nothing. We have taken your place." Here is the theological bias that makes hollow any insistence within Christian leadership that the Middle East situation is to be assessed on "strictly political and moral grounds."

In the previous chapter we referred to the persuasion that Jews have a duty to survive as Jews. It was with trepidation that we spoke of this matter. Any such viewpoint must never arise as a demand from non-Jews, especially Christians. Affirmation of a Jewish obligation to endure as a people can come only from within the community of Jews. At the very most, outsiders may assent to that affirmation.

The shame of Christendom century upon century is to make demands of Jews. The fateful sequel of a demand is an accusation. For what promise is there that the other will ever satisfy any demand of ours in just the way we wish?

Until today, the survival of Jews has meant suffering for them. How can we say to a people that they must suffer? How can we say this to Jews? The Christian community has no right to tell Jews to do anything—whether it be to survive as Jews, or to assimilate, or to do something else. We do not even have the right to tell Jews that they ought to reproach us.

It is not a matter of giving blanket approval to every act of the Israelis. It is a question of having at least the same primal respect for their freedom and dignity that we have for other people.

Through the long, terrible years we defiled our own rights—by our defamation of Jews, by passing by "on the other side." We lost even the right of well-intentioned counsel. Still today the signs of Christian penitence are few. Still today in the United States most antisemites are Christians—this, in face of the truth that "it is the Christian above all who is expected to react most strongly to attacks on Jews" (The Reverend Edward H. Flannery).

Still today there is a serious lack of knowledge among Christians respecting the breadth and depth of Christendom's hostility to, and persecution of, the Jewish people throughout the history of the church. The story is more or less ignored (or, shall we say, suppressed?) in teaching and educational literature. When it is acknowledged, antisemitism is often shrugged off as a relic from the past rather than recognized as a present evil. Much Christian church school literature and Bible study material continue to have a strong potential of fostering negative and prejudicial attitudes toward Jews and Judaism.[1]

In earlier, more "religious" times, Christians would resort to Jesus Christ as their major weapon against "the unbelieving Jews." Today a different weapon seems more fitting and effective: Christians invent a "militant, aggressive" Israel that "threatens world peace" and harms "innocent" Arabs. The weapon has changed; the campaign of vilification is the same.

Franklin H. Littell, the Christian historian and churchman, tells of how ashamed he felt in 1967:

> One of the most shocking experiences of my theological life occurred last June and
> July. I recalled a number of times . . . the traumatic experience that Søren Kierke-

gaard, the Danish littérateur and lay theologian, went through when as a boy he beheld the nakedness of his father. When I saw with an awful sense of human mortality and fallibility the way in which the Protestant spokesmen of the Establishment responded to the need of Israel in June, I saw the nakedness of my father—the theological nakedness as well as the political ineptitude. The incident was not merely personal-autobiographical: I don't see how we can discuss the Christian-Jewish dialogue and the State of Israel without grasping the nettle. We must draw the knife and begin with this time which was so difficult for some of us "younger theologians," men who had hoped that—in the age of the [German] church struggle, in the age of the salvaging of Europe, in the age of the reestablishment of Israel—our fathers in the faith might have learned a new language and a new sense of responsibility towards the Jewish people and Israel.[2]

The spokesmen of the Establishment are not, of course, vulgar antisemites . . . they are too enlightened and humanitarian for that. They are not openly anti-Israel; they are just sympathetic to the governments which pledge Israel's destruction. They are not against Judaism; they just enunciate an emancipated New Covenant which has escaped from the irritating particularism of the Old. They are not openly vindictive toward Jewish history; they just express timeless truth and general humanitarian propositions which avoid the essential Jewishness of Christianity.[3]

From the Roman Catholic side Robert F. Drinan, Dean of the Boston College Law School, testified in 1968: Christians have been so silent about Arab aggression and threatened genocide over a twenty-year period that their conduct can only be identified as sinful. Dean Drinan spoke of the negative or neutral attitude that innumerable American Catholics share toward Israel. He deplored the almost complete absence of thought in Catholic circles about Israel, including the Vatican's failure to give diplomatic recognition to Israel (in contrast to its recognition of Arab countries).[4]

Still the shame does not end. There is today a covert and sophisticated campaign to penetrate the institutional structures of Catholic and Protestant churches in the United States with blatant anti-Israel propaganda, much of it virulently antisemitic. An example is a leaflet providing a Muslim version of the medieval blood libel against Jews and attempting to revive the infamous *Protocols of the Elders of Zion*. A primary resource center for this campaign is Beirut, where Christian groups and leaders openly collaborate in the effort.[5]

Fifty-six Christian missionaries serving in Lebanon included the following charges in a recent open letter to the churches: "the Zionists have driven the Arabs into the desert"; the Palestinian homeland has been seized "by an alien Western political movement"; it may well be that the only way to seek justice is "through armed struggle"; the solution is the "dezionization" of Israel, "an ethnically myopic state," and the substituting of "a pluralistic secular state."[6] Presumably, these missionaries wish to be received as representatives of the Christian gospel. Dezionization means politicide. Is that what these Christians desire?[7]

For years, supporters of the Arab campaign against Israel have maintained an influential voice in major world and national church groups, as evidenced by the pro-Arab bias of inumerable church pronouncements. On May 10, 1970 an international conference of 400 Christian clergymen and laymen issued a "Call from Beirut" urging the total "disappearance of Zionist structures." The major demands of the conference were completely identical with those of Palestinian terrorist organizations dedicated to murder and to the destruction of the people of Israel. Furthermore, under the cloak of attacking Israelis for applying the Bible to narrow political ends, these and other Christians seek to conceal their own subjection of Scripture to anti-Zionist political goals as well as to antisemitic purposes.

It is generally believed that many people in the world would feel guilt and sorrow if the Arab nations were permitted to slaughter the populace of Israel. The anti-Israeli views of many spokesmen within the Christian Establishment prove the absence of any real concern there. A number of church bodies and leaders in the United States convey a strong impression that they look upon Israel as expendable. This contrasts with the large numbers of Americans who are sympathetic to the Israelis. The behavior of the churches in the Middle East conflict reveals the extent to which they have lost any real conscience to condemn lying, plotting, hatred, and bloodshed.

Many church spokesmen express apprehension for the future of Christianity in the Middle East and concern for the welfare and security of Christians in Arab countries. It is true that the effort is often made within Arab nations to identify Christian minorities with alien Western interests. It is also the case that Christians are under great pressures to prove their loyalty to authoritarian regimes, in contrast to Muslims whose fealty is more readily assumed. But the Christian spokesmen often fail to apply the remedy their own diagnosis suggests. If there is in fact marked enmity toward Christians, the answer is anything but political and moral compliance with Arab designs. The only responsible stand is to identify and oppose the enemy. The real threat to the Christian community's independence in the Middle East is the alliance of Islam with Arab chauvinism. By encouraging extremist forces within that alliance and by talking up Arab "aspirations," the churches help sign their own death warrant. The irony of the pro-Arab, anti-Israeli effort within the churches is that religious life and freedom for Christians are flourishing within Israel and are under repression within a number of the very countries the churchmen seek to appease, such as Syria, Iraq, and Egypt.

Church documents are as revealing for what they omit as for what they include. Many of them fail to refer at all to what has been at the root of the conflict in the Middle East: the refusal of Arab nations to accept the reality of Israel.[8]

That groups and individuals beyond the churches have often manifested more concern and sympathy for Israel in her times of peril than the established churches with all their "neutralists" and detractors of Israel is a special source of shame for Christians.[9] The reason for Christian failure cannot be the "complexity" of the Middle East problem; church groups have readily committed themselves publicly and unqualifiedly on infinitely more complex issues, such as the conflict in Southeast Asia. Neither is it a question of the church arbitrarily "taking sides." The issue is not favoritism. It is politicide.

In truth, Christians cannot deny a certain historical-religious fact. The theological wrecking grounds of the past are strewn with various masks assigned to Jesus of Nazareth. He has been coerced into the roles of communist agitator, American advertising executive, Nazi stormtrooper, WASP, black revolutionist, and leader of the New Left. In contrast to all this nonsense, the only humanity Jesus ever had was that of a Jew of Palestine.

The destiny of those who are Christians is tied, whether they wish it or not, to a certain man who, were he living today, could only be identified as an Israeli Jew. This consideration is possessed of infinite psychological and spiritual import. Among psychologists as among theologians, the ambivalence of Christians toward Jesus as a Jew has been noted a number of times. We Christians devise curious stratagems in order to escape the relentless truth of the Jewishness of Jesus.

A favorite among our sleights of hand is to puff Jesus up into a disembodied spirit—not a very original heresy, by any means, in the story of the church. For almost two millennia the church has been trying to divest itself of its Jewish character, which is a polite way of saying that we have sought to get rid of Jesus the Jew. We have mastered well the tools of our anti-Jewish trade. The sharpest one is the pretense that Judaism is nothing but "lifeless legalism." Then when we meet Jews for whom (as for Jesus) the statutes of the Lord rejoice the heart, and the judgments of the Lord are sweeter than honey (Ps. 19:8, 10), we try to say that "something must have gone awry with their Judaism," rather than admitting that the problem is ours.[10]

> *There is something between us now;*
> *The cry you did not raise.*
>
> *You have washed your hands again.*
> *Put down the pitcher.*
> *This water will flow between us.*
>
> *Give me back Jesus;*
> *He is my brother.*
> *He will walk with me*
> *Behind the grey ghetto wall*
> *Into the slaughter-house.*
> *I will lead him into the lethal chamber;*
> *He will lie down upon the poisoned stone;*
> *The little children pricked with the death bubble*
> *Will come unto him.*
>
> *Return to him the yellow badge.*
> *Give me back Jesus;*
> *He is not yours.*[11]

Our shame extends today to Arabs as well as to Jews. Thus, during a period extending back almost a quarter of a century, we in the churches have been guilty of a grave disservice to the Arab peoples, especially to our brothers in Christ, the Arab Christians. We have done almost nothing to combat false teachings about Judaism and theological calumnies against the Jewish people. We have done little to help Arabs learn of the unbroken presence of Jews in Palestine for three thousand and more years. We have helped to perpetuate Arab hostility to Israel, a hostility that can be recognized as unjust only by those who know of and acknowledge historic Jewish rights, along with Arab rights.

A New Spirit, A Renewed Covenant

The dissemination of facts may do little or no good. To learn the actual history of Palestine, of the Jews and their faith, and of Christian denigration of the Jewish people may be too upsetting to one's prejudices. This is a special problem within Christianity (as it is to a lesser extent within Islam), where adherents are often conditioned through religious training to believe the worst things about Jews. (Rosemary Ruether, the Catholic theologian, points out that Christian antisemitism is not something accidental or extrinsic; it is rooted in the Christian gospel itself.[12]) In consequence, changes of attitude require a fundamental moral and spiritual transformation. In New Testament language, only the Spirit of God is able to cast out the demons. The problem is not factual knowledge but reconciliation with one's brother. Yet as long as Christians think they have theological and historical justification for their antipathies toward Jews, there is little reason for them to seek reconciliation.

The Christian community has long journeys to make, morally and theologically, before it will be worthy of equal fellowship with Jews. Yet we may take heart. There are signs of change.

Genuine dialogue with other men is not *knowing that* something is or is not so. Dialogue entails *knowing with:* understanding the other in his own self-understanding. Christians must *know with* Jews—know with them, in their own self-understanding, what it means to be a Jew. It was in this spirit that a group of Catholic and Protestant theologians of the Netherlands recently declared that to separate the Jewish people, in thought or deed, from the land of Israel and Jerusalem is tantamount to challenging their identity as human beings.[13] It was in the same spirit that a number of Christian theologians in the United States stated: "Judaism presupposes inextricable ties with the land of Israel and the city of David, without which Judaism cannot be truly itself. Theologically, it is this dimension to the religion of Judaism which leads us to support [the Israeli decision to reunify] the City of Jerusalem." Morally speaking, it is most essential that when we identify ourselves with a group of human beings, there be nothing exclusivist in our acts. Still other men must be brought within the purview of our concern; otherwise our behavior is unjust. Accordingly, the American theologians continued: The unity of Jerusalem "is the natural condition of the Holy City, and now once again assures the world's religious peoples freedom of worship at the shrines which remain the spiritual centers of their faith." In the same way: "The new situation has also created an opportunity to come to grips decisively with the Arab refugee problem, which must weigh heavily on the world's conscience. We urge both Israel and the Arab countries to exert new initiatives to eliminate once and for all this human suffering, within the framework of an overall settlement of the major issues to be achieved through direct negotiations."[14]

There is a new and refreshing willingness among some churchmen to put themselves in the place of Jews, to *know with* them, to comprehend something of Jewish self-understanding. The editor of *Lutheran Forum* puts the case incisively: For most Jews, to destroy Israel would be equivalent to taking Christ out of Christian faith.[15] Jews cut off from Israel are like Christians deprived of the sacraments.

A constituent group within the World Council of Churches, the Commitee on the Church and the Jewish People, meeting in Racine, Wisconsin in September of 1969, expressed its concern over statements by World Council and other church bodies that overlook vital issues which bulk large in the minds of many people around the world. Specifically, the Committee felt a duty to draw attention to three considerations: (1) The refusal of many to accept Israel's right to exist creates a very real fear among Jews that today's conflict in the Middle East is a struggle for survival, a fear heightened by memories of the Holocaust. (2) Lack of understanding of Israel's right to exist is associated with a failure to comprehend the significance of the historical link and continuous presence of the Jewish people in the land. (3) If it is right to take the plight of Arab refugees seriously, the plight of Jewish refugees from, and residents in, Arab countries cannot be ignored.[16]

A "working paper" on Jewish-Catholic relations was made public in December, 1969 by Lawrence Cardinal Shehan of Baltimore in behalf of the Catholic Secretariat for Promoting Christian Unity. The document emphasizes the increasing cognizance within the Christian church of the "permanent election" of the Jewish people. It points out that fidelity to the covenant is "linked to the gift of a land, which in the Jewish soul has endured as the object of an aspiration that Christians should strive to understand. . . . Christians, whatever the difficulties they may experience, must . . . respect the religious significance of the link between the people and the land. The existence of the State of Israel should not be separated from this perspective, which does not in itself imply any judgment on historical occurrences or on decisions of a purely political order."[17] At the present writing, this statement has not been officially released by the Vatican, and the final, approved version may be changed. However, the draft is being used in the preparation of a Vatican declaration on contemporary Catholic-Jewish relationships.

Scholars and churchmen in different lands are seeking a new Christian understanding of Israel and the Jewish people. The changed spirit within the churches is seen in the persuasion that the Christian community must rid itself forever of the notion that Jews have lost their right to independent peopleness and faith because of a "failure" to become Christians or for some other reason.

If there is a covenant between God and the Jewish people, its disposition lives within the mystery of that We-Thou relationship. Where do outsiders get the prerogative to interfere? As Karl Barth has said, Christians are no more than guests in the house of Israel. Harvey Cox proposes that if Christians would only stand closer to the spiritual descendants of biblical Israel, to so-called religious Jews *and* so-called nonreligious Jews, they would have a much better vantage point for making up their minds theologically. (This proposal has general applicability—to more than the Jewish-Christian relationship.) The closer Christians stand to the Jewish tradition, the more will they be delivered from their obsessional division between religion and the secular domain—a division that, in fact, accounts for much of their inability to achieve theological understanding of the State of Israel. There can be political life without a particular kind of theological interference. But no responsible theology can free itself from politics and morality.

The relating of biblical Israel to the Israel of today is eminently justified, not only through the weight of history, but also on compelling religious and theological grounds. We earlier stressed the many constituent elements of Jewishness, the Jewish *laos*. The Jews of today's Medinat Yisrael (State of Israel) exemplify these different elements.

A group of Christian theologians of Israel, Protestant and Catholic, at recent meetings in Jerusalem considered "Israel" as the term designating the people of God in both Jewish self-understanding and Christian self-understanding. They spoke further of the encounter "of the two peoples of God" in Israel today.[18]

These identifications are most relevant to our present discussion. They help us to relate theologically three fundamental realities:

The Jewish people: the original and abiding people of God's faithfulness.

The Jewish community of Israel (the Yishuv): a contemporary part of the original and abiding people of God's faithfulness (in addition to Jews of the Diaspora).

Christians: those who, through Jesus Christ, are brought into the abiding covenant with the people of God's faithfulness.

The very nature of the Christian's faith binds him to his Jewish brother. St. Paul reminds the Ephesians that before Christ came, they were, as gentiles, "alienated from the commonwealth of Israel, and strangers to the covenants of promise, having no hope and without God in the world." Yet through the grace that burst forth in Jesus they "are no longer strangers and sojourners, but . . . fellow citizens with the saints and members of the household of God, built upon the foundation of the apostles and prophets, Christ Jesus himself being the chief cornerstone . . ." (Eph. 2:12, 19-20). Thus the Christian lives by the trust that he may share in the abiding covenant, through one who was himself a Jew.

Frank M. Cross, Jr. of the Harvard Divinity School applies St. Paul's teaching in Romans 11 to the realm of Jewish-Christian relationships: The church "affirms the validity and eternity" of the election and vocation of Israel. Christians are never permitted to "refer to Judaism as 'another religion,' or as a false form of the biblical faith." It is into the eternal covenant with Israel that Christians are grafted, as a wild olive branch is grafted onto the root of a domestic olive tree. The covenant with Israel "is identical with the new or rather renewed covenant" with the church.[19]

An American church official recently said: "When something happens in the Middle East, Jews spark in a way we don't. For them the future of Israel is the future of their people, but I'm not part of that people. . . ."[20] Here is our whole problem in a nutshell. *Is this churchman really correct? By the very nature of our own faith, we who are Christians are linked to the Jewish people and thereby to the people of Israel.* The Christian *is* involved in the State of Israel, because he *is,* by faith, within the Jewish family. He *is* "part of that people." He is affected in his very existence, not merely as a human being (as a man, he will simply be humanitarian) but as a Christian. It is by virtue of his Christian existence that for him, Israel can never be just one more country. Christianity is devoid of spatial ties to the extent that it is on its own. But through its indissoluble bond with the Jewish people and the Jewish faith, the Christian faith is yoked spiritually to Eretz Yisrael.

The question is whether Christians of today have the spirit to testify that they belong in some way to the family of Jews. If they do not, then Eretz Yisrael can have no peculiar meaning for them. Krister Stendahl is among those who do have that spirit: "Christians would like to be considered honorary Jews for Jesus Christ's sake." Such testimony brings on its own question: "We need to ask, *in spite of it all,* whether [Jews] are willing to let us become part of their family, a peculiar part to be sure, but, even so, relatives who believe themselves to be a peculiar kind of Jew."[21]

On this second choice, we only *ask*; we cannot demand anything. Our qualifications are meager—rather like those of small children. The parallel is apt: The childhood of the church is here in vivid memory. The tears of the Israelites are our tears; the laughter of the Israelites is our laughter. The tears of the Israelis are our tears; the laughter of the Israelis is our laughter. When Israel is attacked, we are attacked. When latter-day churchmen make their pathological and immoral charges against the people of Israel, we are more than ashamed. We receive their accusations as a personal insult, as though our own mother were being defiled. And then we grieve over their heresy-in-action.

Yet we have to be most circumspect with our own accusations, for at least two reasons:

1. "A man had two sons. He went to the first, and said, 'My boy, go and work today in the vineyard.' 'I will, sir,' the boy replied; but he never went. The father came to the second and said the same. 'I will not,' he replied, but afterwards he changed his mind and went. Which of these two did as his father wished?" (Matt. 21:28-31). Suppose, in the end, we refuse to wear the Star of David on our sleeves. And the heretics wear it. . . .

2. It is an irony of history that at the very time "the church is trying desperately to move into a new relationship with the Jewish people her answers should be complicated by political overtones and the clear duty to remain sensitive to the Arab point of view."[22] The "political overtones" do not so much involve what we may have to say about the political problem, as what others may and must say about us. The part of the irony that weighs upon us is our Western coloring. How do we look to others? The literal color is white; our type of work, capitalist; religion, "Zionist"; nationality, imperialist.

It is not strange, therefore, to look to forces of reconciliation from out of a fresh geography—perhaps from the Middle East itself, as utopian as that has to sound for the conceivable future. Here is why, among many reasons, the church in Israel must be strengthened and given a greater voice, particularly in the counsels of the world church community.

Happily, the venting of our fears and hopes does not subvert in the slightest the right reasons for honoring Israel. Yet Eretz Yisrael remains the supreme testing ground for the Jewish-Christian relationship. The Israeli Jew asks the Christian: "Are you prepared to accept me as I am? Here we do not have those pleasant but contrived 'interfaith' dinners so prevalent in the pluralistic United States."

Apart from extremists in both camps, the Jew and the Christian can be in accord that territorial fundamentalism is unacceptable. (A traditional Christian rendering of such fundamentalism is the notion that the Jews "had to return" to the Holy Land to pave the way for the "second coming" of Christ.) Nevertheless, the Christian and the Jew may together, in faith, celebrate Israel—the Jew as host, the Christian as guest. History and morality have opened the door of the sanctuary, although these forces have not built the sanctuary. Following upon acts of thanksgiving, new deeds of stewardship are in order, in gratitude for all the gifts.

A danger for the Christian is that, in concurring that territorial fundamentalism is impossible, he may lurch to the left and lose the theological meaning and lessons in the reborn State of Israel. This is always a temptation. The insurance against it is the realization: Here is not just any people that has been called out from the death march. Here is the people into whose covenant the Christian has been grafted.

The issue for the Christian, as for the Jew, is not in the first instance whether God has ensured the rebirth of Israel. That issue cannot be dealt with until a prior question is faced, a question that has to do with the person of God and his promise to men. Obviously, if we believe that the covenant between God and his ancient people is broken, or for that matter that there "never was" any such covenant, our position upon the meaning of Israel (whether as Jew or as Christian) will be infinitely different from the view we should take if we believe that the covenant abides and that "the gifts and the call of God are irrevocable" (Rom. 11:29). These alternatives demonstrate that no point of view upon the Jewish people, or Israel, or Jewish-Christian relations can ultimately escape religious and theological decisions.[23] We cannot get around these decisions through some moral protest that no people possesses absolute rights to a given territory. It is a question, not of absolute rights, but of the meaning of a people's existence.

> If one's pro-Israel attitude is based on the flimsy foundation of support for the weak as seems so largely to have been the case in Britain, or even worse, on the vested interest of "you scratch my back and I will scratch yours" as seems to have been true of some opinion in the United States, then there should be no surprise at so-called changes of heart and mind. If, however, a Christian attitude is built on a firm religious basis, not only will it not flounder, but neither is it restricted to be for Israel and against the Arabs.[24]

Peter Schneider speaks in behalf of a "theology of restraint," which takes its stand amidst the conflicts of our time but yet, through its very moderation, offers a living example of the way toward reconciliation and peace.

Deeds to Celebrate

Eretz Yisrael is an unfinished world, a crucible, a people in the making.

The Christian knows, or ought to, that all men "have sinned and fall short of the glory of God" (Rom. 3:23). This does not lessen his duty to celebrate human goodness.

We remember human deeds in Israel, deeds we are forbidden to demand, but deeds without which faith is dead. "Would that they had forsaken Me, and obeyed My Commandments" (Rabbi Huna, *Midrash Lamentations*).

Not long ago a group of Arab terrorists were enabled to sit for their matriculation examinations in the local prison at Nablus, Israeli-administered territory. The certificates they received qualify them to enter university in Arab countries or the Hebrew University in Jerusalem.

Hundreds of Arabs from the administered territories, including many refugees, are receiving the same treatment at the Hadassah Medical Center in Jerusalem that any Israeli would receive. Incredibly, the treatment extends as well, regardless of the cost or care involved, to captured terrorists and to numbers of ordinary people who come over from Jordan. No urgent case is ever turned away for lack of funds.[25]

A group of French nuns, who conduct a hospice for Arabs in Jerusalem, recently deplored the "campaign of lies against the Israelis" and testified that in peace and war, their own work has been made particularly happy by the good will of the Israeli authorities, not only toward themselves but, more important, toward Arabs in their care.[26]

In the Gaza Strip, Israeli army officers show concern and compassion for the fate of the previous generation of Arab refugees and also for the new generation. The officers worry about the several thousands of young Arabs who have graduated from high school each year, only to be unable to go on to university or to find jobs.[27] Israel has acted to remedy this situation. At this very moment some 1,200 Arab students from the Gaza Strip are attending university in Egypt at the expense of the Israeli Government.

On the basis of intimate personal experience, Raymond Gunter, former British Minister of Labour, attests that for generosity and kindness, Israeli behavior and policy in the administered areas today are "unique in the history of humanity"—this, in contrast to the tension and oppression that many communications media falsely lead one to expect.[28]

In the Summer of 1969, some 22,000 Arabs from beyond the "cease-fire" lines traveled to Israel or the territories, an increase of 6,000 over the previous summer. During the period from December, 1969 through February, 1970 there was a 20 percent increment in visitors to Israel, non-Jews as well as Jews, in comparison with the same period one year before. Every year witnesses a steady increase.

Israel desires to teach something to humankind, including herself and her neighbors: There is a way to harness the impulses to self-destruction that all men have. That way is through wedding the good life for our fellows to our own self-preservation. Neither goal is reachable without the other.

The Israeli national anthem is Hatikvah (*The Hope*). Jews are the people of hope. May we also be people of hope? Israel offers hope. She offers courage as well. The centuries have taught Jews how to meet adversity. Living even today on the rim of destruction, Israelis do not surrender to despair or cynicism. Savingly, they retain their remarkable sense of humor. Faced with grievous trials, they yet persist in building for a tomorrow of justice and brotherliness. Were their optimism of a utopian kind, were it to wait upon miracles above or beyond human effort, we should have to dismiss it. To give others false or premature hopes is not to serve people but to harm them, by creating illusions. Israeli hopefulness does not rest upon idealistic dreams. It is proven through deeds of understanding and cooperation. It is a tough-minded optimism.

That Jews have stayed so free of hatred despite their history is, from a human standpoint, an unbelievable moral attainment, and, from a theological standpoint, a gift of grace. The leitmotif of Israel is to gain a victory over injustice and hatred, for the sake of justice and love. How can Christians do less than rejoice in this? And how can they do less than celebrate the moral and spiritual stature of a people who, instead of legislating against the churches as the fore- most historic oppressors of Jews, go out of their way to provide freedom of worship for Christians and to engage in interfaith fellowship with them?

Jewish and Christian leaders in Israel are giving of themselves in behalf of amity between Jews and Christians within and beyond the country. Among these leaders are Mothers Alin, Bernes, and Edmond, Elias Chaccour, Jack J. Cohen, Marcel Dubois, David Flusser, Jean Roger Hene, J. W. van der Hoeven, Bruno Hussar, Hans Kosmala, Robert Lindsey, Yona Malachy, Peter Schneider, Uriel Tal, Chaim Wardi, R. J. Zwi Werblowsky, G. Douglas Young, and many others.

Christian penitence is good. Even theology is good, though as nothing com- pared to penitence. Deeds are better than either, when they are penitentially inspired and theologically judicious. There are deeds to celebrate on the strictly Christian side.

Since 1966 an Ecumenical Fraternity of Christians who live and work in Israel has been functioning in Jerusalem. Its purposes are to help the churches gain theological understanding of themselves and of their place in the life of Israel, and to deepen Christian comradeship with Jewry, Judaism, and Israel (people, faith, and land). The Fraternity has established a small center on Mount Zion in an ecumenical setting, adjacent to the American Institute of Holy Land Studies,[29] the Roman Catholic Abbey of the Dormition, and a Greek Orthodox monastery. Nearby are the traditional sites of the "upper room" and King David's tomb. The area is further hallowed by a Jewish sanctuary in remembrance of the Holocaust.[30]

A sublime dimension of Eretz Yisrael for Christians today is their opportunity to reenact and participate in the very kind of life that Jesus lived among his own people, the Jews of Palestine. Christians of our generation are especially blessed: Israel is the one land in the world where they are in the minority and Jews are in the majority. This is good for the Christian soul, for the soul of the church. It reverses the centuries-old pattern of Christian power and over- lordship. Further, the Christian in Israel is part of the larger Israel in a way that is not possible anywhere else.

North of Haifa is an international and interdenominational Christian *moshav*. It is called Nes Ammim, "an ensign to the peoples" (Isa. 11:10). It was begun in 1962 by Dutch, Swiss, and German Protestants. The Christians of Nes Ammim lament the traditional effort to "convert" Jews, an effort that has deepened divi- sions, increased suspicions, and formed a painful contrast to the realities of per- secution and antisemitism. Out of indebtedness to the Jewish people and led by a sense of brotherliness, the inhabitants of Nes Ammim seek to serve Israel through capital investment and economic enterprise, and thereby to foster a spirit of solidarity with Jews. Their main enterprise at present is to raise roses for sale in European markets. After new persecutions of Jews in Iraq early in 1969, the people of Nes Ammim sent the following open letter to the churches:

We have come here to express the basic solidarity between Christianity and Israel. This bond we have learned to see and understand more deeply even in our days. In our presence here, we are representatives and exponents of our Christian churches. Solidarity is tested for its genuineness in times of distress. . . . We have come to recognize by now that the persecution of Jews has been a reality throughout the ages. Too little have we been aware that we were not only witnesses but also co-actors in the tragedies of the massacres that took place in Europe and finally ended in the near-total extinction of Jewry there.

The waves of threatening and hatred that were unleashed in all their ferocity twenty years ago are sweeping on wherever there are Jews. At each new outburst we are thrown back to the situation where the very existence of the Jewish people is at stake.

Three thousand Jews in Iraq are in agony. . . . They live in fear that they will be subject to the mass hatred seething there and in the neighboring countries of Syria, Egypt, and the Lebanon. . . .

Solidarity in times of distress means that we have to identify ourselves with these people, that we have to see their fate as if it were our own, that we have to do all in our power to save them. We can no longer say, "We did not know." There is no excuse to stand aloof or even to be neutral before the violence of evil powers.

We, therefore, address ourselves to the churches, to lay this matter before them in trust and a sure conviction that the plea of Israel to us all will not be in vain.

The Catholic Sisters of Zion work ceaselessly for Christian-Jewish and Jewish-Arab understanding. They are housed both in the Old City of Jerusalem and at Ein Karem nearby. At "Ecce Homo" on the Via Dolorosa the Sisters live above the courtyard of the Romans' Antonia fortress and the Herodian cisterns. They help Jews to learn Arabic and Arabs to learn Hebrew (in a cooperative program with the Hebrew University). Many visitors return again and again, out of archaeological and historical interest, but also because of the Sisters' warmth and understanding of Jesus' own people.[31] The Sisters know their history well: the crucifixion of Jesus was a Roman business. They are gladdened that so many of their guests are Jews. The Sisters of Zion are living examples of a new Christian theology of Israel. True to their own Christian confession, they yet celebrate the faith and witness of the Jewish people, and the ties that bind the two peoples of God's faithfulness.[32]

One way to keep the ecumenical life of Protestants and Catholics from lapsing into Christian self-concentration is through joint endeavors in behalf of such a cause as the welfare of Israel and the Jewish people. Some of us are convinced that the unhappy divisions within Christendom will not be healed, nor the contemporary crisis of faith be resolved, save through the shared patrimony with the original people of God.

There is no substitute for personal experience of Israel. The preeminent answer to arguments over what things are like there, and what the Israelis are like, is to go and see. (Travel costs are lower than ever, and stays at hospices and *kibbutzim* are economical.[33]) Joseph Stimpel, Catholic Bishop of Augsburg, Germany, has resolved to send each of his ordination candidates to spend a month in Israel. As he expressed it: "This is the land where Abraham our father in the faith used to live, and where Jesus preached the gospel of the Kingdom of God." The Bishop added that it is most desirable for his ordinands to meet with Jews and Muslims there, for the mutual benefit of members of the three great faiths that honor one God.[34]

Some deeds are being done; others await us. Concerned Christians can help to expose the politicidal propaganda against Israel that is infiltrating their own denominations and that feeds upon and exploits prejudices already present in the churches.

The roads opened to Christians and others include not only sorrow for past and present sins, but special responsibility for the rights and welfare of the Jewish people. It ought not be necessary to repeat that this does not mean lack of concern for the Arabs or of anyone else.

In the End, Love

For all the trials in the land, the people of Israel go about their business concentrating upon life's happy pursuits and moral opportunities. Nevertheless, the Israelis remain as *ma'apilim,* those who struggle against great odds. A man wrote to an Israeli newspaper: "We Jews are forever and always alone. When we are beaten and pursued, nobody notices. And if we do something to defend ourselves, we are condemned." In coming to the end of this chronicle of Israel's endurance, we wonder: Must these people always be the solitary nation? Must Jews always be the solitary people?

"Is it nothing to you, all you who pass by?" (Lam. 1:12). Perhaps a few will stop—to watch, to pray, to help.

Some will act from wholly humanitarian inspiration. We must not complain. We rejoice.

Were Christian shame and guilt final words, the present would stay wretched and the future would come out bleak. There is a final Christian word, and it is love:

> It is Christian theology, not merely Christian guilt, that commits the Christian to a special love of Jews and Judaism. For they [Jews] "have the adoption as sons, and the glory and the covenants and the legislation and the worship and the promises" (Rom. 9:4), and "the gifts and calling of God are without repentance" (11:29). Our common patrimony makes Jews "most dear'" to Christians (v. 28). Between this part of Christian theology and the actual Christian mentality, long under the influence of the deicidal tradition, there remains a sharp conflict. It is in the interest of Christian truth and love as well as of Jewish-Christian friendship that the conflict must be resolved.
>
> We conclude where we began: it is the Christian above all who is expected to react most strongly to attacks on Jews. It is especially the Christian who is expected to rejoice at the upturn in the fortune of Jews that Zionism, or any other agency, has brought about in our own time. The distance we appear to stand from this horror and rejoicing is the measurement of that estrangement which separates us on the deepest level of our souls.[35]

Our encounter with Israel is at an end. Or perhaps it just begins.

> *It is evening.*
> *I sit beside the Mediterranean.*
> *Waves with foaming lips kiss the stones.*
> *Here I am a guest, soon to leave.*
> *How shall I tie together*
>   *my here with my there?*[36]

Appendix

Proclamation of Israeli Independence

THE LAND OF ISRAEL was the birthplace of the Jewish people. Here their spiritual, religious, and political identity was formed. Here they first achieved statehood, created a culture of national and universal significance, and gave the Bible to the world.

After being forcibly exiled from their Land, the Jewish people kept faith with it in all the countries of their dispersion, never ceasing to pray and hope for their return and the restoration of their political freedom.

Impelled by this historic attachment, Jews strove throughout the centuries to reestablish themselves in the Land of their fathers and regain their statehood. In recent decades they returned en masse. Pioneers and resisters of oppression, they reclaimed the wilderness, revived the Hebrew language, built villages and cities, and created a vigorous community, with its own economic and cultural life. They sought peace yet were ever prepared to defend themselves. They brought the blessings of progress to all the country's inhabitants.

In the year 1897 the First Zionist Congress convened, under the inspiration of Theodor Herzl, and proclaimed the right of the Jewish people to national rebirth in their own country.

This right was recognized by the Balfour Declaration of November 2, 1917, and reaffirmed by the Mandate of the League of Nations, which gave explicit international sanction to the historic connection between the Jewish people and Palestine, and to the right to reconstitute their National Home.

The Nazi Holocaust that recently engulfed the Jewish people—the massacre of millions of Jews in Europe—demonstrated anew the urgency of reestablishing the Jewish State in the Land of Israel, thereby solving the problem of the homelessness of Jews by opening the gates of the homeland to every Jew and lifting the Jewish people to equality in the family of nations.

The survivors of the Holocaust, as well as Jews from other parts of the world, sought unceasingly to enter the Land of Israel, proclaiming their right to lives of dignity, freedom, and labor, and remaining undeterred by restrictions and hardships.

Throughout the Second World War the Jewish people in Palestine contributed their full share in the struggle of the freedom-loving nations against the wickedness of the Nazis. The sacrifices of Jewish soldiers and the strivings of Jewish workers gained Jews the right to be ranked amongst the peoples who founded the United Nations.

On November 29, 1947, the General Assembly of the United Nations adopted a Resolution calling for the establishment of an independent Jewish State in Palestine, and summoning the inhabitants of the country to take whatever steps were necessary to implement that Resolution.

This recognition by the United Nations of the right of the Jewish people to establish their State may not be revoked. It is, moreover, the natural right of the Jewish people to be masters of their fate, along with other nations, in their own sovereign State.

Accordingly, we, the members of the National People's Council, representing the Jewish people of Palestine and the Zionist movement of the world, are met together today in solemn assembly, the day of the termination of the British Mandate for Palestine, and, by virtue of the natural and historic right of the Jewish people and on the strength of the Resolution of the General Assembly of the United Nations, we hereby proclaim the reestablishment of the Jewish State in Palestine, to be called Medinat Yisrael (the State of Israel).

We hereby declare that as from the termination of the Mandate at midnight, this night of the 14th to 15th of May, 1948, and until the establishing of the duly elected authorities of the State in accordance with a Constitution to be drawn up and adopted by a Constituent Assembly not later than October 1, 1948, the present National People's Council shall act as the Provisional Council of State, and its executive organ, the People's Administration, shall constitute the Provisional Government of the State of Israel.

The State of Israel will be open to the immigration of Jews from all countries of their dispersion; it will foster the development of the country for the benefit of all its inhabitants; it will be based on the precepts of freedom, justice, and peace as taught by the prophets of Israel; it will ensure complete equality of social and political rights to all its inhabitants irrespective of religion, race or sex; it will guarantee full freedom of conscience, worship, language, education and culture; it will safeguard the sanctity and inviolability of the shrines and Holy Places of all religions; and it will be faithful to the principles of the Charter of the United Nations.

The State of Israel is prepared to cooperate with the agencies and representatives of the United Nations in implementing the Resolution of the General Assembly of November 29, 1947, and it will take steps to bring about the economic union of the whole of Palestine.

We appeal to the United Nations to assist the Jewish people in the upbuilding of their State and to receive that State into the comity of nations.

We appeal—in the very midst of the wanton aggression launched against us now for months—to the Arab inhabitants of the State of Israel to preserve peace and participate in the upbuilding of the State on the basis of full and equal citizenship and due representation in all its provisional and permanent institutions.

We extend our hand to all neighboring states and their peoples in an offer of peace and unity and appeal to them to cooperate with the independent Jewish nation for the common good of all.

We appeal to the Jewish people all over the world to rally to the side of the Jews of the Land of Israel in the tasks of immigration and development, and to stand by them in the great struggle for the realization of the age-old dream: the redemption of Israel.

Placing our trust in the Rock of Israel, we set our hand to this Proclamation, at this session of the Provisional Council of State, in the City of Tel Aviv, on this Sabbath eve, the fifth day of Iyar, 5708, the fourteenth day of May, 1948.

Notes and References

NOTES TO CHAPTER 1

Preparation for a Portrait

1 In illustration of the explosiveness of our theme, and of the accompanying readiness of some people to stoop to falsehood to advance their cause, we are aware that one of our detractors has circulated the lie that our time in Jordan was limited to "one day at the Amman Airport."

2 The point is developed in Chapter 17. Related matters for debate and discussion in Parts II and III of our study include the rights of minorities in Israel, the feasibility and justice of Israel as a Jewish state, the rights of the Jewish people to the land, and the national claims of the Arabs of erstwhile Palestine.

3 James Muilenberg, "Abraham and the Nations," *Interpretation*, October, 1965, p. 390.

4 Abba Eban, "Reality and Vision in the Middle East," *Foreign Affairs*, July, 1965, p. 633.

5 "Torah" means "teaching," "instruction," "guidance." The application of the term has come to vary with the context and the religious viewpoint of those using it. It may mean a particular commandment, the Ten Commandments (Decalogue), the first five books of the Hebrew Bible (Pentateuch), the whole Bible, or even the entire written and oral Tradition.

6 In Hebrew usage, both classical and modern, the "Holy Land" or the "Land of Israel" is designated simply as "the Land."

7 One exception is the Gypsies. But their very philosophy of life has eschewed attachments to one locale.

NOTES TO CHAPTER 2

From Abraham to the Romans

1 James Parkes, *A History of Palestine from 135 A.D. to Modern Times*, London: Victor Gollancz, 1949, p. 19. In this and the three following chapters, Parkes's study and Abram Leon Sachar's *A History of the Jews* (5th ed., revised, New York: Alfred A. Knopf, 1965) have served as major sources. After our own study was finished, a completely revised version of Parkes's book appeared, published under the title *Whose Land?: A History of the Peoples of Palestine*, Baltimore: Penguin Books, 1970.

2 Gen. 12:1-3. The translation is E. A. Speiser's; the form and structure is James Muilenberg's ("Abraham and the Nations," p. 391).

3 We use the accepted abbreviations for "before the common era" (B.C.E.) and "common era" (C.E.), the era shared by Jews and Christians.

4 Sachar, *A History of the Jews*, p. 31.

5 A significant event had taken place in Judah shortly before the Exile: the core of the Book of Deuteronomy had appeared in written form. As a consequence, a sweeping reform of religious practices was instituted under King Josiah. It has been suggested that while neither the prophets nor this reform succeeded in transforming the nation, nevertheless without these two influences the worship of Yahweh could not have survived the Babylonian destruction of Judah and the resulting Exile. During the Exile the orally-preserved laws and the teachings of the prophets were successfully gathered together, having been reviewed, edited, and newly appreciated in light of intervening events. It was during this period also that the Exodus-tradition gained its preeminent place.

271

[6] However, the Judeans were mainly concerned to revitalize their own culture, not to fashion a composite one. With the Babylonian conquest of Judah, some Judeans had fled to Egypt, establishing communities there that in later centuries became cultural and commercial centers of Jewish life.

[7] The official Hebrew name of the province was Yehud. The Jews had the right to issue their own coins, which bore the consonants YHD.

[8] At the same time, Judah benefited from the Diaspora. The high positions held by Diaspora Jews together with the respect accorded them could not help but enhance Judah's status, despite its small size. Cf. Abba Eban, *My People: The Story of the Jews,* New York: Behrman House-Random House, 1968, pp. 74-5.

[9] Sachar, *A History of the Jews,* p. 98.

[10] Sachar, p. 123; Jules Isaac, *The Teaching of Contempt: Christian Roots of Anti-Semitism,* New York: Holt, Rinehart and Winston, 1964, p. 67.

[11] The Christian Byzantine rulers were to enforce the prohibition against Jewish residence in Jerusalem. However, in the fifth century Empress Eudocia enabled them to return. An exception in the fourth century was the two-year reign of Julian the Apostate, who even gave the Jews permission to rebuild the Temple.

[12] Ben Zion Dinur, "From Bar Kochba's Revolt to the Turkish Conquest," in David Ben Gurion, ed., *The Jews in Their Land,* London: Aldus Books, 1966, p. 167.

[13] Isaac, *The Teaching of Contempt,* pp. 39-73. See also Hannah Vogt, *The Jews: A Chronicle for Christian Conscience,* New York: Association Press, 1967, pp. 42-3, 157-8.

NOTES TO CHAPTER 3

Neglected Years, Renascent Years

[1] Examples include the remains at Capernaum, Chorazin, and Hamath in the Galilee, Beit She'an and Beit Alpha in the Beisan Valley, Jericho and Naaran in the Jordan Valley, Maon and Beersheba in the northwestern and north central Negev. (See *Israeli Mosaics of the Byzantine Period,* New York: New American Library, Inc., 1965, and *The New Israel Atlas,* Jerusalem: Israel Universities Press, 1968, p. 87.) At Beit She'arim, northwest of Nazareth, the ruins of a prosperous town and an elaborate necropolis of this period have been excavated. Further evidence of synagogue building, even when forbidden by imperial law, is to be found in the Emperor's action removing Gamaliel from the office of Patriarch in 415 for defying these and other restrictive laws.

[2] Parkes, *A History of Palestine,* p. 63. In 425 Theodosius II abolished the office as part of his anti-Jewish legislation.

[3] Their interpretations of, and judgments upon, the written Torah became known as the Oral Torah. Judah's compilation, the Mishnah, was to become in turn the basis for further assessment and commentaries on the part of rabbis of contemporary and subsequent generations. When written down, the record of these discussions became known as the Gemara, which together with the Mishnah forms the Talmud. Palestinian Jewry produced the so-called Jerusalem Talmud; the academies of Babylon, the Babylonian Talmud.

For a concise summary of the great significance of the rabbis' efforts during this traumatic period of Jewish history, see James Parkes, "The Palestinian Jews: Did someone forget?," *The New Middle East,* October 1969, p. 31.

[4] Constantine built the Church of the Holy Sepulcher in Jerusalem. Today's building is hardly comparable with the original magnificent structure.

[5] The great majority of traditional Christian sites and shrines were given imperial sanction by that most illustrious of the pilgrims, Constantine's mother, Queen Helena, in collaboration with a Bishop Macarius.

[6] For discussion of this population change, see Parkes, *A History of Palestine,* pp. 65, 76, 81-2; James Parkes, *The Conflict of the Church and the Synagogue,* Cleveland and New York: The World Publishing Co., 1961, pp. 187, 233, 236, 238, 259; and Dinur, "From Bar Kochba's Revolt to the Turkish Conquest," pp. 176, 180-1, 186-7, 191, 198.

[7] Dinur, "From Bar Kochba's Revolt to the Turkish Conquest," pp. 204-5; Parkes, *A History of Palestine,* pp. 87, 90, 92.

8 Ben Zion Dinur, *Israel and the Diaspora*, Philadelphia: The Jewish Publication Society of America, 1969, p. 58; Isaac, *The Teaching of Contempt*, pp. 69-70.

9 Dinur, *Israel and the Diaspora*, pp. 6, 67.

10 *The Historical Connection of the Jewish People with Palestine* (Jewish Agency for Palestine), Tel Aviv: M. Shoham's Press, 1946, p. 19; Dinur, "From Bar Kochba's Revolt to the Turkish Conquest," p. 202. The caliphs were the religio-political heads of Muslim states.

11 The only purely Arab dynasty was this first one, known as the Umayyid Dynasty. Subsequent dynasties were Muslim but not Arab.

12 The Fatimids were caliphs of the North African dynasty (909-1171) who claimed descent from Fatima, Muhammad's daughter, and Ali, his son-in-law.

13 This name derives from the Arabic for "slave." Originally, these people consisted mostly of Turks and Mongols. Subsequently, Circassians were involved.

14 Parkes, *A History of Palestine*, pp. 150, 161.

15 The Druses are a religious sect traceable to the eleventh century c.e. They are an offshoot of Islam.

16 A number of literary works popularized the idea, including Byron's "Hebrew Melodies," the young Disraeli's *Tancred*, and George Eliot's *Daniel Deronda*.

17 The Hasidim were enthusiastic pietists, disciples of Israel ben Eliezer (known as the Baal Shem-Tov, Master of the Good Name), who attracted a great following in eighteenth-century Poland.

18 Yemin Moshe, as the settlement was called, is easily located in today's Jerusalem by means of the windmill across the Hinnom Valley from Mount Zion.

19 Other powers included France, Russia, the United States, Prussia, Sardinia, and Austria. Particularly involved were the powers' own nationals and specific religious institutions.

20 The only Christian settlements that lasted were those of the so-called Templars, pietists who came from Germany in 1868 and stayed until 1939.

21 "Diaspora" is Greek for "dispersion." The Hebrew term *galut* (exile) has expressed the outlook of Jews much more faithfully.

22 One Babylonian Talmudic teaching went so far as to say that a man should not make his permanent home outside the homeland unless famine prevailed in Israel.

23 As a condition of Jewish enfranchisement, Napoleon actually required Jews to renounce the national aspect of Judaism.

24 The reference is to the infamous trial of Alfred Dreyfus, a Jewish officer in the French army, who was accused of treason but finally acquitted.

25 We use the spelling "antisemitism" rather than "anti-Semitism" because, as James Parkes has pointed out, the latter form wrongly insinuates that the phenomenon in question involves a movement against an actual quality called "Semitism." "Antisemitism" means hatred and denigration of the Jewish people, and only that.

26 Leonard J. Fein, *Politics in Israel*, Boston: Little Brown, 1967, p. 14.

27 One significant exception was Socialism and, later on, Marxism, for which Zionism was a throwback to an unacceptable nationalism. Zionism would only siphon off people needed in the revolution.

28 A good deal of the Sultan's opposition stemmed from his increasing difficulties with Russia, which was insisting upon greater privileges especially in the Holy Land. He feared that an increase in Russian Jewish immigration would open the door to further demands.

NOTES TO CHAPTER 4

The Great War and Its Sequels

1 In the preparation of this and the following chapter, Christopher Sykes's study, *Cross Roads to Israel*, has served as one basic source (London: Collins, 1965). Footnote references to Sykes all refer to that volume.

2 As early as 797 the Muslim ruler of Jerusalem permitted Charlemagne, Holy Roman Emperor but also King of the Franks, to build and maintain institutions for the care of Christian pilgrims to the Holy Land. Most leaders of the Crusades, as well as the kings of Jerusalem and

the rulers of other Christian principalities in the East, were French (especially Norman). During the eighteenth and nineteenth centuries, France tried to protect Latin and Maronite Christians against Eastern Christians and Druses in Palestine and Lebanon.

[3] The extent of French demands was uncertain at this juncture.

[4] Sir Henry McMahon, letter to *The Times*, (London) July 23, 1937.

[5] As cited in Sykes, pp. 44-5.

[6] Ronald Bryden, "Zion," *The Observer Magazine* (London), Nov. 5, 1967, pp. 40, 42.

[7] Bryden, "Zion," *The Observer Magazine* (London), Nov. 12, 1967, p. 48.

[8] Parkes, *A History of Palestine*, p. 288.

[9] Benedict's successor, Pius XI, violently opposed the reestablishment of Jews in their homeland.

[10] Sachar, *A History of the Jews*, p. 367.

[11] Sykes, p. 43.

[12] Sykes, pp. 46, 47.

[13] "Agreement between Emir Feisal and Dr. Weizmann January 3, 1919," in Walter Laqueur, ed., *The Israel/Arab Reader*, New York: The Citadel Press, 1969, pp. 19, 20.

[14] "Memorandum Presented to the King-Crane Commission by the General Syrian Congress," in Laqueur, pp. 32-33.

[15] Sykes, p. 69. The Lebanese Christians alone welcomed France's role. They feared domination and persecution by the Muslims.

[16] Sykes cites evidence for this plan; p. 61 and note.

[17] In addition to premeditated Arab attacks in 1920 upon two Jewish settlements in the North, apparently spontaneous rioting occurred in Jerusalem in that same year, with twelve deaths and many injuries.

[18] The Jewish Agency was made responsible for "advising and cooperating with the Administration of Palestine in such economic, social, and other matters as may affect the establishment of the Jewish National Home." The Agency became quasi-governmental in character, possessing wide authority over the Jewish community. Jews regarded it as representative of their interests. Since 1948, the Agency has continued on as the official Jewish body recognized by both the State of Israel and the World Zionist Organization. With headquarters in several world capitals, the Agency engages in comprehensive immigration, settlement, investment, employment, educational, and cultural activities.

[19] However, by the 1930's economic stability and relative prosperity had returned to Palestine, while the Western world remained in dire straits.

[20] Only the heroic determination of one British soldier kept the slaughter from engulfing the entire community of 700. He held the terrorists at bay until British reinforcements arrived. We have sought without success to ascertain his name.

[21] Maurice Samuel, *Light on Israel*, New York: Alfred A. Knopf, 1968, pp. 65, 66.

[22] Nor was the Mufti finished. He had early allied himself with the Axis Powers and hoped to be able to apply Nazi measures against Jews in Palestine. When forced to flee from the region during World War II, he went to Berlin where he gave direct aid in Hitler's "final solution" of the "Jewish problem." After the War, Haj Amin escaped back to the Middle East to resume his quest for personal power and his antisemitic campaign. In 1969 he recruited for the Government of Saudi Arabia its first terrorist organization.

[23] Sykes, p. 218. Mayor Teddy Kollek of Jerusalem has stated that from 1936 to 1939 Arab terrorists killed 9,000 fellow-Arabs, three times the number of combined Jewish and British victims *(The Jerusalem Post* [Weekly Overseas Edition], January 13, 1969). Other Arab deaths resulted mainly from battles against British forces and Jewish settlers.

NOTES TO CHAPTER 5

Resurrection

[1] This action served no real function, since the Committee operated simply as a lackey of the Mufti, despite the silent disapproval many members felt.

[2] In 1938, President Roosevelt called for an international conference to consider the needs of refugees. Great Britain succeeded in keeping the subject of Palestine completely off the agenda. The conference, held at Evian, France, was a total failure. Despite the urgent pleadings of

many spokesmen, the response was shockingly evasive and even self-defensive. Only the Dominican Republic took a humanitarian position. It offered to accept 100,000 Jews from Germany and Austria with the sole stipulation that they be willing to work on the land.

3 When another group, the Arab National Defense Party, signaled its acceptance of the White Paper, a member was murdered by one of the Mufti's assassins.

4 Fein, *Politics in Israel*, p. 25.

5 Many of the Jews accepted into the British forces were given noncombatant positions. Combined efforts by Zionists, President Roosevelt, and even Winston Churchill to permit Palestinian Jews to create a force of their own could budge neither the military leaders in North Africa and the Middle East nor the authorities in Palestine. In opposing such a decision, these men expressed fears of both the Arab reaction and the ultimate use of such a trained unit against the British. It was not until March of 1945 that a Palestinian Jewish force was enabled to go into action under the flag of the Star of David. (Earlier, the Warsaw ghetto fighters had fought the Nazis under the standard of the Star of David—in a sense the first sovereign political act of the Jewish people in nearly 2,000 years.)

6 In the early years, the Nazis allowed some thousands to leave, but only through payments of great sums of money and the running of tremendous risks. The refugees were crowded aboard unseaworthy hulks, and in consequence many of them were drowned. Some were returned to the ports of embarkation and thence to the concentration camps, because no nation would accept them. The comparatively lucky ones were those intercepted by the British Navy and sent to Mauritius.

7 As of September, 1946, 250,000 Jews were still living in German and Austrian camps. Many others outside the camps wanted to leave Europe.

8 In the Summer of 1945 about 8,000 refugees were successfully smuggled past the British blockade. But many others were stopped. In the beginning these latter were returned to Europe. Later on, refugees were sent to internment camps on Cyprus. Some 40,000 were held there by November, 1947.

9 See Munya M. Mardor, *Haganah*, New York: New American Library, 1966. A few exceptions to this policy are reported in other sources.

10 At the end of 1944 the Haganah directly cooperated with the British by rounding up and handing over considerable numbers of these terrorists. But as relations with the British deteriorated, this practice ended.

11 In November of 1944 two young Sternists murdered Lord Moyne, Minister of State in Cairo. The immediate consequence was widespread and indiscriminate anti-Jewish feeling. In July of 1946 the Irgun blew up a wing of the King David Hotel in Jerusalem, where the British Army Secretariat had offices. British, Arab, and Jewish casualties were very high (91 killed, and 41 wounded). This was during a time when Jewish Agency leaders, who had kept trying to forestall such acts, were imprisoned by the British. Some 2,000 other Jews had also been jailed. In September of 1948 the Sternists assassinated the United Nations' mediator, Count Bernadotte.

12 Sykes, p. 341.

13 See Arthur D. Morse, *While Six Million Died: A Chronicle of American Apathy*, New York: Random House, 1967.

14 As cited in Parkes, *A History of Palestine*, p. 353.

15 This was the Morrison Plan, which advocated a federal government involving Jewish and Arab provinces, each to determine its own immigration. The proposal died for lack of adequate consideration.

16 These nations were Australia, Canada, Czechoslovakia, Guatemala, India, Iran, the Netherlands, Peru, Sweden, Uruguay, and Venezuela.

17 Sachar, *A History of the Jews*, p. 432.

18 A minority of three favored a single federal constitution.

19 Sachar, p. 434.

20 The Secretary General of the Arab League had also warned that "the Arabs, if compelled, would fight for Palestine" (cited in Sykes, p. 393).

21 Sykes, p. 388.

22 By the end of December, 1947 some 5,000 Syrian and Lebanese troops had entered the country undeterred by any British force—this, in face of the facts that the Haganah was still considered illegal by the Administration and that Jewish settlements were being subjected to arms searches.

23 According to Sykes, this action was apparently taken on instructions by the Department of State without the knowledge or approval of President Truman. The decision seems to have resulted from pressure by the oil interests combined with concern over the success of the Marshall Plan for Europe, where Arabian oil would be needed.

24 Armistice agreements with the several Arab states were not signed until between February and July, 1949.

NOTES TO CHAPTER 6

The Polarities of Israel

1 It is interesting to note that so many important events in Israel's history are associated with mountains, e.g., the mounts of Sinai, Moriah, Zion, Tabor, Carmel, Masada, and Safed. The psalmist writes: "I will lift up mine eyes unto the hills, from whence cometh my help" (121:1).

2 The terms "Sephardic Jews" and "Ashkenazic Jews" are also used to stand, respectively, for these broad groupings. As Alex Weingrod observes, the words "Oriental" or "Afro-Asian" suggest an identification of the immigrants with certain other peoples with whom they actually have very little in common. Except for the Indian Jews, all these immigrants come from Muslim countries (Israel: Group Relations in a New Society, London: Pall Mall Press, 1965, p. 3). One trouble with the terms "Middle Eastern" and "Eastern" is that they are stretched to include Jews from North Africa. But there is no better terminology. The phrase "Western Jews" is not completely accurate either (Russian Jews are usually referred to in this way) but is usefully applied to Jews from Europe, the Americas, South Africa, and Australia. The point is that "Eastern" and "Western" are not exact geographical expressions.

3 Weingrod, Israel, p. 4.

4 That even individual responsibility and social concerns may together be rejected is suggested in the behavior of the so-called Dizengoffites, so named after Israel's best-known street, Rehov Dizengoff in Tel Aviv, haunt of the country's "espresso generation." As Sraya Shapiro writes, "The Dizengoff habitué has no use for labor and rejects labor-worship, disdains collective and even individual responsibility, rejects pioneering ideals. He is out to tend his own ego, not to improve society, let alone cultivate the desert. At least, that is the reputation he likes to give himself" ("Dizengoff Road," Israel Magazine, I, 4 [1968], 53). Whether this "way of life" will have any decisive consequences for Israeli society is an open question.

5 Women are eligible for exemption on the grounds of religious conviction. In November, 1969 the call-up age for men to serve as reservists was extended from 49 years to 55.

6 Fein, Politics in Israel, pp. 208, 210-11.

NOTES TO CHAPTER 7

From Many Lands . . .

1 Weingrod, Israel, pp. 6-8. Professor Weingrod's study has been of aid in the preparation of this chapter and, to a lesser extent, the next chapter. All references to Weingrod are to that book. In the present section of this chapter their is also some reliance upon A. T. Super, Absorption of Immigrants (Israel Today No. 18), Jerusalem: Israel Digest, 1965, pp. 4-36, together with considerable updating through more recent information.

2 Fein, Politics in Israel, p. 23.

3 According to James Parkes, had the partition plan been implemented, the result would have been a populace of 498,000 Jews and 407,000 settled Arabs plus 90,000 Bedouin Arabs during certain seasons of the year (A History of Palestine, p. 359).

4 Due to lack of funds, there was one period beginning in 1954 when the Jewish Agency had no choice but to follow a selective system for groups of Jews from North Africa. But toward the end of 1955 the monthly rate of entry from North Africa rose to 5,000. During this time, two

of the heavy immigration years were 1956 (55,000) and 1957 (71,000), occasioned by persecution in Egypt (1956 was the year of the Sinai campaign) and the revolt in Hungary, as a consequence of which thousands of refugee Jews opted to settle in Israel.

5 Weingrod, pp. 14, 21.

6 Weingrod, p. 30.

7 Weingrod, pp. 23-7.

8 Ruth Bondy, "Immigrants and Old Timers," *Midstream,* October, 1967, p. 70.

9 Fein, *Politics in Israel,* pp. 54-5.

10 Fein, pp. 146, 191.

11 Bondy, "Immigrants and Old Timers," p. 73.

12 Since we are not engaged in detailed sociological study, we acknowledge an inevitable oversimplification in our categories. The urbane and wealthy newcomer, no matter what his country of origin, obviously has a great headstart over the illiterate and poverty-stricken immigrant. While every newcomer shares certain trials with all other immigrants, different groups incline to react to these in different ways. A case in point is the encounter with the Israeli bureaucracy. The newcomer from Eastern Europe tends to be best prepared to cope with the bureaucracy; the American is infuriated but can often exert the necessary influence to free himself; while the Easterner remains bewildered and helpless until someone comes to rescue him (Geoffrey Wigoder, "Ingathering and Integration," *Conservative Judaism,* Winter, 1965, p. 43). Much of this last-mentioned response is doubtless related to the experiences of Easterners with governmental corruption and authoritarianism before coming to Israel.

13 Weingrod, pp. 13-14.

14 Oded Remba, "The Dilemmas of Israel's Economy," *Midstream,* February, 1969, p. 61.

15 In the country as a whole, Western Jews tend to marry Westerners and Eastern Jews, Easterners. However, the rate of intermarriage is increasing. In 1955 it stood at 11.8 percent; by 1967 it had risen to 15.5 percent (*Statistical Abstract of Israel, 1969,* Jerusalem: Central Bureau of Statistics, p. 68).

16 Wigoder, "Ingathering and Integration," p. 46.

17 Fein, *Politics in Israel,* p. 115.

NOTES TO CHAPTER 8

. . . To One People

1 "The army is not only taken for granted, it is honored. However much the earlier tradition of the Jew eschewed the military, Israelis have come to know the armed forces as their lifeline." Yet "the army does more than reassure Israelis. It undertakes explicit responsibilities in education and integration, and it implicitly provides the most manifest symbol of Israel's nationhood, undiluted by political debate, unencumbered by ideological baggage, unblemished by scandal. There is no question that the army is seen as the most 'pure' of Israel's institutions." Savingly, it remains totally under civilian control (Fein, *Politics in Israel,* pp. 204-5, 209).

2 Between 1970 and 1973, grade nine comes under the Law, and grade ten over the ensuing three years. The extension applies initially to development and border areas and to Jerusalem.

3 Of 127,000 students in post-primary schools in 1967-68, 39,000 paid reduced fees and 55,000 no fees at all (*Statistical Abstract of Israel, 1969,* p. 564).

4 As this is written, the elementary schools are faced with a 10 percent dropout rate in their top classes.

5 Agricultural schools enroll approximately 8 percent of post-primary students, but at least half the graduates never take up farming. Here is an unfortunate case of cultural lag. The old ideal of labor in field or farm has not as yet come to terms with the industrialization of agriculture. However, a realistic plan has now been initiated to establish a number of comprehensive schools in rural and small-town regions offering both academic and vocational courses. Ten of these opened in the Fall of 1968 (Yehuda Kesten, "Education the Secret Weapon," *Israel Magazine,* I, 4 [1968], 68). The passing of a matriculation examination at the conclusion of twelve years of schooling admits a student to university work.

6 The major areas of Israeli scientific concentration include atomic energy, the saving and reclamation of water, desalination of water, artificial rain, crop development, food preserva-

tion, insect control, and electronics. Today in Israel some $40 million a year is expended on research. The nation now ranks third in the world in proportionate numbers of scientists and technologists.

[7] Secondary school teachers are given university training; elementary school teachers tend to go to teachers' training colleges.

[8] In her first twenty-one years Israel built 3,700 schools and other educational institutions. She trained 2,600 doctors, 1,000 dentists, and 2,000 pharmacists. In proportion to her population, Israel ranks second among all countries in the publishing and importing of books. Since 1940, more than 1,100,000 books have been added to public libraries.

[9] Fein, *Politics in Israel*, p. 127.

[10] The law also permits unofficial "recognized" schools, whose funds are in part provided by the State. These are run primarily by the ultra-orthodox Agudat Yisrael for whom the state religious schools are too liberal religiously.

[11] Modern Hebrew has as its components biblical Hebrew, Mishnaic Hebrew, Aramaic, and Medieval and Late Hebrew. The language has been updated through the creation of many new words and idioms. Such work is the responsibility of the Hebrew Language Academy, which is -charged by law with the task of developing the language. Its decisions are binding upon educational institutions, governmental bodies, and local authorities. Cf. Ruth Bondy: "You may speak Hebrew as [the Ukrainian thinker] Ahad Ha'am wrote it, but so long as you are not at home with profanity in Arabic, curses in Russian, the names of engine parts in English and anecdotes in Yiddish, you simply don't know the Israeli national tongue" ("Immigrants and Old-Timers," p. 70).

[12] Between 1951 and 1969, some 315,000 persons attended adult education courses in Hebrew under the auspices of the Ministry of Education and Culture (figures derived from *Statistical Abstract of Israel, 1969*, p. 574). Very many more people have taken radio and privately-sponsored lessons. Since 1948, over a half-million newcomers have learned Hebrew through various courses. Special newspapers for immigrants employ simple Hebrew.

[13] After the sixth century B.C.E., Hebrew ceased to be the major tongue among the Jewish people. It was succeeded by Aramaic, except of course in prayer and study.

[14] Fein, *Politics in Israel*, p. 130.

[15] As recently as 1966, no more than 69 percent of Israeli Jews aged 14 and over used Hebrew as their only or first everyday language, just about the same percentage as in 1948 (*Statistical Abstract of Israel, 1969*, p. 586). Some 250,000 Jews in Israel still do not speak Hebrew, although these are mostly women over 45 (Fein, p. 129).

[16] Hebrew is taught in Arab schools in Israel from the fourth grade, and Arabs can, of course, attend the *ulpanim*.

[17] Hebrew is an everyday language only for some 15 percent of non-Jews in Israel.

[18] Interestingly enough, despite the fact that Arabic is the language of Israel's largest minority, the visitor whose native tongue is English or French can get about in the country with greater ease than if he knew Arabic.

The use or non-use of Hebrew often has a bearing upon wider social and moral questions. For example, the employment of languages other than Hebrew by some Christian churches in Israel helps to counteract any charge of missionary designs upon Israelis.

[19] Trial stays are readily arranged, in the hope that temporary residents will become permanent. The 1968 Zionist Congress initiated a program to encourage immigration from the United States, Great Britain, Europe, South America, and South Africa. Less than a year later the movement could boast over 5,000 members pledged to emigrate to Israel within three years.

[20] Ya'acov Friedler, "Haifa Absorption Centre—How It Works, Where It Helps," *The Jerusalem Post* (Weekly Overseas Edition), April 28, 1969. Much of the financial aid for the nation's absorption program comes through the United Israel Appeal. At present, the average cost of settling one immigrant in Israel is over $2,000.

[21] See Chasya Pincus, "The Story of Youth Aliyah," *Midstream*, February, 1968, pp. 27-43. Youth Aliyah has recently instituted some teaching of potential young immigrants by employing the English and French languages. (Philip Gillon, "Foreign Languages—and Aliya," *The Jerusalem Post* [Weekly Overseas Edition], Nov. 25, 1968). This is the first time that anything but Hebrew has been used in Youth Aliyah teaching.

[22] Cf. Weingrod, *Israel*, pp. 50, 77.

[23] Cf. Weingrod, pp. 77-80.

[24] Weingrod, p. 34.

25 In one town of the upper Galilee some 80,000 people passed through over a fifteen-year period, yet the recent population was only 17,000.

26 Ernest Stock, "Grassroots Politics—Israel Style," *Midstream*, June-July, 1966, p. 5. We do not imply that life in Kiryat Gat is free of social problems. For example, there are complaints about a paucity of cultural opportunities.

27 The climate of Eilat is much like southern Arizona: terribly hot but non-humid. One of the present writers dipped a handkerchief in the waters of the Gulf of Eilat and without wringing it out noted by the clock that in four minutes it was completely dry.

NOTES TO CHAPTER 9

The Communal Settlements

1 Eban, *My People*, p. 493.

2 *Facts About Israel, 1970,* Jerusalem: Ministry of Foreign Affairs, Information Division, pp. 96, 112. Some of the materials in this publication, which is referred to from time to time in our study, tend to portray Israel in a rather rosy light. The publication is to be used with caution.

3 This is not always the case with the aged. An official of Malben, the American Joint Distribution Committee's health and welfare program in Israel, has stated that increasing needs for aid include *kibbutzim* that lack sufficient facilities and funds to care for aging founder-members and parents of younger members. Malben is already assisting 40,000 aged, sick, and handicapped immigrants to Israel (James Feron, *The New York Times*, May 17, 1969).

4 *Kibbutz* children attend the movement's own schools. In many instances there are regional elementary and secondary schools involving a number of settlements. All *kibbutz* children are entitled to attend high school. There is a campaign now afoot to inaugurate a *kibbutz*-sponsored university. The movement already runs its own teacher training college, the nation's largest.

5 In recent years some *kibbutzim* have changed the system to the extent of enabling children to sleep in their homes, using the argument that this fosters psychological security.

6 A variation upon this form of settlement is the *moshav shitufi,* which resembles the collectivist *kibbutz* in its economy and ownership but provides greater individual independence than the *kibbutz,* permitting family possession of homes and family care of children. Accordingly, in contrast to the practice on the *kibbutzim,* most of the women work only part-time.

7 Eban, *My People*, p. 367.

8 An additional reason why large numbers of army officers come from the *kibbutzim* is that the collectives are able to adjust their allocations of manpower to permit the necessary extra training.

9 Fein, *Politics in Israel*, p. 119.

10 H. E. Retik, "The One and Only Labor Party," *Israel Magazine*, I, 10 (1969), 33.

11 This accords with the fact that agricultural endeavor in Israel has in many respects reached or even passed full capacity. The alternative operations in which the *kibbutzim* have increasingly become engaged include factories, food processing, fishing, hotels and restaurants, and handcrafts.

12 Joel Darom, "The Industrialization of the Kibbutz," *Midstream*, December, 1968, pp. 22, 23.

13 Editorial, "Kibbutz University," *The Jerusalem Post* (Weekly Overseas Edition), May 5, 1969.

14 *The Jerusalem Post* (Weekly Overseas Edition), Nov. 3, 1969.

15 As cited in Fein, *Politics in Israel*, p. 117.

NOTES TO CHAPTER 10

Jewish Majority and Arab Minority, I

1 Ernest Stock's report has provided helpful data and commentary in the preparation of this and the next chapter: *From Conflict to Understanding: Relations between Jews and Arabs in Israel since 1948,* New York: Institute of Human Relations Press, 1968. All references to Stock are to that study.

2 We resort to the term "administered areas" because it is quite neutral and because there are serious objections to other phrasing. To say that Israel has "conquered" the areas or even that she "occupies" them does not quite ring true. The point is that Jordan did both these things in 1948 in her war against Israeli independence. "Liberated areas" is another possibility, but this is not sufficiently neutral either. A universally acceptable designation may not become apparent for a long time, and perhaps never.

3 The moral and political question of the reunification of Jerusalem is considered in Chapter 19.

4 Other mixed Arab-Jewish cities in Israel include Jaffa, Haifa, Acre, Lydda, and Ramla. Before 1948, all of these save Haifa were exclusively Arab; now, Arabs are only a minority.

5 Use of the words "Arab-Israeli conflict" to describe one phase of the international situation in the Middle East is thus misleading at this one vital point, however expedient the phrase is as shorthand.

6 Some 32,000 Druses live in northern Israel. Whether these captivating people are to be identified as Arabs depends on the meanings assigned to "Druse" and "Arab." The crucial point is that "Druse" is primarily a religious term, while "Arab" signifies a linguistic and cultural reality. Many of these people will acknowledge only that they are Druses; others will agree that they are Arabs but of course not Muslims. Historically, they have been mistreated and regarded as religious heretics by orthodox Muslims. Their religion is largely secret. By hierarchical decision the Druses extend full fealty to Israel. Because their own internal socio-religious governance is centralized and authoritarian, it is hard to know the extent to which this loyalty is shared among all Druses. At their leaders' express wish, they serve in the Israeli Army, and often distinguish themselves there. Not until the refounding of Israel were they granted complete religious freedom and status.

7 In 1967 the crude birth rate in Israel was 21.5 per 1,000 for Jews and 44.9 for non-Jews.

8 Stock, pp. 16-17.

9 The authorities held that the security measures were dictated by the practical considerations that most Arabs lived in rural areas close to enemy territory and containing very few Jewish residents. The avowed purposes were to prevent collaboration with the enemy, to ensure law and order, and to preclude hostile outbreaks and irredentist activities. Some three quarters of Israeli Arabs were affected by the Military Administration. Although this was not a military government, it did seriously restrict movements of the population and access to certain areas.

10 Cf. the appeal by ten Israeli Arabs to the President of the United Nations General Assembly, November 10, 1960, published under the title *Violation of Human Rights in Israel,* New York: Arab Information Center, 1961. Beyond its criticisms of the Military Administration, this document complained of confiscation of land, the displacement of Israeli Arabs, and job, tax, educational, and racial discrimination.

11 Stock, pp. 24, 46-7.

12 James Feron, *The New York Times,* June 26, 1969.

13 Accordingly, it would be quite in order to treat the Arab-Jewish problem as, at least in part, an instance of the classic conflict between rural and urban life. About forty percent of Israel's Arabs continue to be engaged in agriculture.

14 As far back as 1961, as much as 56 percent of the employed population in the Arab rural settlements would travel to work for Jewish employers (Stock, p. 22).

15 Stock, pp. 23-24.

16 Under Turkish rule there was separation by religious and cultural communities, and this practice was sustained by the British.

17 Stock, p. 8.

18 There has been a sharp contrast between the lot of the Arabs who remained in Israel and those along the West Bank of the Jordan River, the region overrun by the Hashemite Kingdom of Jordan in 1948. The Government of Jordan put few funds into the area and discouraged large business investments there. It preferred to develop the East Bank of the River, the original area of Transjordan.

19 With the Histadrut this was not always so. Before 1955 Arab workers were not admitted to membership; the Histadrut sought to organize them into a separate Palestine Labor League, which it had helped to found in 1927. By 1959, they could achieve full membership. In 1965, the word "Hebrew" was taken from the organization's name, and it was now the official representative of all Israeli workers, Arabs as well as Jews. Part of the Histadrut's program is specifically designed to benefit the Arab community, e.g., it maintains an Arab publishing house (Stock, pp. 67-8, 70).

[20] Four out of every five Arab farmers own their own land; the fifth leases land from the Government.

[21] By 1966, 100 cooperatives were functioning in Arab villages, but most of these involved water supply and housing, rather than the productive side of the economy. One difficulty has been the marked individualism of the Arab farmer. Many attempts to establish cooperatives have failed (Stock, pp. 62, 70-71). This fact becomes ironical as one contemplates Soviet support of the Arabs and the nominal socialist tendencies of Egyptian leaders.

[22] Fein, *Politics in Israel,* p. 58.

[23] *Facts About Israel, 1970,* p. 64.

[24] The 1940's saw only 32.5 percent of Arab children from kindergarten through elementary school age in attendance at school.

[25] James Feron, *The New York Times,* Oct. 29, 1969; *Time,* Nov. 7, 1969, p. 35.

[26] Stock, pp. 32-3

[27] Amnon Rubinstein, "No Man's Land Remains in Jerusalem," *The New York Times Magazine,* May 11, 1969, pp. 128-30.

[28] Notoriously, statistics are readable in all kinds of ways. Thus, it is just as reasonable to emphasize that over a two-year period (from 1966–67 to 1968–69) Arab primary schools improved from a teacher-pupil ratio of 1:30 to that of 1:27, while Jewish primary schools improved only from 1:18.2 to 1:16.7.

[29] In the 1968–69 year some 250 Arab and Druse students were in attendance at the Hebrew University.

[30] It is true that some of the reasons for this lack arise from circumstances beyond anyone's direct culpability, e.g., the relatively large numbers of Arab workers in small establishments, where unionization has been slow to succeed.

[31] Stock, p. 93.

[32] There are some 20-30,000 Bedouin in Israel, with deep roots in the land. Living principally in the Negev, these "lords of the desert" have manfully resisted efforts to alter their nomadic life. The Government is endeavoring to help them settle down, partly because of their interference with the rights of settled peoples but also in order that they might benefit from modern methods of farming, education, social security, and health measures. An example of a new permanent settlement for the Bedouin is Tel Sheba, near Beersheba. While many Bedouin continue to resent outside pressures, numbers of others have confounded skeptics by becoming highly skilled and responsible workers and by showing themselves very happy with a settled, less arduous existence.

NOTES TO CHAPTER 11
Jewish Majority and Arab Minority, II

[1] This latter point was emphasized to us by a highly knowledgeable Anglican churchman and historian who has resided in East Jerusalem for years and who shows anything but a bias in Israel's favor.

[2] Some Christian Arabs in Israel are prone to repeat a saying purporting to come from Muslims: "First we take care of Saturday, then we take care of Sunday," i.e., once the Jews are liquidated, the Christians will come next. We have no interest in broadcasting wild stories, and we have found no independent evidence whatsoever to support any such allegation. We mention the saying here only because it appears to exert a definite influence upon the attitudes of Christian Arabs. It points up the fact of division within the Arab community.

[3] See *The Arab War Against Israel: Statements and Documents,* Jerusalem: Ministry for Foreign Affairs, Information Division, 1967. Included among other documents are the Arab war plans, Egyptian battle orders, the Syrian plan of attack, and a sample of captured Jordanian military operational orders for annihilating Israeli villages.

[4] Stock, *From Conflict to Understanding,* p. 100.

[5] Jack J. Cohen, "Arabs and Jews: From Dilemma to Problems," *The Reconstructionist,* Oct. 6, 1967, p. 22.

[6] Over the two-year period following the War only 45 Arabs were deported from the administered areas and Israel to Jordan for seditious activities. Between the War and January, 1970 only 120 Israeli Arabs had been found guilty of collaborating with Arab terrorist organizations.

[7] This percentage held firm in the October, 1969 elections.

[8] Ze'ev Schul, "Arab Attitudes Still Negative," *The Jerusalem Post* (Weekly Overseas Edition), June 16, 1969. In 1969 Rakah was unable to rouse much support for a divisive policy.

[9] Stock, pp. 25-6.

[10] Cohen, "Arabs and Jews," p. 21.

[11] The testimony is cited in Schul, "Arab Attitudes Still Negative."

[12] Fein, *Politics in Israel*, p. 60.

[13] Stock, p. 50.

[14] Fein, p. 61.

[15] These figures are derived from comparative populations in the Middle East and the United States today. More than 57 million people live in the seven nations that have never made peace with Israel, about nineteen times the number of people in Israel.

[16] The exemption of Arabs from service in the armed forces is a perfect instance of the Israeli dilemma. The publicly emphasized rationale for the policy is avoidance of Arabs having to fight fellow-Arabs and especially blood relatives. Here, surely, is a praiseworthy means of alleviating a conflict of loyalties. At the same time, the exemption testifies implicitly that all is not well. The Arab is all too obviously being assigned to a category different from other citizens. Nor is it possible completely to exclude the fear that were the exemption removed, the nation could have a sizable insurgency on her hands.

[17] Cf. Yehoshafat Harkabi, "The Arab-Israeli Confrontation—An Israeli View," a paper delivered before The Institute for Strategic Studies, Oct. 1-3, 1965, Divonne-les-Bains, France (mimeographed). Harkabi is a professor at the Hebrew University.

[18] Cohen, "Arabs and Jews," p. 9.

[19] American-sponsored organizations that are partially involved in the problems of Arabs include the America-Israel Cultural Foundation, the American Jewish Congress, Hadassah, and the Organization for Rehabilitation Through Training.

[20] Cohen, "Arabs and Jews," p. 16.

NOTES TO CHAPTER 12

Some Issues of Religion, I

[1] Harold Fisch, "Faith in Israel," *Commentary*, February, 1969, p. 64.

[2] The quoted judgment upon Zionism is from a "Semitic Action" group statement (1949). While this particular group is now defunct, various other instances of "Israelism" are not. Numbers of Israeli young people have no particular interest in or concern for problems of the Diaspora. A contemporary exponent of the "Canaanite" outlook is Uri Avneri, a member of Parliament.

[3] Cohen, "Arabs and Jews," p. 17.

[4] "Orthodoxy," *The Encyclopedia of the Jewish Religion*, ed. by R. J. Zwi Werblowsky and Geoffrey Wigoder, New York: Holt, Rinehart and Winston, 1965, p. 293.

[5] The usual meanings of "laic" are "lay" and "secular." However, there are connections with our usage. For one thing, Judaism is a "lay" religion; it has no priests. Again, the Jewish *laos* is in one fundamental respect completely secular: a people of this world, this age *(seculum)* is involved. Cf. James Parkes's concept of the Jews as a "natural community" (in, among many references, *Prelude to Dialogue*, London: Vallentine, Mitchell, 1969, p. 193).

[6] Cf. Eliezer Goldman, *Religious Issues in Israel's Political Life*, Jerusalem: Mador Dati, 1964, p. 11.

[7] One can argue the inappropriateness of such speculation, since Liberal Jews in the West did not possess the fervent Zionist convictions that were widespread among Orthodox Jews elsewhere.

[8] Weingrod, *Israel*, p. 5.

[9] Sachar, *A History of the Jews*, pp. 452-3. Not until 1952 was Ben Gurion forced to yield to the General Zionists—who supported private enterprise—and to include them in the Government.

[10] Goldman, *Religious Issues . . .*, p. 97.

[11] R. J. Zwi Werblowsky, "A Nation Born of Religion," *Israel Magazine*, I, 5 (1968), 21.

[12] Israel inherited from the British the institution of the Chief Rabbinate. There are two

Chief Rabbis, one for the Sephardic community and one for the Ashkenazic community. Israel has about 400 officially appointed rabbis.

[13] The civil courts can neither review nor overturn decisions of a rabbinical or other religious court, unless the competence of such a court to deal with a particular case is in question.

[14] Goldman, *Religious Issues . . .*, p. 63.

[15] In Jerusalem restaurants are closed on the Sabbath; in Tel Aviv they are open.

[16] Goldman, *Religious Issues . . .*, p. 33.

[17] Goldman, p. 43. However, in areas where non-Jews comprise less than 25 percent of the population, the Jewish Sabbath must be the day.

[18] In East Jerusalem a regulation was recently adopted obliging Christian shopkeepers to close on Sunday, and Muslims on Friday.

[19] Cf. Eliezer Whartman, "Religion and Crime," *Israel Magazine*, I, 5 (1968), 29.

[20] The presence of religious parties in the political arena (as in many European states) is a distinctive feature of Israeli life, not only politically speaking but religiously speaking. Reference is made to these bodies in Chapter 14 including some allusion to their political influence and recent fortunes. As yet, no satisfactory information is obtainable on the degree to which religious Jews support the policies of the religious parties in Parliament. Normally, we would anticipate considerable support, but we cannot assume it.

[21] A highly significant exception is the Minister of Religious Affairs. It is inconceivable that in the foreseeable future this individual could be anything but Orthodox. The Ministry of Religious Affairs is a stronghold of the National Religious Party.

[22] Yaaqov Yehoshua, "Moslem Religious Life in Israel," *Christian News From Israel*, Spring, 1970, p. 32.

NOTES TO CHAPTER 13

Some Issues of Religion, II

[1] *Facts About Israel, 1970*, p. 71. Approximately one quarter of the country's Christians, including the Protestants, are not included in the officially recognized religious communities. Among the reasons for the non-recognition of some half-dozen Protestant groups is their small size and the fact that most of their members are foreign nationals. Of course, they are afforded every freedom as private religious associations.

Ironically enough, the British Mandatory Administration never gave official recognition to the Church of England, since that communion entered the picture much after the status quo inherited by Great Britain had been fixed. Not until 1970 was recognition accorded, by Israel, to the Anglican Church (possessing about 2,000 members).

Some 30,000 Christians live in the administered area of the West Bank (Judea and Samaria).

[2] The Department of Christian Communities of the Ministry of Religious Affairs publishes an informative quarterly, *Christian News From Israel*, in English, French, and Spanish, edited by Yona Malachy. A number of courses in Christianity, including New Testament, are offered by Israeli universities. For a brief account of recent developments in relations between the Christian churches and the State of Israel, see the booklet, *Christian Churches in Israel* by S. P. Colbi, Jerusalem: Israel Economist, 1969. Since April, 1969 *The Jerusalem Post* has carried in its Weekend Supplement and Weekly Overseas Edition a feature called "Christian Comment." Its major purpose is to inform readers throughout Israel and the world of different aspects of Christian life and thought in Israel and in other lands.

[3] The Jordanian Government had forbidden visits to Christian holy places except at Christmas and Easter, when limited numbers of Christians were allowed to enter Jordan.

[4] Further commentary related to this matter is included in Chapter 23.

[5] Cf. "Majorities and Minorities in the Middle East," reprint from *Israel Economist* (Jerusalem), February, 1969.

[6] I. S. Ben-Meir, "The Case for Orthodoxy," *Israel Magazine*, I, 5 (1968), 36, 37.

[7] Mendel Kohansky, "Reform Judaism Meets in Israel," *Midstream*, November, 1968, p. 58.

[8] A recent poll sponsored by the *Jewish Chronicle* (London) found that 41 percent of the Israeli public favored recognition of Liberal rabbis, 26 percent opposed it, and 33 percent never heard of the Liberal movement (as reported in Kohansky, p. 59).

[9] Myron M. Fenster, "Religion in Israel," *Congress Bi-Weekly*, Jan. 13, 1969, p. 12.

[10] Kohansky, "Reform Judaism Meets in Israel," p. 54.

[11] If there is just cause, a husband may be compelled to give consent. A wife cannot be compelled to do so, although in exceptional cases the husband is given permission to remarry.

[12] Nonconformist Israeli Jews sometimes object that such a requirement demonstrates how the non-Orthodox or non-religious Jew is discriminated against, in contrast to members of non-Jewish religious groups. What he forgets is that the non-Jew who is a nonconformist is restricted just as stringently. True, the problem is more serious for Jews because of their numbers. But the principle remains the same.

[13] Goldman, *Religious Issues in Israel's Political Life,* pp. 75-6.

[14] Werblowsky, "A Nation Born of Religion," p. 20. In further opposition to Eliezer Goldman's argument, the protest is heard among secularist Israeli Jews that religious control over marriage and divorce is an unwarranted intrusion into the private life of the individual and one that can lead to untold human misery (cf. Ervin Birnbaum, "Old Problems in a New Guise," *Midstream,* May, 1968, p. 30).

[15] However, support from abroad for Liberal Jewish institutions is permitted without any restriction. (Orthodox institutions also receive much support from abroad.)

[16] *The New York Times,* May 13, 1969. In contrast to the recent decision on television, newspapers are still not published on the Jewish Sabbath (*Facts About Israel, 1970,* p. 172). The National Religious Party had earlier (1968) complained to the Government that Israel is "fostering Christian values" through such means as Christian symbolism on postage stamps and Christian radio programs. No changes were made.

[17] As far as we can find out, no finally authoritative information on this issue is as yet available.

[18] The marriage of a noncomformist Israeli Jew will be acknowledged as valid (as will be, presumably, his death) if it takes place outside the country, even if it is not performed in accordance with Orthodox requirements.

Since there is no such thing as civil marriage in Israel, mixed marriages are out of the question. A Jew and a gentile could not be wedded, simply because no social instrument is available for solemnizing the marriage. However, as with a Jewish couple, if such a marriage is contracted outside the country—even as a civil contract—it is treated as valid in Israel.

A problem sometimes arises in marriages outside Israel concerning the status of offspring. If the mother is not registered as a Jew, the children will not be considered Jews unless a process of "conversion" is arranged for them. Otherwise, they eventually meet the same legal problem that a non-Jew faces should he or she wish to marry a Jew.

[19] Kohansky, "Reform Judaism Meets in Israel," p. 59.

[20] According to a recent poll, slightly over half (53 percent) of all Israelis approved an exclusively kosher arrangement in the Defense Forces and governmental and public places. Thirty-nine percent advocated kosher and non-kosher arrangements together (*The Jerusalem Post,* Sept. 30, 1968). With respect to the practice in the armed services, three factors come together: religious scruples, democratic norms, and common sense. To provide both kosher and non-kosher food would be highly impractical. Presumably, non-adherents of *kashruth* are not offended under the present system anywhere to the extent that observant Jews would be offended by the non-availability of kosher food. Indeed, there would be no practicable way for religious Jews to serve in the armed forces without provision for *kashruth.* But the exclusive observance of *kashruth* in other state-supported institutions is much less defensible.

[21] Fisch, "Faith in Israel," p. 65.

[22] Fisch, p. 67.

[23] Herbert Wiener, "The Real Problem of Liberal Judaism in Israel," *Dimensions in American Judaism,* Spring, 1968, pp. 8, 43.

[24] The direction and the hope of a religious movement are sometimes revealed by the identity and behavior of its enemies. A revealing case is the continuing hostility of a small body of ultra-Orthodox Jews in Israel to the form of Orthodoxy that prevails. The ultra-Orthodox accuse the other religionists of having watered down Halachah. Others may adjudge that the accusations actually testify to Orthodox openness to the world. The openness is very slight, but it is there.

The ultra-Orthodox are notoriously represented by the sect Neturei Karta (Guardians of the City), which inhabits the Meah Shearim quarter of Jerusalem. This sect refuses to recognize the State of Israel, contending that the latter is an assembly of dissimulators and idolaters. The true redemption of the people of God must await a divine act in the future. The Zionist movement is human effrontery; all it has done is to imitate the evil nationalistic and political ways of the gentiles. Members of the Neturei Karta employ such devices as stoning moving vehicles on the Sabbath. They comprise fewer than 500 families.

[25] Cf. Kohansky, "Reform Judaism Meets in Israel," p. 58.

NOTES TO CHAPTER 14

Politics in Action

[1] Fein, *Politics in Israel*, pp. 28-9. Professor Fein's valuable study has been a major aid in the preparation of this chapter as well as being of help elsewhere in the present volume. All references to Fein are to the above volume.

[2] Fein, p. 140.

[3] Colin Legum, "Identity Problem," *The Observer* (London), Nov. 10, 1968.

[4] The President, elected by the Knesset, is official Head of State but he is not the Chief Executive. The equivalent of the latter office is that of Prime Minister. A party must receive at least one percent of the vote in order to win a minimum of one seat. The term of office in the Knesset is four years. Apart from the normal ending of its tenure, the Government may fall in any of several ways: through a no-confidence vote in the Knesset, or the resignation of the Prime Minister, or a decision on the part of the Government to resign. When any of these possibilities becomes real, some kind of defection within the governmental coalition is implied. In the event the Government falls, special elections are held. However, the Knesset alone has the power to dissolve itself. The Seventh Knesset of the modern State was elected in October, 1969.

[5] Fein, p. 103. At this particular juncture, Professor Fein seems to be using "State" and "Government" interchangeably. A fundamental contrast between the Israeli and American situations is that in Israel, advocates of the diversion of power live on the political left; in the United States such people have traditionally come from the political right.

[6] Fein, pp. 166, 172.

[7] Fein, p. 181. Since Israel is a democracy, the Government obviously has to be responsive to the demands and interests of the several constituencies: the Knesset itself, the parties in the coalition, its own party, and the wider public.

[8] Fein, p. 105.

[9] Fein, pp. 70-72.

[10] Fein, p. 69. While precise figures on the extent of party membership are not known, it is believed that over forty percent of the adult population has some kind of formal connection with a party.

[11] Fein, p. 144.

[12] In a necessarily cursory treatment we cannot give an exhaustive account of all the factors behind the dominant power of the parties. Another influential historical factor has been the massive work of the political parties in integrating immigrants (to be sure, partly out of self-interest), especially in the period when the State was simply unable to cope with the avalanche.

[13] Mapai, Israel's largest and most powerful party, and the group around which all the governmental coalitions have centered, has sought to balance collectivism and free enterprise, and, internally speaking, has been neither anti-religious nor pro-religious. It is sometimes described as standing for "democratic socialism" somewhat in the tradition of the British Labour Party. Fein speaks of Mapai as "the party of aggregative compromise." Ahduth Avodah (Unity of Labor) is a strongly collectivist party opposed to the religious interests. It insists upon retaining its own independent *kibbutz* movement. Rafi has leaned heavily toward free enterprise. The socialist parties in Israel have depended greatly upon support and direction from different sectors of the *kibbutz* movement.

[14] Mapam is a *kibbutz*-based party, strongly socialist and also anti-religious. It has shown more concern than any other party for the welfare of Israeli Arabs.

[15] Thus, Mapai's purpose in the original merger was to accomplish a controlling majority in the Knesset under its aegis; Ahduth Avodah was attempting to retain its position in the labor bloc and to help check the political ambitions of younger Rafi members; and Rafi was seeking to ensure a complete change in the country's leadership, endeavoring to replace Levi Eshkol by the national hero Moshe Dayan (Ervin Birnbaum, "Old Problems in a New Guise." pp. 26-7). With respect to the Mapam-Israel Labor Party alignment, the Mapam leadership expressed the hope of saving "the Labor Party and Israel socialism from Moshe Dayan and Shimon Peres," of strengthening "the peace and anti-chauvinist majority in the Labor Party," and of achieving a thoroughly socialist society in Israel (*The Jerusalem Post* [Weekly Overseas Edition], Oct. 28, 1968, Nov. 25, 1968).

[16] Lea Ben Dor, "A Two-Party System?," *Congress Bi-Weekly*, Feb. 5, 1968, p. 16.

[17] To the right of the Israel Labor Party is the Independent Liberal Party, which is often sympathetic to labor but whose program is close to the General Zionists. This latter body together with the Herut Party form the Gahal Movement. (The vigorously right-wing Herut

Party has been strongly opposed to the present regime, is constitutionally against governmental intervention in the economy, and has stood for a quite nationalistic foreign policy. It has found a certain appeal among disaffected immigrants.) In February, 1969 the Gahal grouping voted to remain part of the Government coalition. In the October, 1969 elections this grouping captured 26 seats in the Knesset, a gain of 4. In August, 1970 the six Gahal ministers resigned from the Government in opposition to Israel's assent to the American proposal for a temporary cease-fire and a renewal of indirect talks with Egypt through the Jarring U.N. mission. The pity of the non-socialist groups is that even as a united bloc, they have not been able to muster more than half a majority in the Knesset, To the left of the Israel Labor Party stand various groups of much lesser strength. These include two communist and two Arab parties.

18 Birnbaum, "Old Problems in a New Guise," pp. 26-7.

19 Lea Ben Dor, "Twenty Years and Some Progress," *The Jerusalem Post Weekly* (Weekly Overseas Edition), Feb. 3, 1969.

20 Birnbaum, p. 28.

21 The largest of these, the National Religious Party, is a religious-Zionist movement committed to legislation based upon Holy Scripture (the Torah) and, in its politico-economic position, something of a counterpart to Mapai. Agudat Yisrael is pledged to absolute observance of the Torah in the life and administration of the State. Poalei Agudat Yisrael is a worker-oriented counterpart of Agudat Yisrael.

22 Stock, "Grassroots Politics—Israel Style," p. 11.

23 Stock, p. 13.

24 The alleged governmental failure to pay attention to what the public thinks does not prevent Israelis from having their own ideas about the Government. On the basis of a representative sample, the Israel Institute of Applied Social Research concluded that in June, 1968 77 percent of the people believed that the Government was coping effectively with the nation's problems, in contrast to 90 percent in the period immediately after the Six Day War of June 1967. (Terence Smith, *The New York Times,* July 7, 1968).

25 "Changing the Way MK's Are Elected," *The Jerusalem Post* (Weekly Overseas Edition), June 16, 1969. *The Post* editorialized (same date) that even under the new plan, the system is still "more concerned with satisfying the wishes of the parties than of the voters, though it does take a step in the direction of the voters."

26 The City of Jerusalem retains one of these.

27 The major reasons ensuring the political independence (but also the considerable political irrelevance) of the Supreme Court are supplied in Fein, pp. 186-7. Palestine had no system of trial by jury; in Israel today court decisions continue to be rendered by judges alone. Nevertheless, generally speaking, Israeli jurisprudence has been dependent upon and bound to English jurisprudence. Now, however, it is rapidly developing its own autonomy.

28 By disclaiming authority to pass judgment upon parliamentary enactments, the Supreme Court has itself upheld the principle of Knesset sovereignty. One salient factor here is the absence of the kind of constitution that could be used as a standard for judging laws. In her lack of such an instrument, Israel resembles Great Britain. There are, of course, safeguards for such freedoms as speech, religion, and assembly. "The primary reason for the failure to adopt a formalized constitution in Israel has been the realization that on a number of central questions—most notably, the relationship of religion to the State—the societal consensus was insufficient" (Fein, pp. 165-6).

29 Fein, pp. 198, 232.

NOTES TO CHAPTER 15

Ways and Means

1 Yusif Sayigh, "The Israeli Economy in Focus," *The Middle East Newsletter* (Beirut), October, 1968, p. 3.

2 The only proviso is that the money be repaid when the claims are settled.

3 However, the Dead Sea is one of the world's richest sources of chemical deposits. It has potash, magnesium, bromine, and other salts. Copper, phosphates, and additional valuable minerals are mined in the South.

4 Over the two decades beginning in 1948, massive imports had to be secured in order to feed, house, and employ immigrants, to furnish raw materials for industry and agriculture, and to provide capital goods for expansion. The cost of security plus a major increase in imports

for investment and production goods were decisive in widening the trade deficit in 1968 and 1969 (*The Jerusalem Post* [Weekly Overseas Edition], July 21, 1969). The great bulk of defense expenditures must be paid in hard foreign currency.

[5] Remba, "The Dilemmas of Israel's Economy," p. 54.

[6] Between 1950 and 1967, Israel received approximately $9,300,000,000 from abroad. About 53 percent of these capital imports consisted of unilateral transfers requiring no repayment. The sources were world Jewry (mostly American) and the West German and U.S. governments. (Assistance from the latter Government stopped several years ago. In March, 1970 the United States offered $100 million in credits for financing earlier Israeli arms purchases that had been arranged on cash terms. No grants were included.) Somewhat over one-third of the total capital funds were long- and medium-term loans, requiring repayment. The balance were foreign investments (Remba, pp. 55, 59) and funds brought in by immigrants. German reparations payments have ended; restitution payments to individual Israelis continue.

[7] Remba, p. 62.

[8] The *kibbutz* movement today is sometimes identified by its critics as an economic encumbrance, on the alleged ground that it unduly protects small-scale enterprise and retards industrial concentration necessary to progress (a criticism reported by Georges Friedmann, "The Histadrut Paradox," *Midstream*, April, 1967, p. 8). *Kibbutz* spokesmen reply that the economic efficiency of their production and distribution programs has been notably advanced in a number of ways, by means of mechanization and the application of modern technology, and with the aid of their larger federations and even across federation lines. Joint enterprises include transport cooperatives, the sharing of heavy machinery, regional packing plants, and the ownership of industries.

[9] Fein, *Politics in Israel*, pp. 218, 219.

[10] Ben Dor, "A Two-Party System?," p. 16.

[11] Fein, pp. 222-3.

[12] Friedmann, "The Histadrut Paradox," p. 7.

[13] Weingrod, *Israel*, pp. 18-19.

[14] An interesting example of this policy was the establishing in 1969 of Ramat Shalom (Hill of Peace), a settlement on the slopes of Mount Hermon begun by a group of American and British immigrants. This is said to be the first attempt to break away from the communal or cooperative arrangement definitive to Israeli land settlement. Significantly, while Ramat Shalom is an instance of free enterprise, the Government is granting it considerable assistance since it is at once a development project and located in a security area (James Feron, *The New York Times*, April 25, 1969).

[15] One valuable by-product of the 1968 Israel Economic Conference (see below, pp. 162–3) is a Four-Year Development Plan covering 1968-71, prepared by a department in the Office of the Prime Minister.

[16] Avner Hovne, "The Economic Scene in Israel," *Midstream*, May, 1967, p. 12.

[17] For a recent lively discussion of Histadrut history and achievements, see Maurice Carr, "The Jewish Revolution," *Israel Magazine*, II, 6 (March, 1970), 29-37. There are three other labor organizations with a total of about 210,000 members. Two of these are religious and maintain a number of ties with the Histadrut through its trade-union section and welfare services.

[18] Stock, "Grassroots Politics—Israel Style," p. 4.

[19] Friedmann, "The Histadrut Paradox," pp. 3-4.

[20] Friedmann, pp. 5, 9, 10.

[21] Friedmann, pp. 3, 4. Mapai has had much to do with Histadrut policy, a fact that has been identified by left-wing militants as making for undue subjection to "conservative" influences within the labor movement.

[22] Of course, they are labeled "wildcat" strikes insofar as they take place without the Labor Federation's approval.

[23] Friedmann, pp. 4-5. In recent years the State has taken over a number of services previously supplied by the Histadrut. As examples, the Ministry of Labor now supervises employment, and a plan has been adopted to establish a national health service. These developments have not brought joy to the Histadrut leadership.

[24] Over the past few years local production has covered 85 percent of food consumption; only 15 percent of the country's foodstuffs are imported.

[25] In 1968 there was a 12 percent rise in the gross national product, and a like rise was antici-

pated for 1969. As of 1968, general industrial output exceeded $2 billion, and industrial exports rose to some half-billion dollars. In the two and one-half year period following the Six Day War industrial output increased by 30 percent, and industrial production by over 50 percent. The current gross national product is $4.2 billion. Israel's single biggest dollar-earner now is tourism, from which $150 million were gained in 1968. A like amount was expected for 1969.

26 Due to an "overheated" economy in 1966, during which a recession was suffered, the Government instituted a slowdown policy that reduced growth in the national income to 5–6 percent. An inevitable consequence was a rise in unemployment. There had been a steady decline in unemployment between 1953 and 1964, but by May of 1967 the number of jobless had sharply increased to 12 percent of the total labor force. Then came the June War of 1967, which temporarily abolished most unemployment. By April of 1968, the unemployment figure had gone back up to 8 percent, but by the end of the year had subsided to 6 percent. (By 1968 the economic downturn had ended. However, Israeli economists predicted that the nation's increase in output would fall to 8 percent in 1970, as indicative of an economic slowdown. The fact that Israeli unemployed are granted subsistence, in contrast to the plight of unemployed in many other Asian countries, does not make these people feel any less frustrated. A serious complication is that recent unemployment in Israel extended for the first time to highly-trained people. (This has undoubtedly been a spur to emigration from Israel, which has included a considerable number of university-educated persons.) On the other hand, the nation is faced with a shortage of engineers, technicians, teachers, scientists, nurses, social workers, and physicians.

27 Comparatively speaking, Israel is still a poor country. Approximately one out of every six families continues to live below the poverty line (defined at $115 per family per month).

28 Fein, p. 220.

29 It must be noted that most of the increased farm land had already been put to use as long ago as 1953. The total area under cultivation has not expanded appreciably since 1959 (*Statistical Abstract of Israel, 1969*, p. 313). But production has greatly increased because yield per acre has risen, largely due to expanded irrigation. However, Israel's available water resources can at best take care of only 40 percent of the irrigable land. Partly for this reason, new methods of irrigation and arid-area farming are being tried out in the Negev.

30 Howard Blake, "Strictly Business: Interview with Victor M. Carter," *Israel Magazine*, I, 6 (1968), 25.

31 Price inflation has been a continuing problem in Israel, with an annual advance in prices of some 7 percent. However, from May, 1966 until the end of 1967 there was no increase in prices; for the first time since the reestablishment of the State there was complete price stability. Economic development invariably creates inflationary pressures. At the present writing, these pressures are again mounting in Israel.

32 Robert R. Nathan, "A Continuing Effort," *Israel Magazine*, I, 6 (1968), 32.

33 James Feron, *The New York Times*, May 26, 1969, June 29, 1969; *The Jerusalem Post* (Weekly Overseas Edition), July 21, 1969.

34 Aharon Katzir, "Science with Humanism," *Israel Magazine*, I, 7 (1968), 25.

35 Remba, "The Dilemmas of Israel's Economy," p. 58.

36 In 1967 Israel's non-profit organizations spent 825 million Israeli pounds upon health, education, and welfare services. Only 14 percent of this amount came from sources outside Israel, in contrast to 23 percent in 1962 (Yitzhak Tishler, "A Many-Sided Coin," *Israel Magazine*, I, 6 [1968], 13). In 1969, the quota of Israeli bonds put up for sale in the United States totaled $200-million (all repayable with interest). As this is written, support of the territories administered by Israel since the Six Day War of 1967 is costing her between ten and fifteen million dollars per year, although a considerable portion of this is offset through the sale of oil from the Sinai Peninsula and also by a regional trade balance heavily in Israel's favor. During 1969 produce valued at $28.6 million was exported from the West Bank area to Jordan and other countries, under the "open bridges" policy (James Feron, *The New York Times*, Jan. 16, 1970).

37 Fein, p. 215.

38 Tishler, "A Many-Sided Coin," pp. 10, 13. Some criticism has been made of the apparent failure of the Israel Corporation, created at the time of the 1968 Conference, to begin to play a vigorous economic role (see David Drivine, "The Israel Corporation: What to Do With It?," *The Jerusalem Post* [Weekly Overseas Edition], May 12, 1969).

39 Sayigh, "The Israeli Economy in Focus," p. 7.

NOTES TO CHAPTER 16

Israel and the Arab World, I

[1] Unilaterally, Israel arranged with each of the religious bodies the extent of responsibility each wanted to accept for its buildings. The WAQF (Muslim Authority) assumed custody of the Haram esh-Sharif.

[2] Abba Eban, Address to the U.N. General Assembly, Oct. 8, 1968.

[3] In making this judgment, Earl Berger nevertheless claims that Israel's alternatives were very limited (*The Sword and the Covenant: Arab-Israeli Relations 1948-56,* London: Routledge & Kegan Paul, 1965, pp. 96-7). Berger's study is most helpful for an understanding of the 1949–56 period.

[4] Abdullah's attempts to secure an agreement with Israel were thwarted by the Conciliation Commission and by Palestinians in Jordan.

[5] Nasser has plotted both the overthrow and assassination of Hussein at various times. The military enforcement of Nasser's plans to unite both Syria and Jordan to Egypt was prevented only by Israel's presence in the Negev. Egyptian and Saudi Arabian troops have battled one another in Yemen.

[6] Under the programs, Arabs may stay with relatives in Israel or the administered areas for as long as one month (Ray Vickers, "Mideast Indigents," *The Wall Street Journal,* Mar. 6, 1970). Arab students studying abroad are especially encouraged to visit relatives during vacation. Numbers of these students have been touring Israel with Israeli university students. Michael Shashar describes the remarkable free exchange and camaraderie that developed between the Arabs and their hosts during the 1968 visits. In sharp contrast, the Christian Arabs from Bethlehem and the Muslim Arabs from Nablus studiously avoided each other during the entire time ("Summer Escapade," *Israel Magazine,* I, 9 [1968], 60-61).

[7] We are grateful to Mr. M. N. Hawary of Nazareth for providing us with a great deal of information on this subject, more than could be fitted into this brief résumé.

[8] Under the Partition Plan, Israel would have had 5,579 square miles.

[9] Abba Eban, as cited in Berger, *The Sword and the Covenant,* p. 95. This description is just as apt for recent years.

[10] The boycott and blockade cost Israel between $50- and $100 million a year when it was most effective. Both methods are still being practiced. Many major Japanese firms have recently succumbed to Arab pressure (*The New York Times,* Aug. 17, 1969).

[11] A typical Arab broadcast proclaimed: "Peace between us and the Jews is impossible . . . the problem is a matter of life and death and not a dispute over frontiers or interests. . . . This part of the world . . . cannot hold both of us. It is either we or they. . . ." (Cairo Egyptian Home Service, Jan. 12, 1956).

[12] Gil Carl AlRoy, "Dynamics of Violence In the Middle East," *The Reporter,* May 16, 1968, p. 24.

[13] Eban, "Two Years Later," *The Jerusalem Post,* (Weekly Overseas Edition), June 9, 1969.

[14] Nadav Safran, *From War to War: The Arab-Israeli Confrontation, 1948-1967,* New York: Pegasus, 1969, p. 403. This comprehensive work provides valuable insight into the confrontation of Israel and the Arab states.

[15] See Albert B. Sabin, David S. Landes, Allen Pollack, and Herbert Stroup, "The Arabs Need and Want Peace, *But—*," New York: American Professors for Peace in the Middle East, 1968.

[16] Even King Abdullah of Jordan, because of his moderation, was assassinated (1952) by the ex-Mufti's agents. The Governor of Gaza was executed by Egypt for "collaborating" with Israeli forces during the occupation of 1956-57. In 1969 terrorists murdered several Arab community leaders for cooperating with the Israelis, and some men and women in Gaza on suspicion of the same offense. See comments in Sabin and others, "The Arabs Need and Want Peace, *But—*," pp. 14, 17.

[17] At Kfar Etzion, nearby Arab villagers turned the battle into a massacre after a surrender to the Arab Legion was arranged. Only four of 110 men and women managed to survive. In the three other Jewish villages of the Etzion bloc, another 133 people were killed. Thirty-five student volunteers going to the others' assistance were killed and mutilated.

[18] James Parkes, *Voyage of Discoveries,* London: Victor Gollancz, 1969, p. 212; and Sykes, *Cross Roads to Israel,* p. 415.

[19] There were actually very few atrocities by Jewish forces. Sykes mentions Khissas, Sassa, and Katamon (pp. 400-1, 405, 416-17) in addition to Dir Yassin. Because the tragedy at Dir Yassin was widely believed by almost everyone (even by Ben Gurion) to have been an appalling mass murder of innocent villagers by the Irgun, Arab propaganda respecting that event had devastat-

ing effects upon the Arab people. In point of fact, however, Arab survivors substantiate the Irgun report that Dir Yassin was a legitimate, though bloody and unauthorized, battle for a village being used by Iraqi and Palestinian soldiers as a place from which to attack convoys headed for Jerusalem. Numbers of villagers ignored the Irgun's warning to take cover elsewhere and were killed along with the fighters in the bitter house-to-house struggle that ensued. Those who heeded the warning were transported by the Irgun to the Arab lines in or near Jerusalem.

[20] Weingrod, *Israel*, p. 15.

[21] See Elfan Rees, *Century of the Homeless Man*, New York: Carnegie Endowment for International Peace, November, 1957; also, *Bulletin* of the Research Group for European Migration, V, 1, 1957. A number of Congressional committees studied the refugee question. Their reports (e.g., 1953, 1955, 1957, 1961) consistently advocated development projects that would make rehabilitation of the refugees in Arab countries feasible and successful. Many international spokesmen in the United Nations urged similar programs.

[22] Nasser, as quoted in *Zürcher Woche* (Zurich), Sept. 1, 1961. An example of the same exterminationism was expressed by the Lebanese Prime Minister in an address to his Parliament: "The day of the realization of the Arab hope for the return of the refugees . . . means the liquidation of Israel" (in *El Hayat* [Beirut], April 29, 1966).

[23] Since most of the people would have had to be resettled in other parts of the country, Israel's offer was not a minor gesture. The bid for the land was only for security reasons.

NOTES TO CHAPTER 17

Israel and the Arab World, II

[1] Some 6,000 items were involved, including tanks, planes, warships, rocket launchers, anti-aircraft guns, and missile systems.

[2] Hisham Sharabi, "Prelude to War: The Crisis of May–June 1967," *The Arab World*, New York: The Arab Information Center, XIV, 10-11, n.d., pp. 24, 25.

[3] John Badeau contends that Nasser was counting on the world community to prevent a major conflict. Even the Egyptian blockade of the Gulf was an unplanned move prompted by the unexpected total withdrawal of U.N. forces. Nasser's mistaken evaluation and the dramatic support his actions aroused in the Arab world led to his undoing (*The American Approach to the Arab World*, New York: Harper and Row, 1968, p. 169).

[4] Frank Gervasi, *The Case for Israel*, New York: The Viking Press, 1967, Appendix 15, pp. 226 ff.

[5] James Michener, "Israel: A Nation Too Young to Die," *Look*, Aug. 8, 1967, p. 68.

[6] Yaël Dayan, *Israel Journal: June, 1967*, New York: McGraw-Hill Book Company, 1967, p. 16; and "Was It a Bitter Victory?," *The Daily Telegraph Magazine* (London), June 7, 1968, p. 12.

[7] Amos Kenan, "A Letter to All Good People," reprinted from *Israel Horizons*, May, 1968, by American Professors for Peace in the Middle East, p. 4.

[8] *Time*, June 16, 1967, p. 32.

[9] We use "Palestinians" or "Palestinian Arabs" to refer to Arabs, or their descendants, who trace their residency back to what was earlier called Palestine. They may be exiles from the part that is now the State of Israel, or permanent residents of the West Bank or the Gaza Strip. This use of the term "Palestinians" is in actuality inaccurate (and hence used only for the sake of convenience) since Jews of Palestine merit the name just as readily.

[10] In addition to Palestinians, other Arabs also abandoned their homes—according to UNRWA figures, 100,000 Syrians of the Golan Heights (only the Druses remained), and some 35,000 Arabs of the Sinai.

[11] That Israel has learned much since 1949 is illustrated in a remark to us by one Israeli Arab that the Arabs of the territories are being treated much better than the Israeli Arabs were for a good many years.

[12] Almost the entire population of the three Jericho camps fled to the East Bank in 1967.

[13] John Reddaway, "The Palestine Refugees: A Re-Appraisal," *The Middle East Newsletter* (Beirut), March, 1968, p. 3.

[14] *A Statement to the American Christian Community on the Arab-Israeli Conflict*, issued through the Council for Christian Social Action, United Church of Christ, 1969. The statement suggests a settlement combining compensation and a new non-refugee status.

[15] *Fedayeen* literally means "those who sacrifice." "Guerrilla" and "commando" mean regular

fighters trained to harass the enemy's forces—not civilians—by irregular means during a war. "Terrorists" are deliberately indiscriminate in their choice of targets and use of destructive devices. Even though the infiltrators use terrorist methods, some Israelis are willing to call them "guerrillas" in recognition of the seriousness of the situation. This willingness reflects an effort to understand the *fedayeen* and their motivations.

[16] Many of the captured terrorists admit to being enticed into joining up by an offer of good wages. Arab governments have organized, trained, equipped, and paid terrorist bands from the very start.

[17] Nine-year old trainees are taught a *fedayeen* chant: "Oh Zionist, do not think you are safe. Drinking blood is a habit of our men" (*Time,* March 30, 1970, p. 37).

[18] See the letter of Michel Pierre d'Orleans in *The New York Times,* March 3, 1969; also the comments of Hubert Hallin, Secretary-General of the International Organization of Anti-Nazi Underground and Nazi Prisoner Movements, reported in *The Jerusalem Post* (Weekly Overseas Edition), April 21, 1969.

[19] Israel claims that 90 percent are killed, wounded, or captured within 24 hours of crossing the lines. During 1969, 586 Arab saboteurs were killed by the Israeli Defense Forces, and 2,600 suspected saboteurs were arrested, some later to be released. No terrorist is ever executed even though he may have killed an Israeli. Israel has no capital punishment.

[20] Gil Carl AlRoy, "The Prospects of War in the Middle East," *Commentary,* March 1969, p. 56.

[21] For some time after the Six Day War, the Lebanese Government generally tried to keep terrorists from striking from its territory, though it permitted training and recruiting centers. During 1969-70 the Government came under considerable pressure from the terrorist organizations and other Arab governments to permit the terrorists to operate from Lebanese border areas. Thousands of terrorists became active, particularly in the refugee camps, and attacked Israel from across the previously quiet border.

[22] *Time,* March 30, 1970, p. 32.

[23] Yasser Arafat, *Time,* March 30, 1970, p. 32.

[24] George Habash, leader of the Popular Front for the Liberation of Palestine, *Time,* June 13, 1969, p. 42. Habash (a Christian) justifies the most ruthless terrorism with the argument that it is necessary to "shock both an indifferent world and a demoralized Palestine nation."

[25] Sabin and others, "The Arabs Need and Want Peace, But—," pp. 19, 27.

[26] A. L. Goodhart, letter to *The Daily Telegraph* (London), July 29, 1968. Goodhart, former Professor of Jurisprudence at Oxford University, cites the recognized authority Oppenheim-Lauterpacht, *International Law.*

[27] In April, 1970, Israel once again agreed to withhold fire while the canal was repaired. Israelis are only too well aware of the desperate need for water in this dry region. They would much prefer that Israeli and Arab farmers on the two sides of the river be enabled to return to the amicable relationships that existed prior to the Six Day War and the *fedayeen* attacks.

[28] AlRoy, "The Prospects of War in the Middle East," p. 56.

[29] France and Great Britain have sold substantial quantities of heavy arms and aircraft to some Arab countries yet declined to sell to Israel. The French Government has even refused to deliver aircraft for which Israel had paid and which her pilots had test flown.

[30] After the bombing of the factory Israel took the unprecedented step of advising the Egyptians (through the U.N. and the International Red Cross) to defuse a delayed-action bomb that had fallen on the factory and that would probably have caused additional deaths.

[31] Arab inventions of Israeli atrocities require devious maneuvers in order to provide a semblance of authenticity. For example, in April, 1970 Israel raided a military installation at Salahiye, Egypt. Egypt charged that 46 school children were killed in the raid, and more wounded. At least some of the casualties did in fact occur, but the boys were evidently engaged in paramilitary training inside the base. A number of the wounded were still dressed in green khaki uniforms when correspondents were finally permitted to visit them 15 kilometers from the actual scene of the raid. Revealingly, reporters were not allowed to see the "school."

[32] "Talking of the Six Day War," *Israel Magazine,* I, 7 (1968), 65.

[33] Joseph Alsop, *Herald Tribune* (Paris), Sept. 19, 1967.

[34] As cited in Geula Cohen, "Where Do We Go From Here?" *Israel Magazine,* I, 4 (1968), 47.

[35] "Talking of the Six Day War," pp. 65, 69.

[36] As cited in Cohen, "Where Do We Go From Here?," p. 47.

[37] Both statements were made by Shmuel Tamir, "Arab-Israel Parley," *Israel Magazine,* I, 8 (1968), 72. See also Mordechai Bar-On, "Love of Peace," *Israel Magazine,* II, 6 (1970), 14-16.

NOTES TO CHAPTER 18

For Truth and Justice, I

[1] Amos Kenan, "A Letter to All Good People," pp. 2-3.

[2] Henri Baruk, "The Psychology of Hatred," *Israel Magazine*, II, 2 (1969), 19.

[3] As reported in *The New York Times*, April 29, 1969.

[4] M. T. Mehdi, Secretary-General of the Action Committee on American-Arab Relations in New York, said in a letter to *The New York Times* (June 18, 1968) that "it was morally wrong" of Senator Kennedy "to submit to the pressure of the Zionists. . . . [He] is in a very real sense an indirect victim of Zionism."

[5] "Nasser Talks," an interview of Gamal Abdel Nasser by William Attwood, *Look*, March 19, 1968.

[6] Tad Szulc, *The New York Times*, Aug. 22, 1969; *The Jerusalem Post* (Weekly Overseas Edition), Aug. 25, 1969.

[7] *The New York Times*, Sept. 25, 1969.

[8] *The Jerusalem Post* (Weekly Overseas Edition), Aug. 25, 1969; Tad Szulc, *The New York Times*, Aug. 23, 1969. The arsonist was subsequently committed to a mental institution.

[9] Gamal Abdel Nasser, as cited by Raymond H. Anderson, *The New York Times*, Aug. 24, 1969 (our italics).

[10] Statement by Abba Eban at a press conference in Jerusalem, Aug. 24, 1969.

[11] Editorial, "Propaganda Fire," *The Jerusalem Post* (Weekly Overseas Edition), Aug. 25, 1969.

[12] As cited in *Research and Evaluation Report*, New York: Anti-Defamation League of B'nai B'rith, July 8, 1969.

[13] Nasser, as cited in *The New York Times*, Nov. 7, 1969.

[14] Nasser, as cited in *Research and Evaluation Report*.

[15] Nasser, in an address to the National Congress of the Arab Socialist Union, as cited in *The Nasser Doctrine With Which Israel Has to Live*, a statement issued by the Embassy of Israel (Washington), April 1, 1969.

[16] Muhammad Salah ed-Din, as cited in *Al Misri* (Cairo), April 11, 1954.

[17] The full text of the Palestinian National Covenant is reproduced in *New Middle East*, March, 1970, pp. 48-9. See also Yehoshafat Harkabi, "The Palestinians in the Israel-Arab Conflict," *Midstream*, March, 1970, pp. 3-13.

[18] See C. A. Sulzberger, "A Lurch Toward Disaster," *The New York Times*, April 26, 1970.

NOTES TO CHAPTER 19

For Truth and Justice, II

[1] Bernard Lewis, "The Great Powers, the Arabs and the Israelis," *Foreign Affairs*, July, 1969, p. 643.

[2] Cf. Sam Pope Brewer, *The New York Times*, Aug. 27, 1969.

[3] Yosef Tekoah, as cited in *Time*, Jan. 10, 1969, p. 27.

[4] Ya'acov Ben-Israel, "Israel Patient on U Thant's Bias," *The Jerusalem Post* (Weekly Overseas Edition), May 12, 1969. Even neutral diplomats were stunned by Thant's communications.

[5] The Vatican still does not recognize Israel. People in Israel (including Roman Catholics) were deeply grieved by this act of the Pope, as well as by the behavior of other churchmen, simply because no Christian commiseration had been expressed when Israelis were killed or wounded in the preceding terrorist attacks.

[6] Leaders of the National Council of Churches wired their "gratitude" to President Johnson for the American condemnation of the Israeli raid. Ambassador Wiggins identified the raid as "an act of arrogance."

[7] Arthur J. Lelyveld, "Christian Morality and Arab Terrorism" (An American Jewish Congress Statement), *Congress Bi-Weekly*, Jan. 13, 1969, p. 2.

[8] Although Transjordan was carved out of the Palestine Mandate of 1920 by the British, the atlas in general use in Arab schools and a 1964 issue of Jordanian stamps picture the map of "The Hashemite Kingdom of Jordan" as including the entire area of that original Mandate —the land on *both* sides of the Jordan River (Map 4). Jordan did not become a member of the United Nations until 1955.

9 James Parkes maintains that since the only people who would benefit from any attempt to settle all the personal claims going back to 1948 would be a "bevy of lawyers," a far wiser policy would be to "balance the claims of half a million Palestinians against those of the half million Jews in Arab countries and concentrate on the actual needs of the future" (*The Jerusalem Post* [Weekly Overseas Edition], April 20, 1970).

10 Cf. these words from *A Statement to the American Christian Community on the Arab-Israeli Conflict:* "Without the return of the territories occupied by Israel the climate for conciliation over the next decades will be bleak indeed." In the Summer of 1967 the Executive Committees of the National Council of Churches and the World Council of Churches issued public statements insisting that no territorial changes resulting from the armed conflict should be permitted. However, a more recent (May 2, 1969) Policy Statement adopted by the General Board of the N.C.C. does not refer to the territories. It does mention the need of the Palestinian Arabs for "a home that is acceptable to them." On September 1, 1969 the Department of International Affairs, United States Catholic Conference issued a statement that includes among several "requirements" for peace "withdrawal of Israeli armed forces from territories occupied in the recent conflict." The Conference related this requirement to a general settlement.

11 Curtis A. Chambers, "A Perspective on the Middle East," *Together,* April, 1970, p. 31. David Pryce Jones, a British journalist, reported on his own investigation of Israeli prisons and treatment of prisoners in the *Sunday Telegraph* (London), Dec. 21, 1969. The prisoners' lack of bitterness was particularly noted.

12 *The New York Times,* Sept. 17, 1969; *The Jerusalem Post* (Weekly Overseas Edition), Sept. 21, 1969.

13 Nadav Safran, as cited in *Time,* June 23, 1967, p. 25. In his book, *From War to War,* Safran analyzes at length the harmful and fluctuating role of the "big powers."

14 President Eisenhower and Secretary of State Dulles had admitted that they made a mistake in 1957 by insisting that Israel withdraw her forces from the Sinai Peninsula and the Gaza Strip without any guarantee of a real settlement between Egypt and Israel.

15 Document submitted to the U.N. Security Council, cited in *The New York Times,* May 17, 1969.

16 *The Nasser Doctrine With Which Israel Has to Live.*

17 Badeau, *The American Approach to the Arab World,* p. 91.

18 Though the British did everything possible to help the Arabs, up through Israel's War for Independence, the Arabs blamed them for their own defeat (Safran, *From War to War,* p. 100).

19 *The New York Times,* Aug. 31, 1969.

20 *Congressional Record,* P.H. 6617/16, July, 1968.

21 *The New York Times,* Dec. 10, 1969.

22 Cf. C. L. Sulzberger, "Foreign Affairs: Balance Sheet," *The New York Times,* Aug. 15, 1969; "Foreign Affairs: Two Wars in One," *The New York Times,* Aug. 24, 1969. "While it is true that Western Europe could not hold out indefinitely without Middle Eastern oil, it is also true that without oil revenue the economies of most oil-producing countries and their economic dependents would soon collapse" (O. M. Smolansky, "Moscow and the Persian Gulf: An Analysis of Soviet Ambitions and Potential," in T. Cuyler Young, ed., *Middle East Focus: The Persian Gulf,* Princeton: The Princeton University Conference, 1968, p. 153). Because of economic self-interest there will be, nevertheless, continuing pressures in behalf of pro-Arab policies, within the U.S. as well as among other Western investors in Middle East and North African oil. Lobbies in the United States will increase as American businesses expand their Arab markets and add to the numbers of investors.

23 Cf. Dana Adams Schmidt, *The New York Times,* Sept. 17, 1969. Libya alone contributes $84 million a year to the two nations (*The New York Times,* Oct. 5, 1969). Saudi Arabia contributed $3 million in one year to the terrorists (*Time,* Nov. 7, 1969, p. 35).

24 As cited in *The New York Times,* Aug. 30, 1969.

25 Cf. Karl Baehr, "Arab-Israeli Clarification," *The Churchman,* June-July, 1969, p. 11.

26 Typical recent examples in Christian journals of presentations heavily weighted on the Arab side—in substance as in language, and in ways that avoid any serious confrontation with Arab words and actions against the people of Israel—are Wayne H. Cowan, "The Elusive Peace," *Christianity and Crisis,* May 11, 1970, pp. 95-101; and Lillian Harris Dean, "The Mood of the Arabs," *Christian Herald,* June 1970, pp. 12-18.

27 Amnon Rubinstein, "No Man's Land Remains in Jerusalem," p. 131.

28 Benjamin Halpern, letter to *The New York Times,* July 21, 1969.

NOTES TO CHAPTER 20

From Antisemitism to Acceptance

[1] Cf. Willard G. Oxtoby, "Christians and the Mideast Crisis," *The Christian Century*, July 26, 1967, p. 964.

[2] On the question of the roots of antisemitism, see A. Roy Eckardt, *Elder and Younger Brothers*, New York: Charles Scribner's Sons, 1967, chaps. 1-2 and *passim;* Edward H. Flannery, *The Anguish of the Jews*, New York: The Macmillan Company, 1965; James Parkes, *Antisemitism*, Chicago: Quadrangle Books, 1969; also *Israel Magazine*, II, 2 (1969), which is largely devoted to a discussion of the phenomenon of human hatred.

[3] Dr. Cecil Roth clearly demonstrates the falsity of the claim that Jews suffered little under Arab-Muslim rule over the centuries ("Jews in the Arab World," *New Palestine*, 1946, reprinted in *Near East Report*, August, 1967, pp. B-17–B-20). See also Saul S. Friedman, "The Myth of Arab Toleration," *Midstream*, January, 1970, pp. 56-9.

[4] "The Jews in the Arab World," *Time*, Feb. 7, 1969, p. 23.

[5] From an interview with Yehoshafat Harkabi by the authors. Professor Harkabi is a foremost authority on Arab antisemitism, particularly as expressed in literature written in Arabic.

[6] Yehoshafat Harkabi, "The Arab-Israel Confrontation," p. 6.

[7] Stuart E. Rosenberg, "Arab Antisemitism: A Case of Semantics?," *Congress Bi-Weekly*, Nov. 25, 1968, p. 6.

[8] Harkabi, interview.

[9] Bint Al-Shanti, "The Historical Dimensions of this War," in the literary supplement of *Al-Ahram* (Cairo), June 2, 1967, as reprinted in *Midstream*, June-July, 1969, pp. 61-2.

[10] Harkabi, "The Arab-Israel Confrontation," p. 5.

[11] Cf., among other studies, Parkes, *Antisemitism;* and Joshua Trachtenberg, *The Devil and the Jews: The Medieval Conception of the Jews and Its Relation to Modern Antisemitism*, Cleveland: Meridian Books, 1961.

[12] James Parkes, *Arabs and Jews in the Middle East: A Tragedy of Errors*, London: Victor Gollancz Ltd., 1967, p. 15. See also "Nazis in Cairo," *Patterns of Prejudice* (London), May-June 1967, pp. 6-8.

[13] See two articles in *The Wiener Library Bulletin*, Summer, 1967: "Arab Antisemitism—Blood Libel Revived"; and Sylvia G. Haim, "A Muslim View of the 'Protocols' "; also, Harkabi, "The Arab-Israel Confrontation," p. 6.

[14] As cited in *Fact Finding Report: Arab Antisemitism*, a leaflet published by the Anti-Defamation League of B'nai B'rith, July 1969.

[15] As reported by Raymond H. Anderson, *The New York Times*, Aug. 23, 1969. The absurdity of the claim is manifest in the strong tendency within the State Department to take anything but an anti-Arab stance.

[16] Harkabi, p. 6.

[17] Cf. Shimon Shamir, "The Attitude of Arab Intellectuals to the Six-Day War," *Proceedings of the Annual Conference of the American Academic Association for Peace in the Middle East* (Cambridge, Mass., Feb. 15-16, 1969), New York: AAAPME, 1969, pp. 5-24.

[18] *The Observer* (London), April 14, 1968; *The New York Times*, April 10, 1968.

[19] Trachtenberg, *The Devil and the Jews*, p. 181.

[20] Muni Baalbaki, as cited by Shamir, "The Attitude of Arab Intellectuals to the Six-Day War," p. 16.

[21] Edward H. Flannery, "Anti-Zionism and the Christian Psyche," *Journal of Ecumenical Studies*, Spring, 1969, pp. 173-184.

[22] *The Diaries of Theodor Herzl*, New York: Grosset & Dunlap, 1962, pp. 428, 429. Father John Pawlikowski conjectures that this theological position, which condemns the Jewish people to perpetual wandering, is behind the continuing refusal of the Vatican to recognize the State of Israel ("The Middle East Conflict: A Christian Perspective," an address, reproduced in *Congressional Record*, E2844, April 14, 1969).

[23] William Holladay, "Is the Old Testament Zionist?," *The Middle East Newsletter* (Beirut), June-July, 1968, pp. 12, 13.

[24] Holladay, p. 13.

[25] M. T. Mehdi, as cited in Michener, "Israel: A Nation Too Young to Die," p. 74 (italics added).

[26] Cf. Baruk, "The Psychology of Hatred," pp. 19-20.

[27] Baruk, p. 20.

[28] "Arab-Israel Parley," pp. 63, 20, 22.

[29] Cf. Alice and Roy Eckardt, "The Tragic Unity of Enemies: A Report from the Middle East," *The Christian Century*, Jan. 15, 1969, pp. 73-76.

[30] According to results published in January, 1970 of a poll conducted by Public Opinion Research of Israel, just over 40 percent of Israelis favored the integration of the administered territories into Israel (*The New York Times*, Jan. 9, 1970).

[31] Golda Meir, as cited in *Congress Bi-Weekly*, Oct. 17, 1969, p. 19.

[32] Abba Eban developed this theme in an address to the U.N. General Assembly, on June 19, 1967.

NOTES TO CHAPTER 21

Every People's Right, This People's Right

[1] Frederick C. Grant, as cited in Judith H. Banki, *Christian Reactions to the Middle East Crisis*, New York: The American Jewish Committee, 1967, p. 6.

[2] James Parkes, *Arabs and Jews in the Middle East*, pp. 21-2.

[3] Parkes, p. 8.

[4] John Badeau, *The American Approach to the Arab World*, pp. 172, 173.

[5] For example, in a statement by the Russian representative Andrei Gromyko on May 21, 1948.

[6] Parkes, *Arabs and Jews . . .*, pp. 29-30.

[7] Fayez A. Sayegh, *Zionist Colonialism in Palestine*, Beirut: Palestine Liberation Organization, September 1965, p. v.

[8] Joseph Neyer, "'A State Like Any Other State'?," a reprint from *New Politics* distributed by American Professors for Peace in the Middle East, 1968, p. 11.

[9] John Davis, as cited in *The Jerusalem Post* (Weekly Overseas Edition), Oct. 6, 1969.

[10] Cited in *The New York Times*, Oct. 15, 1969.

[11] The information on Israel's domestic and foreign assistance programs for other nations is based primarily upon Harry Essrig and Abraham Segal, *Israel Today* (revised, New York: Union of American Hebrew Congregations, 1968, pp. 247-50; and *Facts About Israel, 1970*, pp. 30-2. See also, *Israel's Programme of International Cooperation*, Jerusalem: Ministry for Foreign Affairs, 1967.

[12] Golda Meir, interview with James Reston in Tel Aviv, *The New York Times*, Feb. 8, 1970. A denial of any Palestinian entity was also made by Foreign Minister Abba Eban on March 9, 1970 (*The Jerusalem Post* [Weekly Overseas Edition], March 16, 1970).

[13] Arie Eliav, as cited in *Time*, Jan. 26, 1970, p. 26.

[14] The words cited are from an article, by Eli Ben-Gal, "One Palestine—Two States," *Le Monde* (Paris), Feb. 11, 1970.

[15] Harkabi, "The Palestinians in the Israel-Arab Conflict," pp. 12, 13.

[16] Only a free plebiscite could reveal the true wishes of the Palestinians. Unfortunately, external Arab constraint would make such expression sadly irrelevant, unless (as seems unlikely) the vote were overwhelmingly on the side of Jordanian overlordship.

[17] Shlomo Argov, "The Present Situation in the Middle East," *Middle East Information Series —IX*, New York: American Academic Association for Peace in the Middle East, January, 1969, pp. 27-8.

[18] Harkabi, "The Palestinians . . .," pp. 9-10.

NOTES TO CHAPTER 22

People-Faith-Land

[1] Cf. Holladay, "Is the Old Testament Zionist?," pp. 11, 12. The import of Holladay's argument is an attempt to trap the people of Israel. Israel is held to be "a political entity" that "does not acknowledge the God of judgment and grace." But of course if Israel were to "acknowledge" such a God, her enemies would immediately accuse her of "theocracy." The only

way out of such immoral maneuvering is to cease applying one kind of standard to Israel and quite different standards to other peoples.

2 Werblowsky, "A Nation Born of Religion," p. 20.

3 A curious failure to understand the distinction between taking religious history literally and taking it seriously characterizes an allegation by John H. Marks that a study of the Jewish people and Israel by one of the present writers exemplifies "literalism" (cf. *Religion in Life,* Summer, 1968, pp. 318-19, and Eckardt, *Elder and Younger Brothers*). The latter study combats religious literalism in similar ways to the present critique of territorial fundamentalism. The distinction between taking religious claims and affirmations literally and taking them seriously is all-important in affirming Israel's *relative* right to the land.

4 Abraham J. Heschel, *Israel: An Echo of Eternity,* New York: Farrar, Straus and Giroux, 1969, p. 113.

5 Heschel, pp. 101, 115, 118.

6 Cf. Reinhold Niebuhr, "The King's Chapel and the King's Court," *Christianity and Crisis,* Aug. 4, 1969, p. 212.

7 Sometimes in the tradition this requirement is expanded: "A Jew is a person who is born of a Jewish mother and has not accepted another faith."

8 In the procedure for registering Israeli residents, the following form has been used: "Any person declaring in good faith that he is a Jew *and is not of another religion,* shall be registered as a Jew and no additional proof shall be required" (cf. Goldman, *Religious Issues in Israel's Political Life,* p. 67).

9 See Chapter 12, page 128.

10 Werblowsky, "A Nation Born of Religion," p. 20.

11 Fein, *Politics in Israel,* p. 136.

12 Cf. Manfred Vogel, "The Dilemma of Identity for the Emancipated Jew," *The Journal of Bible and Religion,* July, 1966, p. 232n.

13 However, the contrast is plain between the Jewish situation on the one side and Christianity on the other. For all its historical origin in Palestine, any existential tie between Christendom and that locale is minimal.

14 *The Jerusalem Post* (Weekly Overseas Edition), June 2, 1969.

15 In the Diaspora thousands of individuals (mostly, but not all, Jews) have helped and continue to help. In the United States, the many organizations and appeals aiding Israel in diverse ways include the America-Israel Cultural Foundation, the American Jewish Committee, the American Jewish Congress, the American Joint Distribution Committee, B'nai B'rith, Hadassah, the Organization for Rehabilitation Through Training, Mizrachi, the United Jewish Appeal, the Zionist Organization of America, and others.

16 David Polish, "Israel—The Meeting of Prophecy and Power," reprint from *Yearbook* of The Central Conference of American Rabbis, 1964, pp. 163, 164, 167 (italics added).

17 David Polish, "The Tasks of Israel and Galut," *Judaism,* Winter, 1969, pp. 3-16 (italics added).

18 Sachar, *A History of the Jews,* p. 432.

NOTES TO CHAPTER 23

From Penitence to Reconciliation

1 Cf. "Judaism and Christian Education: The Strober Report," an editorial in *The Christian Century,* Nov. 5, 1969, p. 1410.

2 Franklin H. Littell, "Israel and the Christian-Jewish Dialogue," in Henry Siegman, editor, *The Religious Dimensions of Israel,* New York: Synagogue Council of America, 1968, p. 41.

3 Franklin H. Littell, as cited in A. Roy Eckardt, "The Jewish-Christian Encounter"; reprint from Central Conference of American Rabbis *Journal,* June, 1968, p. 27. See also Yona Malachy, "The Christian Churches and the Six Day War," *The Wiener Library Bulletin* (London), XXIII, 2-3 (1969), 14-25; and A. Roy Eckardt, "The Reaction of the Churches," *Proceedings of the Annual Conference of the American Academic Association for Peace in the Middle East* (Cambridge, Mass., Feb. 15-16, 1969), New York: AAAPME, 1969, pp. 69-91.

4 Robert F. Drinan, "The State of Israel: Theological Implications for Christians," *Conservative Judaism,* Spring, 1968, pp. 31-2, 33.

5 Statement by Marc H. Tanenbaum, Director of Interreligious Affairs, American Jewish Com-

mittee, before the New York Chapter of that body, Jan. 12, 1969 (mimeographed). See also *Arab Appeals to American Public Opinion Today*, New York: The American Jewish Committee, 1969, pp. 11-12.

[6] As published in the *United Church Herald*, Sept., 1969, pp. 5-6; and a longer version in *Monday Morning*, Sept. 22, 1969, pp. 3-6. Both of these are American church publications.

[7] The statement from Lebanon contrasts sharply with a statement by the United Christian Council in Israel (June 1, 1967) affirming the equal right of all states, nations, and peoples in the region to a peaceful existence. (There is no evidence of official pressures upon either statement.) Were the Christian spokesmen from Israel to take the kind of view the missionaries take, they would call, for example, for the elimination of such states as Lebanon, Syria, Jordan, and Egypt.

[8] Thus, the lengthy Resolution on the Middle East of the National Council of Churches (July 7, 1967) makes no reference whatever to the culpability of the Arab world for the Six Day War. It is entirely silent on Israel's chronic need for defensible borders, her navigation rights, and the role of the U.S.S.R. in fomenting Arab aggression.

[9] At the time of the Six Day War, the Harris Survey showed that 82 percent of the American people believed that Israel's existence must be accepted by the Arab states, while almost 80 percent opposed any U.N. condemnation of Israel's action. In May of 1969, 61 members of the Senate and 243 members of the House of Representatives issued a declaration strongly supporting Israel's cause.

[10] For the opposite (and refreshing) alternative, see Peter Schneider, *Sweeter than Honey: Christian Presence Amid Judaism*, published in the U.S. as *The Dialogue of Christians and Jews*, New York: The Seabury Press, 1967.

[11] Marie Syrkin, "From a Jewish Woman to a Christian Friend."

[12] Rosemary Reuther, "Theological Anti-Semitism in the New Testament," *The Christian Century*, Feb. 14, 1968, pp. 191-96.

[13] Cited in *Christian Attitudes on Jews and Judaism*, no. 5, London: Institute of Jewish Affairs, April, 1969, p. 1.

[14] From an advertisement in *The New York Times*, July 12, 1967.

[15] Glenn C. Stone, in "Symposium: Lutheran Reactions to the Arab-Israel War," *Lutheran Quarterly*, Aug., 1968, p. 284.

[16] As reported by the Ecumenical Press Service (Oct. 16, 1969), Eugene Carson Blake, general secretary of the World Council of Churches, sought to dismiss the Committee's criticism by calling the group an "advisory" body. This is false. It is also false to claim that the World Council of Churches has maintained a "twenty-one year record" of even-handedness on Arab-Israeli relations. On the contrary, World Council statements have been consistently slanted in favor of the Arabs against Israel (H. D. Leuner, "Schäme dich, Weltkirchenrat!" ["Shame on You, World Council of Churches"], *Der Zeuge* [London], November, 1969, pp. 1-2).

[17] As cited in *The Catholic Review*, Dec. 12, 1969.

[18] Peter Schneider, "Ecumenical Fraternity in Israel," *Common Ground* (London), Summer, 1969, p. 17.

[19] Frank M. Cross, Jr., "A Christian Understanding of the Election of Israel," *Andover Newton Quarterly*, March, 1968, pp. 237, 240.

[20] As quoted in *The New York Times*, March 29, 1970.

[21] Krister Stendahl, "Judaism and Christianity II—After a Colloquium and a War," *Harvard Divinity Bulletin*, Autumn, 1967, pp. 5, 7 (italics added).

[22] Peter Schneider, "The State of Israel as a Factor in Christian-Jewish Relationship," a lecture distributed by the Council of Christians and Jews (London), 1964, p. 21.

[23] Cf. Eckardt, *Elder and Younger Brothers*, chaps. 3-8.

[24] Peter Schneider, "A Christian Approach to Middle East Peace," Special Supplement to *The Jerusalem Post*, December 20, 1967, p. 23.

[25] James Feron, *The New York Times*, Jan. 27, 1969.

[26] In a letter to the *Catholic Herald* (London), Oct. 6, 1967.

[27] Tad Szulc, *The New York Times*, April 22, 1969.

[28] Raymond Gunter, as cited in *The Jerusalem Post* (Weekly Overseas Edition), Oct. 13, 1969.

[29] The Institute, under the distinguished presidency of Dr. G. Douglas Young, is a Christian graduate school under American auspices offering studies in the archaeology, history, languages, literatures, and cultures of the Holy Land and the Middle East. For undergraduates who wish

to study in Israel as part of their work toward a degree, a year of suitable study was recently added. A major portion of the teaching is done by Israeli scholars.

30 Schneider, "Ecumenical Fraternity in Israel," pp. 16-21. The full name of the group is Ecumenical Theological Research Fraternity, of which Schneider is Secretary as well as being Adviser on Christian-Jewish Relations to the Anglican Archbishop in Jerusalem. There is also a Jerusalem Students Ecumenical Discussion Group, whose recent activities are specially oriented to Christian students recently come to Israel. The Rainbow Group is an interfaith society of Israeli intellectuals, Jewish and Christian.

31 It is believed that in this courtyard Jesus was condemned by Pontius Pilate, mocked by the soldiers, and started on his way to Calvary.

32 On the Roman Catholic side mention must also be made of St. Isaiah House, established in Jerusalem in 1959, and serving as an instrument of renewal of Jewish-Christian relationships. A new Ecumenical Center under Catholic auspices is being built between Jerusalem and Bethlehem.

33 In July, 1969 ProJeCt Pilgrimage took place, a visit to Israel involving a group of Protestants, Jews, and Catholics from eastern Pennsylvania under the guidance of a minister, rabbi, and priest. To our knowledge, this was the first such pilgrimage from the United States. The group visited sites of peculiar significance to each faith, and shared spiritual experiences, including participation in joint worship.

34 As cited in "Hieronymus," "Christian Comment," *The Jerusalem Post* (Weekly Overseas Edition), Nov. 3, 1969.

35 Flannery, "Anti-Zionism and the Christian Psyche," pp. 183-4.

36 Ephraim Auerbach, *Golden Sunset,* as cited in Sol Liptzin, "Ephraim Auerbach: Sweet Singer of Israel," *Jewish Heritage,* Fall/Winter 1968, p. 46.